THE LAST TWELVE VERSES

OF THE GOSPEL ACCORDING TO

S. MARK

On the next page is exhibited an *exact Fac-simile*, obtained by Photography, of fol. 28 *b* of the Codex Sinaiticus at S. Petersburg, (Tischendorf's א) : shewing the abrupt termination of S. Mark's Gospel at the words ЕΦΟΒΟΥΝΤΟ ΓΑΡ (chap. xvi. 8), as explained at p. 70, and pp. 86—8. The original Photograph, which is here reproduced on a diminished scale, measures in height full fourteen inches and one-eighth; in breadth, full thirteen inches. It was procured for me through the friendly and zealous offices of the English Chaplain at S. Petersburg, the Rev. A. S. Thompson, B.D.; by favour of the Keeper of the Imperial Library, who has my hearty thanks for his liberality and consideration.

It will be perceived that the text begins at S. Mark xvi. 2, and ends with the first words of S. Luke i. 18.

Up to this hour, every endeavour to obtain a Photograph of the corresponding page of the Codex Vaticanus, B, (Nº. 1209, in the Vatican,) has proved unavailing. If the present Vindication of the genuineness of Twelve Verses of the everlasting Gospel should have the good fortune to approve itself to his Holiness, Pope Pius IX., let me be permitted in this unadorned and unusual manner,—(to which I would fain add some circumstance of respectful ceremony if I knew how,)—very humbly to entreat his Holiness to allow me to possess a Photograph, corresponding in size with the original, of the page of Codex B (it is numbered fol. 1303,) which exhibits the abrupt termination of the Gospel according to S. Mark.

J. W. B.

Oriel College, Oxford,
June 14, 1871.

ΚΑΙΔΙΑΓΕΝΟϹΘΗ
ΜΑΤΟΥϹΑΒΒΑΤΟⲨ
ΕϹΧΟΝΤΑΙΕΠΙΤΟ
ΜΝΗΜΑΑΝΑΤΙΛΑ
ΤΟⲤΤΟⲨΗΛΙΟⲨ
ΚΑΙΕΛΕΓΟΝΠΡΟϹ
ΕΑⲨΤΑϹΤΙϹΑΠΟΚⲨ
ⲖΙϹΕΙΗΜΙΝΤΟΝ
ⲖΙΘΟΝΕΚΤΗϹΘⲨ
ΡΑϹΤΟⲨΜΝΗΜΕ
ΟⲨΚΑΙΑΝΑΒΛΕ¥Α
ϹΑΙΘΕⲰΡΟⲨϹΙΝ
ΝΑΚΕΚⲨⲖΙϹΜΕ
ΤΟΝ⳽ⲖΙΘΟΝ·ΗΝΓΑΡ
ΜΕΓΑϹϹⲪΟΔΡΑ·
ΚΑΙΕΙϹΕⲖΘΟⲨϹΑΙΕⲒϹ
ΤΟΜΝΗΜΕΙΟΝΕⲒ
ⲖΟΝΝΕΑΝΙϹΚΟΝ
ΚΑΘΗΜΕΝΟΝΕΝ
ΤΟΙϹΔΕΞΙΟΙϹΠΕΡⲒ
ΒΕΒⲖΗΜΕΝΟΝ⳽ΤⲞ
ⲖΗΝⲖΕⲨΚΗΝΚΑⲒ
ΕΞΕΘΑΜΒΗΘΗ
ϹΑΝ
ΟΔΕⲖΕΓΕΙΑⲨΤΑΙϹ
ΜΗΕΚΘΑΜΒΕΙϹΘⲈ
ⲒΗϹΟⲨΝΖΗΤΕⲒⲦⲈ
ΤΟΝΝΑΖΑΡΗ
ΝΟΝΤΟΝΕϹΤΑⲨ
ΡⲰΜΕΝΟΝΗΓΕⲢ
ΘΗΟⲨΚΕϹΤΙΝ
ⲰΔΕⲒΔΕⲞΤΟΠΟ⳽
ΟΠΟⲨΕΘΗΚΑΝ
ΑⲨΤΟΝ
ΑⲖⲖΑⲨΠΑΓΕΤΕΕⲒ
ΠΑΤΕΤΟΙϹΜΑ
ΘΗΤΑΙϹΑⲨΤΟⲨ
ΚΑΙΤⲰΠΕΤΡⲰ
ΟΤΙΠΡΟΑΓΕⲒⲨ
ΜΑϹΕΙϹΤΗΝΓΑⲖⲒ
ⲖΑΙΑΝΕΚΕⲒ
ΑⲨΤΟΝΟⲮΕϹΘΕ
ΚΑΘⲰϹΕΙΠΕΝ
ⲨΜΙΝ
ΚΑΙΕΞΕⲖΘΟⲨϹΑⲒ
ΕⲪⲨΓΟΝΑΠΟΤΟ⳽
ΜΝΗΜΕⲒΟⲨ
ΕⲒΧΕΝΓΑΡΑⲨΤΑϹ
ΤΡΟΜΟϹΚΑΙΕΚ

ϹΤΑϹⲒϹΚΑⲒΟⲨ
ΔΕΝΙΟⲨΔΕΝΕⲒ
ΠΟΝΕⲪΟΒΟⲨΝ
ΤΟΓΑΡ

ΕⲨΑΓΓΕ
ⲖΙΟ·Ν
ΚΑΤΑΜΑΡΚΟΝ

ΕΠΕΙΔΗΠΕΡΠΟΛΛΟΙ
ΕΠΕΧΕΙΡΗϹΑΝΑΝΑ
ΤΑΞΑϹΘΑΙΔΙΗΓΗϹΙΝ
ΠΕΡΙΤΩΝΠΕΠΛΗ
ΡΟΦΟΡΗΜΕΝΩΝ
ΕΝΗΜΙΝΠΡΑΓΜΑΤ
ΚΑΘΩϹΠΑΡΕΔΟϹΑΝ
ΗΜΙΝΟΙΑΠΑΡΧΗϹΑΥ
ΤΟΠΤΑΙΚΑΙΥΠΗΡΕ
ΤΑΙΓΕΝΟΜΕΝΟΙΤΟΥ
ΛΟΓΟΥΕΔΟΞΕΚΑΜΟΙ
ΠΑΡΗΚΟΛΟΥΘΗΚΟΤΙ
ΑΝΩΘΕΝΠΑϹΙΝΑΚΡΙ
ΒΩϹΚΑΘΕΞΗϹ
ϹΟΙΓΡΑΨΑΙΚΡΑΤΙϹΤΕ
ΘΕΟΦΙΛΕΙΝΑΓΝΩϹ
ΠΕΡΙΩΝΚΑΤΗΧΗΘΗϹ
ΛΟΓΩΝΤΗΝΑϹΦΑ
ΛΙΑΝ ΕΓΕΝΕΤΟΕΝ
ΤΑΙϹΗΜΕΡΑΙϹΗΡΩ
ΔΟΥ ΒΑϹΙΛΕΩϹΤΗϹ
ΙΟΥΔΑΙΑϹΙΕΡΕΥϹΤΙ
ΟΝΟΜΑΤΙΖΑΧΑΡΙΑϹ
ΕΞΕΦΗΜΕΡΙΑϹΑΒΙΑ
ϹΚΑΙΓΥΝΗΑΥΤΩΕΚ
ΤΩΝΘΥΓΑΤΕΡΩΝ
ΑΑΡΩΝ ΚΑΙΤΟΟΝΟ
ΜΑΑΥΤΗϹΕΛΙϹΑΒΕΤ
ΗϹΑΝΔΕΔΙΚΑΙΟΙΑΜ
ΦΟΤΕΡΟΙΕΝΑΝΤΙΟΝ
ΤΟΥΘΥΠΟΡΕΥΟΜΕ
ΝΟΙΕΝΠΑϹΑΙϹΤΑΙϹ
ΕΝΤΟΛΑΙϹΚΑΙΔΙΚΑΙ
ΩΜΑϹΙΝΤΟΥΚΥΑ
ΜΕΜΠΤΟΙΚΑΙΟΥΚ
ΑΥΤΟΙϹΤΕΚΝΟΝΚΑΘ
ΟΤΙΗΝΗΕΛΕΙϹΑΒΕΤ
ϹΤΕΙΡΑΚΑΙΑΜΦΟ
ΤΕΡΟΙΠΡΟΒΕΒΗΚΟ
ΤΕϹΕΝΤΑΙϹΗΜΕΡΑΙϹ
ΑΥΤΩΝΗϹΑΝ
ΕΓΕΝΕΤΟΔΕΕΝΤΩΙΕ
ΡΑΤΕΥΕΙΝΑΥΤΟΝΕ
ΤΗΤΑΞΕΙΤΗϹΕΦΗ
ΜΕΡΙΑϹΑΥΤΟΥΕΝΑ
ΤΙΟΝΤΟΥΘΥΚΑΤΑ
ΤΟΕΘΟϹΤΗϹΙΕΡΑ
ΤΙΑϹΕΛΑΧΕΤΟΥΘΥΜΙΑ

ϹΑΙΕΙϹΕΛΘΩΝΕΙϹ
ΤΟΝΝΑΟΝΤΟΥΚΥ
ΚΑΙΠΑΝΤΟΠΛΗΘΟ
ΗΝΤΟΥΛΑΟΥΠΡΟϹ
ΧΟΜΕΝΟΝΕΞΩΤΗ
ΡΑΤΟΥΘΥΜΙΑΜΑΤ
ΩΦΘΗΔΕΑΥΤΩΑΓ
ΛΟϹΚΥΕϹΤΩϹΕΚΔ
ΞΙΩΝΤΟΥΘΥϹΙΑϹΤ
ΡΙΟΥΤΟΥΘΥΜΙΑΜΑ
ΤΟϹΚΑΙΕΤΑΡΑΧΘΗ
ΖΑΧΑΡΙΑϹΙΔΩΝΚΑΙ
ΦΟΒΟϹΕΠΕΠΕϹΕΝ
ΕΠΑΥΤΟΝ
ΕΙΠΕΝΔΕΠΡΟϹΑΥΤΟ
ΟΑΓΓΕΛΟϹΜΗΦΟΒ
ΖΑΧΑΡΙΑΔΙΟΤΙΕΙϹΗ
ΚΟΥϹΘΗΗΔΕΗϹΙϹ
ϹΟΥΚΑΙΗΓΥΝΗϹΟΥ
ΕΛΕΙϹΑΒΕΤΓΕΝΝΗ
ϹΕΙΥΙΟΝϹΟΥΚΑΙ
ΚΑΛΕϹΕΙϹΤΟΟΝΟΜΑ
ΤΟΥΙΩΑΝΝΗΚΑΙΕ
ϹΤΑΙΧΑΡΑϹΟΙΚΑΙΑ
ΓΑΛΛΙΑϹΙϹΚΑΙΠΟΛ
ΛΟΙΕΠΙΤΗΓΕΝΕϹΕΙ
ΑΥΤΟΥΧΑΡΗϹΟΝΤΑΙ
ΕϹΤΑΙΓΑΡΜΕΓΑϹΕ
ΝΩΠΙΟΝΤΟΥΚΥΚΑΙ
ΟΙΝΟΝΚΑΙϹΙΚΕΡΑΟΥ
ΜΗΠΙΗΚΑΙΠΝϹΑΓΙ
ΟΥΠΛΗϹΘΗϹΕΤΑΙΕ
ΤΙΕΚΚΟΙΛΙΑϹΜΗΤΡ
ΑΥΤΟΥΚΑΙΠΟΛΛΟΥ
ΤΩΝΥΙΩΝΙϹΛΕΠΙ
ϹΤΡΕΨΕΙΕΠΙΚΥΤ
ΘΝΑΥΤΩΝΚΑΙΑΥ
ΤΟϹΠΡΟΕΛΕΥϹΕΤΑΙ
ΕΝΩΠΙΟΝΑΥΤΟΥ
ΕΝΠΝΙΚΑΙΔΥΝΑΜΕΙ
ΗΛΕΙΑΕΠΙϹΤΡ
ΕΨΑΙΚΑΡΔΙΑϹΠΑΤΕ
ΩΝΕΠΙΤΕΚΝΑΚΑΙ
ΑΠΕΙΘΕΙϹΕΝΦΡΟ
ΝΗϹΕΙΔΙΚΑΙΩΝΕ
ΤΟΙΜΑϹΑΙΚΥΛΑΟΝ
ΚΑΤΕϹΚΕΥΑϹΜΕΝΟ
ΚΑΙΕΙΠΕΝΖΑΧΑΡΙΑ

THE

LAST TWELVE VERSES

OF THE GOSPEL ACCORDING TO

S. MARK

VINDICATED AGAINST RECENT CRITICAL OBJECTORS AND ESTABLISHED

BY

JOHN W. BURGON B.D.

VICAR OF S. MARY-THE-VIRGIN'S, FELLOW OF ORIEL COLLEGE, AND GRESHAM LECTURER IN DIVINITY.

WITH FACSIMILES OF CODEX ℵ AND CODEX L

"'Advice to you,' sir, 'in studying Divinity?' Did you say that you 'wished I would give you a few words of advice,' sir? . . . Then let me recommend to you the practice of always *verifying your references,* sir !"
Conversation of the late PRESIDENT ROUTH.

𝕺𝖝𝖋𝖔𝖗𝖉 𝖆𝖓𝖉 𝕷𝖔𝖓𝖉𝖔𝖓:

JAMES PARKER AND CO.

1871.

ISBN 1-888328-00-2

Foreword

The Publishers. This book, *The Last Twelve Verses of Mark*, is published by the Dean Burgon Society, Incorporated (DBS). The Society takes its name from Dean John William Burgon (1813--1888), a conservative Anglican clergyman. The DBS is recognized by the I.R.S. as a non-profit, tax exempt organization. All contributions are tax deductible. The Society's main purpose is stated in its slogan, **"IN DEFENSE OF TRADITIONAL BIBLE TEXTS."** The DBS was founded in 1978, and, since then, has held its annual two-day conference in the United States and Canada. During this time, many excellent messages on textual issues are presented. The messages are available in three forms: (1) video cassettes, (2) audio cassettes, and (3) the printed message book. For information on receiving any of the above, plus a copy of the *"ARTICLES OF FAITH, AND ORGANIZATION"* of the Dean Burgon Society, please write or phone its offices at **609-854-4452.**

The *Dean Burgon News*. The Society has a paper called the *Dean Burgon News*. Within its pages the Society proclaims:

"The DEAN BURGON SOCIETY, INCORPORATED proudly takes its name in honor of John William Burgon (1813--1888), the Dean of Chichester in England, whose tireless and accurate scholarship and contribution in the area of New Testament Textual Criticism; whose defense of the Traditional Greek New Testament Text against its many enemies; and whose firm belief in the verbal inspiration and inerrancy of the Bible, we believe, have all been unsurpassed either before or since his time!"

The Present Reprint. The DEAN BURGON SOCIETY, INCORPORATED is pleased to present, in this form, one of Dean John William Burgon's most convincing books, *The Last Twelve Verses of Mark*. The verses in question are Mark 16:9-20. The arguments of this book, as put forth by Dean Burgon, have seldom been dealt with and never answered successfully. A brief book SUMMARY by DAW is given at the end.

The Importance of Mark 16:9-20. Dean Burgon held that the manner in which these twelve verses are handled by the various textual critics is crucial to their entire methodology. If the critics' textual methods fail to hold up in these twelve verses of the New Testament, their entire system must be rejected. This book shows Dean Burgon's test of strength between the two major opposing forces in the area of textual criticism in his day and in our own, namely: (1) the forces of Bishop B. F. Westcott, Professor F. J. A. Hort, and their followers and (2) the forces of Dean John William Burgon and his followers.

The Fatal Blow to Manuscripts "B" and "Aleph." Because the **only** manuscripts that omit Mark 16:9-20 are "B" (Vaticanus) and "Aleph" (Sinaiticus), we have sub-titled Dean Burgon's book, *The Fatal Blow to Manuscripts "B" and "Aleph."* **At least eighteen uncials, six hundred cursives, every known Lectionary of the East, ten Ancient Versions, and quotations from nineteen Church Fathers bear united witness to the genuineness of Mark 16:9-20!** Since "B" and "Aleph" have failed here, they should be distrusted elsewhere in the New Testament. Despite this failure here, these two manuscripts form the bedrock text of the rash of English versions today, including the New American Standard Version (NASV), New International Version (NIV), Revised Standard Version (RSV), New Revised Standard Version (NRSV) and all the others.

Other Books by Dean Burgon. For those wanting to read four other excellent reprints (presently in Xeroxed format), the following can be ordered from THE DEAN BURGON SOCIETY:

1. *The Revision Revised*, 591 pages for a gift of **$25.00**.
2. *The Traditional Text of the Holy Gospels*, 350 pp. **($15.00)**.
3. *Causes of Corruption of the Holy Gospels*, 316 pp. **($14.00)**.
4. *Inspiration and Interpretation*, 567 pages **($25.00)**.

Please add **$3.00** for postage and handling when you order.

Future Reprints. As funds permit, the DEAN BURGON SOCIETY hopes to bring into reprint-form in the same way as this present book many, if not all, of the above titles. **Can you help us?**

Sincerely for God's Written Words,

D. A. Waite

DAW/w

Rev. D. A. Waite, Th.D., Ph.D.
President, THE DEAN BURGON SOCIETY

**The
Dean Burgon
Society**
In Defense of Traditional Bible Texts
Box 354
Collingswood, New Jersey 08108, U.S.A.

John William Burgon (1813-1888)

ἀμὴν γὰρ λέγω ὑμῖν,
ἕως ἂν παρέλθῃ ὁ οὐρανὸς καὶ ἡ γῆ,
ἰῶτα ἓν ἢ μία κεραία οὐ μὴ παρέλθῃ ἀπὸ τοῦ νόμου,
ἕως ἂν πάντα γένηται.

εὐκοπώτερον δέ ἐστι
τὸν οὐρανὸν καὶ τὴν γῆν παρελθεῖν,
ἢ τοῦ νόμου μίαν κεραίαν πεσεῖν.

ὁ οὐρανὸς καὶ ἡ γῆ παρελεύσονται,
οἱ δὲ λόγοι μου οὐ μὴ παρέλθωσι.

καὶ ἐάν τις ἀφαιρῇ
ἀπὸ τῶν λόγων βίβλου τῆς προφητείας ταύτης,
ἀφαιρήσει ὁ Θεὸς τὸ μέρος αὐτοῦ
ἀπὸ βίβλου τῆς ζωῆς,
καὶ ἐκ τῆς πόλεως τῆς ἁγίας,
καὶ τῶν γεγραμμένων ἐν βιβλίῳ τούτῳ.

TO

SIR ROUNDELL PALMER, Q.C., M.P.,

&c., &c., &c.

DEAR SIR ROUNDELL,

I do myself the honour of inscribing this volume to you. Permit me to explain the reason why.

It is not merely that I may give expression to a sentiment of private friendship which dates back from the pleasant time when I was Curate to your Father,—whose memory I never recal without love and veneration ;—nor even in order to afford myself the opportunity of testifying how much I honour you for the noble example of conscientious uprightness and integrity which you set us on a recent public occasion. It is for no such reason that I dedicate to you this vindication of the last Twelve Verses of the Gospel according to S. Mark.

It is because I desire supremely to submit the argument contained in the ensuing pages to a practised judicial intellect of the loftiest stamp. Recent Editors of the New Testament insist that these "last Twelve Verses" are not genuine. The Critics, almost to a man, avow themselves of the same opinion. Popular Prejudice has been for a long time past warmly enlisted on the same side. I am as convinced as I am of my life, that the reverse is the truth. It is not even with me as it is with certain learned friends of mine, who, admitting the adversary's premisses, content themselves with denying the validity of his inference. However true it may be,—and it is true,—that from those premisses the proposed conclusion does not follow, I yet venture to deny the correctness of those premisses altogether. I insist, on the con-

trary, that the Evidence relied on is untrustworthy,—untrustworthy in every particular.

How, in the meantime, can such an one as I am hope to persuade the world that it is as I say, while the most illustrious Biblical Critics at home and abroad are agreed, and against me? Clearly, the first thing to be done is to secure for myself a full and patient hearing. With this view, I have written a book. But next, instead of waiting for the slow verdict of Public Opinion, (which yet, I know, must come after many days,) I desiderate for the Evidence I have collected, a competent and an impartial Judge. And that is why I dedicate my book to you. *If I can but get this case fairly tried, I have no doubt whatever about the result.*

Whether you are able to find time to read these pages, or not, it shall content me to have shewn in this manner the confidence with which I advocate my cause; the kind of test to which I propose to bring my reasonings. If I may be allowed to say so, —S. Mark's last Twelve Verses shall no longer remain a subject of dispute among men. *I am able to prove that this portion of the Gospel has been declared to be spurious on wholly mistaken grounds: and this ought in fairness to close the discussion. But I claim to have done more. I claim to have shewn, from considerations which have been hitherto overlooked, that its genuineness must needs be reckoned among the things that are absolutely certain.*

I am, with sincere regard and respect,

Dear Sir Roundell,

Very faithfully yours,

JOHN W. BURGON.

ORIEL,
July, 1871.

PREFACE.

THIS volume is my contribution towards the better understanding of a subject which is destined, when it shall have grown into a Science, to vindicate for itself a mighty province, and to enjoy paramount attention. I allude to the Textual Criticism of the New Testament Scriptures.

That this Study is still in its infancy, all may see. The very principles on which it is based are as yet only imperfectly understood. The reason is obvious. It is because the very foundations have not yet been laid, (except to a wholly inadequate extent,) on which the future superstructure is to rise. A careful collation of every extant Codex, (executed after the manner of the Rev. F. H. Scrivener's labours in this department,) is the first indispensable preliminary to any real progress. Another, is a revised Text, not to say a more exact knowledge, of the oldest Versions. Scarcely of inferior importance would be critically correct editions of the Fathers of the Church; and these must by all means be furnished with far completer Indices of Texts than have ever yet been attempted.—There is not a single Father to be named whose Works have been hitherto furnished with even a tolerably complete Index of the places in which he

either quotes, or else clearly refers to, the Text of the
New Testament : while scarcely a tithe of the known
MSS. of the Gospels have as yet been satisfactorily
collated.   Strange to relate, we are to this hour without so much as a satisfactory Catalogue of the Copies
which are known to be extant.

But when all this has been done,—(and the Science
deserves, and requires, a little more public encourage-
ment than has hitherto been bestowed on the arduous
and—let me not be ashamed to add the word—*unre-
munerative* labour of Textual Criticism,)—it will be
discovered that the popular and the prevailing Theory
is a mistaken one. The plausible hypothesis on which
recent recensions of the Text have been for the most
part conducted, will be seen to be no longer tenable.
The latest decisions will in consequence be generally reversed.

I am not of course losing sight of what has been
already achieved in this department of Sacred Learning. While our knowledge of the uncial MSS. has been
rendered tolerably exact and complete, an excellent beginning has been made, (chiefly by the Rev.
F. H. Scrivener, the most judicious living Master
of Textual Criticism,) in acquainting us with the contents of about seventy of the cursive MSS. of the New
Testament. And though it is impossible to deny that
the published Texts of Doctors Tischendorf and Tregelles as *Texts* are wholly inadmissible, yet is it
equally certain that by the conscientious diligence
with which those distinguished Scholars have respec-

tively laboured, they have erected monuments of their learning and ability which will endure for ever. Their Editions of the New Testament will not be superseded by any new discoveries, by any future advances in the Science of Textual Criticism. The MSS. which they have edited will remain among the most precious materials for future study. All honour to them! If in the warmth of controversy I shall appear to have spoken of them sometimes without becoming deference, let me here once for all confess that I am to blame, and express my regret. When they have publicly begged S. Mark's pardon for the grievous wrong they have done *him*, I will very humbly beg their pardon also.

In conclusion, I desire to offer my thanks to the Rev. John Wordsworth, late Fellow of Brasenose College, for his patient perusal of these sheets as they have passed through the press, and for favouring me with several judicious suggestions. To him may be applied the saying of President Routh on receiving a visit from Bishop Wordsworth at his lodgings,— "I see the learned son of a learned Father, sir!"— Let me be permitted to add that my friend inherits the Bishop's fine taste and accurate judgment also.

And now I dismiss this Work, at which I have conscientiously laboured for many days and many nights; beginning it in joy and ending it in sorrow. The College in which I have for the most part written it is designated in the preamble of its Charter and in its Foundation Statutes, (which are already much more than half a thousand years old,) as *Collegium Scholarium in Sacrá Theologiá studentium,—perpetuis temporibus duraturum.* Indebted, under GOD, to the pious munificence of the Founder of Oriel for my opportunities of study, I venture, in what I must needs call evil days, to hope that I have to some extent "employed my advantages," — (the expression occurs in a prayer used by this Society on its three solemn anniversaries,) — as our Founder and Benefactors "would approve if they were now upon earth to witness what we do."

J. W. B.

ORIEL,
July, 1871.

CONTENTS.

CHAPTER V.

THE ALLEGED HOSTILE WITNESS OF CERTAIN OF THE EARLY FATHERS
PROVED TO BE AN IMAGINATION OF THE CRITICS.

CHAPTER VI.

MANUSCRIPT TESTIMONY SHEWN TO BE OVERWHELMINGLY IN FAVOUR
OF THESE VERSES.—PART I.

CHAPTER VII.

MANUSCRIPT TESTIMONY SHEWN TO BE OVERWHELMINGLY IN FAVOUR
OF THESE VERSES.—PART II.

CHAPTER VIII.

THE PURPORT OF ANCIENT SCHOLIA AND NOTES IN MSS. ON THE
SUBJECT OF THESE VERSES, SHEWN TO BE THE REVERSE OF WHAT IS
COMMONLY SUPPOSED.

CHAPTER IX.

INTERNAL EVIDENCE DEMONSTRATED TO BE THE VERY REVERSE OF
UNFAVOURABLE TO THESE VERSES.

CHAPTER X.

THE TESTIMONY OF THE LECTIONARIES SHEWN TO BE ABSOLUTELY
DECISIVE AS TO THE GENUINENESS OF THESE VERSES.

CHAPTER XI.

THE OMISSION OF THESE TWELVE VERSES IN CERTAIN ANCIENT COPIES
OF THE GOSPELS, EXPLAINED AND ACCOUNTED FOR.

CHAPTER XII.

GENERAL REVIEW OF THE QUESTION: SUMMARY OF THE EVIDENCE; AND CONCLUSION OF THE WHOLE SUBJECT.

APPENDIX (A).

APPENDIX (B).

APPENDIX (C).

APPENDIX (D).

APPENDIX (E).

APPENDIX (F).

The Facsimile of CODEX ℵ comes immediately before the Title, and faces the page describing it.

The Facsimile of CODEX L, with its page of description, comes immediately after page 125.

Subjoined, for convenience, are "the Last Twelve Verses."

Ἀναστὰς δὲ πρωὶ πρώτῃ σαββάτου ἐφάνη πρῶτον Μαρίᾳ τῇ Μαγδαληνῇ, ἀφ' ἧς ἐκβεβλήκει ἑπτὰ δαιμόνια. ἐκείνη πορευθεῖσα ἀπήγγειλε τοῖς μετ' αὐτοῦ γενομένοις, πενθοῦσι καὶ κλαίουσι. κἀκεῖνοι ἀκούσαντες ὅτι ζῇ καὶ ἐθεάθη ὑπ' αὐτῆς ἠπίστησαν.

Μετὰ δὲ ταῦτα δυσὶν ἐξ αὐτῶν περιπατοῦσιν ἐφανερώθη ἐν ἑτέρᾳ μορφῇ, πορευομένοις εἰς ἀγρόν. κἀκεῖνοι ἀπελθόντες ἀπήγγειλαν τοῖς λοιποῖς· οὐδὲ ἐκείνοις ἐπίστευσαν.

Ὕστερον ἀνακειμένοις αὐτοῖς τοῖς ἕνδεκα ἐφανερώθη, καὶ ὠνείδισε τὴν ἀπιστίαν αὐτῶν καὶ σκληροκαρδίαν, ὅτι τοῖς θεασαμένοις αὐτὸν ἐγηγερμένον οὐκ ἐπίστευσαν. Καὶ εἶπεν αὐτοῖς, "Πορευθέντες εἰς τὸν κόσμον ἅπαντα, κηρύξατε τὸ εὐαγγέλιον πάσῃ τῇ κτίσει. ὁ πιστεύσας καὶ βαπτισθεὶς σωθήσεται· ὁ δὲ ἀπιστήσας κατακριθήσεται. σημεῖα δὲ τοῖς πιστεύσασι ταῦτα παρακολουθήσει· ἐν τῷ ὀνόματί μου δαιμόνια ἐκβαλοῦσι· γλώσσαις λαλήσουσι καιναῖς· ὄφεις ἀροῦσι· κἂν θανάσιμόν τι πίωσιν, οὐ μὴ αὐτοὺς βλάψει· ἐπὶ ἀρρώστους χεῖρας ἐπιθήσουσι, καὶ καλῶς ἕξουσιν."

Ὁ μὲν οὖν Κύριος, μετὰ τὸ λαλῆσαι αὐτοῖς, ἀνελήφθη εἰς τὸν οὐρανὸν, καὶ ἐκάθισεν ἐκ δεξιῶν τοῦ Θεοῦ· ἐκεῖνοι δὲ ἐξελθόντες ἐκήρυξαν πανταχοῦ, τοῦ Κυρίου συνεργοῦντος, καὶ τὸν λόγον βεβαιοῦντος διὰ τῶν ἐπακολουθούντων σημείων. Ἀμήν.

(9) Now when JESUS was risen early the first day of the week, He appeared first to Mary Magdalene, out of whom He had cast seven devils. (10) And she went and told them that had been with Him, as they mourned and wept. (11) And they, when they had heard that He was alive, and had been seen of her, believed not. (12) After that He appeared in another form unto two of them, as they walked, and went into the country. (13) And they went and told it unto the residue: neither believed they them. (14) Afterward He appeared unto the eleven as they sat at meat, and upbraided them with their unbelief and hardness of heart, because they believed not them which had seen Him after He was risen. (15) And He said unto them, "Go ye into all the world, and preach the Gospel to every creature. (16) He that believeth and is baptized shall be saved; but he that believeth not shall be damned. (17) And these signs shall follow them that believe; In My Name shall they cast out devils; they shall speak with new tongues; (18) they shall take up serpents; and if they drink any deadly thing, it shall not hurt them; they shall lay hands on the sick, and they shall recover." (19) So then after the LORD had spoken unto them, He was received up into Heaven, and sat on the Right Hand of GOD. (20) And they went forth, and preached every where, the LORD working with them, and confirming the word with signs following. Amen.

THE LAST TWELVE VERSES OF THE GOSPEL ACCORDING TO S. MARK.

CHAPTER I.

THE CASE OF THE LAST TWELVE VERSES OF S. MARK'S GOSPEL, STATED.

These Verses generally suspected at the present time.   The popularity of this opinion accounted for.

IT has lately become the fashion to speak of the last Twelve Verses of the Gospel according to S. Mark, as if it were an ascertained fact that those verses constitute no integral part of the Gospel. It seems to be generally supposed, (1) That the evidence of MSS. is altogether fatal to their claims ; (2) That "the early Fathers" witness plainly against their genuineness; (3) That, from considerations of "internal evidence" they must certainly be given up. It shall be my endeavour in the ensuing pages to shew, on the contrary, That manuscript evidence is so overwhelmingly in their favour that no room is left for doubt or suspicion :—That there is not so much as *one* of the Fathers, early or late, who gives it as his opinion that these verses are spurious :— and, That the argument derived from internal considerations proves on inquiry to be baseless and unsubstantial as a dream.

But I hope that I shall succeed in doing more. It shall be my endeavour to shew not only that there really is no reason whatever for calling in question the genuineness of this portion of Holy Writ, but also that there exist sufficient reasons for feeling confident that it must needs be genuine. This is clearly as much as it is possible for me

to achieve. But when this has been done, I venture to hope
that the verses in dispute will for the future be allowed to
retain their place in the second Gospel unmolested.

It will of course be asked,—And yet, if all this be so,
how does it happen that both in very ancient, and also in
very modern times, this proposal to suppress twelve verses
of the Gospel has enjoyed a certain amount of popularity?
At the two different periods, (I answer,) for widely different
reasons.

(1.) In the ancient days, when it was the universal belief
of Christendom that the Word of GOD must needs be consistent with itself in every part, and prove in every part
(like its Divine Author) perfectly "faithful and true," the
difficulty (which was deemed all but insuperable) of bringing certain statements in S. Mark's last Twelve Verses into
harmony with certain statements of the other Evangelists,
is discovered to have troubled Divines exceedingly. "In
fact," (says Mr. Scrivener,) "it brought suspicion upon these
verses, and caused their omission in some copies seen by
Eusebius." That the maiming process is indeed attributable
to this cause and came about in this particular way, I am
unable to persuade myself; but, if the desire to provide an
escape from a serious critical difficulty did not actually
occasion that copies of S. Mark's Gospel were mutilated, it
certainly was the reason why, in very early times, such
mutilated copies were viewed without displeasure by some,
and appealed to with complacency by others.

(2.) But times are changed. We have recently been
assured on high authority that the Church has reversed her
ancient convictions in this respect: that *now*, "most sound
theologians have no dread whatever of acknowledging minute
points of disagreement" (i.e. minute *errors*) "in the fourfold narrative even of the life of the Redeemer[a]." There
has arisen in these last days a singular impatience of Dogmatic Truth, (especially Dogma of an unpalatable kind,)
which has even rendered popular the pretext afforded by
these same mutilated copies for the grave resuscitation of
doubts, never as it would seem seriously entertained by any

[a] Abp. Tait's *Harmony of Revelation and the Sciences*, (1864,) p. 21.

of the ancients; and which, at all events for 1300 years and upwards, have deservedly sunk into oblivion.

Whilst I write, *that* "most divine explication of the chiefest articles of our Christian belief," the Athanasian Creed [b], is made the object of incessant assaults [c]. But then it is remembered that statements quite as "uncharitable" as any which this Creed contains are found in the 16th verse of S. Mark's concluding chapter; are in fact the words of Him whose very Name is Love. The precious *warning clause*, I say, (miscalled "damnatory [d],") which an impertinent officiousness is for glossing with a rubric and weakening with an apology, proceeded from Divine lips,—at least if these concluding verses be genuine. How shall this inconvenient circumstance be more effectually dealt with than by accepting the suggestion of the most recent editors, that S. Mark's concluding verses are an unauthorised addition to his Gospel? "If it be acknowledged that the passage has a harsh sound," (remarks Dean Stanley,) "unlike the usual utterances of Him who came not to condemn but to save, the discoveries of later times have shewn, almost beyond doubt, that it is *not a part of S. Mark's Gospel, but an addition by another hand;* of which the weakness in the external evidence coincides with the internal evidence in proving its later origin [e]."

Modern prejudice, then,—added to a singularly exaggerated estimate of the critical importance of the testimony

[b] See by all means Hooker, E. P., v. xlii. 11—13.

[c] Abp. Tait is of opinion that it "should not retain its place in the public Service of the Church:" and Dean Stanley gives sixteen reasons for the same opinion,—the fifteenth of which is that "many excellent laymen, including King George III., have declined to take part in the recitation." (*Final*) *Report of the Ritual Commission*, 1870, p. viii. and p. xvii.

[d] In the words of a thoughtful friend, (Rev. C. P. Eden),—"*Condemnatory* is just what these clauses are *not.* I understand myself, in uttering these words, not to condemn a fellow creature, but to acknowledge a truth of Scripture, GOD's judgment namely on the sin of unbelief. The further question,— In whom the sin of unbelief is found; *that* awful question I leave entirely in His hands who is the alone Judge of hearts; who made us, and knows our infirmities, and whose tender mercies are over all His works."

[e] "The Athanasian Creed," by the Dean of Westminster (*Contemporary Review*, Aug., 1870, pp. 158, 159).

of our two oldest Codices, (another of the "discoveries of
later times," concerning which I shall have more to say
by-and-by,)—must explain why the opinion is even popular
that the last twelve verses of S. Mark are a spurious appendix to his Gospel.

Not that Biblical Critics would have us believe that the
Evangelist left off at verse 8, intending that the words,—
"neither said they anything to any man, for they were
afraid," should be the conclusion of his Gospel. "No one
can imagine," (writes Griesbach,) "that Mark cut short the
thread of his narrative at that place [f]." It is on all hands
eagerly admitted, that so abrupt a termination must be held
to mark an incomplete or else an uncompleted work.   How,
then, in the original autograph of the Evangelist, is it supposed that the narrative proceeded? This is what no one
has even ventured so much as to conjecture.   It is assumed,
however, that the original termination of the Gospel, whatever it may have been, has perished.   We appeal, of course,
to its actual termination: and,—Of what nature then, (we
ask,) is the supposed necessity for regarding the last twelve
verses of S. Mark's Gospel as a spurious substitute for what
the Evangelist originally wrote? What, in other words,
has been the history of these modern doubts; and by what
steps have they established themselves in books, and won
the public ear?

To explain this, shall be the object of the next ensuing
chapters.

[f] *Commentarius Criticus,* ii. 197.

CHAPTER II.

THE HOSTILE VERDICT OF BIBLICAL CRITICS SHEWN TO BE QUITE OF RECENT DATE.

Griesbach the first to deny the genuineness of these Verses (p. 6).—
Lachmann's fatal principle (p. 8) *the clue to the unfavourable
verdict of Tischendorf* (p. 9), *of Tregelles* (p. 10), *of Alford*
(p. 12); *which has been generally adopted by subsequent Scholars
and Divines* (p. 13).—*The nature of the present inquiry explained*
(p. 15.)

IT is only since the appearance of Griesbach's second edition [1796—1806] that Critics of the New Testament have
permitted themselves to handle the last twelve verses of
S. Mark's Gospel with disrespect.   Previous critical editions
of the New Testament are free from this reproach.   "There
is no reason for doubting the genuineness of this portion of
Scripture," wrote Mill in 1707, after a review of the evidence (as far as he was acquainted with it) for and against.
Twenty-seven years later, appeared Bengel's edition of the
New Testament (1734); and Wetstein, at the end of another
seventeen years (1751-2), followed in the same field.   Both
editors, after rehearsing the adverse testimony *in extenso*,
left the passage in undisputed possession of its place.   Alter
in 1786-7, and Birch in 1788 [a], (suspicious as the latter evidently was of its genuineness,) followed their predecessors'
example.   But Matthaei, (who also brought his labours to
a close in the year 1788,) was not content to give a silent
suffrage.   He had been for upwards of fourteen years a laborious collator of Greek MSS. of the New Testament, and
was so convinced of the insufficiency of the arguments which
had been brought against these twelve verses of S. Mark,

[a] *Quatuor Evangelia Graece cum variantibus a textu lectionibus Codd.
MSS. Bibliothecae Vaticanae, etc. Jussu et sumtibus regiis edidit Andreas
Birch, Havniae,* 1788.   A copy of this very rare and sumptuous folio may be
seen in the King's Library (Brit. Mus.)

that with no ordinary warmth, no common acuteness, he
insisted on their genuineness.

"With Griesbach," (remarks Dr. Tregelles[b],) "Texts which
may be called really critical begin;" and Griesbach is the
first to insist that the concluding verses of S. Mark are spurious.
That he did not suppose the second Gospel to have always
ended at verse 8, we have seen already[c]. He was of opinion,
however, that "at some very remote period, the original
ending of the Gospel perished,—disappeared perhaps *from
the Evangelist's own copy,*—and that the present ending was
by some one substituted in its place." Griesbach further invented the following elaborate and extraordinary hypothesis
to account for the existence of S. Mark xvi. 9—20.

He invites his readers to believe that when, (before the
end of the second century,) the four Evangelical narratives
were collected into a volume and dignified with the title of
"The Gospel,"—S. Mark's narrative was furnished by some
unknown individual with its actual termination in order to
remedy its manifest incompleteness; and that this volume
became the standard of the Alexandrine recension of the
text: in other words, became the fontal source of a mighty
family of MSS. by Griesbach designated as "Alexandrine."
But there will have been here and there in existence isolated
copies of one or more of the Gospels; and in all of these,
S. Mark's Gospel, (by the hypothesis,) will have ended
abruptly at the eighth verse. These copies of single Gospels, when collected together, are presumed by Griesbach
to have constituted "the Western recension." If, in codices
of this family also, the self-same termination is now all but
universally found, the fact is to be accounted for, (Griesbach says,) by the natural desire which possessors of the
Gospels will have experienced to supplement their imperfect
copies as best they might. "Let this conjecture be accepted," proceeds the learned veteran,—(unconscious apparently that he has been demanding acceptance for at least
half-a-dozen wholly unsupported as well as entirely gratuitous conjectures,)—"and every difficulty disappears; and

---

[b] *Account of the Printed Text,* p. 83.   [c] See above, p. 3.

it becomes perfectly intelligible how there has crept into almost every codex which has been written, from the second century downwards, a section quite different from the original and genuine ending of S. Mark, which disappeared before the four Gospels were collected into a single volume." —In other words, if men will but be so accommodating as to assume that the conclusion of S. Mark's Gospel disappeared before any one had the opportunity of transcribing the Evangelist's inspired autograph, they will have no difficulty in understanding that the present conclusion of S. Mark's Gospel was not really written by S. Mark.

It should perhaps be stated in passing, that Griesbach was driven into this curious maze of unsupported conjecture by the exigencies of his "Recension Theory;" which, inasmuch as it has been long since exploded, need not now occupy us. But it is worth observing that the argument already exhibited, (such as it is,) breaks down under the weight of the very first fact which its learned author is obliged to lay upon it. Codex B.,—the solitary manuscript witness for *omitting* the clause in question, (for Codex א had not yet been discovered,)—had been already claimed by Griesbach as a chief exponent of his so-called "Alexandrine Recension." But then, on the Critic's own hypothesis, (as we have seen already,) Codex B. ought, on the contrary, to have *contained* it. How was that inconvenient fact to be got over? Griesbach quietly remarks in a foot-note that Codex B. "*has affinity* with the Eastern family of MSS."—The misfortune of being saddled with a worthless theory was surely never more apparent. By the time we have reached this point in the investigation, we are reminded of nothing so much as of the weary traveller who, having patiently pursued an *ignis fatuus* through half the night, beholds it at last vanish; but not until it has conducted him up to his chin in the mire.

Neither Hug, nor Scholz his pupil,—who in 1808 and 1830 respectively followed Griesbach with modifications of his recension-theory,—concurred in the unfavourable sentence which their illustrious predecessor had passed on the concluding portion of S. Mark's Gospel. The latter even

eagerly vindicated its genuineness[d]. But with Lachmann,
—whose unsatisfactory text of the Gospels appeared in
1842, — originated a new principle of Textual Revision;
the principle, namely, of paying exclusive and absolute
deference to the testimony of a few arbitrarily selected
ancient documents; no regard being paid to others of
the same or of yet higher antiquity. This is not the
right place for discussing this plausible and certainly most
convenient scheme of textual revision. That it leads to
conclusions little short of irrational, is certain. I notice it
only because it supplies the clue to the result which, as far
as S. Mark xvi. 9—20 is concerned, has been since arrived
at by Dr. Tischendorf, Dr. Tregelles, and Dean Alford[e],—
the three latest critics who have formally undertaken to
reconstruct the sacred Text.

They agree in assuring their readers that the genuine
Gospel of S. Mark extends no further than ch. xvi. ver. 8:
in other words, that all that follows the words ἐφοβοῦντο
γάρ is an unauthorized addition by some later hand; "a
fragment,"—distinguishable from the rest of the Gospel not
less by internal evidence than by external testimony. This
verdict becomes the more important because it proceeds from
men of undoubted earnestness and high ability; who cannot
be suspected of being either unacquainted with the evidence
on which the point in dispute rests, nor inexperienced in
the art of weighing such evidence. Moreover, their verdict
has been independently reached; is unanimous; is unhesitating; has been eagerly proclaimed by all three on many
different occasions as well as in many different places[f]; and

---

[d] "Eam esse authenticam rationes internae et externae probant gravissimae."

[e] I find it difficult to say what distress the sudden removal of this amiable
and accomplished Scholar occasions me, just as I am finishing my task.
I consign these pages to the press with a sense of downright reluctance,—
(constrained however by the importance of the subject,)—seeing that *he* is no
longer among us either to accept or to dispute a single proposition. All I can
do is to erase every word which might have occasioned him the least an-
noyance; and indeed, as seldom as possible to introduce his respected name.
An open grave reminds one of the nothingness of earthly controversy; as
nothing else does, or indeed can do.

[f] Tischendorf, besides eight editions of his laborious critical revision of the
Greek Text, has edited our English "Authorized Version" (Tauchnitz, 1869,)

may be said to be at present in all but undisputed possession of the field [g]. The first-named Editor enjoys a vast reputation, and has been generously styled by Mr. Scrivener, "the first Biblical Critic in Europe." The other two have produced text-books which are deservedly held in high esteem, and are in the hands of every student. The views of such men will undoubtedly colour the convictions of the next generation of English Churchmen. It becomes absolutely necessary, therefore, to examine with the utmost care the grounds of their verdict, the direct result of which is to present us with a mutilated Gospel. If they are right, there is no help for it but that the convictions of eighteen centuries in this respect must be surrendered. But if Tischendorf and Tregelles are wrong in this particular, it follows of necessity that doubt is thrown over the whole of their critical method. The case is a crucial one. Every page of theirs incurs suspicion, if their deliberate verdict in *this* instance shall prove to be mistaken.

1. Tischendorf disposes of the whole question in a single sentence. "That these verses were not written by Mark,"

with an "Introduction" addressed to unlearned readers, and the various readings of Codd. ℵ, B and A, set down in English at the foot of every page.—Tregelles, besides his edition of the Text of the N. T., is very full on the subject of S. Mark xvi. 9—20, in his "Account of the Printed Text," and in his "Introduction to the Textual Criticism of the N. T." (vol. iv. of Horne's *Introd.*)—Dean Alford, besides six editions of his Greek Testament, and an abridgment "for the upper forms of Schools and for passmen at the Universities," put forth two editions of a "N. T. for English Readers," and three editions of "the Authorized Version newly compared with the original Greek and revised;"—in every one of which it is stated that these twelve verses are "probably an addition, placed here in very early times."

[g] The Rev. F. H. Scrivener, Bp. Ellicott, and Bp. Wordsworth, are honourable exceptions to this remark. The last-named excellent Divine reluctantly admitting that "this portion may not have been penned by S. Mark himself;" and Bishop Ellicott (*Historical Lectures*, pp. 26-7) asking "Why may not this portion have been written by S. Mark at a later period?;"—both alike resolutely insist on its genuineness and canonicity. To the honour of the best living master of Textual Criticism, the Rev. F. H. Scrivener, (of whom I desire to be understood to speak as a disciple of his master,) be it stated that he has never at any time given the least sanction to the popular outcry against this portion of the Gospel. "Without the slightest misgiving" he has uniformly maintained the genuineness of S. Mark xvi. 9—20. (*Introduction*, pp. 7 and 429—32.)

(he says,) "admits of satisfactory proof." He then recites
in detail the adverse external testimony which his predecessors had accumulated; remarking, that it is abundantly
confirmed by internal evidence. Of this he supplies a solitary sample; but declares that the whole passage is "abhorrent" to S. Mark's manner. "The facts of the case being
such," (and with this he dismisses the subject,) "a healthy
piety reclaims against the endeavours of those who are for
palming off as Mark's what the Evangelist is so plainly
shewn to have known nothing at all about [h]." A mass of
laborious annotation which comes surging in at the close
of verse 8, and fills two of Tischendorf's pages, has the effect
of entirely divorcing the twelve verses in question from the
inspired text of the Evangelist. On the other hand, the evidence *in favour* of the place is despatched in less than twelve
lines. What can be the reason that an Editor of the New
Testament parades elaborately every particular of the evidence, (such as it is,) *against* the genuineness of a considerable portion of the Gospel; and yet makes summary work
with the evidence in its favour? That Tischendorf has at
least entirely made up his mind on the matter in hand is
plain. Elsewhere, he speaks of the Author of these verses
as "*Pseudo Marcus* [i]."

2. Dr. Tregelles has expressed himself most fully on this
subject in his "Account of the Printed Text of the Greek
New Testament" (1854). The respected author undertakes
to shew "that the early testimony that S. Mark did not
write these verses is confirmed by existing monuments."
Accordingly, he announces as the result of the propositions
which he thinks he has established, "that the *book of Mark
himself* extends no further than ἐφοβοῦντο γάρ." He is the

---

[h] "Hæc non a Marco scripta esse argumentis probatur idoneis," (p. 320.)
"Quæ testimonia aliis corroborantur argumentis, ut quod conlatis prioribus
versu 9. parum apte adduntur verba ἀφ' ἧς ἐκβεβ. item quod singula multifariam a Marci ratione abhorrent." (p. 322.)—I quote from the 7th Leipsic
ed.; but in Tischendorf's 8th ed. (1866, pp. 403, 406,) the same verdict is
repeated, with the following addition:—"Quæ quum ita sint, sanæ erga
sacrum textum pietati adversari videntur qui pro apostolicis venditare per-
gunt quæ a Marco aliena esse tam luculenter docemur." (p. 407.)

Evangelia Apocrypha, 1853, Proleg. p. lvi.

only critic I have met with to whom it does not seem incredible that S. Mark did actually conclude his Gospel in
this abrupt way: observing that "perhaps we do not know
enough of the circumstances of S. Mark when he wrote his
Gospel to say whether he did or did not leave it with a complete termination." In this modest suggestion at least Dr.
Tregelles is unassailable, since we know absolutely nothing
whatever about "the circumstances of S. Mark," (or of any
other Evangelist,) "when he wrote his Gospel:" neither
indeed are we quite sure *who* S. Mark *was*. But when he
goes on to declare, notwithstanding, "that the remaining
twelve verses, by whomsoever written, have a full claim
to be received as an authentic part of the second Gospel;"
and complains that "there is in some minds a kind of
timidity with regard to Holy Scripture, as if all our notions
of its authority depended on our knowing who was the
writer of each particular portion; instead of simply seeing
and owning that it was given forth from GOD, and that it
is as much His as were the Commandments of the Law
written by His own finger on the tables of stone[k];"—the
learned writer betrays a misapprehension of the question
at issue, which we are least of all prepared to encounter in
such a quarter. We admire his piety but it is at the expense of his critical sagacity. For the question is not at all
one of *authorship*, but only one of *genuineness*. Have the
codices been *mutilated* which do *not* contain these verses?
If they have, then must these verses be held to be *genuine*.
But on the contrary, Have the codices been *supplemented*
which contain them? Then are these verses certainly *spurious*. There is no help for it but they must either be held
to be an integral part of the Gospel, and therefore, in default
of any proof to the contrary, as certainly by S. Mark as any
other twelve verses which can be named; or else an unauthorized addition to it. If they belong to the post-apostolic age it is idle to insist on their Inspiration, and to
claim that this "authentic anonymous addition to what
Mark himself wrote down" is as much the work of GOD
"as were the Ten Commandments written by His own

[k] pp. 253, 7—9.

finger on the tables of stone." On the other hand, if they "ought as much to be received as part of our second Gospel as the last chapter of Deuteronomy (unknown as the writer is) is received as the right and proper conclusion of the book of Moses,"—it is difficult to understand why the learned editor should think himself at liberty to sever them from their context, and introduce the subscription ΚΑΤΑ ΜΑΡΚΟΝ after ver. 8. In short, "How persons who believe that these verses did not form a part of the original Gospel of Mark, but were added afterwards, can say that they have a good claim to be received as an authentic or genuine part of the second Gospel, that is, a portion of canonical Scripture, passes comprehension." It passes even Dr. Davidson's comprehension; (for the foregoing words are his;) and Dr. Davidson, as some of us are aware, is not a man to stick at trifles [1].

3. Dean Alford went a little further than any of his pre-decessors. He says that this passage "was placed as a com-pletion of the Gospel soon after the Apostolic period,—the Gospel itself having been, for some reason unknown to us, left incomplete. The most probable supposition" (he adds) "is, that *the last leaf of the original Gospel was torn away.*" The italics in this conjecture (which was originally Gries-bach's) are not mine. The internal evidence (declares the same learned writer) "preponderates vastly against the au-thorship of Mark;" or (as he elsewhere expresses it) against "its genuineness as a work of the Evangelist." Accord-ingly, in his Prolegomena, (p. 38) he describes it as "*the remarkable fragment* at the end of the Gospel." After this, we are the less astonished to find that he *closes the second Gospel at ver.* 8; introduces the Subscription there; and en-closes the twelve verses which follow within heavy brackets. Thus, whereas from the days of our illustrious countryman

---

[1] In his first edition (1848, vol. i. p. 163) Dr. Davidson pronounced it "mani-festly untenable" that S. Mark's Gospel was the last written; and assigned A.D. 64 as "its most probable" date. In his second (1868, vol. ii. p. 117), he says:—"When we consider that *the Gospel was not written till the second century*, internal evidence loses much of its force against the authenticity of these verses."—*Introduction to N. T.*

Mill (1707), the editors of the N. T. have either been silent on the subject, or else have whispered only that this section of the Gospel is to be received with less of confidence than the rest,—it has been reserved for the present century to convert the ancient suspicions into actual charges. The latest to enter the field have been the first to execute Griesbach's adverse sentence pronounced fifty years ago, and to load the blessed Evangelist with bonds.

It might have been foreseen that when Critics so conspicuous permit themselves thus to handle the precious deposit, others would take courage to hurl their thunderbolts in the same direction with the less concern. "It is probable," (says Abp. Thomson in the *Bible Dictionary*,) "that this section is from a different hand, and was annexed to the Gospels soon after the times of the Apostles [m]."—The Rev. T. S. Green [n], (an able scholar, never to be mentioned without respect,) considers that "the hypothesis of very early interpolation satisfies the body of facts in evidence,"— which "point unmistakably in the direction of a spurious origin."—"In respect of Mark's Gospel," (writes Professor Norton in a recent work on the *Genuineness of the Gospels*,) "there is ground for believing that the last twelve verses were not written by the Evangelist, but were added by some other writer to supply a short conclusion to the work, which some cause had prevented the author from completing [o]."— Professor Westcott—who, jointly with the Rev. F. J. A. Hort, announces a revised Text—assures us that "the original text, from whatever cause it may have happened, terminated abruptly after the account of the Angelic vision." The rest "was added at another time, and probably by another hand." "It is in vain to speculate on the causes of this abrupt close." "The remaining verses cannot be regarded as part of the original narrative of S. Mark [p]."—Meyer insists that this is an "apocryphal fragment," and reproduces all the arguments, external and internal, which have ever been

---

[m] Vol. ii. p. 239.   [n] *Developed Criticism*, [1857], p. 53.

[o] Ed. 1847, i. p. 17. He recommends this view to his reader's acceptance in five pages,—pp. 216 to 221.

[p] *Introduction to the Study of the Gospels*, p. 311.

arrayed against it, without a particle of misgiving. The "note" with which he takes leave of the subject is even insolent[q]. A comparison (he says) of these "fragments" (ver. 9—18 and 19) with the parallel places in the other Gospels and in the Acts, shews how vacillating and various were the Apostolical traditions concerning the appearances of our LORD after His Resurrection, and concerning His Ascension. ("Hast thou killed, and also taken possession?")

Such, then, is the hostile verdict concerning these last twelve verses which I venture to dispute, and which I trust I shall live to see reversed. The writers above cited will be found to rely (1.) on the external evidence of certain ancient MSS.; and (2.) on Scholia which state "that the more ancient and accurate copies terminated the Gospel at ver. 8." (3.) They assure us that this is confirmed by a formidable array of Patristic authorities. (4.) Internal proof is declared not to be wanting. Certain incoherences and inaccuracies are pointed out. In fine, "the phraseology and style of the section" are declared to be "unfavourable to its authenticity;" not a few of the words and expressions being "foreign to the diction of Mark."—I propose to shew that all these confident and imposing statements are to a great extent either mistakes or exaggerations, and that the slender residuum of fact is about as powerless to achieve the purpose of the critics as were the seven green withs of the Philistines to bind Samson.

In order to exhibit successfully what I have to offer on this subject, I find it necessary to begin (in the next chapter) at the very beginning. I think it right, however, in this place to premise a few plain considerations which will be of use to us throughout all our subsequent inquiry; and which indeed we shall never be able to afford to lose sight of for long.

The question at issue being simply this,—Whether it is reasonable to suspect that the last twelve verses of S. Mark are a spurious accretion and unauthorized supplement to his Gospel, or not?—the whole of our business clearly resolves itself into an examination of what has been urged in proof

[q] *Critical and Exegetical Commentary,* 1855, 8vo. pp. 182, 186—92.

that the former alternative is the correct one. Our opponents maintain that these verses did not form part of the
original autograph of the Evangelist. But it is a known
rule in the Law of Evidence that *the burthen of proof lies on
the party who asserts the affirmative of the issue*[r]. We have
therefore to ascertain in the present instance what the supposed proof is exactly worth ; remembering always that in
this subject-matter a *high degree of probability* is the only
kind of proof which is attainable. When, for example, it is
contended that the famous words in S. John's first Epistle
(1 S. John v. 7, 8,) are not to be regarded as genuine, the
fact that they are away from almost every known Codex
is accepted as a proof that they were also away from the
autograph of the Evangelist. On far less weighty evidence,
in fact, we are at all times prepared to yield the hearty
assent of our understanding in this department of sacred
science.

And yet, it will be found that evidence of overwhelming
weight, if not of an entirely different kind, is required in
the present instance : as I proceed to explain.

1. When it is contended that our LORD's reply to the
young ruler (S. Matt. xix. 17) *was not* Τί με λέγεις ἀγαθόν ;
οὐδεὶς ἀγαθὸς, εἰ μὴ εἷς, ὁ Θεός,—it is at the same time insisted that *it was* Τί με ἐρωτᾷς περὶ τοῦ ἀγαθοῦ ; εἷς ἐστὶν
ὁ ἀγαθός. It is proposed to omit the former words *only* because an alternative clause is at hand, which it is proposed
to substitute in its room.

2. Again. When it is claimed that some given passage
of the Textus Receptus,—S. Mark xv. 28, for example,
(καὶ ἐπληρώθη ἡ γραφὴ ἡ λέγουσα, Καὶ μετὰ ἀνόμων ἐλο-
γίσθη,) or the Doxology in S. Matth. vi. 13,—is spurious,
all that is pretended is that certain words are an unauthorized addition to the inspired text ; and that by simply
omitting them we are so far restoring the Gospel to its
original integrity.—The same is to be said concerning *every
other charge of interpolation which can be named.* If the
celebrated "pericopa de adulterâ," for instance, be indeed

---

[r] In the Roman law this principle is thus expressed,—" Ei incumbit pro-
batio qui dicit, non qui negat." Taylor *on the Law of Evidence*, 1868, i. p. 369.

not genuine, we have but to leave out those twelve verses
of S. John's Gospel, and to read chap. vii. 52 in close sequence
with chap. viii. 12; and we are assured that we are put in
possession of the text as it came from the hands of its inspired Author.   Nor, (it must be admitted), is any difficulty
whatever occasioned thereby ; for there is no reason assignable why the two last-named verses should *not* cohere ; (there
is no internal improbability, I mean, in the supposition ;)
neither does there exist any *à priori* reason why a considerable portion of narrative should be looked for in that particular part of the Gospel.

3. But the case is altogether different, as all must see,
when it is proposed to get rid of the twelve verses which
for 1700 years and upwards have formed the conclusion of
S. Mark's Gospel ; no alternative conclusion being proposed
to our acceptance.   For let it be only observed what this
proposal practically amounts to and means.

(*a*.) And first, it does *not* mean that S. Mark himself, with
design, brought his Gospel to a close at the words ἐφοβοῦντο
γάρ.   *That* supposition would in fact be irrational.   It does
not mean, I say, that by simply leaving out those last
twelve verses we shall be restoring the second Gospel to its
original integrity.   And this it is which makes the present
a different case from every other, and necessitates a fuller,
if not a different kind of proof.

(*b*.) What then ?   It means that although an abrupt and
impossible termination would confessedly be the result of
omitting verses 9—20, no nearer approximation to the original autograph of the Evangelist is at present attainable.
Whether S. Mark was *interrupted* before he could finish his
Gospel,—(as Dr. Tregelles and Professor Norton suggest ;)—
in which case it will have been published by its Author
in an unfinished state: or whether "*the last leaf was torn
away*" before a single copy of the original could be procured,—(a view which is found to have recommended itself
to Griesbach ;)—in which case it will have once had a different termination from at present ; which termination however, by the hypothesis, has since been irrecoverably lost ;—
(and to one of these two wild hypotheses the critics are

logically reduced;)—*this* we are not certainly told. The critics are only agreed in assuming that S. Mark's Gospel *was at first without the verses which at present conclude it.*

But this assumption, (that a work which has been held to be a complete work for seventeen centuries and upwards was originally incomplete,) of course requires *proof.* The foregoing improbable theories, based on a gratuitous assumption, are confronted *in limine* with a formidable obstacle which must be absolutely got rid of before they can be thought entitled to a serious hearing. It is a familiar and a fatal circumstance that the Gospel of S. Mark has been furnished with its present termination ever since the second century of the Christian æra [*]. In default, therefore, of distinct historical evidence or definite documentary proof that *at some earlier period than that* it terminated abruptly, nothing short of the utter unfitness of the verses which at present conclude S. Mark's Gospel to be regarded as the work of the Evangelist, would warrant us in assuming that they are the spurious accretion of the post-apostolic age: and as such, at the end of eighteen centuries, to be deliberately rejected. We must absolutely be furnished, I say, with internal evidence of the most unequivocal character; or else with external testimony of a direct and definite kind, if we are to admit that the actual conclusion of S. Mark's Gospel is an unauthorized substitute for something quite different that has been lost. I can only imagine one other thing which could induce us to entertain such an opinion; and that would be the *general* consent of MSS., Fathers, and Versions in leaving these verses out. Else, it is evident that we are logically *forced* to adopt the far easier supposition that (*not* S. Mark, but) *some copyist of the third century* left a copy of S. Mark's Gospel unfinished; which unfinished copy became the fontal source of the mutilated copies which have come down to our own times [†].

---

[*] This is freely allowed by all. "Certiores facti sumus hanc pericopam jam in secundo sæculo lectam fuisse tanquam hujus evangelii partem." Tregelles *N. T.* p. 214.

[†] This in fact is how Bengel (N. T. p. 526) accounts for the phenomenon:—
"Fieri potuit ut librarius, scripto versu 8, reliquam partem scribere differret,

I have thought it right to explain the matter thus fully
at the outset; not in order to prejudge the question, (for
that could answer no good purpose,) but only in order that
the reader may have clearly set before him the real nature
of the issue. "Is it reasonable to suspect that the concluding verses of S. Mark are a spurious accretion and unauthorized supplement to his Gospel, or not?" *That* is the question which we have to consider,—the *one* question. And
while I proceed to pass under careful review all the evidence
on this subject with which I am acquainted, I shall be again
and again obliged to direct the attention of my reader to its
bearing on the real point at issue. In other words, we shall
have again and again to ask ourselves, how far it is rendered
probable by each fresh article of evidence that S. Mark's
Gospel, when it left the hands of its inspired Author, was an
unfinished work ; the last chapter ending abruptly at ver. 8 ?

I will only point out, before passing on, that the course
which has been adopted towards S. Mark xvi. 9—20, by the
latest Editors of the New Testament, is simply illogical.
Either they regard these verses as *possibly* genuine, or else
as *certainly* spurious. If they entertain (as they say they
do) a decided opinion that they are *not* genuine, they ought
(if they would be consistent) *to banish them from the text* [u].
Conversely, *since they do not banish them from the text,* they
have no right to pass a fatal sentence upon them ; to designate their author as "pseudo-Marcus;" to handle them in
contemptuous fashion. The plain truth is, these learned men
are better than their theory ; the worthlessness of which they
are made to *feel* in the present most conspicuous instance.
It reduces them to perplexity. It has landed them in inconsistency and error.—They will find it necessary in the
end to reverse their convictions. They cannot too speedily
reconsider their verdict, and retrace their steps.

et id exemplar, casu non perfectum, alii quasi perfectum sequerentur, praeser-
tim quum ea pars cum reliquâ historiâ evangelicâ minus congruere videretur."
  [u] It is thus that Tischendorf treats S. Luke xxiv. 12, and (in his latest edition) S. John xxi. 25.

CHAPTER III.

THE EARLY FATHERS APPEALED TO, AND OBSERVED TO BEAR FAVOURABLE WITNESS.

Patristic evidence sometimes the most important of any (p. 20).—*The importance of such evidence explained* (p. 21).—*Nineteen Patristic witnesses to these Verses, produced* (p. 23).—*Summary* (p. 30).

THE present inquiry must be conducted solely on grounds of Evidence, external and internal. For the full consideration of the former, seven Chapters will be necessary [a]: for a discussion of the latter, one seventh of that space will suffice [b]. We have first to ascertain whether the external testimony concerning S. Mark xvi. 9—20 is of such a nature as to constrain us to admit that it is highly probable that those twelve verses are a spurious appendix to S. Mark's Gospel.

1. It is well known that for determining the Text of the New Testament, we are dependent on three chief sources of information: viz. (1.) on MANUSCRIPTS,—(2.) on VERSIONS,—(3.) on FATHERS. And it is even self-evident that the *most ancient* MSS.,—the *earliest* Versions,—the *oldest* of the Fathers, will probably be in every instance the most trustworthy witnesses.

2. Further, it is obvious that a really ancient Codex of the Gospels must needs supply more valuable critical help in establishing the precise Text of Scripture than can possibly be rendered by any Translation, however faithful: while Patristic citations are on the whole a less decisive authority, even than Versions. The reasons are chiefly these : — (*a.*) Fathers often quote Scripture loosely, if not licentiously; and sometimes *allude* only when they seem to *quote*. (*b.*) They appear to have too often depended on their memory, and sometimes are demonstrably loose and inac-

---

[a] Chap. III.—VIII., also Chap. X.   [b] Chap. IX.

c 2

curate in their citations; the same Father being observed
to quote the same place in different ways. (*c.*) Copyists and
Editors may not be altogether depended upon for the exact
form of such supposed quotations. Thus the evidence of
Fathers must always be to some extent precarious.

3. On the other hand, it cannot be too plainly pointed
out that when,—instead of certifying ourselves of the *actual
words employed* by an Evangelist, their precise *form* and
exact *sequence*, — our object is only to ascertain whether
a considerable passage of Scripture is genuine or not; is to
be rejected or retained; was known or was not known in the
earliest] ages of the Church; then, instead of supplying the
least important evidence, Fathers become by far the most
valuable witnesses of all. This entire subject may be conveniently illustrated by an appeal to the problem before us.

4. Of course, if we possessed copies of the Gospels coeval
with their authors, nothing could compete with such evidence. But then unhappily nothing of the kind is the case.
The facts admit of being stated within the compass of a few
lines. We have one Codex (the Vatican, B) which is thought
to belong to the first half of the iv[th] century; and another,
the newly discovered Codex Sinaiticus, (at St. Petersburg, א)
which is certainly not quite so old,—perhaps by 50 years.
Next come two famous codices; the Alexandrine (in the
British Museum, A) and the Codex Ephraemi (in the Paris
Library, C), which are probably from 50 to 100 years more
recent still. The Codex Bezae (at Cambridge, D) is considered by competent judges to be the depository of a recension of the text as ancient as any of the others. Notwithstanding its strangely depraved condition therefore,—
the many "monstra potius quam variae lectiones" which it
contains, — it may be reckoned with the preceding four,
though it must be 50 or 100 years later than the latest of
them. After this, we drop down, (as far as S. Mark is concerned,) to 2 uncial MSS. of the viii[th] century,—7 of the
ix[th],—4 of the ix[th] or x[th c], while cursives of the xi[th] and xii[th]

---

[e] Viz. E, L, [viii]: K, M, V, Γ, Δ, Λ (quœre), Π (Tisch. *ed.* 8va.) [ix]:
G, X, S, U [ix, x]. The following uncials are defective here,—F (ver. 9—19),
H (ver. 9—14), I, N, O, P, Q, R, T, W, Y, Z.

centuries are very numerous indeed,—the copies increasing
in number in a rapid ratio as we descend the stream of Time.
Our primitive manuscript witnesses, therefore, are but *five*
in number at the utmost.   And of these it has never been
pretended that the oldest is to be referred to an earlier date
than the beginning of the iv[th] century, while it is thought
by competent judges that the last named may very possibly
have been written quite late in the vi[th].

5. Are we then reduced to this fourfold, (or at most five-
fold,) evidence concerning the text of the Gospels,—on evidence of not quite certain date, and yet (as we all believe) not
reaching further back than to the iv[th] century of our æra?
Certainly not.   Here, FATHERS come to our aid.   There are
perhaps as many as an hundred Ecclesiastical Writers older
than the oldest extant Codex of the N. T.: while between
A.D. 300 and A.D. 600, (within which limits our five oldest
MSS. may be considered certainly to fall,) there exist about
two hundred Fathers more.   True, that many of these have
left wondrous little behind them; and that the quotations
from Holy Scripture of the greater part may justly be described as rare and unsatisfactory.   But what then?   From
the three hundred, make a liberal reduction; and an hundred writers will remain who *frequently* quote the New
Testament, and who, when they do quote it, are probably
as trustworthy witnesses to the Truth of Scripture as either
Cod. ℵ or Cod. B.   We have indeed heard a great deal too
much of the precariousness of this class of evidence: not
nearly enough of the gross inaccuracies which disfigure the
text of those two Codices.   Quite surprising is it to discover
to what an extent Patristic quotations from the New Testament have evidently retained their exact original form.
What we chiefly desiderate at this time is a more careful
revision of the text of the Fathers, and more skilfully
elaborated indices of the works of each: *not one* of them
having been hitherto satisfactorily indexed.   It would be
easy to demonstrate the importance of bestowing far more
attention on this subject than it seems to have hitherto
enjoyed: but I shall content myself with citing a single
instance; and for this, (in order not to distract the reader's

attention), I shall refer him to the Appendix [d]. What is at
least beyond the limits of controversy, whenever *the genuineness of a considerable passage of Scripture* is the point in dispute, the testimony of Fathers who undoubtedly recognise
that passage, is beyond comparison the most valuable testimony we can enjoy.

6. For let it be only considered what is implied by
a Patristic appeal to the Gospel. It amounts to this:—
that a conspicuous personage, probably a Bishop of the
Church,—one, therefore, whose history, date, place, are all
more or less matter of notoriety,—gives us his written assurance that the passage in question was found in that copy of
the Gospels which he was accustomed himself to employ;
the uncial codex, (it has long since perished) *which belonged to
himself,* or to the Church which he served. It is evident, in
short, that any objection to quotations from Scripture in the
writings of the ancient Fathers can only apply to the *form*
of those quotations; not to their *substance.* It is just as
certain that a verse of Scripture was actually read by the
Father who unmistakedly refers to it, as if we had read it
with him; even though the gravest doubts may be entertained as to the 'ipsissima verba' which were found in his
own particular copy. He may have trusted to his memory:
or copyists may have taken liberties with his writings: or
editors may have misrepresented what they found in the
written copies. The *form* of the quoted verse, I repeat, may
have suffered almost to any extent. The *substance,* on the
contrary, inasmuch as it lay wholly beyond their province,
may be looked upon as an indisputable *fact.*

7. Some such preliminary remarks, (never out of place
when quotations from the Fathers are to be considered,)
cannot well be withheld when the most venerable Ecclesiastical writings are appealed to. The earliest of the Fathers
are observed to quote with singular licence,—to *allude* rather
than to quote. Strange to relate, those ancient men seem
scarcely to have been aware of the grave responsibility they
incurred when they substituted expressions of their own for
the utterances of the SPIRIT. It is evidently not so much

---

[d] See Appendix (A), on the true reading of S. Luke ii. 14.

that their *memory* is in fault, as their *judgment,*—in that
they evidently hold themselves at liberty to paraphrase, to
recast, to reconstruct [e].

I. Thus, it is impossible to resist the inference that PAPIAS
refers to S. Mark xvi. 18 when he records a marvellous
tradition concerning "Justus surnamed Barsabas," "how
that after drinking noxious poison, through the LORD'S grace
he experienced no evil consequence [f]." He does not give
the words of the Evangelist. It is even surprising how completely he passes them by; and yet the allusion to the place
just cited is manifest. Now, Papias is a writer who lived so
near the time of the Apostles that he made it his delight
to collect their traditional sayings. His date (according to
Clinton) is A.D. 100.

II. JUSTIN MARTYR, the date of whose first Apology is
A.D. 151, is observed to say concerning the Apostles that,
after our LORD'S Ascension,—ἐξελθόντες πανταχοῦ ἐκήρυξαν [g]: which is nothing else but a quotation from the last
verse of S. Mark's Gospel,—ἐκεῖνοι δὲ ἐξελθόντες ἐκήρυξαν
πανταχοῦ. And thus it is found that the conclusion of
S. Mark's Gospel was familiarly known within fifty years
of the death of the last of the Evangelists.

III. When IRENÆUS, in his third Book against Heresies,
deliberately quotes and remarks upon the 19th verse of the
last chapter of S. Mark's Gospel [h], we are put in possession of

---

[e] Consider how Ignatius (*ad Smyrn.*, c. 3) quotes S. Luke xxiv. 39; and
how he refers to S. John xii. 3 in his Ep. *ad Ephes.* c. 17.

[f] Ἱστορεῖ [sc. Παπίας] ἕτερον παράδοξον περὶ Ἰοῦστον τὸν ἐπικληθέντα Βαρσαβᾶν γεγονὸς,—evidently a slip of the pen for Βαρσαβᾶν τὸν ἐπικληθέντα Ἰοῦστον
(see Acts i. 23, quoted by Eusebius immediately afterwards,)—ὡς δηλητήριον
φάρμακον ἐμπιόντος καὶ μηδὲν ἀηδὲς διὰ τὴν τοῦ Κυρίου χάριν ὑπομείναντος.
Euseb. *Hist. Eccl.* iii. 39.

[g] *Apol.* I. c. 45.—The supposed quotations in c. 9 from the Fragment *De
Resurrectione* (Westcott and others) are clearly references to S. Luke xxiv.,—
not to S. Mark xvi.

[h] lib. iii. c. x. *ad fin.* (ed. Stieren, i. p. 462). "In fine autem Evangelii ait
Marcus, *et quidem Dominus Jesus, postquam locutus est eis, receptus est in
caelos, et sedet ad dexteram Dei.*" Accordingly, against S. Mark xvi. 19 in
Harl. MS. 5647 (= Evan. 72) occurs the following marginal scholium, which
Cramer has already published.—Εἰρηναῖος ὁ τῶν Ἀποστόλων πλησίον, ἐν τῷ
πρὸς τὰς αἱρέσεις γ΄ λόγῳ τοῦτο ἀνήνεγκεν τὸ ῥητὸν ὡς Μάρκῳ εἰρημένον.

the certain fact that the entire passage now under consideration was extant in a copy of the Gospels which was used by the Bishop of the Church of Lyons sometime about the year A.D. 180, and which therefore cannot possibly have been written much more than a hundred years after the date of the Evangelist himself: while it *may* have been written by a contemporary of S. Mark, and probably *was* written by one who lived immediately after his time.—Who sees not that this single piece of evidence is in itself sufficient to outweigh the testimony of any codex extant? It is in fact a mere trifling with words to distinguish between "Manuscript" and "Patristic" testimony in a case like this: for (as I have already explained) the passage quoted from S. Mark's Gospel by Irenæus is to all intents and purposes *a fragment from a dated manuscript;* and *that* MS., demonstrably older by at least one hundred and fifty years than the oldest copy of the Gospels which has come down to our times.

IV. Take another proof that these concluding verses of S. Mark were in the second century accounted an integral part of his Gospel. HIPPOLYTUS, Bishop of Portus near Rome (190—227), a contemporary of Irenæus, quotes the 17th and 18th verses in his fragment Περὶ Χαρισμάτων[1].

---

[1] First published as his by Fabricius (vol. i. 245.) Its authorship has never been disputed. In the enumeration of the works of Hippolytus (inscribed on the chair of his marble effigy in the Lateran Museum at Rome) is read,—ΠΕΡΙ ΧΑΡΙΣΜΑΤΩΝ ; and by that name the fragment in question is actually designated in the third chapter of the (so called) "Apostolical Constitutions," (τὰ μὲν οὖν πρῶτα τοῦ λόγου ἐξεθέμεθα περὶ τῶν Χαρισμάτων, κ.τ.λ.),—in which singular monument of Antiquity the fragment itself is also found. It is in fact nothing else but the first two chapters of the "Apostolical Constitutions;" of which the iv[th] chapter is also claimed for Hippolytus, (though with evidently far less reason,) and as such appears in the last edition of the Father's collected works, (*Hippolyti Romani quæ feruntur omnia Græce,* ed. Lagarde, 1858,)—p. 74.

The work thus assigned to Hippolytus, (evidently on the strength of the heading,—Διατάξεις τῶν αὐτῶν ἁγίων Ἀποστόλων περὶ χειροτονιῶν, διὰ Ἱππολύτου,) is part of the "Octateuchus Clementinus," concerning which Lagarde has several remarks in the preface to his *Reliquiæ Juris Ecclesiastici Antiquissimæ,* 1856. The composition in question extends from p. 5 to p. 18 of the last-named publication. The exact correspondence between the "Octateuchus Clementinus" and the Pseudo-Apostolical Constitutions will be found to ex-

Also in his Homily on the heresy of Noetus[k], Hippolytus
has a plain reference to this section of S. Mark's Gospel.
To an inattentive reader, the passage alluded to might seem
to be only the fragment of a Creed; but this is not the
case.   In the Creeds, CHRIST is *invariably* spoken of as
ἀνελθόντα : in the Scriptures, *invariably* as ἀναληφθέντα[l].
So that when Hippolytus says of Him, ἀναλαμβάνεται εἰς
οὐρανοὺς καὶ ἐκ δεξιῶν Πατρὸς καθίζεται, the reference must
needs be to S. Mark xvi. 19.

V. At the Seventh COUNCIL OF CARTHAGE held under
Cyprian, A.D. 256, (on the baptizing of Heretics,) Vincentius, Bishop of Thibari, (a place not far from Carthage,) in
the presence of the eighty-seven assembled African bishops,
quoted two of the verses under consideration[m]; and Augustine, about a century and a half later, in his reply, recited
the words afresh[n].

VI. The Apocryphal ACTA PILATI (sometimes called the
" Gospel of Nicodemus") Tischendorf assigns without hesitation to the iii[rd] century; whether rightly or wrongly
I have no means of ascertaining.   It is at all events a very
ancient forgery, and it contains the 15th, 16th, 17th and
18th verses of this chapter[o].

VII. This is probably the right place to mention that ver.
15 is clearly alluded to in two places of the (so-called) " APO-
STOLICAL CONSTITUTIONS[p];" and that verse 16 is quoted (with

tend no further than the single chapter (the iv[th]) specified in the text. In
the meantime the fragment περὶ χαρισμάτων (containing S. Mark xvi. 17, 18,)
is identical throughout. It forms the first article in Lagarde's *Reliquiæ*, extending from p. 1 to p. 4, and is there headed Διδασκαλία τῶν ἁγίων 'Αποστόλων
περὶ χαρισμάτων.

   [k] *Ad fin.* See Routh's *Opuscula*, i. p. 80.

   [l] For which reason I cordially subscribe to Tischendorf's remark (ed. 8va.
p. 407), " Quod idem [Justinus] Christum ἀνεληλυθότα εἰς τοὺς οὐράνους dicit,
[*Apol.* I. c. 50 ?] minus valet."

   [m] " In nomine meo manum imponite, daemonia expellite," (Cyprian *Opp.*
p. 237 [*Reliqq. Sacr.* iii. p. 124,] quoting S. Mark xvi. 17, 18,)—" *In nomine
meo daemonia ejicient* .... super egrotos *manus imponent* et bene habebunt."

   [n] *Responsa ad Episcopos*, c. 44, (*Reliqq.* v. 248.)

   [o] *Evangelia Apocrypha*, ed. Tischendorf, 1853, pp. 243 and 351: also
Proleg. p. lvi.

   [p] In *l.* vii. c. 7 (*ad fin.*),—λαβόντες ἐντολὴν παρ' αὐτοῦ κηρύξαι τὸ εὐαγγέλιον

no variety of reading from the *Textus receptus* ^q) in an earlier
part of the same ancient work. The "Constitutions" are
assigned to the iiird or the ivth century ^r.

VIII and IX. It will be shewn in Chapter V. that EUSE-
BIUS, the Ecclesiastical Historian, was profoundly well acquainted with these verses. He discusses them largely, and
(as I shall prove in the chapter referred to) was by no means
disposed to question their genuineness. His Church History
was published A.D. 325.

MARINUS also, (whoever that individual may have been,)
a contemporary of Eusebius,—inasmuch as he is introduced
to our notice by Eusebius himself as asking a question concerning the last twelve verses of S. Mark's Gospel without
a trace of misgiving as to the genuineness of that about
which he inquires,—is a competent witness in their favor
who has hitherto been overlooked in this discussion.

X. Tischendorf and his followers state that Jacobus Nisibenus quotes these verses. For "Jacobus Nisibenus" read
"APHRAATES the Persian Sage," and the statement will be
correct. The history of the mistake is curious.

Jerome, in his Catalogue of Ecclesiastical writers, makes
no mention of Jacob of Nisibis,—a famous Syrian Bishop
who was present at the Council of Nicæa, A.D. 325. Gen-
nadius of Marseille, (who carried on Jerome's list to the
year 495) asserts that the reason of this omission was Jerome's ignorance of the Syriac language; and explains that
Jacob was the author of twenty-two Syriac Homilies ^s. Of
these, there exists a very ancient Armenian translation;
which was accordingly edited as the work of Jacobus Nisibenus with a Latin version, at Rome, in 1756. Gallandius
reprinted both the Armenian and the Latin; and to Gallandius (vol. v.) we are referred whenever "Jacobus Nisibenus"
is quoted.

εἰς ὅλον τὸν κόσμον: and in *l.* viii. *c.* 1,—ἡμῖν τοῖς ἀποστόλοις μέλλουσι τὸ
εὐαγγέλιον καταγγέλλειν πάσῃ τῇ κτίσει. Observe, this immediately follows
the quotation of verses 17, 18.

   ^q *Lib.* vi. *c.* 15.—The quotation (at the beginning of *lib.* viii.) of the 17th
and 18th verses, has been already noticed in its proper place. *Supra*, p. 24.

   ^r Scrivener's *Introduction*, p. 421.

   ^s *Apud* Hieron. *Opp. ed.* Vallars., ii. 951-4.

But the proposed attribution of the Homilies in question, —though it has been acquiesced in for nearly 1400 years,— is incorrect. Quite lately the Syriac originals have come to light, and they prove to be the work of Aphraates, "the Persian Sage,"—a Bishop, and the earliest known Father of the Syrian Church. In the first Homily, (which bears date A.D. 337), verses 16, 17, 18 of S. Mark xvi. are quoted [t],— yet not from the version known as the Curetonian Syriac, nor yet from the Peshito exactly [u].—Here, then, is another wholly independent witness to the last twelve verses of S. Mark, coeval certainly with the two oldest copies of the Gospel extant,—B and א.

XI. AMBROSE, Archbishop of Milan (A.D. 374—397) freely quotes this portion of the Gospel,—citing ver. 15 four times: verses 16, 17 and 18, each three times: ver. 20, once [x].

XII. The testimony of CHRYSOSTOM (A.D. 400) has been all but overlooked. In part of a Homily claimed for him by his Benedictine Editors, he points out that S. Luke alone of the Evangelists describes the Ascension : S. Matthew and S. John not speaking of it,—S. Mark recording the event only. Then he quotes verses 19, 20. "This" (he adds) "is the end of the Gospel. Mark makes no extended mention of the Ascension [y]." Elsewhere he has an unmistakable reference to S. Mark xvi. 9 [z].

XIII. JEROME, on a point like this, is entitled to more attention than any other Father of the Church. Living at a very early period, (for he was born in 331 and died in 420,) — endowed with extraordinary Biblical learning, — a man of excellent judgment,—and a professed Editor of

[t] See Dr. Wright's ed. of " Aphraates," (4to. 1869,) i. p. 21. I am entirely indebted to the learned Editor's *Preface* for the information in the text.

[u] From Dr. Wright, and my brother Archdeacon Rose.

[x] Vol. i. 796 E and vol. ii. 461 D quote ver. 15 : 1429 B quotes ver. 15 and 16 : vol. ii. 663 B, C quotes ver. 15 to 18. Vol. i. 127 A quotes ver. 16 to 18. Vol. i. 639 E and vol. ii. 400 A quote ver. 17, 18. Vol. i. 716 A quotes ver. 20.

[y] *Opp.* iii. 765 A, B.

[z] Καὶ μὴν τὸ εὐαγγέλιον τοὐναντίον λέγει, ὅτι ᾗ Μαρίᾳ πρώτῃ [ὤφθη]. Chrys. *Opp.* x. 355 B.

the New Testament, for the execution of which task he
enjoyed extraordinary facilities, — his testimony is most
weighty. Not unaware am I that Jerome is commonly
supposed to be a witness on the opposite side: concerning
which mistake I shall have to speak largely in Chapter V.
But it ought to be enough to point out that we should not
have met with these last twelve verses in the Vulgate, had
Jerome held them to be spurious [a]. He familiarly quotes
the 9th verse in one place of his writings [b]; in another place
he makes the extraordinary statement that in certain of the
copies, (especially the Greek,) was found after ver. 14 *the
reply of the eleven Apostles,* when our SAVIOUR "upbraided
them with their unbelief and hardness of heart, because
they believed not them which had seen Him after He was
risen [c]." To discuss so weak and worthless a forgery,—no
trace of which is found in any MS. in existence, and of
which nothing whatever is known except what Jerome here
tells us,—would be to waste our time indeed. The fact remains, however, that Jerome, besides giving these last twelve
verses a place in the Vulgate, quotes S. Mark xvi. 14, as
well as ver. 9, in the course of his writings.

XIV. It was to have been expected that AUGUSTINE would
quote these verses: but he more than quotes them. He
brings them forward again and again [d],—discusses them as
the work of S. Mark,—remarks that "in diebus Pascha-
libus," S. Mark's narrative of the Resurrection was publicly

---

[a] "Cogis" (he says to Pope Damasus) "ut post exemplaria Scripturarum
toto orbe dispersa quasi quidam arbiter sedeam; et quia inter se variant, quae
sint illa quae cum Graecâ consentiant veritate decernam.—Haec praesens
praefatiuncula pollicetur quatuor Evangelia . . . . codicum Graecorum emen-
data conlatione, sed et veterum."

[b] Vol. i. p. 327 C (*ed.* Vallars.)

[c] *Contra Pelagianos,* II. 15, (Opp. ii. 744-5) :—"In quibusdam exemplaribus
et maxime in Graecis codicibus, juxta Marcum in fine Evangelii scribitur :
*Postea quum accubuissent undecim, apparuit eis Jesus, et exprobravit incre-
dulitatem et duritiam cordis eorum, quia his qui viderant eum resurgentem,
non crediderunt. Et illi satisfaciebant dicentes : Sæculum istud iniquitatis
et incredulitatis substantia est, quae non sinit per immundos spiritus veram
Dei apprehendi virtutem : idcirco jam nunc revela justitiam tuam.*"

[d] e.g. ver. 12 in vol. ii. 515 C (Ep. 149); Vol. v. 988 C.—Verses 15, 16, in
vol. v. 391 E, 985 A: vol. x. 22 F.

read in the Church [e]. All this is noteworthy. Augustine flourished A.D. 395—430.

XV. and XVI. Another very important testimony to the genuineness of the concluding part of S. Mark's Gospel is furnished by the unhesitating manner in which NESTORIUS, the heresiarch, quotes ver. 20 ; and CYRIL OF ALEXANDRIA accepts his quotation, adding a few words of his own [f]. Let it be borne in mind that this is tantamount to the discovery of *two* dated codices containing the last twelve verses of S. Mark,—and *that* date *anterior* (it is impossible to say by how many years) to A.D. 430.

XVII. VICTOR OF ANTIOCH, (concerning whom I shall have to speak very largely in Chapter V.,) flourished about A.D. 425. The critical testimony which he bears to the genuineness of these verses is more emphatic than is to be met with in the pages of any other ancient Father. It may be characterized as the most conclusive testimony which it was in his power to render.

XVIII. HESYCHIUS of Jerusalem, by a singular oversight, has been reckoned among the impugners of these verses. He is on the contrary their eager advocate and champion. It seems to have escaped observation that towards the close of his " Homily on the Resurrection," (published in the works of Gregory of Nyssa, and erroneously ascribed to that Father,) Hesychius appeals to the 19th verse, and quotes it as S. Mark's at length [g]. The date of Hesychius is uncertain ; but he may, I suppose, be considered to belong to the vi[th] century. His evidence is discussed in Chapter V.

XIX. This list shall be brought to a close with a reference to the SYNOPSIS SCRIPTURAE SACRAE,—an ancient work

---

[e] Vol. v. 997 F, 998 B, C.

[f] ἐξελθόντες γάρ, φησι, διεκήρυσσον τὸν λόγον πανταχοῦ. τοῦ Κυρίου συνεργοῦντος, καὶ τὸν λόγον βεβαιοῦντος, διὰ τῶν ἐπακολουθησάντων σημείων. Nestorius c. *Orthodoxos :* (Cyril. Alexand. adv. Nestorian. Opp. vol. vi. 46 B.) To which, Cyril replies,— τῇ παρ' αὐτοῦ δυναστείᾳ χρώμενοι, διεκηρύττοντο καὶ εἰργάζοντο τὰς θεοσημείας οἱ θεσπέσιοι μαθηταί. *(Ibid.* D.) This quotation was first noticed by Matthaei (*Enthym. Zig.* i. 161.)

[g] ὁμοίως δὲ καὶ τὸ παρὰ τῷ Μάρκῳ γεγραμμένον· 'Ο μὲν οὖν Κύριος—ἐκ δεξιῶν τοῦ Θεοῦ. Greg. Nyss. *Opp.* iii. 415.

ascribed to Athanasius [h], but probably not the production of
that Father.   It is at all events of much older date than
any of the later uncials; and it rehearses in detail the contents of S. Mark xvi. 9—20 [i].

It would be easy to prolong this enumeration of Patristic
authorities; as, by appealing to Gregentius in the vi[th] century,
and to Gregory the Great, and Modestus, patriarch of Constantinople in the vii[th];—to Ven. Bede and John Damascene
in the viii[th];—to Theophylact in the xi[th];—to Euthymius
in the xii[th][k]: but I forbear.   It would add no strength to my
argument that I should by such evidence support it; as the
reader will admit when he has read my X[th] chapter.

It will be observed then that *three* competent Patristic
witnesses of the ii[nd] century,—*four* of the iii[rd],—*six* of the
iv[th],—*four* of the vth,—and *two* (of uncertain date, but probably) of the vi[th],—have admitted their familiarity with
these "last Twelve Verses."   Yet do they not belong to one
particular age, school, or country.   They come, on the contrary, from every part of the ancient Church: Antioch and

---

[h] Athanasii *Opp.* vol. ii. p. 181 F, 182 A.   See the *Præfat.*, pp. vii., viii.

[i] In dismissing this enumeration, let me be allowed to point out that there
must exist many more Patristic citations which I have overlooked.   The necessity one is under, on occasions like the present, of depending to a great extent
on "Indices," is fatal; so scandalously inaccurate is almost every Index of
Texts that can be named.   To judge from the Index in Oehler's edition of
Tertullian, that Father quotes these twelve verses not less than eight times.
According to the Benedictine Index, Ambrose does not quote them so much
as once.   Ambrose, nevertheless, quotes five of these verses no less than fourteen times; while Tertullian, as far as I am able to discover, does not quote
S. Mark xvi. 9—20 at all.

Again.   One hoped that the Index of Texts in Dindorf's new Oxford ed. of
Clemens Alex. was going to remedy the sadly defective Index in Potter's ed.
But we are still exactly where we were.   S. John i. 3 (or 4), so remarkably
quoted in vol. iii. 433, l. 8: S. John i. 18, 50, memorably represented in vol. iii.
412, l. 26: S. Mark i. 13, interestingly referred to in vol. iii. 455, lines 5, 6, 7:
—are nowhere noticed in the Index.   The Voice from Heaven at our SAVIOUR'S
Baptism,—a famous misquotation (vol. i. 145, l. 14),—does not appear in the
Index of quotations from S. Matthew (iii. 17), S. Mark (i. 11), or S. Luke
(iii. 22.)

[k] Gregentius *apud* Galland. xi. 653 E.—Greg. Mag. (Hom. xxix. in Evang.)
—Modestus *apud* Photium *cod.* 275.—Johannis Damasceni *Opp.* (ed. 1712)
vol. i. 608 E.—Bede, and Theophylact (who quotes *all* the verses) and Euthymius *in loc.*

Constantinople,—Hierapolis, Cæsarea and Edessa,—Carthage, Alexandria and Hippo,—Rome and Portus.   And thus, upwards of nineteen early codexes have been to all intents and purposes inspected for us in various lands by unprejudiced witnesses,—*seven* of them at least of more ancient date than the oldest copy of the Gospels extant.

I propose to recur to this subject for an instant when the reader has been made acquainted with the decisive testimony which ancient Versions supply.   But the Versions deserve a short Chapter to themselves.

CHAPTER IV.

THE EARLY VERSIONS EXAMINED, AND FOUND TO YIELD
UNFALTERING TESTIMONY TO THE GENUINENESS OF
THESE VERSES.

*The Peshito,—the Curetonian Syriac,—and the Recension of Thomas
of Hharkel* (p. 33.)*—The Vulgate* (p. 34)*—and the Vetus Itala*
(p. 35)*—the Gothic* (p. 35)*—and the Egyptian Versions* (p. 35).*—
Review of the Evidence up to this point,* (p. 36).

It was declared at the outset that when we are seeking to
establish in detail *the Text* of the Gospels, the testimony
of Manuscripts is incomparably the most important of all.
To early Versions, the second place was assigned. To Patristic citations, the third. But it was explained that whenever (as here) the only question to be decided is whether
a considerable portion of Scripture be genuine or not, then,
Patristic references yield to no class of evidence in importance. To which statement it must now be added that second
only to the testimony of Fathers on such occasions is to be
reckoned the evidence of the oldest of the Versions. The
reason is obvious. (*a.*) We know for the most part the approximate date of the principal ancient Versions of the New
Testament :—(*b.*) Each Version is represented by at least one
very ancient Codex :—and (*c.*) It may be safely assumed that
Translators were never dependant on a single copy of the
original Greek when they executed their several Translations. Proceed we now to ascertain what evidence the oldest
of the Versions bear concerning the concluding verses of
S. Mark's Gospel : and first of all for the Syriac.

I. "Literary history," (says Mr. Scrivener,) " can hardly
afford a more powerful case than has been established for
the identity of the Version of the Syriac now called the
' Peshito' with that used by the Eastern Church long before the great schism had its beginning, in the native land

of the blessed Gospel." The Peshito is referred by common consent to the iind century of our æra ; and is found to contain the verses in question.

II. This, however, is not all. Within the last thirty years, fragments of *another* very ancient Syriac translation of the Gospels, (called from the name of its discoverer " THE CURE-TONIAN SYRIAC,") have come to light[a] : and in this translation also the verses in question are found[b]. This fragmentary codex is referred by Cureton to the middle of the vth century. At what earlier date the Translation may have been executed,—as well as how much older the original Greek copy may have been which this translator employed,—can of course only be conjectured. But it is clear that we are listening to another truly primitive witness to the genuineness of the text now under consideration ;—a witness (like the last) vastly more ancient than either the Vatican Codex B, or the Sinaitic Codex ℵ ; more ancient, therefore, than any Greek copy of the Gospels in existence. We shall not be thought rash if we claim it for the iiird century.

III. Even this, however, does not fully represent the sum of the testimony which the Syriac language bears on this subject. Philoxenus, Monophysite Bishop of Mabug (Hierapolis) in Eastern Syria, caused a revision of the Peshito Syriac to be executed by his Chorepiscopus Polycarp, A.D. 508 ; and by the aid of three[c] approved and accurate Greek manuscripts, this revised version of Polycarp was again revised by Thomas of Hharkel, in the monastery of Antonia at Alexandria, A.D. 616. The Hharklensian Revision, (commonly called the " PHILOXENIAN,") is therefore an extraordinary monument of ecclesiastical antiquity indeed : for, being the Revision of a revised Translation of the New Testament known to have been executed from MSS. which must have been at least as old as the vth century, it ex-

---

[a] Dr. Wright informs me (1871) that some more leaves of this Version have just been recovered.

[b] By a happy providence, one of the fragments contains the last four verses.

[c] In the margin, against S. Matth. xxviii. 5, Thomas writes,—" *In tribus codicibus Græcis,* et in uno Syriaco antiquæ versionis, non inventum est nomen, ' Nazarenus.' "—Cf. ad xxvii. 35.—Adler's *N. T. Verss. Syrr.*, p. 97.

hibits the result of what may be called a collation of copies
made at a time when only four of our extant uncials were
in existence.   Here, then, is a singularly important accumu-
lation of manuscript evidence on the subject of the verses
which of late years it has become the fashion to treat as
spurious.   And yet, neither by Polycarp nor by Thomas
of Hharkel, are the last twelve verses of S. Mark's Gospel
omitted [d].

To these, if I do not add the "Jerusalem version,"—(as
an independent Syriac translation of the Ecclesiastical Sections, perhaps of the vth century, is called [e],)—it is because
our fourfold Syriac evidence is already abundantly. sufficient.
In itself, it far outweighs in respect of antiquity anything
that can be shewn on the other side.   Turn we next to the
Churches of the West.

IV. That Jerome, at the bidding of Pope Damasus (A.D.
382), was the author of that famous Latin version of the
Scriptures called THE VULGATE, is known to all.   It seems
scarcely possible to overestimate the critical importance of
such a work,—executed at such a time,—under such auspices,
—and by a man of so much learning and sagacity as Jerome.
When it is considered that we are here presented with the
results of a careful examination of the best Greek Manuscripts to which a competent scholar had access in the
middle of the fourth century,—(and Jerome assures us that

---

[d] That among the 437 various readings and marginal notes on the Gospels
relegated to the Philoxenian margin, should occur the worthless supplement
which is only found besides in Cod. L. (see ch. viii.)—is not at all surprising.
Of these 437 readings and notes, 91 are not found. in White's Edition; while
105 (the supplement in question being one of them) are found in White only.
This creates a suspicion that in part at least the Philoxenian margin must
exhibit traces of the assiduity of subsequent critics of the Syriac text.   (So
Adler on S. Matth. xxvi. 40.)   To understand the character of some of those
marginal notes and annotations, the reader has but to refer to Adler's learned
work, (pp. 79—134) and examine the notes on the following places :—S. Matth.
xv. 21 : xx. 28 (= D): xxvi. 7.   S. Mk. i. 16 : xii. 42.   S. Lu. x. 17 (= B D):
42 (= B ℵ L): xi. 1 : 53.   S. Jo. ii. 1 [3] (=ℵ) : iii. 26: vii. 39 (partly
= B) : x. 8, &c. &c.

[e] This work has at last been published in 2 vols. 4to., Verona, 1861-4,
under the following title :—*Evangeliarium Hierosolymitanum ex Codice Vaticano Palaestino demprompsit, edidit, Latine vertit, Prolegomenis et Glossario
adornavit, Comes* FRANCISCUS MINISCALCHI ERIZZO.

he consulted several,)—we learn to survey with diminished complacency our own slender stores (if indeed any at all exist) of corresponding antiquity. It is needless to add that the Vulgate contains the disputed verses: that from no copy of this Version are they away. Now, in such a matter as this, Jerome's testimony is very weighty indeed.

V. The Vulgate, however, was but the revision of a much older translation, generally known as the VETUS ITALA. This Old Latin, which is of African origin and of almost Apostolic antiquity, (supposed of the ii[nd] century,) conspires with the Vulgate in the testimony which it bears to the genuineness of the end of S. Mark's Gospel[f] :—an emphatic witness that in the African province, from the earliest time, no doubt whatever was entertained concerning the genuineness of these last twelve verses.

VI. The next place may well be given to the venerable version of the Gothic Bishop Ulphilas,—A.D. 350. Himself a Cappadocian, Ulphilas probably derived his copies from Asia Minor. His version is said to have been exposed to certain corrupting influences ; but the unequivocal evidence which it bears to the last verses of S. Mark is at least unimpeachable, and must be regarded as important in the highest degree[g]. The oldest extant copy of the GOTHIC of Ulphilas is assigned to the vth or early in the vi[th] century : and the verses in question are there also met with.

VII. and VIII. The ancient Egyptian versions call next for notice : their testimony being so exceedingly ancient and respectable. The MEMPHITIC, or dialect of Lower Egypt, (less properly called the "Coptic" version), which is assigned to the iv[th] or v[th] century, contains S. Mark xvi. 9—20.—Fragments of the THEBAIC, or dialect of Upper Egypt, (a distinct version and of considerably earlier date,

---

[f] It does not sensibly detract from the value of this evidence that *one* ancient codex, the "Codex Bobbiensis" (k), which Tregelles describes as "a revised text, in which the influence of ancient MSS. is discernible," [*Printed text*, &c. p. 170.] and which therefore may not be cited in the present controversy,—exhibits after ver. 8 a Latin translation of the spurious words which are also found in Cod. L.

[g] "Quod Gothicum testimonium haud scio an critici satis agnoverint, vel pro dignitate aestimaverint." Mai, *Nova Patt. Bibl.* iv. 256.

less properly called the " Sahidic,") survive in MSS. of
very nearly the same antiquity: and one of these fragments happily contains the last verse of the Gospel according to S. Mark. The Thebaic version is referred to the
iiird century.

After this mass of evidence, it will be enough to record
concerning the Armenian version, that it yields inconstant
testimony: some of the MSS. ending at ver. 8; others
putting after these words the subscription, ($\epsilon\dot{v}a\gamma\gamma\acute{\epsilon}\lambda\iota o\nu$ $\kappa a\tau\grave{a}$
$Má\rho\kappa o\nu$,) and then giving the additional verses with a new
subscription: others going on without any break to the
end. This version may be as old as the vth century; but
like the Ethiopic [iv—vii?] and the Georgian [vi?] it
comes to us in codices of comparatively recent date. All
this makes it impossible for us to care much for its testimony. The two last-named versions, whatever their disadvantages may be, at least bear constant witness to the
genuineness of the verses in dispute.

1. And thus we are presented with a mass of additional
evidence, — so various, so weighty, so multitudinous, so
venerable,—in support of this disputed portion of the Gospel, that it might well be deemed in itself decisive.

2. For these Versions do not so much shew what individuals held, as what Churches have believed and taught
concerning the sacred Text,—mighty Churches in Syria
and Mesopotamia, in Africa and Italy, in Palestine and
Egypt.

3. We may here, in fact, conveniently review the progress
which has been hitherto made in this investigation. And
in order to bar the door against dispute and cavil, let us
be content to waive the testimony of Papias as precarious,
and that of Justin Martyr as too fragmentary to be decisive.
Let us frankly admit that the citation of Vincentius à
Thibari at the viith Carthaginian Council is sufficiently in-
exact to make it unsafe to build upon it. The " Acta Pilati" and the " Apostolical Constitutions," since their date
is somewhat doubtful, shall be claimed for the ivth century
only, and not for the iiird. And now, how will the evidence stand for the last Twelve Verses of S. Mark's Gospel?

(*a*) In the vth century, to which Codex A and Codex C are referred, (for Codex D is certainly later,) at least three famous Greeks and the most illustrious of the Latin Fathers, —(*four* authorities in all,)—are observed to recognise these verses.

(*b*) In the iv[th] century, (to which Codex B and Codex א probably belong, five Greek writers, one Syriac, and two Latin Fathers,—besides the Vulgate, Gothic and Memphitic Versions,—(*eleven* authorities in all,)—testify to familiar acquaintance with this portion of S. Mark's Gospel.

(*c*) In the iii[rd] century, (and by this time MS. evidence has entirely forsaken us,) we find Hippolytus, the Curetonian Syriac, and the Thebaic Version, bearing plain testimony that at that early period, in at least *three* distinct provinces of primitive Christendom, no suspicion whatever attached to these verses. Lastly,—

(*d*) In the ii[nd] century, Irenæus, the Peshito, and the Italic Version as plainly attest that in Gaul, in Mesopotamia and in the African province, the same verses were unhesitatingly received within a century (more or less) of the date of the inspired autograph of the Evangelist himself.

4. Thus, we are in possession of the testimony of *at least six* independent witnesses, of a date considerably anterior to the earliest extant Codex of the Gospels. They are all of the best class. They deliver themselves in the most unequivocal way. And their testimony to the genuineness of these Verses is unfaltering.

5. It is clear that nothing short of direct adverse evidence of the weightiest kind can sensibly affect so formidable an array of independent authorities as this. What must the evidence be which shall set it entirely aside, and induce us to believe, with the most recent editors of the inspired Text, that the last chapter of S. Mark's Gospel, as it came from the hands of its inspired author, ended abruptly at ver. 8?

The grounds for assuming that his "last Twelve Verses" are spurious, shall be exhibited in the ensuing chapter.

CHAPTER V.

It would naturally follow to shew that manuscript evidence confirms the evidence of the ancient Fathers and of
the early Versions of Scripture. But it will be more satisfactory that I should proceed to examine without more
delay the testimony, which, (as it is alleged,) is borne by
a cloud of ancient Fathers against the last twelve verses of
S. Mark. " The absence of this portion from some, from
many, or from most copies of his Gospel, or that it was not
written by S. Mark himself," (says Dr. Tregelles,) " is attested by Eusebius, Gregory of Nyssa, Victor of Antioch,
Severus of Antioch, Jerome, and by later writers, especially
Greeks[a]." The same Fathers are appealed to by Dr. David-
son, who adds to the list Euthymius; and by Tischendorf and
Alford, who add the name of Hesychius of Jerusalem. They
also refer to "many ancient Scholia." "These verses"
(says Tischendorf) "are not recognised by the sections of
Ammonius nor by the Canons of Eusebius : Epiphanius and
Cæsarius bear witness to the fact[b]." " In the Catenæ on
Mark" (proceeds Davidson) "the section is not explained.
Nor is there any trace of acquaintance with it on the part of
Clement of Rome or Clement of Alexandria;"—a remark
which others have made also ; as if it were a surprising circumstance that Clement of Alexandria, who appears to have
no reference to the last chapter of *S. Matthew's* Gospel, should

---

[a] *Account of the Printed Text,* p. 247.　　　[b] *Gr. Test.* p. 322.

be also without any reference to the last chapter of *S. Mark's:* as if, too, it were an extraordinary, thing that Clement of Rome should have omitted to quote from the last chapter of S. Mark, — seeing that the same Clement does not quote from S. Mark's Gospel *at all.* . . . The alacrity displayed by learned writers in accumulating hostile evidence, is certainly worthy of a better cause. Strange, that their united industry should have been attended with such very unequal success when their object was to exhibit the evidence *in favour of* the present portion of Scripture.

(1) Eusebius then, and (2) Jerome; (3) Gregory of Nyssa and (4) Hesychius of Jerusalem; (5) Severus of Antioch, (6) Victor of Antioch, and (7) Euthymius:—Do the accomplished critics just quoted,—Doctors Tischendorf, Tregelles, and Davidson, really mean to tell us that "it is attested" by these seven Fathers that the concluding section of S. Mark's Gospel "was not written by S. Mark himself?" Why, there is *not one* of them who says so: while some of them say the direct reverse. But let us go on. It is, I suppose, because there are Twelve Verses to be demolished that the list is further eked out with the names of (8) Ammonius, (9) Epiphanius, and (10) Cæsarius,—to say nothing of (11) the anonymous authors of Catenæ, and (12) "later writers, especially Greeks."

I. I shall examine these witnesses one by one : but it will be convenient in the first instance to call attention to the evidence borne by,

GREGORY OF NYSSA.

This illustrious Father is represented as expressing himself as follows in his second "Homily on the Resurrection [c]:"— "In the more accurate copies, the Gospel according to Mark has its end at 'for they were afraid.' In some copies, however, this also is added,—'Now when He was risen early the first day of the week, He appeared first to Mary Magdalene, out of whom He had cast seven devils.'"

---

[c] 'Εν μὲν τοῖς ἀκριβεστέροις ἀντιγράφοις τὸ κατὰ Μάρκον εὐαγγέλιον μέχρι τοῦ ἐφοβοῦντο γάρ, ἔχει τὸ τέλος. ἐν δέ τισι πρόσκειται καὶ ταῦτα ἀναστὰς δὲ πρωὶ πρώτῃ σαββάτων (sic) ἐφάνη πρῶτον Μαρίᾳ τῇ Μαγδαληνῇ ἀφ' ἧς ἐκβεβλή-κει ἑπτὰ δαιμόνια.   *Opp.* (ed. 1638) iii. 411 B.

That this testimony should have been so often appealed to as proceeding from Gregory of Nyssa [d], is little to the credit of modern scholarship. One would have supposed that the gravity of the subject,—the importance of the issue, —the sacredness of Scripture, down to its minutest jot and tittle,—would have ensured extraordinary caution, and in-duced every fresh assailant of so considerable a portion of the Gospel to be very sure of his ground before reiterating what his predecessors had delivered. And yet it is evident that not one of the recent writers on the subject can have investigated this matter for himself. It is only due to their known ability to presume that had they taken ever so little pains with the foregoing quotation, they would have found out their mistake.

(1.) For, in the first place, the second " Homily on the Resurrection" printed in the iii[rd] volume of the works of Gregory of Nyssa, (and which supplies the critics with their quotation,) is, as every one may see who will take the trouble to compare them, *word for word the same Homily* which Combefis in his " Novum Auctarium," and Gallandius in his " Bibliotheca Patrum" printed as the work of Hesy-chius, and vindicated to that Father, respectively in 1648 and 1776 [*]. Now, if a critic chooses to risk his own reputa-tion by maintaining that the Homily in question is indeed by Gregory of Nyssa, and is not by Hesychius,—well and good. But since the Homily can have had but one author, it is surely high time that one of these two claimants should be altogether dropped from this discussion.

(2.) Again. Inasmuch as page after page of the same Homily is observed to reappear, *word for word*, under the name of " Severus of Antioch," and to be unsuspiciously printed as his by Montfaucon in his " Bibliotheca Coisli-niana" (1715), and by Cramer in his "Catena[e]" (1844),— although it may very reasonably become a question among critics whether Hesychius of Jerusalem or Severus of An-

---

[d] Tregelles, *Printed Text*, p. 248, also in Horne's *Introd.* iv. 434-6. So Nor-ton, Alford, Davidson, and the rest, following Wetstein, Griesbach, Scholz, &c.

[*] *Nov. Auct.* i. 743-74.—*Bibl. Vett. PP.* xi. 221-6.

[e] *Bibl. Coisl.* pp. 68-75.— *Catena,* i. 243-51.

tioch was the actual author of the Homily in question [f], yet
it is plain that critics must make their election between the
two names; and not bring them *both* forward. No one,
I say, has any right to go on quoting "Severus" *and* "Hesychius,"—as Tischendorf and Dr. Davidson are observed to
do:—"Gregory of Nyssa" *and* "Severus of Antioch,"—as
Dr. Tregelles is found to prefer.

(3.) In short, here are three claimants for the authorship
of one and the same Homily. To whichever of the three
we assign it,—(and competent judges have declared that
there are sufficient reasons for giving it to Hesychius rather
than to Severus,—while *no one* is found to suppose that
Gregory of Nyssa was its author,)—*who* will not admit that
no further mention must be made of the other two?

(4.) Let it be clearly understood, therefore, that henceforth
the name of "Gregory of Nyssa" must be banished from
this discussion. So must the name of "Severus of Antioch."
The memorable passage which begins,—"In the more accurate copies, the Gospel according to Mark has its end
at 'for they were afraid,'"—is found in *a Homily which
was probably written by Hesychius, presbyter of Jerusalem,—
a writer of the vi*[th] *century.* I shall have to recur to his work
by-and-by. The next name is

EUSEBIUS,

II. With respect to whom the case is altogether different. What that learned Father has delivered concerning
the conclusion of S. Mark's Gospel requires to be examined
with attention, and must be set forth much more in detail.
And yet, I will so far anticipate what is about to be offered,
as to say at once that if any one supposes that Eusebius has
anywhere plainly "stated that it is *wanted in many MSS.* [g],"
—he is mistaken. Eusebius nowhere says so. The reader's
attention is invited to a plain tale.

It was not until 1825 that the world was presented by

---

[f] Dionysius Syrus (i.e. the Monophysite Jacobus Bar-Salibi [see Dean Payne
Smith's *Cat. of Syrr. MSS.* p. 411] who died A.D. 1171) in his *Exposition of
S. Mark's Gospel* (published at Dublin by Dudley Loftus, 1672, 4to.) seems
(at p. 59) to give this homily to Severus.—I have really no independent opinion on the subject.　　　　　　　　[g] Alford, *Greek Test.* i. p. 433.

Cardinal Angelo Mai[h] with a few fragmentary specimens
of a lost work of Eusebius on the (so-called) Inconsistencies
in the Gospels, from a MS. in the Vatican[i]. These, the
learned Cardinal republished more accurately in 1847, in
his "Nova Patrum Bibliotheca[k];" and hither we are invariably referred by those who cite Eusebius as a witness
against the genuineness of the concluding verses of the
second Gospel.

It is much to be regretted that we are still as little as
ever in possession of the lost work of Eusebius. It appears
to have consisted of three Books or Parts; the former two
(addressed "to Stephanus") being discussions of difficulties
at the beginning of the Gospel,—the last ("to Marinus")
relating to difficulties in its concluding chapters[l]. The
Author's plan, (as usual in such works), was, first, to set
forth a difficulty in the form of a Question; and straightway, to propose a Solution of it,—which commonly assumes
the form of a considerable dissertation. But whether we are
at present in possession of so much as a single entire specimen of these "Inquiries and Resolutions" exactly as it came
from the pen of Eusebius, may reasonably be doubted. That

---

[h] *Scriptorum Vett. Nova Collectio,* 4to. vol. i. pp. 1—101.

[i] At p. 217, (*ed.* 1847), Mai designates it as "Codex Vat. Palat. cxx pul-
cherrimus, sæculi ferme x." At p. 268, he numbers it rightly,—ccxx. We
are there informed that the work of Eusebius extends from fol. 61 to 96 of
the Codex.

[k] Vol. iv. pp. 219—309.

[l] See *Nova P. P. Bibliotheca,* iv. 255.—That it was styled "Inquiries with
their Resolutions" (Ζητήματα καὶ Λύσεις), Eusebius leads us to suppose by
himself twice referring to it under that name, (*Demonstr. Evang. lib.* vii. 3 :
also in the Preface to Marinus, *Mai,* iv. 255 :) which his abbreviator is also
observed to employ (*Mai,* iv. 219, 255.) But I suspect that he and others so
designate the work only from the nature of its contents; and that its actual
title is correctly indicated by Jerome,—*De Evangeliorum Diaphoniâ :* "Edidit" (he says) "de Evangeliorum Diaphoniâ," (*De Scriptt. Illustt.* c. 81.)
Again, Διαφωνία Εὐαγγελίων, (*Hieron. in Matth.* i. 16.) Consider also the
testimony of Latinus Latinius, given below, p. 44, note (q). 'Indicated' by
Jerome, I say : for the entire title was probably, Περὶ τῆς δοκούσης ἐν τοῖς
εὐαγγελίοις κ.τ.λ. διαφωνίας. The Author of the Catena on S. Mark edited by
Cramer (i. p. 266), quotes an opinion of Eusebius ἐν τῷ πρὸς Μαρῖνον περὶ τῆς
δοκούσης ἐν τοῖς εὐαγγελίοις περὶ τῆς ἀναστάσεως διαφωνίας : words which are
extracted from the same MS. by Simon, *Hist. Crit. N. T.* p. 89.

the work which Mai has brought to light is but a highly
condensed exhibition of the original, (and scarcely that,) its
very title shews; for it is headed,—" An abridged selection
from the 'Inquiries and Resolutions [of difficulties] in the
Gospels' by Eusebius[m]." Only *some* of the original Questions, therefore, are here noticed at all: and even these have
been subjected to so severe a process of condensation and
abridgment, that in some instances *amputation* would probably be a more fitting description of what has taken place.
Accordingly, what were originally two Books or Parts, are
at present represented by XVI. " Inquiries," &c., addressed
" to Stephanus;" while the concluding Book or Part is represented by IV. more, "to Marinus,"—of which, *the first*
relates to our LORD's appearing to Mary Magdalene after
His Resurrection. Now, since the work which Eusebius addressed to Marinus is found to have contained " Inquiries,
with their Resolutions, concerning our SAVIOUR's *Death* and
Resurrection[n],"—while a quotation professing to be derived from "the *thirteenth* chapter" relates to Simon the
Cyrenian bearing our SAVIOUR's Cross[o];—it is obvious that
the original work must have been very considerable, and
that what Mai has recovered gives an utterly inadequate
idea of its extent and importance[p]. It is absolutely neces-

---

[m] 'Εκλογὴ ἐν συντόμῳ ἐκ τῶν συντεθέντων ὑπὸ Εὐσεβίου πρὸς Στέφανον [and
πρὸς Μαρῖνον] περὶ τῶν ἐν τοῖς Εὐαγγελίοις ζητημάτων καὶ λύσεων. *Ibid.*
pp. 219, 255.—(See the plate of fac-similes facing the title of vol. i. ed. 1825.)

[n] Εὐσέβιος . . . . ἐν ταῖς πρὸς Μαρῖνον ἐπὶ ταῖς περὶ τοῦ θείου πάθους καὶ τῆς
ἀναστάσεως ζητήσεσι καὶ ἐκλύσεσι, κ.τ.λ. I quote the place from the less
known Catena of Cramer, (ii. 389,) where it is assigned to Severus of Antioch:
but it occurs also in *Corderii Cat. in Joan.* p. 436. (See Mai, iv. 299.)

[o] This passage is too grand to be withheld:—Οὐ γὰρ ἦν ἄξιός τις ἐν τῇ πόλει
'Ιουδαίων, (ὥς φησιν Εὐσέβιος κεφαλαίῳ ιγ' πρὸς Μαρῖνον,) τὸ κατὰ τοῦ διαβόλου
τρόπαιον τὸν σταυρὸν βαστάσαι· ἀλλ' ὁ ἐξ ἀγροῦ, ὃς μηδὲν ἐπικεκοινώνηκε τῇ
κατὰ Χριστοῦ μιαιφονίᾳ. (*Possini Cat. in Marcum*, p. 343.)

[p] Mai, iv. p. 299.—The Catenæ, inasmuch as their compilers are observed
to have been very curious in such questions, are evidently full of *disjecta mem-
bra* of the work. These are recognisable for the most part by their form; but
sometimes they actually retain the name of their author. Accordingly, Catenæ
have furnished Mai with a considerable body of additional materials; which (as
far as a MS. Catena of Nicetas on S. Luke, [Cod. A. apu Vat. 1611,] enabled
him,) he has edited with considerable industry; throwing them into a kind of
Supplement. (Vol. iv. pp. 268—282, and pp. 283—298.) It is only surprising

sary that all this should be clearly apprehended by any one
who desires to know exactly what the alleged evidence of
Eusebius concerning the last chapter of S. Mark's Gospel is
worth,—as I will explain more fully by-and-by. Let it,
however, be candidly admitted that there seems to be no
reason for supposing that whenever the lost work of Eusebius comes to light, (and it has been seen within about
300 years[q],) it will exhibit anything essentially different
from what is contained in the famous passage which has
given rise to so much debate, and which may be exhibited
in English as follows. It is put in the form of a reply to
one "Marinus," who is represented as asking, first, the following question :—

"How is it, that, according to Matthew [xxviii. 1], the
SAVIOUR appears to have risen 'in the end of the Sabbath ;'
but, according to Mark [xvi. 9], 'early the first day of the
week' ?"—Eusebius answers,

"This difficulty admits of a twofold solution. He who is for

---

that with the stores at his command, Mai has not contrived to enlighten us
a little more on this curious subject. It would not be difficult to indicate sundry passages which he has overlooked. Neither indeed can it be denied that
the learned Cardinal has executed his task in a somewhat slovenly manner.
He does not seem to have noticed that what he quotes at pp. 357-8—262—283
—295, is to be found in the *Catena* of Corderius at pp. 448-9—449—450—457.
—He quotes (p. 300) from an unedited Homily of John Xiphilinus, (*Cod. Vat.*
p. 160,) what he might have found in Possinus ; and in Cramer too, (p. 446.)
He was evidently unacquainted with Cramer's work, though it had been published 3 (if not 7) years before his own,—else, at p. 299, instead of quoting
Simon, he would have quoted Cramer's *Catenæ*, i. 266.—It was in his power to
solve his own shrewd doubt, (at p. 299,—concerning the text of a passage in
Possinus, p. 343,) seeing that the Catena which Possinus published was transcribed by Corderius from a MS. in the Vatican. (Possini *Præfat.* p. ii.) In
the Vatican, too, he might have found the fragment he quotes (p. 300) from
p. 364 of the *Catena* of Possinus. In countless places he might, by such references, have improved his often manifestly faulty text.

q Mai quotes the following from Latinus Latinius (*Opp.* ii. 116.) to Andreas
Masius. Sirletus (Cardinalis) "scire te vult in Siciliâ inventos esse ... libros
tres Eusebii Cæsariensis *de Evangeliorum Diaphoniâ*, qui ut ipse sperat brevi
in lucem prodibunt." The letter is dated 1563.

I suspect that when the original of this work is recovered, it will be found
that Eusebius digested his "Questions" *under heads* : e.g. περὶ τοῦ τάφου, καὶ
τῆς δοκούσης διαφωνίας (p. 264) : περὶ τῆς δοκούσης περὶ τῆς ἀναστάσεως διαφωνίας. (p. 299.)

getting rid of the entire passage[r], will say that it is not met
with in *all* the copies of Mark's Gospel : the accurate copies,
at all events, making the end of Mark's narrative come after
the words of the young man who appeared to the women
and said, ' Fear not ye ! Ye seek JESUS of Nazareth,' &c. :
to which the Evangelist adds,—' And when they heard it,
they fled, and said nothing to any man, for they were
afraid.'   For at those words, in almost all copies of the
Gospel according to Mark, comes the end.   What follows,
(which is met with seldom, [and only] in some copies, certainly not in all,) might be dispensed with ; especially if it
should prove to contradict the record of the other Evangelists.   This, then, is what a person will say who is for
evading and entirely getting rid of a gratuitous problem.

   " But another, on no account daring to reject anything
whatever which is, under whatever circumstances, met with
in the text of the Gospels, will say that here are two readings, (as is so often the case elsewhere ;) and that *both* are to
be received,—inasmuch as by the faithful and pious, *this*
reading is not held to be genuine rather than *that ;* nor *that*
than *this.*"

It will be best to exhibit the whole of what Eusebius has
written on this subject,—as far as we are permitted to know
it,—continuously.   He proceeds :—

   " Well then, allowing this piece to be really genuine, our
business is to interpret the sense of the passage[s].   And certainly, if I divide the meaning into two, we shall find that
it is not opposed to what Matthew says of our SAVIOUR's
having risen ' in the end of the Sabbath.'   For Mark's ex-

---

   [r] I translate according to the sense,—the text being manifestly corrupt.
Τὴν τοῦτο φάσκουσαν περικοπήν is probably a gloss, explanatory of τὸ κεφάλαιον
αὐτό.   In strictness, the κεφάλαιον begins at ch. xv. 42, and extends to the end
of the Gospel.   There are 48 such κεφάλαια in S. Mark.   But this term was
often loosely employed by the Greek Fathers, (as "capitulum" by the Latins,)
to denote *a passage* of Scripture, and it is evidently so used here.   Περικοπή,
on the contrary, in this place seems to have its true technical meaning, and to
denote the liturgical *section,* or "lesson."

   [s] 'Ανάγνωσμα (like περικοπή, spoken of in the foregoing note,) seems to be
here used in its technical sense, and to designate the liturgical *section,* or
"lectio."   See Suicer, *in voce.*

pression, ('Now when He was risen early the first day of the
week,') we shall read with a pause, putting a comma after
'Now when He was risen,'—the sense of the words which
follow being kept separate. Thereby, we shall refer [Mark's]
'when He was risen' to Matthew's 'in the end of the Sabbath,' (for it was *then* that He *rose*); and all that comes
after, expressive as it is of a distinct notion, we shall connect with what follows; (for it was '*early*, the first day of the
week,' that 'He *appeared to Mary Magdalene*.')   This is in
fact what John also declares; for he too has recorded that
'early,' 'the first day of the week,' [JESUS] appeared to
the Magdalene.   Thus then Mark also says that He appeared to her early : not that He *rose* early, but long before,
(according to that of Matthew, 'in the end of the Sabbath :'
for though He *rose* then, He did not *appear to Mary* then,
but 'early.')   In a word, two distinct seasons are set before
us by these words : first, the season of the Resurrection,—
which was 'in the end of the Sabbath;' secondly, the season
of our SAVIOUR's Appearing,—which was 'early.'   The former[t], Mark writes of when he says, (it requires to be read
with a pause,)—'Now, when He was risen.'   Then, after
a comma, what follows is to be spoken,—'Early, the first
day of the week, He appeared to Mary Magdalene, out of
whom He had cast seven devils[u].'"—Such is the entire passage.   Little did the learned writer anticipate what bitter
fruit his words were destined to bear !

1. Let it be freely admitted that what precedes is calculated at first sight to occasion nothing but surprise and
perplexity.   For, in the first place, there really is *no problem
to solve.*   The discrepancy suggested by "Marinus" at the
outset, is plainly imaginary, the result (chiefly) of a strange
misconception of the meaning of the Evangelist's Greek,
—as in fact no one was ever better aware than Eusebius
himself.   "These places of the Gospels would never have
occasioned any difficulty," he writes in the very next page,

---

[t] The text of Eusebius seems to have experienced some disarrangement
and depravation here.

[u] Mai, *Bibl. P.P. Nova*, iv. 255-7. For purposes of reference, the original
of this passage is given in the Appendix (B).

(but it is the commencement of his reply to the *second* question of Marinus,)—"if people would but abstain from assuming that Matthew's phrase (ὀψὲ σαββάτων) refers to *the evening of the Sabbath-day* : whereas, (in conformity with the established idiom of the language,) it obviously refers to an advanced period of the ensuing night [v]." He proceeds:—"The self-same moment therefore, or very nearly the self-same, is intended by the Evangelists, only under different names : and there is no discrepancy whatever between Matthew's,—'in the end of the Sabbath, as it began to dawn toward the first day of the week,' and John's—'The first day of the week cometh Mary Magdalen early, when it was yet dark.' The Evangelists indicate by different expressions one and the same moment of time, but in a broad and general way." And yet, if Eusebius knew all this so well, why did he not say so at once, and close the discussion? I really cannot tell; except on one hypothesis, —which, although at first it may sound somewhat extraordinary, the more I think of the matter, recommends itself to my acceptance the more. I suspect, then, that the discussion we have just been listening to, is, essentially, *not an original production :* but that Eusebius, having met with the suggestion in some older writer, (in Origen probably,) reproduced it in language of his own,—doubtless because he thought it ingenious and interesting, but not by any means because he regarded it as true. Except on some such theory, I am utterly unable to understand how Eusebius can have written so inconsistently. His admirable remarks just quoted, are obviously a full and sufficient answer,—the proper answer in fact,—to the proposed difficulty : and it is a memorable circumstance that the ancients generally were so sensible of this, that they are found to have *invariably* [x] substituted

---

[v] Mai, iv. 257. So far, I have given the substance only of what Eusebius delivers with wearisome prolixity. It follows,—ὥστε τὸν αὐτὸν σχεδὸν νοεῖσθαι καιρὸν, ἢ τὸν σφόδρα ἐγγὺς, παρὰ τοῖς εὐαγγελισταῖς διαφόροις ὀνόμασι τετηρημένον. μηδέν τε διαφέρειν Ματθαῖον ἰρηκότα " ὀψὲ—τάφον" [xxviii. 1.] 'Ιωάννου φήσαντος "τῇ δὲ μιᾷ—ἔτι οὔσης σκοτίας." [xx. 1.] πλατυκῶς γὰρ ἕνα καὶ τὸν αὐτὸν δηλοῦσι χρόνον διαφόροις ῥήμασι.—For the principal words in the text, see the Appendix (B) *ad fin.*

[x] I allude to the following places :—Combefis, *Novum Auctarium*, col. 780.

what Eusebius wrote in reply to the *second* question of
Marinus for what he wrote in reply to *the first;* in other
words, for the dissertation which is occasioning us all this
difficulty.

2. But next, even had the discrepancy been real, the
remedy for it which is here proposed, and which is advocated with such tedious emphasis, would probably prove
satisfactory to no one.   In fact, the entire method advocated
in the foregoing passage is hopelessly vicious.   The writer
begins by advancing statements which, if he believed them
to be true, he must have known are absolutely fatal to the
verses in question.   This done, he sets about discussing the
possibility of reconciling an isolated expression in S. Mark's
Gospel with another in S. Matthew's : just as if on *that*
depended the genuineness or spuriousness of the entire context : as if, in short, the major premiss in the discussion
were some such postulate as the following :—" Whatever
in one Gospel cannot be proved to be entirely consistent
with something in another Gospel, is not to be regarded
as genuine."   Did then the learned Archbishop of Cæsarea
really suppose that a comma judiciously thrown into the
empty scale might at any time suffice to restore the equili-
brium, and even counterbalance the adverse testimony of
almost every MS. of the Gospels extant ?   Why does he not
at least deny the truth of the alleged facts to which he
began by giving currency, if not approval ; and which, so
long as they are allowed to stand uncontradicted, render all
further argumentation on the subject simply nugatory ?   As
before, I really cannot tell,—except on the hypothesis which
has been already hazarded.

3. Note also, (for this is not the least extraordinary feature of the case,) what vague and random statements those
are which we have been listening to.   The entire section

—Cod. Mosq. 138, (printed by Matthaei, *Anectt. Græc.* ii. 62.)—also Cod.
Mosq. 139, (see N. T. ix. 223-4.)—Cod. Coislin. 195 *fol.* 165.—Cod. Coislin. 23,
(published by Cramer, *Catt.* i. 251.)—Cod. Bodl. ol. Meerman Auct. T. i. 4,
fol. 169.—Cod. Bodl. Laud. Gr. 33, *fol.* 79.—Any one desirous of knowing
more on this subject will do well to begin by reading Simon *Hist. Crit. du
N. T.* p. 89. See Mai's foot-note, iv. p. 257.

(S. Mark xvi. 9—20,) "*is not met with in all* the copies:" at all events *not* "*in the accurate*" ones.   Nay, it is "*met with seldom.*"   In fact, it is *absent from* "*almost all*" copies.   But, —Which of these four statements is to stand?   The first is comparatively unimportant.   Not so the second.   The last two, on the contrary, would be absolutely fatal,—if trustworthy?   But *are* they trustworthy?

To this question only one answer can be returned.   The exaggeration is so gross that it refutes itself.   Had it been merely asserted that the verses in question were wanting in *many* of the copies,—even had it been insisted that *the best copies* were without them,—well and good: but to assert that, in the beginning of the fourth century, from "*almost all*" copies of the Gospels they were away,—is palpably untrue. What had become then of the MSS. from which the Syriac, the Latin, *all* the ancient Versions were made?   How is the contradictory evidence of *every copy of the Gospels in existence but two* to be accounted for?   With Irenæus and Hippolytus, with the old Latin and the Vulgate, with the Syriac, and the Gothic, and the Egyptian versions to refer to, we are able to assert that the author of such a statement was guilty of monstrous exaggeration.   We are reminded of the loose and random way in which the Fathers,—(giants in Interpretation, but very children in the Science of Textual Criticism,)—are sometimes observed to speak about the state of the Text in their days.   We are reminded, for instance, of the confident assertion of an ancient Critic that the true reading in S. Luke xxiv. 13 is not "three-score" but "*an hundred* and three-score;" for that so "the accurate copies" used to read the place, besides Origen and Eusebius.   And yet (as I have elsewhere explained) the reading ἑκατὸν καὶ ἑξήκοντα is altogether impossible.   "Apud nos mixta sunt omnia," is Jerome's way of adverting to an evil which, serious as it was, was yet not nearly so great as he represents; viz. the unauthorized introduction into one Gospel of what belongs of right to another.   And so in a multitude of other instances.   The Fathers are, in fact, constantly observed to make critical remarks about the ancient copies which simply *cannot* be correct.

E

And yet the author of the exaggeration under review, be it
observed, is clearly *not Eusebius*.   It is evident that *he* has
nothing to say against the genuineness of the conclusion of
S. Mark's Gospel.   Those random statements about the copies
with which he began, do not even purport to express his
own sentiments.   Nay, Eusebius in a manner repudiates
them ; for he introduces them with a phrase which separates
them from himself : and, " This then is what a person will
say,"—is the remark with which he finally dismisses them.
It would, in fact, be to make this learned Father stultify
himself to suppose that he proceeds gravely to discuss a
portion of Scripture which he had already deliberately rejected as spurious.   But, indeed, the evidence before us
effectually precludes any such supposition.   " Here are two
readings," he says, "(as is so often the case elsewhere :)
both of which are to be received,—inasmuch as by the faithful and pious, *this* reading is not held to be genuine rather
than *that ;* nor *that* than *this.*"   And thus we seem to be
presented with the actual opinion of Eusebius, as far as it
can be ascertained from the present passage,—if indeed he
is to be thought here to offer any personal opinion on the
subject at all ; which, for my own part, I entirely doubt.
But whether we are at liberty to infer the actual sentiments
of this Father from anything here delivered or not, quite
certain at least is it that to print only the first half of the
passage, (as Tischendorf and Tregelles have done,) and then
to give the reader to understand that he is reading the
adverse testimony of Eusebius as to the genuineness of the
end of S. Mark's Gospel, is nothing else but to misrepresent
the facts of the case ; and, however unintentionally, to deceive those who are unable to verify the quotation for
themselves.

It has been urged indeed that Eusebius cannot have recognised the verses in question as genuine, because a scholium purporting to be his has been cited by Matthaei from
a Catena at Moscow, in which he appears to assert that
"according to Mark," our SAVIOUR " is not recorded to have
appeared to His Disciples after His Resurrection :" whereas
in S. Mark xvi. 14 it is plainly recorded that " Afterwards

He appeared unto the Eleven as they sat at meat." May
I be permitted to declare that I am distrustful of the proposed inference, and shall continue to feel so, until I know
something more about the scholium in question? Up to the
time when this page is printed I have not succeeded in ob-
taining from Moscow the details I wish for: but they must
be already on the way, and I propose to embody the result
in a "Postscript" which shall form the last page of the
Appendix to the present volume.

Are we then to suppose that there was no substratum of
truth in the allegations to which Eusebius gives such prominence in the passage under discussion? By no means.
The mutilated state of S. Mark's Gospel in the Vatican
Codex (B) and especially in the Sinaitic Codex (‌א) sufficiently establishes the contrary. Let it be freely conceded,
(but in fact it has been freely conceded already,) that there
must have existed in the time of Eusebius *many* copies of
S. Mark's Gospel which were without the twelve concluding
verses. I do but insist that there is nothing whatever in
that circumstance to lead us to entertain one serious doubt
as to the genuineness of these verses. I am but concerned
to maintain that there is nothing whatever in the evidence
which has hitherto come before us,—certainly not *in the
evidence of Eusebius,*—to induce us to believe that they are
a spurious addition to S. Mark's Gospel.

III. We have next to consider what

JEROME

has delivered on this subject. So great a name must needs
command attention in any question of Textual Criticism:
and it is commonly pretended that Jerome pronounces emphatically against the genuineness of the last twelve verses
of the Gospel according to S. Mark. A little attention to
the actual testimony borne by this Father will, it is thought,
suffice to exhibit it in a wholly unexpected light; and induce us to form an entirely different estimate of its practical bearing upon the present discussion.

It will be convenient that I should premise that it is in
one of his many exegetical Epistles that Jerome discusses
this matter. A lady named Hedibia, inhabiting the furthest

extremity of Gaul, and known to Jerome only by the ardour
of her piety, had sent to prove him with hard questions.
He resolves her difficulties from Bethlehem [y] : and I may
be allowed to remind the reader of what is found to have
been Jerome's practice on similar occasions,—which, to
judge from his writings, were of constant occurrence.   In
fact, Apodemius, who brought Jerome the Twelve problems
from Hedibia, brought him Eleven more from a noble
neighbour of hers, Algasia [z].   Once, when a single mes-
senger had conveyed to him out of the African province
a quantity of similar interrogatories, Jerome sent two Egyptian monks the following account of how he had proceeded
in respect of the inquiry,—(it concerned 1 Cor. xv. 51,)—
which they had addressed to him :—"Being pressed for
time, I have presented you with the opinions of all the
Commentators; for the most part, translating their very
words; in order both to get rid of your question, and to
put you in possession of ancient authorities on the subject."
This learned Father does not even profess to have been in
the habit of delivering his own opinions, or speaking his
own sentiments on such occasions.   "This has been hastily
dictated," he says in conclusion,—(alluding to his constant
practice, which was to dictate, rather than to write,)—
"in order that I might lay before you what have been the
opinions of learned men on this subject, as well as the arguments by which they have recommended their opinions.
My own authority, (who am but nothing,) is vastly inferior
to that of our predecessors in the LORD."   Then, after special commendation of the learning of Origen and Eusebius,
and the valuable Scriptural expositions of many more,—
"My plan," (he says,) "is to read the ancients; to prove
all things, to hold fast that which is good; and to abide
stedfast in the faith of the Catholic Church.—I must now
dictate replies, either original or at second-hand, to other
Questions which lie before me [a]."   We are not surprised,
after this straightforward avowal of what was the method

[y] Ep. cxx. *Opera*, (ed. Vallars.) vol. i. pp. 811– 43.

[z] *Ibid.* p. 844.

[a] *Ibid.* p. 793—810.   See especially pp. 794, 809, 810.

on such occasions with this learned Father, to discover that, instead of hearing *Jerome* addressing *Hedibia*, — (who had interrogated him concerning the very problem which is at present engaging our attention,)—we find ourselves only listening to *Eusebius* over again, addressing *Marinus*.

" This difficulty admits of a two-fold solution," Jerome begins ; as if determined that no doubt shall be entertained as to the source of his inspiration. Then, (making short work of the tedious disquisition of Eusebius,)—" Either we shall reject the testimony of Mark, which is met with in scarcely any copies of the Gospel,—almost all the Greek codices being without this passage :—(especially since it seems to narrate what contradicts the other Gospels :)—or else, we shall reply that both Evangelists state what is true : Matthew, when he says that our Lord rose ' late in the week :' Mark,—when he says that Mary Magdalene saw Him ' early, the first day of the week.' For the passage must be thus pointed,—' When He was risen :' and presently, after a pause, must be added,—' Early, the first day of the week, He appeared to Mary Magdalene.' He therefore who had risen late in the week, according to Matthew,—Himself, early the first day of the week, according to Mark, appeared to Mary Magdalene. And this is what John also means, shewing that it was early on the next day that He appeared."—To understand how faithfully in what precedes Jerome treads in the footsteps of Eusebius, it is absolutely necessary to set the Latin of the one over against the Greek of the other, and to compare them. In order to facilitate this operation, I have subjoined both originals at foot of the page: from which it will be apparent that Jerome is here not so much adopting the sentiments of Eusebius as simply *translating his words* [b].

[b] " Hujus quæstionis duplex solutio est. [Τούτου διττὴ ἂν εἴη ἡ λύσις.] Aut enim non recipimus Marci testimonium, quod in raris fertur [σπανίως ἔν τισι φερόμενα] Evangeliis, omnibus Græciæ libris pene hoc capitulum [τὸ κεφάλαιον αὐτὸ] in fine non habentibus ; [ἐν τούτῳ γὰρ σχεδὸν ἐν ἅπασι τοῖς ἀντιγράφοις τοῦ κατὰ Μάρκον εὐαγγελίου περιγέγραπται τὸ τέλος] ; præsertim cum diversa atque contraria Evangelistis ceteris narrare videntur [μάλιστα εἴπερ ἔχοιεν ἀντιλογίαν τῇ τῶν λοιπῶν εὐαγγελιστῶν μαρτυρίᾳ.] Aut hoc respondendum, quod uterque verum dixerit [ἑκατέραν παραδεκτέαν ὑπάρχειν...συγχωρουμένου

This, however, is not by any means the strangest feature of the case. That Jerome should have availed himself ever so freely of the materials which he found ready to his hand in the pages of Eusebius cannot be regarded as at all extraordinary, after what we have just heard from himself of his customary method of proceeding. It would of course have suggested the gravest doubts as to whether we were here listening to the personal sentiment of this Father, or not; but that would have been all. What are we to think, however, of the fact ‚that *Hedibia's question to Jerome* proves on inspection to be nothing more than a translation of *the very question which Marinus had long before addressed to Eusebius?* We read on, perplexed at the coincidence; and speedily make the notable discovery that her next question, and her next, are *also* translations *word for word* of the next two of Marinus. For the proof of this statement the reader is again referred to the foot of the page°. It is at least decisive:

εἶναι ἀληθοῦς.] Matthæus, quando Dominus surrexerit vespere sabbati : Marcus autem, quando tum viderit Maria Magdalena, id est, mane prima sabbati. Ita enim distinguendum est, Cum autem resurrexisset : [μετὰ διαστολῆς ἀναγνωστέον 'Αναστὰς δέ :] et, parumper, spiritu coarctato inferendum, Prima sabbati mane apparuit Mariæ Magdalenæ : [εἶτα ὑποστίξαντες ῥητέον, Πρωὶ τῇ μιᾷ τῶν σαββάτων ἐφάνη Μαρίᾳ τῇ Μαγδαληνῇ.] Ut qui vespere sabbati, juxta Matthæum surrexerat, [παρὰ τῷ Ματθαίῳ, ὀψὲ σαββάτων· τοτε γὰρ ἐγήγερτο.] ipse mane prima sabbati, juxta Marcum, apparuerit Mariæ Magdalenæ. [πρωὶ γὰρ τῇ μιᾷ τοῦ σαββάτου ἐφάνη Μαρίᾳ τῇ Μαγδαληνῇ.] Quod quidem et Joannes Evangelista significat, mane Eum alterius diei visum esse demonstrans." [τοῦτο γοῦν ἐδήλωσε καὶ ὁ 'Ιωάννης πρωὶ καὶ αὐτὸς τῇ μιᾷ τοῦ σαββάτου ὦφθαι αὐτὸν μαρτυρήσας.]

For the Latin of the above, see *Hieronymi Opera*, (ed. Vallars.) vol. i. p. 819 : for the Greek, with its context, see Appendix (B).

° ἠρώτας τὸ πρῶτον,—Πῶς παρὰ μὲν τῷ Ματθαίῳ ὀψὲ σαββάτων φαίνεται ἐγεγερμένος ὁ Σωτὴρ, παρὰ δὲ τῷ Μάρκῳ πρωὶ τῇ μιᾷ τῶν σαββάτων; [Eusebius ad Marinum, (Mai, iv. 255.)]

Primum quæris,—Cur Matthæus dixerit, vespere autem Sabbati illucescente in una Sabbate Dominum resurrexisse ; et Marcus mane resurrectionem ejus factam esse commemorat. [Hieronymus ad Hedibiam, (Opp. i. 818-9.)]

Πῶς, κατὰ τὸν Ματθαῖον, ὀψὲ σαββάτων ἡ Μαγδαληνὴ τεθεαμένη τὴν ἀνάστασιν, κατὰ τὸν 'Ιωάννην ἡ αὐτὴ ἑστῶσα κλαίει παρὰ τῷ μνημείῳ τῇ μιᾷ τοῦ σαββάτου. [Ut suprà, p. 257.]

Quomodo, juxta Matthæum, vespere Sabbati, Maria Magdalene vidit Dominum resurgentem ; et Joannes Evangelista refert eam mane una sabbati juxta sepulcrum flere ? [Ut suprà, p. 819.]

and the fact, which admits of only one explanation, can be
attended by only one practical result. It of course shelves
the whole question as far as the evidence of Jerome is concerned. Whether Hedibia was an actual personage or not,
let those decide who have considered more attentively than
it has ever fallen in my way to do that curious problem,—
What was the ancient notion of the allowable in Fiction ?
That different ideas have prevailed in different ages of the
world as to where fiction ends and fabrication begins ;—that
widely discrepant views are entertained on the subject even
in our own age ;—all must be aware. I decline to investigate the problem on the present occasion. I do but claim
to have established beyond the possibility of doubt or cavil
that what we are here presented with *is not the testimony of
Jerome at all.* It is evident that this learned Father amused
himself with translating for the benefit of his Latin readers
a part of the (lost) work of Eusebius ; (which, by the way,
he is found to have possessed in the same abridged form in
which it has come down to ourselves :)—and he seems to
have regarded it as allowable to attribute to " Hedibia" the
problems which he there met with. (He may perhaps have
known that Eusebius before him had attributed them, with
just as little reason, to " Marinus.") In that age, for aught
that appears to the contrary, it may have been regarded as
a graceful compliment to address solutions of Scripture difficulties to persons of distinction, who possibly had never
heard of those difficulties before ; and even to represent the
Interrogatories which suggested them as originating with
themselves. I offer this only in the way of suggestion, and
am not concerned to defend it. The only point I am concerned to establish is that Jerome is here a *translator*, not
an original author : in other words, that it is *Eusebius* who
here speaks, and not Jerome. For a critic to pretend that it

Πῶς, κατὰ τὸν Ματθαῖον, ὀψὲ σαββάτων ἡ Μαγδαληνὴ μετὰ τῆς ἄλλης Μαρίας
ἀψαμένη τῶν ποδῶν τοῦ Σωτῆρος, ἡ αὐτὴ πρωὶ τῇ μιᾷ τοῦ σαββάτου ἀκούει μή μου
ἅπτου, κατὰ τὸν Ἰωάννην. [*Ut suprà*, p. 262.]

Quomodo, juxta Matthæum, Maria Magdalene vespere Sabbati cum alterâ
Mariâ advoluta sit pedibus Salvatoris ; cum, secundum Joannem, audierit à
Domino, Noli me tangere. [*Ut suprà*, p. 821.]

is in *any* sense the testimony of Jerome which we are here
presented with ; that Jerome is one of those Fathers "who,
even though they copied from their predecessors, were yet
competent to transmit the record of a fact [d],"—is entirely to
misunderstand the case.   The man who translates,—not
adopts, but *translates,—the problem* as well as its solution :
who deliberately asserts that it emanated from a Lady inhabiting the furthest extremity of Gaul, who nevertheless was
demonstrably not its author : who goes on to propose as
hers question after question *verbatim as he found them written
in the pages of Eusebius ;* and then resolves them one by one
in the very language of the same Father :—such a writer has
clearly conducted us into a region where his individual responsibility quite disappears from sight.   We must hear no
more about Jerome, therefore, as a witness against the genuineness of the concluding verses of S. Mark's Gospel.

On the contrary.   Proof is at hand that Jerome held these
verses to be genuine.   The proper evidence of this is supplied
by the fact that he gave them a place in his revision of the
old Latin version of the Scriptures.   If he had been indeed
persuaded of their absence from *"almost all the Greek codices,"*
does any one imagine that he would have suffered them to
stand in the Vulgate ?   If he had met with them in *"scarcely
any copies of the Gospel,"*—do men really suppose that he
would yet have retained them ?   To believe this would, again,
be to forget what was the known practice of this Father ;
who, because he found the expression "without a cause"
(εἰκή,—S. Matth. v. 22,) only "in certain of his codices," but
not "in the true ones," *omitted* it from the Vulgate.   Because,
however, he read "righteousness" (where we read "alms")
in S. Matth. vi. 1, he exhibits *"justitiam"* in his revision of
the old Latin version.   On the other hand, though he knew
of MSS. (as he expressly relates) which read "works" for
"children" (ἔργων for τέκνων) in S. Matth. xi. 19, he does
not admit that (manifestly corrupt) reading,—which, however, is found both in the Codex Vaticanus and the Codex
Sinaiticus.   Let this suffice.   I forbear to press the matter
further.   It is an additional proof that Jerome accepted the

[d] Tregelles, *Printed Text,* p. 247.

conclusion of S. Mark's Gospel that he actually quotes it, and on more than one occasion : but to prove this, is to prove more than is here required[e]. I am concerned only to demolish the assertion of Tischendorf, and Tregelles, and Alford, and Davidson, and so many more, concerning the testimony of Jerome ; and I have demolished it. I pass on, claiming to have shewn that the name of Jerome as an adverse witness must never again appear in this discussion.

IV. and V. But now, while the remarks of Eusebius are yet fresh in the memory, the reader is invited to recal for a moment what the author of the " Homily on the Resurrection," contained in the works of Gregory of Nyssa (above, p. 39), has delivered on the same subject. It will be remembered that we saw reason for suspecting that not

SEVERUS OF ANTIOCH, but

HESYCHIUS OF JERUSALEM,

(both of them writers of the vi[th] century,) has the better claim to the authorship of the Homily in question[f],—which, however, cannot at all events be assigned to the illustrious Bishop of Nyssa, the brother of Basil the Great. "In the more accurate copies," (says this writer,) " the Gospel according to Mark has its end at ' for they were afraid.' In some copies, however, this also is added,—' Now when He was risen early the first day of the week, He appeared first to Mary Magdalene, out of whom He had cast seven devils.' This, however, seems to contradict to some extent what we before delivered ; for since it happens that the hour of the night when our SAVIOUR rose is not known, how does it come to be here written that He rose ' early ?' But the saying will prove to be no ways contradictory, if we read with skill. We must be careful intelligently to introduce a comma after, ' Now when He was risen :' and then to proceed,—' Early in the Sabbath He appeared first to Mary Magdalene :' in order that ' when He was risen ' may refer (in conformity with what Matthew says) to the foregoing season ; while ' early ' is connected with the appearance to Mary."[*]—I presume it would be to abuse a reader's patience to offer any remarks on all this. If a careful perusal of the foregoing passage

<hr />

[e] See above, p. 28.   [f] See above, p. 40-1.   [*] See the Appendix (C) § 2.

does not convince him that Hesychius is here only reproducing what he had read in Eusebius, nothing that I can say will .persuade him of the fact.　The *words* indeed are by no means the same; but the sense is altogether identical. He seems to have also known the work of Victor of Antioch. However, to remove all doubt from the reader's mind that the work of Eusebius was in the hands of Hesychius while he wrote, I have printed in two parallel columns and transferred to the Appendix what must needs be conclusive[g]; for it will be seen that the terms are only not identical in which Eusebius and Hesychius discuss that favourite problem with the ancients,—the consistency of S. Matthew's ὀψὲ τῶν σαββάτων with the πρωὶ of S. Mark.

It is, however, only needful to read through the Homily in question to see that it is an attempt to weave into one piece a quantity of foreign and incongruous materials.　It is in fact not a Homily at all, (though it has been thrown into that form;) but a Dissertation,— into which, Hesychius, (who is known to have been very curious in questions of that kind[h],) is observed to introduce solutions of most of those famous difficulties which cluster round the sepulchre of the world's Redeemer on the morning of the first Easter Day[i]; and which the ancients seem to have delighted in discussing,—as, the number of the Marys who visited the sepulchre; the angelic appearances on the morning of the Resurrection; and above all the seeming discrepancy, already adverted to, in the Evangelical notices of the time at which our LORD rose from the dead.　.I need not enter more particularly into an examination of this (so-called) 'Homily': but I must not dismiss it without pointing out that its author

---

[g]　See the Appendix (C) § 1.—For the statement in line 5, see § 2.

[h]　In the *Eccl. Græc. Monumenta* of Cotelerius, (iii. 1—53,) may be seen the discussion of 60 problems, headed,—Συναγωγὴ ἀποριῶν καὶ ἐπιλύσεων, ἐκλεγεῖσα ἐν ἐπιτομῇ ἐκ τῆς εὐαγγελικῆς συμφωνίας τοῦ ἁγίου Ἡσυχίου πρεσβυτέρου Ἱεροσολύμων.　From this it appears that Hesychius, following the example of Eusebius, wrote a work on "Gospel Harmony,"—of which nothing but an abridgment has come down to us.

[i]　He says that he writes,—Πρὸς τὴν τοῦ ὑποκειμένου προβλήματος λύσιν, καὶ τῶν ἄλλων τῶν κατὰ τὴν ἐξέτασιν τῶν ῥητῶν ἀναφυομένων ζητήσεων, κ.τ.λ. Greg. Nyss. *Opp.* iii. 400 c.

at all events cannot be thought to have repudiated the concluding verses of S. Mark : for at the end of his discourse,
he quotes the 19th verse entire, without hesitation, in confirmation of one of his statements, and declares that the
words are written by S. Mark [k].

I shall not be thought unreasonable, therefore, if I contend
that Hesychius is no longer to be cited as a witness in this
behalf: if I point out that it is entirely to misunderstand
and misrepresent the case to quote *a passing allusion of his to
what Eusebius had long before delivered on the same subject,* as
if it exhibited his own individual teaching. It is demonstrable [l] that he is not bearing testimony to the condition of
the MSS. of S. Mark's Gospel in his own age : neither, indeed, is he bearing testimony *at all.* He is simply amusing
himself, (in what is found to have been his favourite way,)
with reconciling an apparent discrepancy in the Gospels ;
and he does it by adopting certain remarks of Eusebius.
Living so late as the vi[th] century ; conspicuous neither for
his judgment nor his learning ; a copyist only, so far as his
remarks on the last verses of S. Mark's Gospel are concerned ;—this writer does not really deserve the space and
attention we have been compelled to bestow upon him.

VI. We may conclude, by inquiring for the evidence
borne by

VICTOR OF ANTIOCH.

And from the familiar style in which this Father's name
is always introduced into the present discussion, no less than
from the invariable practice of assigning to him the date
" A.D. 401," it might be supposed that " Victor of Antioch "
is a well-known personage. Yet is there scarcely a Commentator of antiquity about whom less is certainly known.
Clinton (who enumerates cccxxii " Ecclesiastical Authors "
from A.D. 70 to A.D. 685 [m]) does not even record his name.
The recent " Dictionary of Greek and Roman Biography "
is just as silent concerning him.   Cramer (his latest editor)

---

[k] ὁμοίως δὲ καὶ τὸ παρὰ τῷ Μάρκῳ γεγραμμένον· Ὁ μὲν οὖν Κύριος, κ.τ.λ.
Greg. Nyss. *Opp.* iii. 415 D.—See above, p. 29, note (g).

[l] See below, chap. X.

[m] *Fasti Romani,* vol. ii. Appendix viii. pp. 395—495.

calls his very existence in question; proposing to attribute
his Commentary on S. Mark to Cyril of Alexandria [n]. Not
to delay the reader needlessly,—Victor of Antioch is an interesting and unjustly neglected Father of the Church;
whose date,—(inasmuch as he apparently quotes sometimes
from Cyril of Alexandria who died A.D. 444, and yet seems
to have written soon after the death of Chrysostom, which
took place A.D. 407), may be assigned to the first half of the
v[th] century,—suppose A.D. 425—450. And in citing him
I shall always refer to the best (and most easily accessible)
edition of his work,—that of Cramer (1840) in the first
volume of his " Catenae."

But a far graver charge is behind. From the confident
air in which Victor's authority is appealed to by those who
deem the last twelve verses of S. Mark's Gospel spurious,
it would of course be inferred that his evidence is hostile
to the verses in question; whereas his evidence to their
genuineness is the most emphatic and extraordinary on
record. Dr. Tregelles asserts that " his *testimony* to the
absence of these twelve verses from some or many copies,
stands in contrast to his own *opinion* on the subject." But
Victor delivers *no* " opinion:" and his " testimony " is the
direct reverse of what Dr. Tregelles asserts it to be. This
learned and respected critic has strangely misapprehended
the evidence [o].

I must needs be brief in this place. I shall therefore
confine myself to those facts concerning " Victor of Antioch,"
or rather concerning his work, which are necessary for the
purpose in hand [p].

Now, his Commentary on S. Mark's Gospel,—as all must
see who will be at the pains to examine it,—is to a great
extent a compilation. The same thing may be said, no
doubt, to some extent, of almost every ancient Commentary
in existence. But I mean, concerning this particular work,

---

[n] Vol. i. *Præfat.* p. xxviii. See below, note (p).

[o] " Victor Antiochenus" (writes Dr. Tregelles in his N. T. vol. i. p. 214,)
" dicit ὅτι νενόθευται τὸ παρὰ Μάρκῳ τελευταῖον ἕν τισι φερόμενον."

[p] For additional details concerning Victor of Antioch, and his work, the
studious in such matters are referred to the Appendix (D).

that it proves to have been the author's plan not so much
to give the general results of his acquaintance with the
writings of Origen, Apollinarius, Theodorus of Mopsuestia,
Eusebius, and Chrysostom ; as, with or without acknowledgment, to transcribe largely (but with great license)
from one or other of these writers. Thus, the whole of his
note on S. Mark xv. 38, 39, is taken, without any hint that
it is not original, (much of it, *word for word*,) from Chrysostom's 88th Homily on S. Matthew's Gospel[q]. The
same is to be said of the first twelve lines of his note on
S. Mark xvi. 9. On the other hand, the latter half of the
note last mentioned professes to give the substance of what
Eusebius had written on the same subject. It is in fact an
extract from those very "Quaestiones ad Marinum" concerning which so much has been offered already. All this,
though it does not sensibly detract from the interest or the
value of Victor's work, must be admitted entirely to change
the character of his supposed evidence. He comes before
us rather in the light of a Compiler than of an Author : his
work is rather a "Catena" than a Commentary : and as
such in fact it is generally described. Quite plain is it, at
all events, that the sentiments contained in the sections last
referred to, are *not Victor's at all.* For one half of them,
no one but Chrysostom is responsible : for the other half, no
one but Eusebius.

But it is Victor's familiar use of the writings of Eusebius,
—especially of those Resolutions of hard Questions " concerning the seeming Inconsistencies in the Evangelical accounts
of the Resurrection," which Eusebius addressed to Marinus,
—on which the reader's attention is now to be concentrated.
Victor cites that work of Eusebius *by name* in the very *first*
page of his Commentary. That his *last* page also contains
a quotation from it, (also *by name*), has been already pointed
out[r]. Attention is now invited to what is found concerning
S. Mark xvi. 9—20 in the *last page but one* (p. 444) of

---

[q] *Opp.* vol. vii. p. 825 E—826 B : or, in Field's edition, p. 527, line 3 to 20.
[r] Cramer, i. p. 266, lines 10, 11,—ὥς φησιν Εὐσέβιος ὁ Καισαρείας ἐν τῷ πρὸς
Μαρῖνον κ.τ.λ. And at p. 446, line 19,—Εὐσέβιός φησιν ὁ Καισαρείας κ.τ.λ.

Victor's work.   It shall be given in English; because I will
convince unlearned as well as learned readers. Victor, (after
quoting four lines from the 89th Homily of Chrysostom[s]),
reconciles (exactly as Eusebius is observed to do[t]) the notes
of time contained severally in S. Matth. xxviii. 1, S. Mark
xvi. 2, S. Luke xxiv. 1, and S. John xx. 1.   After which,
he proceeds as follows:—

"In certain copies of Mark's Gospel, next comes,—' Now
when [JESUS] was risen early the first day of the week, He
appeared to Mary Magdalene;'—a statement which seems
inconsistent with Matthew's narrative. This might be met
by asserting, that the conclusion of Mark's Gospel, though
found in certain copies, is spurious, However, that we may
not seem to betake ourselves to an off-hand answer, we
propose to read the place thus:—' Now when [JESUS] was
risen:' then, after a comma, to go on,—' early the first day
of the week He appeared to Mary Magdalene.' In this
way we refer [Mark's] ' Now when [JESUS] was risen' to
Matthew's ' in the end of the sabbath,' (for *then* we believe
Him to have *risen;*) and all that comes after, expressive as
it is of a different notion, we connect with what follows.
Mark relates that He who ' arose (according to Matthew) *in
the end of the Sabbath,' was seen* by Mary Magdalene ' *early.*'
This is in fact what John also declares; for he too has recorded that ' early,' ' the first day of the week,' [JESUS]
appeared to the Magdalene. In a word, two distinct seasons
are set before us by these words: first, the season of the
Resurrection, — which was ' in the end of the Sabbath;'
secondly, the season of our SAVIOUR's Appearing,— which
was ' early [u].' "

No one, I presume, can read this passage and yet hesitate
to admit that he is here listening to Eusebius "ad Marinum" over again.   But if any one really retains a particle
of doubt on the subject, he is requested to cast his eye to
the foot of the present page; and even an unlearned reader,

[s] Compare Cramer's *Vict. Ant.* i. p. 444, line 6—9, with Field's *Chrys.* iii.
p. 539, line 7—21.

[t] Mai, iv. p. 257-8.

[u] Cramer, vol. i. p. 444, line 19 to p. 445, line 4.

surveying the originals with attention, may easily convince himself that *Victor is here nothing else but a copyist* [x]. That the work in which Eusebius reconciles " seeming discrepancies in the Evangelical narratives," was actually lying open before Victor while he wrote, is ascertained beyond dispute. He is observed in his next ensuing Comment to quote from it, and to mention Eusebius as its author. At the end of the present note he has a significant allusion to Eusebius :—

---

[x] The following is the original of what is given above :—'Επειδὴ δὲ ἔν τισι τῶν ἀντιγράφων πρόσκειται τῷ παρόντι εὐαγγελίῳ, "ἀναστὰς δὲ τῇ μιᾷ τοῦ σαββάτου πρωΐ, ἐφάνη (see below *) Μαρίᾳ τῇ Μαγδαληνῇ," δοκεῖ δὲ τοῦτο διαφωνεῖν τῷ ὑπὸ Ματθαίου εἰρημένῳ, ἐρούμεν ὡς δυνατὸν μὲν εἰπεῖν ὅτι νενόθευται τὸ παρὰ Μάρκῳ τελευταῖον ἔν τισι φερόμενον. πλὴν ἵνα μὴ δόξωμεν ἐπὶ τὸ ἔτοιμον καταφεύγειν, οὕτως ἀναγνωσόμεθα· "ἀναστὰς δὲ," καὶ ὑποστίξαντες ἐπάγωμεν, "πρωΐ τῇ μιᾷ τοῦ σαββάτου ἐφάνη Μαρίᾳ τῇ Μαγδαληνῇ." ἵνα [*The extract from* VICTOR *is continued below in the right hand column : the left exhibiting the text of* EUSEBIUS ' *ad Marinum.*']

(EUSEBIUS.)

τὸ μὲν "ἀναστὰς," ἀν[απέμψωμεν P] ἐπὶ τὴν παρὰ τῷ Ματθαίῳ "ὀψὲ σαββάτων." (τότε γὰρ ἐγήγερτο.) τὸ δὲ ἑξῆς, ἑτέρας ὂν διανοίας ὑποστατικὸν, συνάψωμεν τοῖς ἐπιλεγομένοις.

("πρωΐ" γὰρ "τῇ μιᾷ τοῦ σαββάτου ἐφάνη Μαρίᾳ τῇ Μαγδαληνῇ.")

τοῦτο γοῦν ἐδήλωσε καὶ ὁ Ἰωάννης "πρωΐ" καὶ αὐτὸς "τῇ μιᾷ τοῦ σαββάτου" ὦφθαι αὐτὸν τῇ Μαγδαληνῇ μαρτυρήσας.

[31 words are here omitted.]

ὡς παρίστασθαι ἐν τούτοις καιροὺς δύο· τὸν μὲν γὰρ τῆς ἀναστάσεως τὸν "ὀψὲ τοῦ σαββάτου." τὸν δὲ τῆς τοῦ Σωτῆρος ἐπιφανείας, τὸν "πρωΐ."

[EUSEBIUS, *apud Mai,* iv. p. 256.]

(VICTOR.)

τὸ μὲν "ἀναστὰς," ἀναπέμψωμεν ἐπὶ τὴν παρὰ τῷ Ματθαίῳ "ὀψὲ σαββάτων." (τότε γὰρ ἐγηγέρθαι αὐτὸν πιστεύομεν.) τὸ δὲ ἑξῆς, ἑτέρας ὂν διανοίας παραστατικὸν, συνάψωμεν τοῖς ἐπιλεγομένοις·

(τὸν γὰρ "ὀψὲ σαββάτων" κατὰ Ματθαῖον ἐγηγερμένον ἱστορεῖ "πρωΐ" ἑωρακέναι Μαρίαν τὴν Μαγδαληνήν.)

τοῦτο γοῦν ἐδήλωσε καὶ Ἰωάννης, "πρωΐ" καὶ αὐτὸς "τῇ μιᾷ τῶν σαββάτων" ὦφθαι αὐτὸν τῇ Μαγδαληνῇ μαρτυρήσας.

ὡς παρίστασθαι ἐν τούτοις καιροὺς δύο· τὸν μὲν τῆς ἀναστάσεως, τὸν "ὀψὲ τοῦ σαββάτου" τὸν δὲ τῆς τοῦ Σωτῆρος ἐπιφανείας, τὸ "πρωΐ."

[VICTOR ANTIOCH., *ed. Cramer,* i. p. 444-5: (*with a few slight emendations of the text from* Evan. Cod. Reg. 178.)]

---

* Note, that Victor *twice* omits the word πρῶτον, and *twice* reads τῇ μιᾷ τοῦ σαββάτου, (instead of πρώτῃ σαββάτου), *only because Eusebius had inadvertently* (thrice times) *done the same thing* in the place from which Victor is copying. See Mai *Nova P.P. Bibl.* iv. p. 256, line 19 and 26 : p. 257 line 4 and 5.

"I know very well," he says, "what has been suggested *by
those who are at the pains to remove the apparent inconsistencies
in this place*[y]." But when writing on S. Mark xvi. 9—20,
he does more. After abridging, (as his manner is,) what
Eusebius explains with such tedious emphasis, (giving the
substance of five columns in about three times as many
lines,) he adopts the exact expressions of Eusebius,—follows
him in his very mistakes,—and finally transcribes his words.
The reader is therefore requested to bear in mind that what
he has been listening to is *not the testimony of Victor at all:*
but *the testimony of Eusebius.* This is but one more echo
therefore of a passage of which we are all beginning by this
time to be weary; so exceedingly rash are the statements
with which it is introduced, so utterly preposterous the proposed method of remedying a difficulty which proves after
all to be purely imaginary.

What then *is* the testimony of Victor? Does he offer any
independent statement on the question in dispute, from
which his own private opinion (though nowhere stated) may
be lawfully inferred? Yes indeed. Victor, though frequently a Transcriber only, is observed every now and then
to come forward in his own person, and deliver his individual sentiment[z]. But nowhere throughout his work
does he deliver such remarkable testimony as in this place.
Hear him!

"*Notwithstanding that in very many copies of the present
Gospel, the passage beginning, 'Now when [JESUS] was risen
early the first day of the week, He appeared first to Mary Mag-
dalene,' be not found,—(certain individuals having supposed it to
be spurious,)—yet* WE, AT ALL EVENTS, INASMUCH AS IN VERY
MANY WE HAVE DISCOVERED IT TO EXIST, HAVE, OUT OF ACCU-
RATE COPIES, SUBJOINED ALSO THE ACCOUNT OF OUR LORD'S
ASCENSION, (FOLLOWING THE WORDS 'FOR THEY WERE AFRAID,')
IN CONFORMITY WITH THE PALESTINIAN EXEMPLAR OF MARK

---

[y] οὐκ ἀγνοῶ δὲ ὡς διαφόρους ὀπτασίας γεγενῆσθαί φασιν οἱ τὴν δοκοῦσαν δια-
φωνίαν διαλῦσαι σπουδάζοντες. Vict. Ant. *ed. Cramer,* vol. i. p. 445, l. 23-5:
referring to what Eusebius says *apud Mai,* iv. 264 and 265 (§ iiii): 287—290
(§§ v, vi, vii.)

[z] e.g. in the passage last quoted.

WHICH EXHIBITS THE GOSPEL VERITY: THAT IS TO SAY, FROM THE WORDS, 'NOW WHEN [JESUS] WAS RISEN EARLY THE FIRST DAY OF THE WEEK,' &C., DOWN TO 'WITH SIGNS FOLLOWING. AMEN[a].''—And with these words Victor of Antioch brings his Commentary on S. Mark to an end.

Here then we find it roundly stated by a highly intelligent Father, writing in the first half of the vth century,—

(1.) That the reason why the last Twelve Verses of S. Mark are absent from some ancient copies of his Gospel is *because they have been deliberately omitted by Copyists :*

(2.) That the ground for such omission was the *subjective judgment* of individuals,—*not* the result of any appeal to documentary evidence. Victor, therefore, clearly held that the Verses in question had been *expunged* in consequence of their (seeming) inconsistency with what is met with in the other Gospels :

(3.) That he, on the other hand, had convinced himself by reference to "very many" and "accurate" copies, that the verses in question are genuine :

(4.) That in particular the Palestinian Copy, which enjoyed the reputation of "exhibiting the genuine text of S. Mark," contained the Verses in dispute.—To *Opinion*, therefore, Victor opposes *Authority.* He makes his appeal to the most trustworthy documentary evidence with which he is acquainted; and the deliberate testimony which he delivers is a complete counterpoise and antidote to the loose phrases of Eusebius on the same subject:

(5.) That in consequence of all this, following the Palestinian Exemplar, he had from accurate copies *furnished his own work with the Twelve Verses in dispute;*—which is a categorical refutation of the statement frequently met with that the work of Victor of Antioch is *without* them.

We are now at liberty to sum up; and to review the progress which has been hitherto made in this Inquiry.

Six Fathers of the Church have been examined who are commonly represented as bearing hostile testimony to the last Twelve Verses of S. Mark's Gospel; and they have been

---

[a] For the original of this remarkable passage the reader is referred to the Appendix (E).

easily reduced to *one*.   Three of them, (Hesychius, Jerome,
Victor,) prove to be echoes, not voices.   The remaining two,
(Gregory of Nyssa and Severus,) are neither voices nor
echoes, but merely *names :* GREGORY OF NYSSA having really
no more to do with this discussion than Philip of Macedon;
and " Severus" and " Hesychius" representing one and the
same individual.   Only by a Critic seeking to mislead his
reader will any one of these five Fathers be in future cited
as witnessing against the genuineness of S. Mark xvi. 9—20.
Eusebius is the solitary witness who survives the ordeal of
exact inquiry [b].   But,

I. EUSEBIUS, (as we have seen), instead of proclaiming his
distrust of this portion of the Gospel, enters upon an elaborate proof that its contents are not inconsistent with what
is found in the Gospels of S. Matthew and S. John.   His
testimony is reducible to two innocuous and wholly uncon-
nected propositions: the first,—That there existed in his
day a vast number of copies in which the last chapter of
S. Mark's Gospel ended abruptly at ver. 8; (the correlative
of which of course would be that there also existed a vast
number which were furnished with the present ending.)   The
second,—That by putting a comma after the word 'Ἀναστάς,
S. Mark xvi. 9, is capable of being reconciled with S. Matth.
xxviii. 1 [c]. . . . . I profess myself unable to understand how
it can be pretended that Eusebius would have subscribed to
the opinion of Tischendorf, Tregelles, and the rest, that the
Gospel of S. Mark was never finished by its inspired Author,
or was mutilated before it came abroad; at all events, that
the last Twelve Verses are spurious.

---

[b] How shrewdly was it remarked by Matthaei, eighty years ago,—" Scholia
certe, in quibus de integritate hujus loci dubitatur, omnia *ex uno fonte pro-
manarunt.*   Ex eodem fonte Hieronymum etiam hausisse intelligitur ex ejus
loco quem laudavit Wetst. ad ver. 9.—Similiter Scholiastæ omnes in principio
hujus Evangelii in disputatione de lectione ἐν ἡσαΐᾳ τῷ προφήτῃ ex uno pen-
dent.   *Fortasse Origenes auctor est hujus dubitationis.*" (N. T. vol. ii. p. 270.)
—The reader is invited to remember what was offered above in p. 47
(line 23.)

[c] It is not often, I think, that one finds in MSS. a point actually inserted
after 'Ἀναστὰς δέ.   Such a point is found, however, in Cod. 34 (= Coisl. 195,)
and Cod. 22 (= Reg. 72,) and doubtless in many other copies.

II. The observations of Eusebius are found to have been adopted, and in part transcribed, by an unknown writer of the vi[th] century,—whether HESYCHIUS or SEVERUS is not certainly known: but if it were Hesychius, then it was not Severus; if Severus, then not Hesychius. This writer, however, (whoever he may have been,) is careful to convince us that individually he entertained *no doubt whatever* about the genuineness of this part of Scripture, for he says that he writes in order to remove the (hypothetical) objections of others, and to silence their (imaginary) doubts. Nay, he freely *quotes the verses as genuine*, and declares that they were read in his day on a certain Sunday night in the public Service of the Church. . . . To represent such an one,—(it matters nothing, I repeat, whether we call him "Hesychius of Jerusalem" or "Severus of Antioch,")—as a hostile witness, is simply to misrepresent the facts of the case. He is, on the contrary, the strenuous champion of the verses which he is commonly represented as impugning.

III. As for JEROME, since that illustrious Father comes before us in this place as a *translator* of Eusebius only, he is no more responsible for what Eusebius says concerning S. Mark xvi. 9—20, than Hobbes of Malmesbury is responsible for anything that Thucydides has related concerning the Peloponnesian war. Individually, however, it is certain that Jerome was convinced of the genuineness of S. Mark xvi. 9—20: for in two different places of his writings he not only quotes the 9th and 14th verses, but he exhibits all the twelve in the Vulgate.

IV. Lastly, VICTOR OF ANTIOCH, who wrote in an age when Eusebius was held to be an infallible oracle on points of Biblical Criticism, — having dutifully rehearsed, (like the rest,) the feeble expedient of that illustrious Father for harmonizing S. Mark xvi. 9 with the narrative of S. Matthew, —is observed to cite the statements of Eusebius concerning *the last Twelve Verses* of S. Mark, only in order to refute them. Not that he opposes opinion to opinion,—(for the opinions of Eusebius and of Victor of Antioch on this behalf were probably identical;) but statement he meets with counter-statement,—fact he confronts with fact. Scarcely can anything be imagined more emphatic than his testimony, or more conclusive.

For the reader is requested to observe that here is an Ecclesiastic, writing in the first half of the vth century, who *expressly witnesses to the genuineness* of the Verses in dispute. He had made reference, he says, and ascertained their existence in very many MSS. (ὡς ἐν πλείστοις). He had derived his text from "accurate" ones: (ἐξ ἀκριβῶν ἀντι-γράφων.) More than that: he leads his reader to infer that he had personally resorted to the famous Palestinian Copy, the text of which was held to exhibit the inspired verity, and had satisfied himself that the concluding section of S. Mark's Gospel *was there.* He had, therefore, been either to Je-rusalem, or else to Cæsarea; had inquired for those venerable records which had once belonged to Origen and Pamphilus[d]; and had inspected them. Testimony more express, more weighty,—I was going to say, more decisive,—can scarcely be imagined. It may with truth be said to close the present discussion.

With this, in fact, Victor lays down his pen. So also may I. I submit that nothing whatever which has hitherto come before us lends the slightest countenance to the modern dream that S. Mark's Gospel, as it left the hands of its in-spired Author, ended abruptly at ver. 8. Neither Eusebius nor Jerome; neither Severus of Antioch nor Hesychius of Jerusalem; certainly not Victor of Antioch; least of all Gregory of Nyssa,—yield a particle of support to that mon-strous fancy. The notion is an invention, a pure imagina-tion of the Critics ever since the days of Griesbach.

It remains to be seen whether the MSS. will prove some-what less unaccommodating.

VII. For it can be of no possible avail, at this stage of the discussion, to appeal to

EUTHYMIUS ZIGABENUS,

the Author of an interesting Commentary, or rather Compi-lation on the Gospels, assigned to A.D. 1116. Euthymius lived, in fact, full five hundred years too late for his testimony to be of the slightest importance. Such as it is, however, it is

---

[d] Scrivener's *Introduction,* pp. 47, 125, 431.

not unfavourable. He says,—"Some of the Commentators
state that here," (viz. at ver. 8,) "the Gospel according to
Mark finishes ; and that what follows is a spurious addition." (Which clearly is his version of the statements of one
or more of the four Fathers whose testimony has already
occupied so large a share of our attention.) "This portion we
must also interpret, however," (Euthymius proceeds,) "since
there is nothing in it prejudicial to the truth[c]."—But it is
idle to linger over such a writer. One might almost as well
quote "Poli *Synopsis*," and then proceed to discuss it. The
cause must indeed be desperate which seeks support from
a quarter like this. What possible sanction can an Ecclesiastic of the xii[th] century be supposed to yield to the hypothesis that S. Mark's Gospel, as it left the hands of its inspired Author, was an unfinished work ?

It remains to ascertain what is the evidence of the MSS.
on this subject. And the MSS. require to be the more
attentively studied, because it is to *them* that our opponents
are accustomed most confidently to appeal. On them in
fact they rely. The nature and the value of the most ancient
Manuscript testimony available, shall be scrupulously investigated in the next two Chapters.

[c] Φασὶ δέ τινες τῶν ἐξηγητῶν ἐνταῦθα συμπληροῦσθαι τὸ κατὰ Μάρκον εὐαγ-
γέλιον· τὰ δὲ ἐφεξῆς προσθήκην εἶναι μεταγενεστέραν. Χρὴ δὲ καὶ ταύτην
ἑρμηνεῦσαι μηδὲν τῇ ἀληθείᾳ λυμαινομένην.—Euthym. Zig. (*ed.* Matthaei, 1792),
in loc.

CHAPTER VI.

MANUSCRIPT TESTIMONY SHEWN TO BE OVERWHELM-INGLY IN FAVOUR OF THESE VERSES.—Part I.

S. Mark xvi. 9—20, *contained in every MS. in the world except two.—Irrational Claim to Infallibility set up on behalf of Cod.* B (p. 73) *and Cod.* א (p. 75).—*These two Codices shewn to be full of gross Omissions* (p. 78),—*Interpolations* (p. 80),—*Corruptions of the Text* (p. 81),—*and Perversions of the Truth* (p. 83).—*The testimony of Cod.* B *to S. Mark* xvi. 9—20, *shewn to be favorable, notwithstanding* (p. 86).

THE two oldest Copies of the Gospels in existence are the famous Codex in the Vatican Library at Rome, known as "Codex B;" and the Codex which Tischendorf brought from Mount Sinai in 1859, and which he designates by the first letter of the Hebrew alphabet (א). These two manuscripts are probably not of equal antiquity[a]. An interval of fifty years at least seems to be required to account for the marked difference between them. If the first belongs to the beginning, the second may be referred to the middle or latter part of the iv[th] century. But the two Manuscripts agree in this,—that *they are without the last twelve verses of S. Mark's Gospel.* In both, after ἐφοβοῦντο γάρ (ver. 8), comes the subscription: in Cod. B,—ΚΑΤΑ ΜΑΡΚΟΝ; in Cod. א,—ΕΤΑΓΓΕΛΙΟΝ ΚΑΤΑ ΜΑΡΚΟΝ.

Let it not be supposed that we have any *more* facts of this class to produce. All has been stated. It is not that the evidence of Manuscripts is one,—the evidence of Fathers and Versions another. The very reverse is the case. Manuscripts, Fathers, and Versions alike, are *only not unanimous* in bearing consistent testimony. But the consentient witness

---

[a] For some remarks on this subject the reader is referred to the Appendix (F).

of the MSS. is even extraordinary. With the exception of the two uncial MSS. which have just been named, there is *not one* Codex in existence, uncial or cursive,—(and we are acquainted with, at least, eighteen other uncials [b], and about six hundred cursive Copies of this Gospel,)—which leaves out the last twelve verses of S. Mark.

The inference which an unscientific observer would draw from this fact, is no doubt in this instance the correct one. He demands to be shewn the Alexandrine (A) and the Parisian Codex (C),—neither of them probably removed by much more than fifty years from the date of the Codex Sinaiticus, and both unquestionably *derived from different originals;*— and he ascertains that no countenance is lent by either of those venerable monuments to the proposed omission of this part of the sacred text. He discovers that the Codex Bezae (D), the only remaining very ancient MS. authority,—notwithstanding that it is observed on most occasions to exhibit an extraordinary sympathy with the Vatican (B),—here sides with A and C against B and ℵ. He inquires after all the other uncials and all the cursive MSS. in existence, (some of them dating from the xth century,) and requests to have it explained to him *why* it is to be supposed that all these many witnesses,—belonging to so many different patriarchates, provinces, ages of the Church, — have entered into a grand conspiracy to bear false witness on a point of this magnitude and importance? But he obtains no intelligible answer to this question. How, then, is an unprejudiced student to draw any inference but one from the premises? *That* single peculiarity (he tells himself) of bringing the second Gospel abruptly to a close at the 8th verse of the xvi[th] chapter, is absolutely fatal to the two Codices in question. It is useless to din into his ears that those Codices are probably both of the iv[th] century,—unless men are prepared to add the assurance that a Codex of the iv[th] century is *of necessity* a more trustworthy witness to the text of the Gospels than a Codex of the vth. The omission of these twelve verses, I repeat, in itself, destroys his confidence in

[b] Viz. A, C [v]; D [vi]; E, L [viii]; F, K, M, V, Γ, Δ, Λ (quære), Π [ix]; G, H, X, S, U [ix, x].

Cod. B and Cod. ℵ: for it is obvious that a copy of the Gospels which has been so seriously mutilated in one place may have been slightly tampered with in another. He is willing to suspend his judgment, of course. The two oldest copies of the Gospels in existence are entitled to great reverence *because* of their high antiquity. They must be allowed a most patient, most unprejudiced, most respectful, nay, a most indulgent hearing. But when all this has been freely accorded, on no intelligible principle can more be claimed for any two MSS. in the world.

The rejoinder to all this is sufficiently obvious. Mistrust will no doubt have been thrown over the evidence borne to the text of Scripture in a thousand other places by Cod. B and Cod. ℵ, *after demonstration that those two Codices exhibit a mutilated text* in the present place. But what else is this but the very point requiring demonstration? Why may not these two be right, and all the other MSS. wrong?

I propose, therefore, that we reverse the process. Proceed we to examine the evidence borne by these two witnesses on certain *other* occasions which admit of *no* difference of opinion; or next to none. Let us endeavour, I say, to ascertain *the character of the Witnesses* by a patient and unprejudiced examination of their Evidence,—not in one place, or in two, or in three; but on several important occasions, and throughout. If we find it invariably consentient and invariably truthful, then of course a mighty presumption will have been established, the very strongest possible, that their adverse testimony in respect of the conclusion of S. Mark's Gospel must needs be worthy of all acceptation. But if, on the contrary, our inquiries shall conduct us to the very opposite result,—what else can happen but that our confidence in these two MSS. will be hopelessly shaken? We must in such case be prepared to admit that it is just as likely as not that this is only *one more occasion* on which these " two false witnesses" have conspired to witness falsely. If, at this juncture, extraneous evidence of an entirely trustworthy kind can be procured to confront them : above all, if some one ancient witness of unimpeachable veracity can be found who shall bear contradictory evidence : what other alternative will be left us but to reject their testimony in respect of S. Mark xvi. 9—20 with something like indignation; and to acquiesce in the belief of universal Christendom for eighteen hundred years that these twelve verses are just as much entitled to our unhesitating acceptance as any other twelve verses in the Gospel which can be named?

I. It is undeniable, in the meantime, that for the last quarter of a century, it has become the fashion to demand for the readings of Codex B something very like absolute deference. The grounds for this superstitious sentiment, (for really I can describe it in no apter way,) I profess myself unable to discover. Codex B comes to us without a history: without recommendation of any kind, except that of its antiquity. It bears traces of careless transcription in every page. The mistakes which the original transcriber made are of perpetual recurrence. "They are chiefly omissions, of one, two, or three words; but sometimes of half a verse, a whole verse, or even of several verses .... I hesitate not to assert that it would be easier to find a folio containing three or four such omissions than to light on one which should be without any [e]." In the Gospels alone, Codex B leaves out words or whole clauses no less than 1,491 times [d] : of which by far the largest proportion is found in S. Mark's Gospel. Many of these, no doubt, are to be accounted for by the proximity of a "like ending [e]." The Vatican MS. (like the Sinaitic [f]) was originally de-

---

[e] Vercellone, — *Del antichissimo Codice Vaticano della Bibbia Greca,* Roma, 1860. (pp. 21.)

[d] *Dublin Univ. Mag.* (Nov. 1859,) p. 620, quoted by Scrivener, p. 93.

[e] ὁμοιοτέλευτον.

[f] See Scrivener's *Introduction* to his ed. of the Codex Bezæ, p. xxiii. The passage referred to reappears at the end of his Preface to the 2nd ed. of his *Collation of the Cod. Sinaiticus.*—Add to his instances, this from S. Matth. xxviii. 2, 3 :—

ΚΑΙ ΕΚΑΘΗΤΟ Ε
ΠΑΝω ΑΥΤΟΥ [ΗΝ ΔΕ
Η ΕΙΔΕΑ ΑΥΤΟΥ] ωC
ΑCΤΡΑΠΗ

It is plain why the scribe of אּ wrote επανω αυτου ως αστραπη.—The next is from S. Luke xxiv. 31 :—

ΔΙΗΝΤΓΗ
CAN ΟΙ ΟΦΘΑΛΜΟΙ

rived from an older Codex which contained about twelve
or thirteen letters in a line [g].   And it will be found that
some of its omissions which have given rise to prolonged

КАΙ [ЄΠЄΓΝШCAN AYTŌ
КАΙ] AYTOC AΦAN
TOC ЄΓЄΝЄTO

Hence the omission of και επεγνωσαν αυτον in א.—The following explains
the omission from א (and D) of the Ascension at S. Luke xxiv. 52:—

AΠ AYTШN КАΙ [AN
ЄΦЄPЄTO ЄIC TON
OYPANON КАΙ] AY
TOI ΠPOCKYNHCI

The next explains why א reads περικαλυψαντες επηρωτων αυτον in S. Luke
xxii. 64:—

ΔЄPONTЄC КАΙ ΠЄ
PIKAΛYΨANTЄC Є
[TYΠTON AYTOY TO
ΠPOCШΠON КАΙ Є]
ΠHPШTШN AYTŌ

The next explains why the words και πας εις αυτην βιαζεται are absent
in א (and G) at S. Luke xvi. 16:—

ЄYAΓΓЄ
ΛIZЄTAI [КАΙ ΠAC
ЄIC AYTHN ΒI
AZЄTAI] ЄYKOΠШ
TЄPON ΔЄ ЄCTIN TŌ

[g] In this way, (at S. John xvii. 15, 16), the obviously corrupt reading of
Cod. B (ινα τηρησης αυτους εκ του κοσμου)—which, however, was the reading
of the copy used by Athanasius (*Opp.* p. 1035: *al. ed.* p. 825)—is explained:—

ЄK TOY [ΠONHPOY.
ЄK TOY] KOCMOY
OYK ЄICIN KAΘШC

Thus also is explained why B (with א, A, D, L) omits a precious clause in
S. Luke xxiv. 42:—

OΠTOY MЄPOC КАΙ
[AΠO MЄΛICCI
OY KHPIOY КАΙ]
ΛABШN ЄNШΠION

And why the same MSS. (all but A) omit an important clause in S. Luke
xxiv. 53:—

ЄN TШ IЄPШ [AIN
OYNTЄC КАΙ] ЄYΛO
ΓOYNTЄC TON O̅N̅

And why B (with א, L) omits an important clause in the history of the Temptation (S. Luke iv. 5):—

КАΙ ANAΓAΓШN AY
TON [ЄIC OPOC YΨH
ΛON] ЄΔIΞЄN AYTШ

discussion are probably to be referred to nothing else but the oscitancy of a transcriber with such a codex before him[h]: without having recourse to any more abstruse hypothesis; without any imputation of bad faith;—*certainly without supposing that the words omitted did not exist in the inspired autograph of the Evangelist.* But then it is undeniable that some of the omissions in Cod. B are not to be so explained. On the other hand, I can testify to the fact that the codex is disfigured throughout with *repetitions*. The original scribe is often found to have not only written the same words twice over, but to have failed whenever he did so to take any notice with his pen of what he had done.

What then, (I must again inquire,) are the grounds for the superstitious reverence which is entertained in certain quarters for the readings of Codex B? If it be a secret known to the recent Editors of the New Testament, they have certainly contrived to keep it wondrous close.

II. More recently, a claim to co-ordinate primacy has been set up on behalf of the Codex Sinaiticus. Tischendorf is actually engaged in remodelling his seventh Leipsic edition, chiefly in conformity with the readings of his lately discovered MS.[i] And yet the Codex in question abounds with "errors of the eye and pen, to an extent not unparalleled, but happily rather unusual in documents of firstrate importance." On many occasions, 10, 20, 30, 40 words are dropped through very carelessness[k]. "Letters and words, even whole sentences, are frequently written twice

---

[h] In this way the famous omission (א, B, L) of the word δευτεροπρώτῳ, in S. Luke vi. 1, is (to say the least) capable of being explained:—

ΕΓΕΝΕΤΟ Δ Ε ΕΝ CAB
ΒΑΤω Δ[ΕΥΤΕΡΟ
ΠΡωΤω Δ]ΙΑΠΟΡΕΥΕ
CΘΑΙ

and of υιου Βαραχιου (א) in S. Matth. xxvii. 35 :—

ΑΙΜΑΤΟC ΖΑΧΑΡΙΟΥ
[ΥΙΟΥ ΒΑΡΑΧΙΟΥ]
ΟΝ ΕΦΟΝΕΥCΑΤΕ

[i] He has reached the 480th page of vol. ii. (1 Cor. v. 7.)

[k] In this way 14 words have been omitted from Cod. א in S. Mark xv. 47— xvi. 1:—19 words in S. Mark i. 32-4:—20 words in S. John xx. 5, 6:—39 words in S. John xix. 20, 21.

over, or begun and immediately cancelled : while that gross
blunder . . . whereby a clause is omitted because it happens to
end in the same words as the clause preceding, occurs no less
than 115 times in the New Testament.   Tregelles has freely
pronounced that 'the state of the text, as proceeding from
the first scribe, may be regarded as *very rough*[1].' "   But
when "the first scribe" and his "very rough" performance
have been thus unceremoniously disposed of, one would
like to be informed what remains to command respect in
Codex א?   Is, then, *manuscript authority* to be confounded
with *editorial caprice*,—exercising itself upon the corrections
of "at least ten different revisers," who, from the vi[th] to the
xii[th] century, have been endeavouring to lick into shape
a text which its original author left "*very rough ?*"

The co-ordinate primacy, (as I must needs call it,) which,
within the last few years, has been claimed for Codex B
and Codex א, threatens to grow into a species of tyranny,—
from which I venture to predict there will come in the end
an unreasonable and unsalutary recoil.   It behoves us, therefore, to look closely into this matter, and to require a reason
for what is being done.   The text of the sacred deposit is
far too precious a thing to be sacrificed to an irrational, or
at least a superstitious devotion to two MSS.,—simply because they may possibly be older by a hundred years than
any other which we possess.   "Id verius quod prius," is an
axiom which holds every bit as true in Textual Criticism as
in Dogmatic Truth.   But on that principle, (as I have already
shewn,) the last twelve verses of S. Mark's Gospel are fully
established [m]; and by consequence, the credit of Codd. B
and א sustains a severe shock.   Again, "Id verius quod
prius;" but it does not of course follow that a Codex of
the iv[th] century shall exhibit a more correct text of Scripture than one written in the vth, or even than one written
in the xth.   For the proof of this statement, (if it can be supposed to require proof,) it is enough to appeal to Codex D.
That venerable copy of the Gospels is of the vi[th] century.

[1] Scrivener's *Full Collation*, &c., p. xv.; quoting Tregelles' N. T. Part II.
page ii.)
[m] See Chap. IV. p. 37.

It is, in fact, one of our five great uncials.   No older MS. of
the Greek Text is known to exist,—excepting always A, B, C
and ℵ.   And yet *no* text is more thoroughly disfigured by
corruptions and interpolations than that of Codex D.   In the
Acts, (to use the language of its learned and accurate Editor,)
"it is hardly an exaggeration to assert that it reproduces
the *textus receptus* much in the same way that one of the
best Chaldee Targums does the Hebrew of the Old Testament: so wide are the variations in the diction, so constant
and inveterate the practice of expanding the narrative by
means of interpolations which seldom recommend themselves
as genuine by even a semblance of internal probability [n]."
Where, then, is the *à priori* probability that two MSS. of the
iv[th] century shall have not only a superior claim to be heard,
but almost an exclusive right to dictate which readings are
to be rejected, which retained?

How ready the most recent editors of the New Testament
have shewn themselves to hammer the sacred text on the
anvil of Codd. B and ℵ,—not unfrequently in defiance of the
evidence of all other MSS., and sometimes to the serious
detriment of the deposit,—would admit of striking illustration were this place for such details.   Tischendorf's English
"*New Testament,*"—"with various readings from the three
most celebrated manuscripts of the Greek Text" translated
at the foot of every page,—is a recent attempt (1869) to
popularize the doctrine that we have to look exclusively to
two or three of the oldest copies, if we would possess the
Word of GOD in its integrity.   Dean Alford's constant appeal
in his revision of the Authorized Version (1870) to "the
oldest MSS.," (meaning thereby generally Codd. ℵ and B
with one or two others [o]), is an abler endeavour to fami-
liarize the public mind with the same belief.   I am bent on
shewing that there is nothing whatever in the character of
either of the Codices in question to warrant this servile
deference.

(*a*) And first,—Ought it not sensibly to detract from our

---

[n] Scrivener's *Introduction to Con. Bezae*, p. liv.

[o] *e.g.* in S. John i. 42 (meaning only ℵ, B, L): iv. 42 (ℵ, B, C): v. 12
(ℵ, B, C, L): vi. 22 (A, B, L), &c.

opinion of the value of their evidence to discover that *it is
easier to find two consecutive verses in which the two MSS. differ,
the one from the other, than two consecutive verses in which they
entirely agree?* Now this is a plain matter of fact, of which
any one who pleases may easily convince himself. But the
character of two witnesses who habitually contradict one
another has been accounted, in every age, precarious. On
every such occasion, only one of them can possibly be speaking the truth. Shall I be thought unreasonable if I confess that these *perpetual* inconsistencies between Codd. B
and א,—grave inconsistencies, and occasionally even gross
ones,—altogether destroy my confidence in either?

(*b*) On the other hand, discrepant as the testimony of
these two MSS. is throughout, they yet, strange to say,
conspire every here and there in exhibiting minute corruptions of such an unique and peculiar kind as to betray
a (probably not very remote) common corrupt original.
These coincidences in fact are so numerous and so extraordinary as to establish a real connexion between those two
codices; and that connexion is fatal to any claim which
might be set up on their behalf as wholly independent
witnesses [P].

(*c*) Further, it is evident that both alike have been subjected, probably during the process of transcription, to the
same depraving influences. But because such statements
require to be established by an induction of instances, the
reader's attention must now be invited to a few samples of
the grave blemishes which disfigure our two oldest copies
of the Gospel.

1. And first, since it is the omission of the end of S. Mark's
Gospel which has given rise to the present discussion, it
becomes a highly significant circumstance that the original

[P] e.g. S. Matth. x. 25; xii. 24, 27: S. Luke xi. 15, 18, 19 (βεεζεβουλ).—
1 Cor. xiii. 3 (καυχησωμαι).—S. James i. 17 (αποσκιασματος).—Acts i. 5 (εν πν.
βαπ. αγ.).—S. Mark vi. 20 (ηπορει).—S. Matth. xiv. 30 (ισχυρον).—S. Luke iii.
32 (Ιωβηλ).—Acts i. 19 (ιδια omitted).—S. Matth. xxv. 27 (τα αργυρια).—
S. Matth. xvii. 22 (συστρεφομενων).—S. Luke vi. 1 (δευτεροπρωτω omitted).—
See more in Tischendorf's *Prolegomena* to his 4to. reprint of the *Cod. Sin.*
p. xxxvi. On this head the reader is also referred to Scrivener's very interesting *Collation of the Cod. Sinaiticus*, Introduction, p. xliii. *seq.*

scribe of Cod. ℵ had *also* omitted the *end of the Gospel according to S. John* [q]. In this suppression of ver. 25, Cod. ℵ stands *alone* among MSS. A cloud of primitive witnesses vouch for the genuineness of the verse. Surely, it is nothing else but the *reductio ad absurdum* of a theory of recension, (with Tischendorf in his last edition,) to accommodate our printed text to the vicious standard of the original penman of Cod. ℵ, and bring the last chapter of S. John's Gospel to a close at ver. 24!

Cod. B, on the other hand, omits the whole of those two solemn verses wherein S. Luke describes our LORD's "Agony and bloody Sweat," together with the act of the ministering Angel [r]. As to the genuineness of those verses, recognised as they are by Justin Martyr, Irenæus, Hippolytus, Epiphanius, Didymus, Gregory of Nazianzus, Chrysostom, Theodoret, by all the oldest versions, and by almost every MS. in existence, including Cod. ℵ,—it admits of *no* doubt. Here then is proof positive that in order to account for omissions from the Gospel in the oldest of the uncials, there is no need whatever to resort to the hypothesis that such portions of the Gospel are not the genuine work of the Evangelist. "The admitted error of Cod. B in this place," (to quote the words of Scrivener,) "ought to make some of its advocates more chary of their confidence in cases where it is less countenanced by other witnesses than in the instance before us."

Cod. B (not Cod. ℵ) is further guilty of the "grave error" (as Dean Alford justly styles it,) of omitting that solemn record of the Evangelist:—"Then said JESUS, Father, forgive them; for they know not what they do." It also withholds the statement that the inscription on the Cross was "in letters of Greek, and Latin, and Hebrew [s]." Cod ℵ, on the other hand, omits the confession of the man born blind (ὁ δὲ ἔφη, πιστεύω κύριε· καὶ προσεκύνησεν αὐτῷ) in S. John ix. 38.—Both Cod. ℵ and Cod. B retain nothing but the

---

[q] See Tischendorf's note in his reprint of the Cod. Sin., *Prolegg.* p. lix.

[r] Ὤφθη δὲ αὐτῷ ἄγγελος—καταβαίνοντα ἐπὶ τὴν γῆν. S. Luke xxii. 43, 44.

[s] ὁ δὲ Ἰησοῦς—τί ποιοῦσι, (xxiii. 34):—γράμμασιν Ἑλληνικοῖς καὶ Ῥωμαϊκοῖς καὶ Ἑβραϊκοῖς, (xxiii. 38.)

word υἱόν of the expression τὸν υἱὸν αὐτῆς τὸν πρωτότοκον,
in S. Matth. i. 25; and suppress altogether the important
doctrinal statement ὁ ὢν ἐν τῷ οὐρανῷ, in S. John iii. 13:
as well as the clause διελθὼν διὰ μέσου αὐτῶν· καὶ παρῆγεν
οὕτως, in S. John viii. 59.   Concerning all of which, let it
be observed that I am neither imputing motives nor pre-
tending to explain *the design* with which these several serious
omissions were made.   All that is asserted is, that they cannot be imputed to the carelessness of a copyist, but were
intentional: and I insist that they effectually dispose of the
presumption that when an important passage is observed to
be wanting from Cod. B or Cod. ℵ, its absence is to be accounted for by assuming that it was also absent *from the
inspired autograph of the Evangelist.*

2. To the foregoing must be added the many places where
the text of B or of ℵ, or of both, has clearly been *interpolated.*
There does not exist in the whole compass of the New Testament a more monstrous instance of this than is furnished
by the transfer of the incident of the piercing of our Redeemer's side from S. John xix. 24 to S. Matth. xxvii., in
Cod. B and Cod. ℵ, where it is introduced at the end of
ver. 49,—in defiance of reason as well as of authority[t].
"This interpolation" (remarks Mr. Scrivener) "which would
represent the Saviour as pierced while yet living, is a good
example of the fact that some of our highest authorities
may combine in attesting a reading unquestionably false[u]."
Another singularly gross specimen of interpolation, in my
judgment, is supplied by the purely apocryphal statement
which is met with in Cod. ℵ, at the end of S. Matthew's account of the healing of the Centurion's servant,—καὶ ὑπο-
στρεψας ο εκατονταρχος εις τον οικον αυτου εν αυτη τη ωρα,
ευρεν τον παιδα υγιαινοντα (viii. 13.)—Nor can anything
well be weaker than the substitution (for ὑστερήσαντος οἴνου,
in S. John ii. 3) of the following[v], which is found *only* in
Cod. ℵ:—οινον ουκ ειχον, οτι συνετελεσθη ο οινος του γαμου.

---

[t] αλλος δε λαβων λογχην ενυξεν αυτου την πλευραν, και εξηλθεν υδωρ και αιμα.
Yet B, C, L and ℵ contain this!   [u] *Coll. of the Cod. Sin.*, p. xlvii.
[v] So, in the margin of the Hharklensian revision.

But the inspired text has been depraved in the same licentious way throughout, by the responsible authors of Cod. B and Cod. ℵ, although such corruptions have attracted little notice from their comparative unimportance. Thus, the reading (in ℵ) ημας δει εργαζεσθαι τα εργα του πεμψαντος ημας (S. John ix. 4) carries with it its own sufficient condemnation; being scarcely rendered more tolerable by B's substitution of με for the second ημας.—Instead of τεθεμελίωτο γὰρ ἐπὶ τὴν πέτραν (S. Luke vi. 48), B and ℵ present us with the insipid gloss, δια το καλως οικοδομεισθαι αυτην. — In the last-named codex, we find the name of "Isaiah" (ησαιου) thrust into S. Matth. xiii. 35, in defiance of authority and of *fact*.—Can I be wrong in asserting that the reading ο μονογενης θεος (for υἱός) in S. John i. 18, (a reading found in Cod. B and Cod. ℵ alike,) is undeserving of serious attention?—May it not also be confidently declared that, in the face of all MS. evidence [x], no future Editors of the New Testament will be found to accept the highly improbable reading ο ανθρωπος ο λεγομενος Ιησους, in S. John ix. 11, although the same two Codices conspire in exhibiting it?—or, on the authority of *one* of them (ℵ), to read εν αυτω ζωη εστιν [y] (for ἐν αὐτῷ ζωὴ ἦν) in S. John i. 4?—Certain at least it is that no one will *ever* be found to read (with B) εβδομηκοντα δυο in S. Luke x. 1,—or (with ℵ) ο εκλεκτος του θεου (instead of ὁ υἱὸς τοῦ θεοῦ) in S. John i. 34.—But let me ask, With what show of reason can the pretence of *Infallibility*, (as well as the plea of Primacy), be set up on behalf of a pair of MSS. licentiously corrupt as these have already been *proved* to be? For the readings above enumerated, be it observed, are either critical depravations of the inspired Text, or else unwarrantable interpolations. They *cannot* have resulted from careless transcription.

3. Not a few of the foregoing instances are in fact of a kind

---

[x] Note, that it is a mistake for the advocates of this reading to claim the *Latin* versions as allies. Ἀπεκρίθη ἐκεῖνος, Ἄνθρωπος λεγόμενος Ἰησοῦς κ.τ.λ. is not "Respondit, Ille homo qui dicitur Jesus," (as both Tischendorf and Tregelles assume;) but "*Respondit ille,* Homo," &c.,—as in verses 25 and 36.

[y] This reading will be found discussed in a footnote (p) at the end of Chap. VII.,—p. 110.

to convince me that the text with which Cod. B and Cod. א
were chiefly acquainted, must have been once and again
subjected to a clumsy process of *revision.* Not unfrequently,
as may be imagined, the result (however tasteless and infelicitous) is not of serious importance; as when, (to give
examples from Cod. א,) for τὸν ὄχλον ἐπικεῖσθαι αὐτῷ (in
S. Luke v. 1) we are presented with συναχθηναι τον οχλον :—
when for ζῶν ἀσώτως (in S. Luke xv. 13) we read εις χωραν
μακραν; and for οἱ ἐξουσιάζοντες αὐτῶν (in S. Luke xxii. 25),
we find οι αρχοντες των [εθνων] εξουσιαζουσιν αυτων, και,
(which is only a weak reproduction of S. Matth. xx. 25):—
when again, for σκοτία ἤδη ἐγεγόνει (in S. John vi. 17), we
are shewn κατελαβεν δε αυτους η σκοτια : and when, for
καὶ τίς ἐστιν ὁ παραδώσων αὐτόν (in S. John vi. 64) we are
invited to accept και τις ην ο μελλων αυτον παραδιδοναι [z].
But it requires very little acquaintance with the subject to
foresee that this kind of license may easily assume serious
dimensions, and grow into an intolerable evil. Thus, when
the man born blind is asked by the HOLY ONE if he believes
ἐπὶ τὸν υἱὸν τοῦ Θεοῦ (S. John. ix. 35), we are by no means
willing to acquiesce in the proposed substitute, τον υιον του
ανθρωπου: neither, when the SAVIOUR says, γινώσκομαι ὑπὸ
τῶν ἐμων (S. John x. 14) are we at all willing to put up
with the weak equivalent γινωσκουσι με τα εμα. Still less is
και εμοι αυτους εδωκας any equivalent at all for καὶ τὰ ἐμὰ
πάντα σά ἐστι, καὶ τὰ σὰ ἐμά, in S. John xvii. 10: or, αλλοι

---

[z] The following may be added from Cod. א :—μεγάλοι αὐτῶν (in S. Mark x.
42) changed into βασιλεις: ειπεν (in S. Mark xiv. 58) substituted for ἡμεῖς
ἠκούσαμεν αὐτου λέγοντος: εβδομηκοντα τεσσαρων (in S. Lu. ii. 37) for ὀγδοηκ :
and εωρακεν σε (in S. Jo. viii. 57) for ἑώρακας :—in all which four readings
Cod. א is without support. [Scrivener, *Coll. Cod. Sin.* p. li.] The epithet
μεγαν, introduced (in the same codex) before λιθον in S. Mark xv. 46; and και
πατριας inserted into the phrase ἐξ οἴκου Δαβὶδ in S. Lu. i. 27,—are two more
specimens of mistaken officiousness. In the same infelicitous spirit, Cod. B
and Cod. א concur in omitting ἰσχυρόν (S. Matt. xiv. 30), and in substituting
πυκνα for πυγμῇ, and ραντισωνται for βαπτίσωνται in S. Mark vii. 3 and 4:—
while the interpolation of τασσομενος after ἐξουσίαν in S. Matth. viii. 9, because
of the parallel place in S. Luke's Gospel; and the substitution of ανθρωπος
αυστηρος ει (from S. Luke xix. 21) for σκληρὸς εἶ ἄνθρωπος in S. Matth. xxv. 24,
are proofs that yet another kind of corrupting influence has been here at work
besides those which have been already specified.

ζωσουσιν σε, και ποιησουσιν σοι οσα ου θελεις, for ἄλλος σε ζώσει. καὶ οἴσει ὅπου οὐ θέλεις, in S. John xxi. 18. Indeed, even when our LORD is not the speaker, such licentious depravation of the text is not to be endured. Thus, in S. Luke xxiii. 15, Cod. B and Cod. א conspire in substituting for ἀνέπεμψα γὰρ ὑμᾶς πρὸς αὐτόν,—ανεπεμψεν γαρ αυτον προς ημας; which leads one to suspect the copyist was misled by the narrative in ver. 7. Similar instances might be multiplied to an indefinite extent.

Two yet graver corruptions of the truth of the Gospel, (but they belong to the same category,) remain to be specified. Mindful, I suppose, of S. James' explanation "how that *by works* a man is justified," the author of the text of Codices B and א has ventured to alter our LORD's assertion (in S. Matth. xi. 19,) "Wisdom is justified of *her children*," into "Wisdom is justified by *her works;*" and, in the case of Cod. א, his zeal is observed to have so entirely carried him away, that he has actually substituted εργων for τέκνων in the parallel place of S. Luke's Gospel.—The other example of error (S. Matth. xxi. 31) is calculated to provoke a smile. Finding that our SAVIOUR, in describing the conduct of the two sons in the parable, says of the one,— ὕστερον δὲ μεταμεληθεὶς ἀπῆλθεν, and of the other,—καὶ οὐκ ἀπῆλθεν; some ancient scribe, (who can have been but slenderly acquainted with the Greek language,) seems to have conceived the notion that a more precise way of identifying the son who "*afterwards* repented and went," would be to designate him as ὁ ὕστερος. Accordingly, in reply to the question,—τίς ἐκ τῶν δύο ἐποίησεν τὸ θέλημα τοῦ πατρός; we are presented (but *only in Cod.* B) with the astonishing information,—λεγουσιν ο υστερος. And yet, seeing clearly that this made nonsense of the parable, some subsequent critic is found to have *transposed the order of the two sons:* and in that queer condition the parable comes down to us in the famous Vatican Codex B.

4. Some of the foregoing instances of infelicitous tampering with the text of the Gospels are, it must be confessed, very serious. But it is a yet more fatal circumstance in connexion with Cod. B and Cod. א that they are convicted

of certain perversions 'of the truth of Scripture which *must*
have been made with deliberation and purpose. Thus, in
S. Mark xiv, they exhibit a set of passages—(verses 30, 68,
72)—"which bear clear marks of wilful and critical correction,
thoroughly carried out in Cod. ℵ, only partially in Cod. B ;
the object being so far to assimilate the narrative of Peter's
denial with those of the other Evangelists, as to suppress
the fact, vouched for by S. Mark only, that the cock crowed
twice. (In Cod. ℵ, δίς is omitted in ver. 30,"—ἐκ δευτέρου
and δίς in ver. 72,—"and καὶ ἀλέκτωρ ἐφώνησε in ver. 68:
the last change being countenanced by B ᵃ.") One such
discovery, I take leave to point out, is enough to destroy
all confidence in the text of these two manuscripts : for it
proves that another kind of corrupting influence,—besides
carelessness, and accident, and tasteless presumption, and
unskilful assiduity,—has been at work on Codices B and ℵ.
We are constrained to approach these two manuscripts with
suspicion in all cases where a supposed critical difficulty in
harmonizing the statements of the several Evangelists will
account for any of the peculiar readings which they exhibit.

Accordingly, it does not at all surprise me to discover
that in both Codices the important word ἐξελθοῦσαι (in
S. Matth. xxviii. 8) has been altered into ἀπελθουσαι. I
recognise in that substitution of ἀπο for ἔξ the hand of one
who was not aware that the women, when addressed by the
Angel, were *inside the sepulchre;* but who accepted the belief (it is found to have been as common in ancient as in
modern times) that they beheld him " sitting on the stone ᵇ."
—In consequence of a similar misconception, both Codices
are observed to present us with the word " *wine*" instead of
" *vinegar*" in S. Matthew's phrase ὄξος μετὰ χολῆς μεμιγ-
μένον: which results from a mistaken endeavour on the
part of some ancient critic to bring S. Matth. xxvii. 34 into

ᵃ Scrivener, *Coll. Cod. Sin.* p. xlvii.

ᵇ Add to the authorities commonly appealed to for ἐξελθ. Chrys. ⁸³⁴ (twice,)
(also quoted in Cramer's *Cat.* ²⁴¹). The mistake adverted to in the text is at
least as old as the time of Eusebius, (Mai, iv. p. 264 = 287), who asks,—Πῶς
παρὰ τῷ Ματθδίῳ ἡ Μαγδαληνὴ Μαρία μετὰ τῆς ἄλλης Μαρίας ἔξω τοῦ μνήματος
ἑώρακεν τὸν ἕνα ἄγγελον ἐπικαθήμενον τῷ λίθῳ τοῦ μνήματος, κ.τ.λ.

harmony with S. Mark xv. 23. The man did not perceive
that the cruel insult of the " vinegar and gall" (which the
SAVIOUR tasted but would not drink) was quite a distinct
thing from the proffered mercy of the " myrrhed wine"
which the SAVIOUR put away from Himself altogether.

So again, it was in order to bring S. Luke xxiv. 13 into
harmony with a supposed fact of geography that Cod. ℵ
states that Emmaus, (which Josephus also places at sixty
stadia from Jerusalem), was *" an hundred* and sixty" stadia
distant. The history of this interpolation of the text is
known. It is because some ancient critic (Origen probably)
erroneously assumed that *Nicopolis* was the place intended.
The conjecture met with favour, and there are not wanting
scholia to declare that this was the reading of "the accurate" copies,—notwithstanding the physical impossibility
which is involved by the statement[e].—Another geographical
misconception under which the scribe of Cod. ℵ is found to
have laboured was that Nazareth (S. Luke i. 26) and Caper-
naum (S. Mark i. 28) were *in Judæa.* Accordingly he has
altered the text in both the places referred to, to suit his
private notion[d].—A yet more striking specimen of the preposterous method of the same scribe is supplied by his substitution of Καισαριας for Σαμαρείας in Acts viii. 5,—
evidently misled by what he found in viii. 40 and xxi. 8.
—Again, it must have been with a view of bringing Revelation into harmony with the (supposed) facts of physical
Science that for the highly significant Theological record
καὶ ἐσκοτίσθη ὁ ἥλιος at the Crucifixion[e], has been substituted both in B and ℵ, του ηλιου εκλιποντος,—a state-

---

[e] Tischendorf accordingly *is forced,* for once, to reject the reading of his
oracle ℵ,—witnessed to though it be by Origen and Eusebius. His discussion
of the text in this place is instructive and even diverting. How is it that such
an instance as the present does not open the eyes of Prejudice itself to the
danger of pinning its faith to the consentient testimony even of Origen, of
Eusebius, and of Cod. ℵ? . . . . The reader is reminded of what was offered
above, in the lower part of p. 49.

[d] A similar perversion of the truth of Scripture is found at S. Luke iv. 44,
(cf. the parallel place, S. Matth. iv. 23 : S. Mark i. 39). It does not mend the
matter to find ℵ supported this time by Codd. B, C, L, ℘, R.

[e] S. Lu. xxiii. 45 :—ὅπερ οὐδέποτε πρότερον συνέβη, ἀλλ᾽ ἢ ἐν Αἰγύπτῳ μόνον,
ὅτε τὸ πάσχα τελεῖσθαι ἔμελλε· καὶ γὰρ ἐκεῖνα τούτων τύπος ἦν. (Chrys. vii. 824 c.)

ment which (as the ancients were perfectly well aware[f])
introduces into the narrative an astronomical contradiction.
—It may be worth adding, that Tischendorf with singular
inconsistency admits into his text the astronomical contradiction, while he rejects the geographical impossibility.—
And this may suffice concerning the text of Codices B
and א.

III. We are by this time in a condition to form a truer
estimate of the value of the testimony borne by these two
manuscripts in respect of the last twelve verses of S. Mark's
Gospel. If we were disposed before to regard their omission
of an important passage as a serious matter, we certainly
cannot any longer so regard it. We have by this time seen
enough to disabuse our minds of every prejudice. Codd. B
and א are the very reverse of infallible guides. Their de-
flections from the Truth of Scripture are more constant, as
well as more licentious by far, than those of their younger
brethren : their unauthorized omissions from the sacred text
are not only far more frequent but far more flagrant also.
And yet the main matter before us,—*their omission of the last
twelve verses of S. Mark's Gospel,*—when rightly understood,
proves to be an entirely different phenomenon from what an
ordinary reader might have been led to suppose. Attention
is specially requested for the remarks which follow.

IV. To say that in the Vatican Codex (B), which is unquestionably the oldest we possess, S. Mark's Gospel ends
abruptly at the 8th verse of the xvi[th] chapter, and that the

---

[f] ὅπως δὲ μὴ εἴπωσί τινες ἔκλειψιν εἶναι τὸ γεγενημένον, ἐν τῇ τεσσαρεσκαιδε-
κάτῃ ἡμέρᾳ τῆς σελήνης γέγονε τὸ σκότος :—ὅτε ἔκλειψιν συμβῆναι ἀμήχανον.
So Victor of Antioch, in his Catena on S. Mark (ed. Possin.) He makes the
remark twice : first (p. 351) in the midst of an abridgment of the beginning of
Chrysostom's 88th Homily on S. Matthew : next (p. 352) more fully, after quoting " the great Dionysius " of Alexandria. See also an interesting passage on
the same subject in Cramer's *Catena in Matth.* i. p. 237,—from whom derived, I know not ; but professing to be from Chrysostom. (Note, that the
10 lines ἐξ ἀνεπιγράφου, beginning p. 236, line 33 = Chrys. vii. 824, D, E.)
The very next words in Chrysostom's published Homily (p. 825 A.) are as follows :—Ὅτε γὰρ οὐκ ἦν ἔκλειψις, ἀλλ' ὀργή τε καὶ ἀγανάκτησις, οὐκ ἐντεῦθεν
μόνον δῆλον ἦν, ἀλλὰ καὶ ἀπὸ τοῦ καιροῦ· τρεῖς γὰρ ὥρας παρέμεινεν, ἡ δὲ ἔκλειψις
ἐν μιᾷ γίνεται καιροῦ ῥοπῇ.—Anyone who would investigate this matter further
should by all means read Matthaei's long note on S. Luke xxiii. 45.

customary subscription (ΚΑΤΑ ΜΑΡΚΟΝ) follows,—is true; but
it is far from being *the whole* truth.   It requires to be stated
in addition that the scribe, whose plan is found to have been
to begin every fresh book of the Bible at the top of *the next
ensuing column* to that which contained the concluding words
of the preceding book, has at the close of S. Mark's Gospel
deviated from his else invariable practice.   He has left in
this place one column entirely vacant.   It is *the only vacant
column* in the whole manuscript;—a blank space *abundantly
sufficient to contain the twelve verses which he nevertheless withheld.   Why* did he leave that column vacant?   *What* can have
induced the scribe on this solitary occasion to depart from
his established rule?   The phenomenon,—(I believe I was the
first to call distinct attention to it,)—is in the highest degree significant, and admits of only one interpretation.   *The
older MS.* from which Cod. B was copied must have infallibly
contained the twelve verses in dispute.   The copyist was instructed to leave them out,—and he obeyed: but he prudently left a blank space *in memoriam rei*.   Never was blank
more intelligible!   Never was silence more eloquent!   By
this simple expedient, strange to relate, the Vatican Codex
is made to *refute itself* even while it seems to be bearing testimony against the concluding verses of S. Mark's Gospel,
by withholding them: for it forbids the inference which,
under ordinary circumstances, must have been drawn from
that omission.   It does more.   By *leaving room* for the
verses it omits, it brings into prominent notice at the end of
fifteen centuries and a half, *a more ancient witness than itself.*
The venerable Author of the original Codex from which
Codex B was copied, is thereby brought to view.   And thus,
our supposed adversary (Codex B) proves our most useful
ally: for it procures us the testimony of an hitherto unsuspected witness.   The earlier scribe, I repeat, unmistakably
comes forward at this stage of the inquiry, to explain that
he at least is prepared to answer for the genuineness of these
Twelve concluding Verses with which the later scribe, his
copyist, from his omission of them, might unhappily be
thought to have been unacquainted.

It will be perceived that nothing is gained by suggesting

that the scribe of Cod. B. *may* have copied from a MS. which
exhibited the same phenomenon which he has himself reproduced. This, by shifting the question a little further
back, does but make the case against Cod. ℵ the stronger.

But in truth, after the revelation which has been already
elicited from Cod. B, the evidence of Cod. ℵ may be very
summarily disposed of. I have already, on independent
grounds, ventured to assign to that Codex a somewhat later
date than is claimed for the Codex Vaticanus [g]. My opinion
is confirmed by observing that the Sinaitic contains no such
blank space at the end of S. Mark's Gospel as is conspicuous
in the Vatican Codex. I infer that the Sinaitic was copied
from a Codex which had been already mutilated, and reduced to the condition of Cod. B ; and that the scribe, only
because he knew not what it meant, exhibited S. Mark's
Gospel in consequence as if it really had no claim to those
twelve concluding verses which, nevertheless, *every* authority
we have hitherto met with has affirmed to belong to it
of right.

Whatever may be thought of the foregoing suggestion,
it is at least undeniable that Cod. B and Cod. ℵ are at variance on the main point. They *contradict* one another concerning the twelve concluding verses of S. Mark's Gospel. For
while Cod. ℵ refuses to know anything at all about those
verses, Cod. B admits that it remembers them well, by vo-
lunteering the statement that they were found in the older
codex, of which it is in every other respect a faithful repre-
sentative. The older and the better manuscript (B), therefore, refutes its junior (ℵ). And it will be seen that logically
this brings the inquiry to a close, as far as the evidence of
the manuscripts is concerned. We have referred to the
oldest extant copy of the Gospels in order to obtain its testimony : and,—" Though without the Twelve Verses concerning which you are so solicitous," (it seems to say,) " I yet
hesitate not to confess to you that an older copy than myself,
—the ancient Codex from which I was copied,—actually did
contain them."

The problem may, in fact, be briefly stated as follows. Of

<hr>

[g] See above, p. 70, and the Appendix (F).

the four oldest Codices of the Gospels extant,—B, ℵ, A, C,—
two (B and ℵ) are *without* these twelve verses : two (A and C)
are *with* them.   Are these twelve verses then an unauthorized *addition* to A and C? or are they an unwarrantable
omission from B and ℵ?   B itself declares plainly that from
itself they are an omission.   And B is the oldest Codex of
the Gospel in existence.   What candid mind will persist in
clinging to the solitary fact that from the single Codex ℵ
these verses are away, in proof that " S. Mark's Gospel was
at first without the verses which at present conclude it ? "

Let others decide, therefore, whether the present discussion has not already reached a stage at which an unprejudiced Arbiter might be expected to address the prosecuting
parties somewhat to the following effect :—

" This case must now be dismissed.   The charge brought
by yourselves against these Verses was, that they are an unauthorized addition to the second Gospel ; a spurious appendix, of which the Evangelist S. Mark can have known
nothing.   But so far from substantiating this charge, you
have not adduced a single particle of evidence which renders it even probable.

" The appeal was made by yourselves to Fathers and to
MSS.   It has been accepted.   And with what result?

(*a*) " Those many Fathers whom you represented as hostile, prove on investigation to be reducible to *one*, viz. Eusebius : and Eusebius, as we have seen, *does not say* that the
verses are spurious, but on the contrary labours hard to
prove that they may very well be genuine.   On the other
hand, there are earlier Fathers than Eusebius who quote
them without any signs of misgiving.   In this way, the
positive evidence in their favour is carried back to the ii[nd]
century.

(*b*) " Declining the testimony of the Versions, you insisted
on an appeal to MSS.   On the MSS., in fact, you still make
your stand,—or rather you rely on *the oldest* of them ; for,
(as you are aware,) *every MS. in the world except the two
oldest* are against you.

" I have therefore questioned the elder of those two MSS. ;
and it has volunteered the avowal that an older MS. than

itself—*the Codex from which it was copied*—was furnished
with those very Verses which you wish me to believe that
some older MS. still must needs have been without. What
else can be said, then, of your method but that it is frivolous? and of your charge, but that it is contradicted by
the evidence to which you yourselves appeal?

" But it is illogical; that is, it is unreasonable, besides.

" For it is high time to point out that even if it so happened that the oldest known MS. was observed to be without
these twelve concluding verses, it would still remain a thing
unproved (not to say highly improbable) that from the autograph of the Evangelist himself they were also away. Supposing, further, that no Ecclesiastical writer of the ii[nd] or
iii[rd] century could be found who quoted them: even so, it
would not follow that there existed no such verses for a primitive Father to quote. The earliest of the Versions might
in addition yield faltering testimony; but even so, *who* would
be so rash as to raise on such a slender basis the monstrous
hypothesis, that S. Mark's Gospel when it left the hands of
its inspired Author was without the verses which at present
conclude it? How, then, would you have proposed to account for the consistent testimony of an opposite kind yielded
by every other known document in the world?

" But, on the other hand, what are the facts of the case?
(1) The earliest of the Fathers,—(2) the most venerable of
the Versions,—(3) the oldest MS. of which we can obtain
any tidings,—*all* are observed to *recognize these Verses.*
'Cadit quaestio' therefore. The last shadow of pretext has
vanished for maintaining with Tischendorf that 'Mark the
Evangelist knew nothing of' these verses :—with Tregelles
that 'The book of Mark himself extends no further than
ἐφοβοῦντο γάρ:'—with Griesbach that 'the *last leaf of the
original Gospel was probably torn away.'* . . . It is high time,
I say, that this case were dismissed. But there are also costs
to be paid. Cod. B and Cod. ℵ are convicted of being 'two
false witnesses,' and must be held to go forth from this inquiry with an injured reputation."

This entire subject is of so much importance that I must
needs yet awhile crave the reader's patience and attention.

CHAPTER VII.

*The other chief peculiarity of Codices B and ℵ (viz. the omission of the
words ἐν Ἐφέσῳ from Ephes. i. 1) considered. — Antiquity unfavourable to the omission of those words (p. 93).—The Moderns
infelicitous in their attempts to account for their omission (p. 100).—
Marcion probably the author of this corruption of the Text of Scripture (p. 106).—Other peculiarities of Codex ℵ disposed of (p. 109).*

THE subject which exclusively occupied our attention
throughout the foregoing chapter admits of apt and powerful illustration. Its vast importance will be a sufficient
apology for the particular disquisition which follows, and
might have been spared, but for the plain challenge of the
famous Critic to be named immediately.

"There are two remarkable readings," (says Tischendorf,
addressing English readers on this subject in 1868,) "which
are very instructive towards determining the age of the
manuscripts [ℵ and B], and *their authority.*" He proceeds
to adduce,—

1. The absence from both, of the last Twelve Verses of
S. Mark's Gospel,—concerning which, the reader probably
thinks that by this time he has heard enough. Next,—

2. He appeals to their omission of the words ἐν Ἐφέσῳ
from the first verse of S. Paul's Epistle to the Ephesians,—
*another peculiarity, in which Codd. ℵ and B stand quite alone
among MSS.*

I. Here is an extraordinary note of sympathy between
two copies of the New Testament indeed. Altogether unique
is it: and that it powerfully corroborates the general opinion

of their high antiquity, no one will deny. But how about
" their *authority*"? Does the coincidence also raise our
opinion of *the trustworthiness of the Text*, which these two
MSS. concur in exhibiting? for *that* is the question which
has to be considered,—the *only* question. The ancientness of
a reading is one thing: its genuineness, (as I have explained
elsewhere,) quite another. The questions are entirely distinct. It may even be added that while the one is really of
little moment, the latter is of all the importance in the
world. I am saying that it matters very little whether
Codd. א and B were written in the beginning of the iv[th]
century, or in the beginning of the vth : whereas it matters
much, or rather it matters *everything,* whether they exhibit
the Word of God faithfully, or occasionally with scandalous
license. How far the reading which results from the suppression of the last two words in the phrase τοῖς ἁγίοις τοῖς
οὖσιν ἐν Ἐφέσῳ, is *critically allowable* or not, I forbear to
inquire. That is not the point which we have to determine.
The one question to be considered is,—May it *possibly* be
the true reading of the text after all? Is it any way
credible that S. Paul began his Epistle to the Ephesians as
follows :—Παῦλος ἀπόστολος Ἰησοῦ Χριστοῦ διὰ θελήματος
Θεοῦ, τοῖς ἁγίοις τοῖς οὖσι καὶ πιστοῖς ἐν Χριστῷ Ἰησοῦ? ...
If it be eagerly declared in reply that the thing is simply
incredible: that the words ἐν Ἐφέσῳ are required for the
sense ; and that the commonly received reading is no doubt
the correct one: then,—there is an end of the discussion.
Two extraordinary notes of sympathy between two Manuscripts will have been appealed to as crucial proofs of the
trustworthiness of the Text of those Manuscripts : (for of their
high *Antiquity,* let me say it once more, there can be no
question whatever :) and it will have been proved in one
case,—admitted in the other,—that *the omission is unwarrantable.*—If, however, on the contrary, it be maintained that
the words ἐν Ἐφέσῳ probably had no place in the original
copy of this Epistle, but are to be regarded as an unauthorized
addition to it,—then, (as in the case of the Twelve Verses
omitted from the end of S. Mark's Gospel, and which it was
also pretended are an unauthorized supplement,) we demand

to be shewn the evidence on the strength of which this opinion is maintained, in order that we may ascertain what it is precisely worth.

Tischendorf,—the illustrious discoverer and champion of Codex א, and who is accustomed to appeal triumphantly to its omission of the words ἐν Ἐφέσῳ as *the other* conclusive proof of the trustworthiness of its text,—may be presumed to be the most able advocate it is likely to meet with, as well as the man best acquainted with what is to be urged in its support. From him, we learn that the evidence for the omission of the words in question is as follows:—"In the beginning of the Epistle to the Ephesians we read, 'to the saints which are at Ephesus;' but Marcion (A.D. 130—140), did not find the words 'at Ephesus' in his copy. The same is true of Origen (A.D. 185—254); and Basil the Great (who died A.D. 379), affirmed that those words were wanting in *old* copies. And this omission accords very well with the encyclical or general character of the Epistle. At the present day, our ancient Greek MSS., and all ancient Versions, contain the words 'at Ephesus;' yea (*sic*), even Jerome knew no copy with a different reading. Now, only the Sinaitic and the Vatican correspond with the *old* copies of Basil, and those of Origen and Marcion [a]."—This then is the sum of the evidence. Proceed we to examine it somewhat in detail.

(1) And first, I take leave to point out that the learned writer is absolutely without authority for his assertion that "Marcion *did not find* the words ἐν Ἐφέσῳ in his copy" of S. Paul's Epistle to the Ephesians. Tischendorf's one pretence for saying so is Tertullian's statement that certain heretics, (Marcion he specifies by name,) had given to S. Paul's "Epistle to the Ephesians" the unauthorized title of "Epistle *to the Laodiceans* [b]." This, (argues Tischendorf,) Marcion could not have done had he found ἐν Ἐφέσῳ in the first verse [c]. But the proposed inference is clearly invalid.

---

[a] Tischendorf's "*Introduction*" to his (Tauchnitz) edition of the English N. T., 1869,—p. xiii.

[b] "Epistola quam nos 'ad Ephesios' præscriptam habemus, hæretici vero 'ad Laodicenos.'" *Adv. Marcion.* lib. v. c. xi, p. 309 (ed. Oehler.)

[c] "'Titulum' enim 'ad Laodicenos' ut addidisse accusatur a Tertulliano,

For, with what show of reason can Marcion,—whom Tertullian taxes with having dared "*titulum interpolare*" in the
case of S. Paul's "Epistle to the Ephesians,"—be *therefore*,
assumed to have read the first verse differently from ourselves? Rather is the directly opposite inference suggested by the very language in which Tertullian (who
was all but the contemporary of Marcion) alludes to the
circumstance [d].

Those, however, who would really understand the work
of the heretic, should turn from the African Father,—(who
after all does but say that Marcion and his crew feigned
concerning S. Paul's Epistle to the *Ephesians*, that it was
addressed to the *Laodiceans*,)—and betake themselves to the
pages of Epiphanius, who lived about a century and a half
later. This Father had for many years made Marcion's
work his special study [e], and has elaborately described it,
as well as presented us with copious extracts from it [f].   And

ita in salutatione verba ἐν Ἐφέσῳ omnino non legisse censendus est." (N. T.
in loc.)

[d] "Ecclesiæ quidem veritate Epistolam istam 'ad Ephesios' habemus emissam, non 'ad Laodicenos;' sed Marcion ei titulum aliquando interpolare gestiit, quasi et in isto diligentissimus explorator." *Adv. Marcion.* lib. v. c. xvii,
pp. 322-3 (ed. Oehler.)

[e] ἀπὸ ἐτῶν ἱκανῶν. (Epiphan. *Opp.* i. 310 c.)

[f] He describes its structure minutely at vol. i. pp. 309—310, and from pp.
312-7; 318—321. [Note, by the way, the gross blunder which has crept
into the printed text of Epiphanius at p. 321 D: pointed out long since by
Jones, *On the Canon*, ii. 38.] His plan is excellent. Marcion had rejected
every Gospel except S. Luke's, and of S. Paul's Epistles had retained only
ten,—viz. (1st) Galatians, (2nd and 3rd) I and II Corinthians, (4th) Romans,
(5th and 6th) I and II Thessalonians, (7th) *Ephesians*, (8th) Colossians, (9th)
Philemon, (10th) Philippians. Even these he had mutilated and depraved.
And yet out of that one mutilated Gospel, Epiphanius selects 78 passages,
(pp. 312-7), and out of those ten mutilated Epistles, 40 passages more (pp. 318
—21); by means of which 118 texts he undertakes to refute the heresy of
Marcion. (pp. 322—50: 350—74.) [It will be perceived that Tertullian goes
over Marcion's work in much the same way.] .. Very beautiful, and well worthy
of the student's attention, (though it comes before us in a somewhat incorrect
form,) is the remark of Epiphanius concerning the living energy of GOD's Word,
even when dismembered and exhibited in a fragmentary shape. Ὅλου γὰρ τοῦ
σώματος ζῶντος, ὡς εἰπεῖν, τῆς θείας γραφῆς, ποῖον ηὕρισκε (sc. Marcion) μέλος
νεκρὸν κατὰ τὴν αὐτοῦ γνώμην, ἵνα παρεισαγάγῃ ψεῦδος κατὰ τῆς ἀληθείας; ....
παρέκοψε πολλὰ τῶν μελῶν, κατέσχε δὲ ἐνιά τινα παρ' ἑαυτῷ· καὶ αὐτὰ δὲ τὰ
κατασχεθέντα ἔτι ζῶντα οὐ δύναται νεκροῦσθαι, ἀλλ' ἐκεῖ μὲν τὸ ζωτικὸν τῆς
ἐμφάσεως, κἄν τε μυρίως παρ' αὐτῷ κατὰ λεπτὸν ἀποτμηθείη. (p. 375 B.)

the account in Epiphanius proves that Tischendorf is mistaken in the statement which he addresses to the English reader, (quoted above;) and that he would have better consulted for his reputation if he had kept to the "ut videtur" with which (in his edition of 1859) he originally broached his opinion. It proves in fact to be no matter of opinion at all. Epiphanius states distinctly that *the Epistle to the Ephesians* was one of the ten Epistles of S. Paul which Marcion *retained*. In his "Apostolicon," or collection of the (mutilated) Apostolical Epistles, the "Epistle to the Ephesians," (identified by the considerable quotations which Epiphanius makes from it[g],) stood (he says) *seventh* in order; while the (so called) "Epistle to the Laodiceans,"— a distinct composition therefore,—had the *eleventh*, that is, the last place assigned to it[h]. That this latter Epistle contained a corrupt exhibition ‸ of Ephes. iv. 5 is true enough. Epiphanius records the fact in two places[i]. But then it is to be borne in mind that he charges Marcion with having derived that quotation *from the Apocryphal Epistle to the Laodiceans*[k]; instead of taking it, as he ought to have done, from the genuine Epistle to the Ephesians. The passage, when faithfully exhibited, (as Epiphanius points out,) by its very form refutes the heretical tenet which the context of Marcion's spurious epistle to the Laodiceans was intended to establish; and which the verse in question, in its interpolated form, might seem to favour[l].—I have entered into

He seems to say of Marcion,—

> Fool! to suppose thy shallow wits
> Could quench a life like that. Go, learn
> That cut into ten thousand bits
> Yet every bit would breathe and burn!

[g] He quotes Ephes. ii. 11, 12, 13, 14: v. 14: v. 31. (See Epiphanius, *Opp.* i. p. 318 and 371-2.)

[h] *Ibid.* p. 318 C (= 371 B), and 319 A (= 374 A.)

[i] *Ibid.* p. 319 and 374. But note, that through error in the copies, or else through inadvertence in the Editor, the depravation commented on at p. 374 B, C, is lost sight of at p. 319 B.

[k] See below, at the end of the next note.

[l] Προσέθετο δὲ ἐν τῷ ἰδίῳ Ἀποστολικῷ καλουμένῳ καὶ τῆς καλουμένης πρὸς Λαοδικέας:—"Εἷς Κύριος, μία πίστις, ἓν βάπτισμα, εἷς Χριστός, εἷς Θεὸς, καὶ Πατὴρ πάντων, ὁ ἐπὶ πάντων καὶ διὰ πάντων καὶ ἐν πᾶσιν." (Epiphan. *Opp.* vol. i. p. 374.) Here is obviously a hint of τριῶν ἀνάρχων ἀρχῶν διαφορὰς πρὸς

this whole question more in detail perhaps than was necessary : but I was determined to prove that Tischendorf's
statement that "Marcion (A.D. 130—140) did not find the
words 'at Ephesus' in his copy,"—is absolutely without
foundation.   It is even *contradicted* by the known facts of
the case.   I shall have something more to say about Marcion
by-and-by; who, it is quite certain, read the text of Ephes.
i. 1 exactly as we do.

(2.) The *only* Father who so expresses himself as to warrant the inference that the words ἐν Ἐφέσῳ were absent
from his copy, is Origen, in the beginning of the third century.   "Only in the case of the Ephesians," (he writes),
"do we meet with the expression 'the Saints which are:'
and we inquire,—Unless that additional phrase be simply
redundant, what can it possibly signify?   Consider, then,
whether those who have been partakers of *His* nature who
revealed Himself to Moses by the Name of I AM, may not,
in consequence of such union with Him, be designated as
'those *which are:'* persons, called out, of a state of *not-
being,* so to speak, into a state of *being* ᵐ."—If Origen had
read τοῖς ἁγίοις τοῖς οὖσιν ἐν Ἐφέσῳ in his copy, it is
to me incredible that he would have gone so very far out
of his way to miss the sense of such a plain, and in fact,

ἀλλήλας ἐχουσῶν: [Μαρκίωνος γὰρ τοῦ ματαιόφρονος δίδαγμα, εἰς τρεῖς ἀρχὰς
τῆς μοναρχίας τομὴν καὶ διαίρεσιν. Athanas. i. 231 ᴇ.] but, (says Epiphanius),
οὐχ οὕτως ἔχει ἡ τοῦ ἁγίου Ἀποστόλου ὑπόθεσις καὶ ἠσφαλισμένον κήρυγμα.
ἀλλὰ ἄλλως παρὰ τὸ ὅν ποιήτευμα.   Then he contrasts with the 'fabrication'
of Marcion, the inspired verity,—Eph. iv. 5 : declaring ἕνα Θεὸν, τὸν αὐτὸν
πατέρα πάντων,—τὸν αὐτὸν ἐπὶ πάντων, καὶ ἐν πᾶσι, κ.τ.λ.—p. 374 c.

Epiphanius reproaches Marcion with having obtained materials ἐκτὸς τοῦ
Εὐαγγελίου καὶ τοῦ Ἀποστόλου· οὐ γὰρ ἔδοξε τῷ ἐλεεινοτάτῳ Μαρκίωνι ἀπὸ τῆς
πρὸς Ἐφεσίους ταύτην τὴν μαρτυρίαν λέγειν, (sc. the words quoted above,) ἀλλὰ
τῆς πρὸς Λαοδικέας, τῆς μὴ οὔσης ἐν τῷ Ἀποστόλῳ. (p. 375 ᴀ.)   (Epiphanius
here uses Ἀπόστολος in its technical sense,—viz. as synonymous with S. Paul's
Epistles.)

ᵐ Ὡριγένης δέ φησι,—Ἐπὶ μόνων Ἐφεσίων εὕρομεν κείμενον τὸ "τοῖς ἁγίοις
τοῖς οὖσι·" καὶ ζητοῦμεν, εἰ μὴ παρέλκει προσκείμενον τὸ "τοῖς ἁγίοις τοῖς οὖσι,"
τί δύναται σημαίνειν; ὅρα οὖν εἰ μὴ ὥσπερ ἐν τῇ Ἐξόδῳ ὄνομά φησιν ἑαυτοῦ ὁ
χρηματίζων Μωσεῖ τὸ ΩΝ οὕτως οἱ μετέχοντες τοῦ ὄντος γίνονται "ὄντες," καλού-
μενοι οἱονεὶ ἐκ τοῦ μὴ εἶαι εἰς τὸ εἶναι. "ἐξελέξατο γὰρ ὁ Θεὸς τὰ μὴ ὄντα,"
φησὶν ὁ αὐτὸς Παῦλος, "ἵνα τὰ ὄντα καταργήσῃ."—Cramer's *Catena in Ephes.*
i. 1,—vol. vi. p. 102.

unmistakable an expression. Bishop Middleton, and Michaelis before him,—*reasoning however only from the place in Basil,* (to be quoted immediately,)—are unwilling to allow that the words ἐν Ἐφέσῳ were ever away from the text. It must be admitted as the obvious inference from what Jerome has delivered on this subject (*infrâ*, p. 98 *note* (s)) that he, too, seems to know nothing of the reading (if reading it can be called) of Codd. B and ℵ.

(3) The influence which Origen's writings exercised over his own and the immediately succeeding ages of the Church, was prodigious. Basil, bishop of Cæsarea in Cappadocia, writing against the heresy of Eunomius about 150 years later,—although he read ἐν Ἐφέσῳ in his own copy of S. Paul's Epistles,—thought fit to avail himself of Origen's suggestion. It suited his purpose. He was proving the eternal existence of the SON of GOD. Even *not to know* GOD (he remarks) is *not to be:* in proof of which, he quotes S. Paul's words in 1 Cor. i. 28 :—"Things *which are not,* hath GOD chosen." "Nay," (he proceeds,) the same S. Paul, " in his Epistle to the Ephesians, inasmuch as he is addressing persons who by intimate knowledge were truly joined to Him who 'IS,' designates them specially as ' those *which are :*' saying,—'To the Saints *which are,* and faithful in CHRIST JESUS.' " That this fancy was not original, Basil makes no secret. He derived it, (he says,) from "those who were before us;" a plain allusion to the writings of Origen. But neither was *the reading* his own, either. This is evident. He had *found* it, he says,—(an asseveration indispensable to the validity of his argument,)—but only after he had made *search* [n],—"*in the old copies* [o]." No doubt, Origen's strange fancy must have been even *unintelligible* to Basil when first he met with it. In plain terms, it sounds to this day incredibly foolish,—when read apart from the mutilated text which alone suggested it to Origen's fervid ima-

[n] Consider S. John i. 42, 44, 46 : v. 14 : ix. 35 : xii. 14, &c.

[o] Ἀλλὰ καὶ τοῖς Ἐφεσίοις ἐπιστέλλων ὡς γνησίως ἡνωμένοις τῷ Ὄντι δι' ἐπιγνώσεως, "ὄντας" αὐτοὺς ἰδιαζόντως ὠνόμασεν, εἰπών· "τοῖς ἁγίοις τοῖς οὖσι, καὶ πιστοῖς ἐν Χριστῷ Ἰησοῦ." οὕτω γὰρ καὶ οἱ πρὸ ἡμῶν παραδεδώκασι, καὶ ἡμεῖς ἐν τοῖς παλαιοῖς τῶν ἀντιγράφων εὑρήκαμεν. Note also what immediately follows. (Basil *Opp.* i. p. 254 E, 255 A.)

H

gination.—But what there is in all this to induce us to suspect that Origen's reading was after all the *right* one, and *ours* the *wrong*, I profess myself wholly at a loss to discover. Origen himself complains bitterly of the depraved state of the copies in his time; and attributes it (1) to the carelessness of the scribes: (2) to the rashness of correctors of the text: (3) to the licentiousness of individuals, adopting some of these corrections and rejecting others, according to their own private caprice[q].

(4) Jerome, a man of severer judgment in such matters than either Origen or Basil, after rehearsing the preceding gloss, (but only to reject it,) remarks that "certain persons" had been "over-fanciful" in putting it forth. He alludes probably to Origen, whose Commentary on the Ephesians, in three books, he expressly relates that he employed[r]: but he does not seem to have apprehended that Origen's text *was without the words ἐν Ἐφέσῳ.* If he *was* acquainted with Origen's *text*, (of which, however, his writings afford no indication,) it is plain that he disapproved of it. Others, he says, understand S. Paul to say not "the Saints *which are*:" but, —"the Saints and faithful *which are at Ephesus*[s]."

(5) The witnesses have now all been heard: and I submit that there has been elicited from their united evidence nothing at all calculated to shake our confidence in the universally received reading of Ephesians i. 1. The facts of the case are so scanty that they admit of being faithfully stated in a single sentence. Two MSS. of the ivth century, (exhibiting in other respects several striking notes of vicious sympathy,) are found to conspire in omitting a clause in Ephesians i. 1, which, (necessary as it is to the sense,) may be inferred to have been absent from Origen's copy: and

[q] See the places quoted by Scrivener, *Introd.* pp. 381—91; particularly p. 385. [r] Hieron. *Opp.* vol. vii. p. 543:—"Illud quoque in Præfatione commoneo, ut sciatis Origenem tria volumina in hanc Epistolam conscripsisse, quem et nos ex parte sequuti sumus."

[s] "Quidam curiosius quam necesse est putant ex eo quod Moysi dictum est 'Haec dices filiis Israel, QUI EST misit me,' etiam eos qui Ephesi sunt [Note this. Cf. "qui sunt Ephesi," *Vulg.*] sancti et fideles, essentiae vocabulo nuncupatos: ut . . . ab Eo 'qui est,' hi 'qui sunt' appellentur . . . . Alii vero simpliciter, non ad eos 'qui sint,' sed 'qui Ephesi sancti et fideles sint' scriptum arbitrantur." Hieron. *Opp.* vii. p. 545 A, B.

Basil testifies that it was absent from " the old copies" to which he himself obtained access. This is really the whole of the matter : in which it is much to be noted that Origen does not say that he *approved* of this reading. Still less does Basil. They both witness to *the fact* that the words ἐν Ἐφέσῳ were omitted from *some* copies of the iii[rd] century, just as Codd. B and א witness to the same fact in the iv[th]. But what then? Origen is known occasionally to go out of his way to notice readings confessedly worthless; and, why not here? For not only is the text all but *unintelligible* if the words ἐν Ἐφέσῳ be omitted : but (what is far more to the purpose) the direct evidence of *all* the copies, whether uncial or cursive[t],—and of *all* the Versions,—is *against* the omission. In the face of this overwhelming mass of unfaltering evidence to insist that Codd. B and א must yet be accounted right, and all the rest of Antiquity wrong, is simply irrational. To uphold the authority, in respect of this nonsensical reading, of *two* MSS. confessedly untrustworthy in countless other places,—against *all* the MSS.— *all* the Versions,—is nothing else but an act of vulgar prejudice. I venture to declare,—(and with this I shall close the discussion and dismiss the subject,)—*that there does not exist one single instance in the whole of the New Testament* of a reading even probably correct in which the four following notes of spurious origin concur,—which nevertheless are observed to attach to the two readings which have been chiefly discussed in the foregoing pages: viz.

1. The adverse testimony of *all the uncial MSS. except two.*

2. The adverse testimony of all, or *very nearly all*, the cursive MSS.

---

[t] The cursive "Cod. N°. 67 **" (or "67²") is improperly quoted as "omitting" (Tisch.) these words. The reference is to a MS. in the Imperial Library at Vienna, (Nessel 302 : Lambec. 34, which = our Paul 67), collated by Alter (N. T. 1786, vol. ii. pp. 415—558), who says of it (p. 496),—"*cod. ἐν ἐφέσῳ punctis notat.*" . . . . . The MS. must have a curious history. H. Treschow describes it in his *Tentamen Descriptionis Codd. aliquot Graece,* &c. Havn. 1773, pp. 62—73.—Also, A. C. Hwiid in his *Libellus Criticus de indole Cod. MS. Graeci N. T. Lambec. xxxiv.* &c. Havn. 1785.—It appears to have been corrected by some Critic,—perhaps from Cod. B itself.

3. The adverse testimony of *all the Versions,* without exception.

4. The adverse testimony of *the oldest Ecclesiastical Writers.*
To which if I do not add, as I reasonably might,—

5. *The highest inherent improbability,*—
it is only because I desire to treat this question purely as one *of Evidence.*

II. Learned men have tasked their ingenuity *to account for* the phenomenon on which we have been bestowing so many words. The endeavour is commendable; but I take leave to remark in passing that if we are to set about discovering reasons at the end of fifteen hundred years for every corrupt reading which found its way into the sacred text during the first three centuries subsequent to the death of S. John, we shall have enough to do. Let any one take up the Codex Bezae, (with which, by the way, Cod. B shews marvellous sympathy [u],) and explain if he can why there is a grave omission, or else a gross interpolation, in almost every page; and how it comes to pass that Cod. D "reproduces the ' textus receptus' of the Acts much in the same way that one of the best Chaldee Targums does the Hebrew of the Old Testament; so wide are the variations in the diction, so constant and inveterate the practice of expounding the narrative by means of interpolations which seldom recommend themselves as genuine by even a semblance of internal probability [x]." Our business as Critics is not *to invent theories* to account for the errors of Copyists; but rather to ascertain where they have erred, where not. What with the inexcusable depravations of early Heretics,—the preposterous emendations of ancient Critics,—the injudicious assiduity of Harmonizers,—the licentious caprice of individuals;—what with errors resulting from the inopportune recollection of similar or parallel places, — or from the familiar phraseology of the Ecclesiastical Lections,—or from the inattention of Scribes, — or from marginal glosses;— however arising, endless are the corrupt readings of the oldest MSS. in existence; and it is by no means safe to

---

[u] So indeed does Cod. ℵ occasionally. See Scrivener's *Collation,* p. xlix.

[x] Scrivener's *Introduction to Codex Bezae,* p. liv.

follow up the detection of a depravation of the text with a theory to account for its existence. Let me be allowed to say that such theories are seldom satisfactory. *Guesses* only they are at best.

Thus, I profess myself wholly unable to accept the suggestion of Ussher,—(which, however, found favour with Garnier (Basil's editor), Bengel, Benson, and Michaelis; and has since been not only eagerly advocated by Conybeare and Howson following a host of German Critics, but has even enjoyed Mr. Scrivener's distinct approval;)—that the Epistle to the Ephesians " was *a Circular* addressed to other Asiatic Cities besides the capital Ephesus,—to Laodicea perhaps among the rest (Col. iv. 16); and that while some Codices may have contained the name of Ephesus in the first verse, *others may have had another city substituted, or the space after* τοῖς οὖσιν *left utterly void*ʸ." At first sight, this conjecture has a kind of interesting plausibility which recommends it to our favour. On closer inspection,—(i) It is found to be not only gratuitous; but (ii) altogether unsupported and unsanctioned by the known facts of the case; and (what is most to the purpose) (iii) it is, as I humbly think, demonstrably erroneous. I demur to it,—

(1) Because of its exceeding Improbability : for (*a*) when S. Paul sent his Epistle to the Ephesians we know that Tychicus, the bearer of itᶻ, was charged with *a distinct Epistle* to the Colossians ᵃ: an Epistle nevertheless so singularly like the Epistle to the Ephesians that it is scarcely credible S. Paul would have written those two several Epistles to two of the Churches of Asia, and yet have sent only a duplicate of one of them, (*that* to the Ephesians,) furnished with a different address, to so large and important a place as Laodicea, for example. (*b*) Then further, the provision which S. Paul made at this very time for communicating with the Churches of Asia which he did not separately address is found to have been different. The Laodiceans were to read in their public assembly S. Paul's " *Epistle to the Colossians*," which the Colossians were ordered to send them. The Colos-

ʸ Scrivener, *Coll. of Cod. Sin.* p. xlv.

ᶻ Eph. vi. 21, 22.   ᵃ Coloss. iv. 7, 16.

sians in like manner were to read the Epistle,—(to whom
addressed, we know not),—which S. Paul describes as τὴν ἐκ
Λαοδικείας [b].   If then it had been S. Paul's desire that the
Laodiceans (suppose) should read publicly in their Churches
his Epistle to the Ephesians, surely, he would have charged
the Ephesians to procure that *his Epistle to them should be
read in the Church of the Laodiceans.*   Why should the
Apostle be gratuitously assumed to have simultaneously
adopted one method with the Churches of *Colosse* and Laodicea,—another with the Churches of *Ephesus* and Laodicea,
—in respect of his epistolary communications?

(2) (*a*) But even supposing, for argument's sake, that
S. Paul *did* send duplicate copies of his Epistle to the Ephesians to certain of the principal Churches of Asia Minor,—
why should he have left the salutation *blank*, ("carta bianca,"
as Bengel phrases it [c],) for Tychicus to fill up when he got
into Asia Minor?   And yet, by the hypothesis, nothing short
of *this* would account for the reading of Codd. B and ℵ.

(*b*) Let the full extent of the demand which is made on
our good nature be clearly appreciated.   We are required to
believe that there was (1) A copy of what we call S. Paul's
"Epistle to the Ephesians" sent into Asia Minor by S. Paul
with a blank address; i.e. "with the space after τοῖς οὖσιν
left utterly void:" (2) That Tychicus neglected to fill up
that blank: and, (what is remarkable) (3) That no one was
found to fill it up for him.   Next, (4) That the same copy
became the fontal source of the copy seen by Origen, and
(5) Of the "old copies" seen by Basil; as well as (6) Of
Codd. B and ℵ.   And even this is not all.   The same hypothesis constrains us to suppose that, on the contrary, (7) *One
other* copy of this same "Encyclical Epistle," filled up with
the Ephesian address, became the archetype of *every other
copy of this Epistle in the world.* . . . . . But of what nature,
(I would ask,) is the supposed necessity for building up such
a marvellous structure of hypothesis,—of which the top story
overhangs and overbalances all the rest of the edifice?   The
thing which puzzles us in Codd. B and ℵ is not that we find
the name of *another City* in the salutation of S. Paul's "Epis-

---

[b] *Ubi supra.*   [c] *Gnomon,* in Ephes. i. 1, *ad init.*

tle to the Ephesians," but that we find the name of *no* city
at all; nor meet with any vacant space there.

(*c*) On the other hand, supposing that S. Paul actually did
address to different Churches copies of the present Epistle,
and was scrupulous (as of course he was) to fill in the addresses himself before the precious documents left his hands,
—then, doubtless, each several Church would have received,
cherished, and jealously guarded its own copy. But if *this* had
been the case, (or indeed if Tychicus had filled up the blanks
for the Apostle,) is it not simply incredible that we should
never have heard a word about the matter until now ? unaccountable, above all, that there should nowhere exist traces
of *conflicting testimony* as to the Church to which S. Paul's
Epistle to the Ephesians was addressed ? whereas *all* the
most ancient writers, without exception,—(Marcion himself
[A.D. 140 [d]], the "Muratorian" fragment [A.D. 170 or earlier],
Irenæus [A.D. 175], Clemens Alexandrinus, Tertullian, Origen,
Dionysius Alexandrinus, Cyprian, Eusebius,)—and all copies
wheresoever found, give one unvarying, unfaltering witness.
Even in Cod. B. and Cod. ℵ, (and this is much to be noted,)
the superscription of the Epistle attests that it was addressed
"to the Ephesians." Can we be warranted (I would respectfully inquire) in inventing facts in the history of an Apostle's
practice, in order to account for what seems to be after all
only an ordinary depravation of his text [e] ?

[d] See above, pp. 93—6. As for the supposed testimony of Ignatius (*ad Ephes.*
c. xii.), see the notes, ed. Jacobson. See also Lardner, vol. ii.

[e] Let it be clearly understood by the advocates of this expedient for account-
ing for the state of the text of Codd. B. and ℵ, that nothing whatever is gained
for the credit of those two MSS. by their ingenuity. Even if we grant them
all they ask, the Codices in question remain, by their own admission, *defective.*

Quite plain is it, by the very hypothesis, that one of two courses alone remains open to them in editing the text: either (1) *To leave a blank space* after
τοῖς οὖσιν : or else, (2) *To let the words ἐν Ἐφέσῳ stand,*—which I respectfully
suggest is the wisest thing they can do. [For with Conybeare and Howson
(*Life and Letters of S. Paul,* ii. 491), to eject the words "at Ephesus" from
the text of Ephes. i. 1, and actually to substitute in their room the words "in
Laodicea,"—is plainly abhorrent to every principle of rational criticism. The
remarks of C. and H. on this subject (pp. 486 ff) have been faithfully met and
sufficiently disposed of by Dean Alford (vol. iii. *Prolegg.* pp. 13-8) ; who infers,
"in accordance with the prevalent belief of the Church in all ages, that this
Epistle was *veritably addressed to the Saints in Ephesus,* and *to no other*

(3) But, in fact, it is high time to point out that such
"*a Circular*" as was described above, (each copy furnished
with a blank, to be filled up with the name of a different
City,) would be a document without parallel in the annals of
the primitive Church.　It is, as far as I am aware, essentially a modern notion.　I suspect, in short, that the suggestion before us is only another instance of the fatal misapprehension which results from the incautious transfer of the
notions suggested by some familiar word in a living language
to its supposed equivalent in an ancient tongue.　Thus, because κύκλιος or ἐγκύκλιος confessedly signifies "circularis,"
it seems to be imagined that ἐγκύκλιος ἐπιστολή may mean
"a Circular Letter."　Whereas it really means nothing of
the sort; but—"*a Catholic Epistle* [f]."

An "*Encyclical*," (and *that* is the word which has been
imported into the present discussion), was quite a different
document from what *we* call "a Circular."　Addressed to
no one Church or person in particular, it was Catholic or
General,—the common property of all to whom it came.
The General (or Catholic) Epistles of S. James, S. Peter,
S. John are "Encyclical [g]."　So is the well-known Canonical
Epistle which Gregory, Bp. of Neocæsaræa in Pontus, in the
middle of the third century, sent to the Bishops of his
province [h].　As for "*a blank circular*," to be filled up with

---

Church."]　In the former case, they will be exhibiting a curiosity ; viz. they
will be shewing us how (they think) a duplicate (" carta bianca ") copy of the
Epistle looked with "the space after τοῖς οὖσι left utterly void :" in the latter,
they will be representing the archetypal copy which was sent to the Metro-
politan see of Ephesus.　But by printing the text thus,—τοῖς ἁγίοις τοῖς οὖσιν
[ἐν 'Εφέσῳ] καὶ πιστοῖς κ.τ.λ., they are acting on an entirely different theory.
They are merely testifying their mistrust of the text of every MS. in the world
except Codd. B and ℵ.　This is clearly to forsake the "Encyclical" hypothesis
altogether, and to put Ephes. i. 1 on the same footing as any other disputed
text of Scripture which can be named.

　[f] 'Εγκύκλιον ἐπιστολήν, vel ἐγκύκλια γράμματα Christophorsonus et alii inter-
pretantur *literas circulares :* ego cum viris doctis malim *Epistolas* vel *literas
publicas*, ad omnes fideles pertinentes, quas Græci aliàs vocant ἐπιστολὰς
καθολικάς.—Suicer *in voce*.

　[g] Καθολικαὶ λέγονται αὗται, οἱονεὶ ἐγκύκλιοι.—See Suicer *in voce,* 'Εγκύκλιος.

　[h] Routh's *Reliquiæ,* vol. iii. p. 266.—"Tum ex Conciliis, tum ex aliis Patrum
scriptis notum est, consuevisse primos Ecclesiae Patres acta et decreta Conci-
liorum passim ad omnes Dei Ecclesias mittere per epistolas, quas non uni

the words " in Ephesus," " in Laodicea," &c.,—its like (I repeat) is wholly unknown in the annals of Ecclesiastical
Antiquity.   The two notions are at all events inconsistent
and incompatible.   If S. Paul's Epistle to the Ephesians
was "a Circular," then it was not " Encyclical :" if it was
" Encyclical" then it was not " a Circular."

Are we then deliberately to believe, (for to this necessity
we are logically reduced,) that the Epistle which occupies
the fifth place among S. Paul's writings, and which from
the beginning of the second century,—that is, from the
very dawn of Historical evidence,—has been known as
" the Epistle to the Ephesians," was an " Encyclical," "Catholic" or " General Epistle,"—addressed τοῖς ἁγίοις τοῖς
οὖσι, καὶ πιστοῖς ἐν Χριστῷ 'Ιησοῦ ?   There does not live
the man who will accept so irrational a supposition.   The
suggestion therefore by which it has been proposed to account for the absence of the words ἐν 'Εφέσῳ in Ephes. i. 1
is not only in itself in the highest degree improbable, and
contradicted by all the evidence to which we have access ;
but it is even inadmissible on critical grounds, and must
be unconditionally surrendered [i].   It is observed to collapse
before every test which can be applied to it.

privatim dicârunt, sed publice describi ab omnibus, dividi passim et pervulgari,
atque cum omnibus populis communicari voluerunt.   Hac igitur epistolae
ἐγκύκλιοι vocatae sunt, quia κυκλόσε, quoquò versum et in omnem partem
mittebantur."—Suicer *in voc.*

[i] "On the whole," says Bishop Middleton, (*Doctrine of the Greek Art.*
p. 355) "I see nothing so probable as the opinion of Macknight (on Col. iv. 16,)
—'that the Apostle sent the Ephesians word by Tychicus, who carried their
letter, to send a copy of it to the Laodiceans ; with an order to them to com-
municate it to the Colossians.' "—This suggestion is intended to meet *another*
difficulty, and leaves the question of the reading of Ephes. i. 1 untouched.
It proposes only to explain what S. Paul means by the enigmatical expression
which is found in Col. iv. 16.

Macknight's suggestion, though it has found favour with many subsequent
Divines, appears to me improbable in a high degree.   S. Paul is found not to
have sent *the Colossians* "word by Tychicus, who carried their letter, to send
a copy of it to the Laodiceans."   He charged them, himself, to do so.   Why;
at the same instant, is the Apostle to be thought to have adopted two such
different methods of achieving one and the same important end ?   And why,
instead of this roundabout method of communication, were not *the Ephesians*
ordered,—if not by S. Paul himself, at least by Tychicus,—to send a copy of

III. Altogether marvellous in the meantime it is to me,—
if men must needs account for the omission of the words
ἐν ᾿Εφέσῳ from this place,—that they should have recourse
to wild, improbable, and wholly unsupported theories, like
those which go before; while an easy,—I was going to say
the obvious,—solution of the problem is close at hand, and
even solicits acceptance.

Marcion the heretic, (A.D. 140) is distinctly charged by
Tertullian (A.D. 200), and by Jerome a century and a half
later, with having abundantly mutilated the text of Scripture, and of S. Paul's Epistles in particular. Epiphanius
compares the writing which Marcion tampered with to
a moth-eaten coat[k]. "Instead of a stylus," (says Tertullian,) "Marcion employed a knife." "What wonder if he
omits syllables, since often he omits whole pages[l]?" S. Paul's
Epistle to the Ephesians, Tertullian even singles out by
name; accusing Marcion of having furnished it with a new
title. All this has been fully explained above, from page 93
to page 96.

Now, that Marcion recognised as S. Paul's Epistle *"to
the Ephesians"* that Apostolical writing which stands fifth
in our Canon, (but which stood seventh in his,) is just as
certain as that he recognised as such S. Paul's Epistles to
the Galatians, Corinthians, Romans, Thessalonians, Colos-

their Epistle to Colosse direct? And why do we find the Colossians charged
to read publicly τὴν ἐκ Λαοδικείας, which (by the hypothesis) would have been
only a copy,—instead of τὴν ἐξ ᾿Εφέσου, which, (by the same hypothesis,) would
have been the original? Nay, why is it not designated by S. Paul, τὴν πρὸς
᾿Εφεσίους,—(if indeed it was his Epistle to the Ephesians which is alluded to,)
instead of τὴν ἐκ Λαοδικείας; which would hardly be an intelligible way of
indicating the document? Lastly, why are not the Colossians ordered to com-
municate a copy of their Epistle to the illustrious Church of the *Ephesians*
also, which had been originally addressed by S. Paul? If the Colossians must
needs read the Epistle (so like their own) which the Apostle had just written
to the Ephesians, surely the Ephesians must also be supposed to have required
a sight of the Epistle which S. Paul had at the same time written to the
Colossians!

[k] Epiphan. *Opp.* i. 311 D.

[l] "Marcion exerte et palam machæra non stilo usus est, quoniam ad mate-
riam suam cædem Scripturarum confecit." (Tertullian *Præscript. Hær.* c. 38,
p. 50.) "Non miror si syllabas subtrahit, cum paginas totas plerumque sub-
ducat." (*Adv. Marcion.* lib. v, c. xvii, p. 455.)

sians, Philippians. All this has been fully explained in
a preceding page [m].

But it is also evident that Marcion put forth as S. Paul's
another Epistle,—of which all we know for certain is, that it
contained portions of the Epistle to the Ephesians, and pur-
ported to be addressed by S. Paul " to the Laodiceans." To
ascertain with greater precision the truth of this matter at the
end of upwards of seventeen centuries is perhaps impossible.
Nor is it necessary. Obvious is it to suspect that not only
did this heretical teacher at some period of his career prefix
a new heading to certain copies of the Epistle to the Ephesians, but also that some of his followers industriously erased
from certain other copies the words ἐν Ἐφέσῳ in ver. 1,—as
being *the only two words in the entire Epistle* which effectually
refuted their Master. It was not needful, (be it observed,)
to multiply copies of the Epistle for the propagation of
Marcion's deceit. Only two words had to be erased,—*the
very two words whose omission we are trying to account for,—*
in order to give some colour to his proposed attribution of
the Epistle, ("quasi in isto diligentissimus explorator,")—to
the Laodiceans. One of these mutilated copies will have
fallen into the hands of Origen,—who often complains of the
corrupt state of his text: while the critical personages for
whom Cod. B and Cod. ℵ were transcribed will probably
have been acquainted with other such mutilated copies. Are
we not led, as it were by the hand, to take some such view
of the case? In this way we account satisfactorily, and on
grounds of historic evidence, for the omission which has
exercised the Critics so severely.

I do not lose sight of the fact that the Epistle to the
Ephesians ends without salutations, without personal notices
of any kind. But in this respect it is not peculiar [n]. *That,*
—joined to a singular absence of identifying allusion,—sufficiently explains why Marcion selected this particular Epistle for the subject of his fraud. But, to infer from this circumstance, in defiance of the Tradition of the Church Universal, and in defiance of its very Title, that the Epistle is

---

[m] See above p. 95, and see note (f) p. 94.

[n] See, by all means, Alford on this subject, vol. iii. *Prolegg.* pp. 13—15.

'Encyclical,' in the technical sense of that word ; and to go
on to urge this characteristic as an argument in support of
the omission of the words ἐν Ἐφέσῳ,—is clearly the device of
an eager Advocate; not the method of a calm and unprejudiced Judge.   True it is that S. Paul,—who, writing to
the Corinthians from Ephesus, says "*the Churches of Asia
salute you,*" (1 Cor. xvi. 19,)—may have known very well
that an Epistle of his "to the Ephesians," would, as a matter of course, be instantly communicated to others besides
the members of that particular Church: and in fact this
may explain why there is nothing specially "Ephesian" in
the contents of the Epistle.   The Apostle,—(as when he
addressed "the Churches of Galatia,")—may have had certain of the other neighbouring Churches in his mind while
he wrote.   But all this is wholly foreign to the question
before us : the one *only* question being *this*,—Which of the
three following addresses represents what S. Paul must be
considered to have actually written in the first verse of his
"Epistle to the Ephesians"?—

(1) τοῖς ἁγίοις τοῖς οὖσιν ἐν Ἐφέσῳ καὶ πιστοῖς ἐν X. Ἰ.

(2) τοῖς ἁγίοις τοῖς οὖσιν ἐν . . . . . . καὶ πιστοῖς ἐν X. Ἰ.

(3) τοῖς ἁγίοις τοῖς οὖσι, καὶ πιστοῖς ἐν X. Ἰ.

What I have been saying amounts to this : that it is absolutely unreasonable for men to go out of their way to invent
a theory wanting every element of probability in order to
account for the omission of the words ἐν Ἐφέσῳ from
S. Paul's Epistle to the Ephesians ; while they have under
their eyes the express testimony of a competent witness of
the ii[nd] century that a certain heretic, named Marcion, "presumed to prefix an unauthorized title to that very Epistle,"
("Marcion ei titulum aliquando interpolare gestiit,")—which
title obviously *could not stand unless those two words were first
erased from the text.*   To interpolate that new title, and to
erase the two words which were plainly inconsistent with it,
were obviously correlative acts which must always have been
performed together.

But however all this may be, (as already pointed out,)
the only question to be determined by us is,—whether it
be credible that the words ἐν Ἐφέσῳ are an unauthorized

addition; foisted into the text of Ephes. i. 1 as far back as
the Apostolic age: an interpolation which, instead of dying
out, and at last all but disappearing, has spread and established itself, until the words are found in every copy,—are
represented in every translation,—have been recognised in
every country,—witnessed to by every Father,—received in
every age of the Church? I repeat that the one question
which has to be decided is, not *how* the words ἐν Ἐφέσῳ came
to be put in, or came to be left out; but simply whether, on
an impartial review of the evidence, it be reasonable (with
Tischendorf, Tregelles, Conybeare and Howson, and so many
more,) to suspect their genuineness and enclose them in
brackets? Is it *credible* that the words ἐν Ἐφέσῳ are a spurious and unauthorized addition to the inspired autograph
of the Apostle?... We have already, as I think, obtained
a satisfactory answer to this question. It has been shewn,
as conclusively as in inquiries of this nature is possible, that
in respect of the reading of Ephesians i. 1, Codd. B and א
are even *most* conspicuously at fault.

IV. But if these two Codices are thus convicted of error
in respect of the one remaining text which their chief up-
holders have selected, and to which they still make their
most confident appeal,—what remains, but to point out that
it is high time that men should be invited to disabuse their
minds of the extravagant opinion which they have been so
industriously taught to entertain of the value of the two
Codices in question? It has already degenerated into an
unreasoning prejudice, and threatens at last to add one more
to the already overgrown catalogue of " vulgar errors."

V. I cannot, I suppose, act more fairly by Tischendorf
than by transcribing in conclusion his remarks on the four
remaining readings of Codex א to which he triumphantly
appeals: promising to dismiss them all with a single remark.
He says, (addressing unlearned readers,) in his " Introduction" to the Tauchnitz (English) New Testament ᵒ :—

" To these examples, others might be added. Thus, Origen
says on John i. 4, that in some copies it was written, 'in
Him *is* life,' for 'in Him *was* life.' This is a reading which

---

ᵒ p. xiv.—See above, pp. 8, 9, note (f).

we find in sundry quotations before the time of Origen[p];
but now, among all known Greek MSS. it is *only in the
Sinaitic, and the famous old Codex Bezae*, a copy of the
Gospels at Cambridge; yet it is also found in most of the
early Latin versions, in the most ancient Syriac, and in
the oldest Coptic.—Again, in Matth. xiii. 35, Jerome ob-

[p] One is rather surprised to find the facts of the case so unfairly represented
in addressing unlearned readers; who are entitled to the largest amount of
ingenuousness, and to entire sincerity of statement. The facts are these :—
(1) Valentt. (*apud* Irenæum), (2) Clemens Alex., and (3) Theodotus (*apud*
Clem.) read ἐστι: but then (1) Irenæus himself, (2) Clemens Alex., and
(3) Theodotus (*apud* Clem.) *also* read ἦν. These testimonies, therefore, clearly
neutralize each other. Cyprian also has *both* readings.—Hippolytus, on the
other hand, reads ἐστι; but Origen, (though he remarks that ἐστι is "perhaps
not an improbable reading,") reads ἦν *ten or eleven times.* Ἦν is also the reading of Eusebius, of Chrysostom, of Cyril, of Nonnus, of Theodoret,—of the
Vulgate, of the Memphitic, of the Peshito, and of the Philoxenian Versions;
as well as of B, A, C,—in fact of *all the MSS. in the world*, except of א and D.
All that remains to be set on the other side are the Thebaic and Cureton's
Syriac, together with most copies of the early Latin.
And now, with the evidence thus all before us, will any one say that it is
lawfully a question for discussion which of these two readings must exhibit the
genuine text of S. John i. 4 ? (For I treat it as a question of authority, and
reason from *the evidence,*—declining to import into the argument what may be
called *logical* considerations; though I conceive them to be all on my side.)
I suspect, in fact, that the inveterate practice of the primitive age of reading
the place after the following strange fashion,—ὃ γέγονεν ἐν αὐτῷ ζωὴ ἦν, was
what led to this depravation of the text. Cyril in his Commentary [heading of
lib. i, c. vi.] so reads S. John i. 3, 4. And to substitute ἐστί (for ἦν) in such
a sentence as *that*, was obvious. . . . Chrysostom's opinion is well known, "Let
us beware of putting the full stop" (he says) "at the words οὐδὲ ἕν,—as do the
heretics." [He alludes to Valentinus, Heracleon (Orig. *Opp.* i. 130), and to
Theodotus (*apud* Clem. Alex.). But it must be confessed that Irenæus, Hippolytus (*Routh, Opusc.* i. 68), Clemens Alex., Origen, Concil. Antioch. (A.D. 269,
Routh iii. 293), Theophilus Antioch., Athanasius, Cyril of Jer.,—besides of the
Latins, Tertullian, Lactantius, Victorinus (*Routh* iii. 459), and Augustine,—
point the place in the same way. "It is worth our observation," (says Pearson,) "that Eusebius citing the place of S. John to prove that the HOLY GHOST
was made by the SON, leaves out those words twice together by which the
Catholics used to refute that heresy of the Arians, viz. ὃ γέγονεν."]
Chrysostom proceeds,—" In order to make out that THE SPIRIT is a creature, they read Ὁ γέγονε, ἐν αὐτῷ ζωὴ ἦν; by which means, the Evangelist's
language is made unintelligible." (*Opp.* viii. 40.)—This punctuation is nevertheless adopted by Tregelles,—but not by Tischendorf. The Peshito, Epiphanius (quoted in Pearson's note, referred to *infrà*), Cyprian, Jerome and the
Vulgate divide the sentence as we do.—See by all means on this subject Pearson's *note* (z), ART. viii, (ii. p. 262 ed. Burton). Also Routh's *Opusc.* i. 88-9.

serves that in the third century Porphyry, the antagonist of Christianity, had found fault with the Evangelist Matthew for having said, 'which was spoken by the prophet Esaias.' A writing of the second century had already witnessed to the same reading; but Jerome adds further that well-informed men had long ago removed the name of Esaias. Among all our MSS. of a thousand years old and upwards, there *is not a solitary example containing the name of Esaias in the text referred to,—except the Sinaitic,* to which a few of less than a thousand years old may be added.—Once more, Origen quotes John xiii. 10 six times; but *only the Sinaitic and several ancient Latin MSS.* read it the same as Origen: 'He that is washed needeth not to wash, but is clean every whit.'—In John vi. 51, also, where the reading is very difficult to settle, the *Sinaitic is alone among all Greek copies* indubitably correct; and Tertullian, at the end of the second century, confirms the Sinaitic reading: 'If any man eat of my bread, he shall live for ever. The bread that I will give for the life of the world is my flesh.' We omit to indicate further illustrations of this kind, although there are many others like them [q]."

Let it be declared without offence, that there appears to

[q] It may not be altogether useless that I should follow this famous Critic of the text of the N. T. over the ground which he has himself chosen. He challenges attention for the four following readings of the Codex Sinaiticus:—

(1.) S. JOHN i. 4: *εν αυτω ζωη εστιν.*—(2.) S. MATTH. xiii. 35: *το ρηθεν δια ησαΐου του προφητου.*—(3.) S. JOHN xiii. 10: *ο λελουμενος ουχ εχι χρειαν νιψασθαι.*—(4.) S. JOHN vi. 51: *αν τις φαγη εκ του εμου αρτου, ζησει εις τον αιωνα·—ο αρτος ον εγω δωσω υπερ της του κοσμου ζωης η σαρξ μου εστιν.* (And this, Dr. Tischendorf asserts to be "indubitably correct.")

On inspection, these four readings prove to be exactly what might have been anticipated from the announcement that they are almost the private property of the single Codex ℵ. The last three are absolutely worthless. They stand self-condemned. To examine is to reject them: the second (of which Jerome says something *very* different from what Tisch. pretends) and fourth being only two more of those unskilful attempts at critical emendation of the inspired Text, of which this Codex contains so many sorry specimens: the third being clearly nothing else but the result of the carelessness of the transcriber. Misled by the like ending (*δμοιοτέλευτον*) he has *dropped a line*: thus:—

ΟΥΧ ЄΧΙ ΧΡЄΙΑΝ [ЄΙ
ΜΗ ΤΟΥϹ ΠΟΔΑϹ] ΝΙ
ΨΑϹΘΑΙ ΑΛΛΑ ЄϹΤΙΝ

The first, I have discussed briefly in the foregoing footnote (p) p. 110.

exist in the mind of this illustrious Critic a hopeless confusion between the *antiquity* of a Codex and the *value* of its
readings.   I venture to assert that a reading is valuable or
the contrary, exactly in proportion to the probability of its
being true or false.   Interesting it is sure to be, be it what
it may, if it be found in a very ancient codex,—interesting
and often instructive : but the editor of Scripture must
needs bring every reading, wherever found, to this test at
last :—Is it to be thought that what I am here presented
with is what the Evangelist or the Apostle actually wrote ?
If an answer in the negative be obtained to this question,
then, the fact that one, or two, or three of the early Fathers
appear to have so read the place, will not avail to impart to
the rejected reading one particle of *value*.   And yet Tischendorf thinks it enough in *all* the preceding passages to assure
his reader that a given reading in Cod. ℵ was recognised by
Origen, by Tertullian, by Jerome.   To have established this
one point he evidently thinks sufficient.   There is implied in
all this an utterly false major premiss : viz. That Scriptural
quotations found in the writings of Origen, of Tertullian, of
Jerome, must needs be the *ipsissima verba* of the SPIRIT.
Whereas it is notorious " that the worst corruptions to which
the New Testament has ever been subjected originated within
a hundred years after it was composed : that Irenæus and
the whole Western, with a portion of the Syrian Church,
used far inferior manuscripts to those employed by Stunica,
or Erasmus, or Stephens, thirteen centuries later, when
moulding the Textus Receptus[r]."   And one is astonished
that a Critic of so much sagacity, (who of course knows
better,) should deliberately put forth so gross a fallacy,—
not only without a word of explanation, a word of caution,
but in such a manner as inevitably to mislead an unsuspect-
ing reader.   Without offence to Dr. Tischendorf, I must be
allowed to declare that, in the remarks we have been considering, he shews himself far more bent on glorifying the
"Codex Sinaiticus" than in establishing the Truth of the
pure Word of GOD.   He convinces me that to have found

---

[r]   Scrivener's *Introduction*, p. 386.   The whole Chapter deserves careful study.

an early uncial Codex, is every bit as fatal as to have "taken a gift." Verily, "*it doth blind the eyes of the wise*[a]."

And with this, I shall conclude my remarks on these two famous Codices. I humbly record my deliberate conviction that when the Science of Textual Criticism, which is at present only in its infancy, comes to be better understood ; (and a careful collation of every existing Codex of the New Testament is one indispensable preliminary to its being ever placed on a trustworthy basis;) a very different estimate will be formed of the importance of not a few of those readings which at present are received with unquestioning submission, chiefly on the authority of Codex B and Codex א. On the other hand, it is perfectly certain that no future collations, no future discoveries, will ever make it credible that the last Twelve Verses of S. Mark's Gospel are a spurious supplement to the Evangelical Narrative ; or that the words ἐν Ἐφέσῳ are an unauthorized interpolation of the inspired Text.

And thus much concerning Codex B and Codex א.

I would gladly have proceeded at once to the discussion of the " Internal Evidence," but that the external testimony commonly appealed to is not yet fully disposed of. There remain to be considered certain ancient "Scholia" and "Notes," and indeed whatever else results from the critical inspection of ancient MSS., whether uncial or cursive : and all this may reasonably claim one entire Chapter to itself.

[a] Deut. xvi. 19.

1

CHAPTER VIII.

THE PURPORT OF ANCIENT SCHOLIA, AND NOTES IN MSS.
ON THE SUBJECT OF THESE VERSES, SHEWN TO BE
THE REVERSE OF WHAT IS COMMONLY SUPPOSED.

*Later Editors of the New Testament the victims of their predecessors'
inaccuracies.—Birch's unfortunate mistake (p. 117).—Scholz' serious blunders (p. 119 and pp. 120-1).—Griesbach's sweeping misstatement (pp. 121-2).—The grave misapprehension which has resulted from all this inaccuracy of detail (pp. 122-3).*

*Codex L (p. 123).—Ammonius not the author of the so-called "Am-
monian" Sections (p. 125).—Epiphanius (p. 132).—"Caesarius,"
a misnomer.—"The Catenae," misrepresented (p. 133).*

IN the present Chapter, I propose to pass under review
whatever manuscript testimony still remains unconsidered ;
our attention having been hitherto exclusively devoted to
Codices B and ℵ. True, that the rest of the evidence may
be disposed of in a single short sentence :—*The Twelve Verses
under discussion are found in every copy of the Gospels in existence with the exception of Codices B and ℵ.* But then,

I. We are assured,—(by Dr. Tregelles for example,)—that
"a Note or a Scholion stating the absence of these verses
from *many*, from *most*, or from the *most correct* copies (often
from Victor or Severus) is found in twenty-five other cursive
Codices[a]." Tischendorf has nearly the same words: "Scholia"
(he says) "in very many MSS. state that the Gospel of Mark
in the most ancient (and most accurate) copies ended at the
ninth verse." That distinguished Critic supports his assertion by appealing to seven MSS. in particular,—and referring generally to "about twenty-five others." Dr. Davidson
adopts every word of this blindfold.

1. Now of course if all that precedes were true, this department of the Evidence would become deserving of serious

---

[a] *Printed Text*, p. 254.

attention. But I simply *deny the fact.* I entirely deny that the "Note or Scholion" which these learned persons affirm to be of such frequent occurrence has any existence whatever, —except in their own imaginations. On the other hand, I assert that notes or scholia which state the exact reverse, (viz. that "in the older" or "the more accurate copies" the last twelve verses of S. Mark's Gospel *are contained,*) recur even perpetually. The plain truth is this:—These eminent persons have taken their information at second-hand,— partly from Griesbach, partly from Scholz,—without sus- picion and without inquiry. But then they have slightly misrepresented Scholz; and Scholz (1830) slightly misunder- stood Griesbach; and Griesbach (1796) took liberties with Wetstein; and Wetstein (1751) made a few serious mis- takes. The consequence might have been anticipated. The Truth, once thrust out of sight, certain erroneous statements have usurped its place,—which every succeeding Critic now reproduces, evidently to his own entire satisfaction; though not, it must be declared, altogether to his own credit. Let me be allowed to explain in detail what has occurred.

2. Griesbach is found to have pursued the truly German plan of setting down *all* the twenty-five MSS.[b] and *all* the five Patristic authorities which up to his time had been cited as bearing on the genuineness of S. Mark xvi. 9—20 : giving the former *in numerical order*, and stating generally concerning them that in one or other of those authorities it would be found recorded "that the verses in question were anciently *wanting* in some, or in most, or in almost all the Greek copies, or in the most accurate ones :—or else that they were *found* in a few, or in the more accurate copies, or in many, or in most of them, specially in the Palestinian Gospel." The learned writer (who had made up his mind long before that the verses in question are to be rejected) no doubt perceived that this would be the most convenient way of disposing of the evidence for and against : but one is at a loss to understand how English scholars can have acquiesced in such a slipshod statement for well nigh

[b] Viz. Codd. L, 1, 22, 24, 34, 36, 37, 38, 39, 40, 41,—108, 129, 137, 138, 143, 181, 186, 195, 199, 206, 209, 210, 221, 222.

a hundred years.   A very little study of the subject would have shewn them that Griesbach derived the first eleven of his references from Wetstein [c], the last fourteen from Birch [d]. As for Scholz, he unsuspiciously adopted Griesbach's fatal enumeration of Codices ; adding five to the number; and only interrupting the series here and there, in order to insert the quotations which Wetstein had already supplied from certain of them.   With Scholz, therefore, rests the blame of everything which has been written since 1830 concerning the MS. evidence for this part of S. Mark's Gospel; subsequent critics having been content to adopt his statements without acknowledgment and without examination.   Unfortunately Scholz did his work (as usual) in such a slovenly style, that besides perpetuating old mistakes he invented new ones; which, of course, have been reproduced by those who have simply translated or transcribed him. And now I shall examine his note " (z) [e]", with which practically all that has since been delivered on this subject by Tischendorf, Tregelles, Davidson, and the rest, is identical.

(1.) Scholz (copying Griesbach) first states that in two MSS. in the Vatican Library [f] the verses in question " are marked with an asterisk."   The original author of this statement was Birch, who followed it up by explaining the fatal signification of this mark [g].   From that day to this, the asterisks in Codd. Vatt. 756 and 757 have been religiously reproduced by every Critic in turn ; and it is universally taken for granted that they represent two ancient

---

[c] Wetstein quoted 14 Codices in all : but Griesbach makes no use of his reference to Reg. 2868, 1880, and 2282 (leg. 2242 ?) which = Evan. 15, 19, 299 (?) respectively.

[d] *Variae Lectiones*, &c. (1801, p. 225-6.)—He cites Codd. Vatt. 358, 756, 757, 1229 (= our 129, 137, 138, 143): Cod. Zelada (= 181) : Laur. vi. 18, 34 (= 186, 195): Ven. 27 (= 210) : Vind. Lamb. 38, 39, Kol. 4 (= 221, 222, 108): Cod. iv. (*leg.* 5 ?) S. Mariæ Bened. Flor. (= 199) : Codd. Ven. 6, 10 (= 206, 209.)

[e] *Nov. Test.* vol. i. p. 199.

[f] Vat. 756, 757 = our Evan. 137, 138.

[g] Quo signo tamquam censoria virgula usi sunt librarii, qua Evangelistarum narrationes, in omnibus Codicibus non obvias, tamquam dubias notarent.— *Variae Lectiones*, &c. p. 225.

witnesses against the genuineness of the last twelve verses of
the Gospel according to S. Mark.

And yet, (let me say it without offence,) a very little
attention ought to be enough to convince any one familiar
with this subject that the proposed inference is absolutely
inadmissible. For, in the first place, a *solitary* asterisk (not
at all a rare phenomenon in ancient MSS.[h]) has of necessity
no such signification. And even if it does sometimes indicate that all the verses which follow are suspicious, (of
which, however, I have never seen an example,) it clearly
could not have that signification here,—for a reason which
I should have thought an intelligent boy might discover.

Well aware, however, that I should never be listened to,
with Birch and Griesbach, Scholz and Tischendorf, and indeed every one else against me,—I got a learned friend at
Rome to visit the Vatican Library for me, and inspect the
two Codices in question *. That he would find Birch right
in his facts, I had no reason to doubt; but I much more
than doubted the correctness of his proposed inference from
them. I even felt convinced that the meaning and purpose
of the asterisks in question would be demonstrably different
from what Birch had imagined.

Altogether unprepared was I for the result. It is found
that the learned Dane has here made one of those (venial,
but) unfortunate blunders to which every one is liable who
registers phenomena of this class in haste, and does not
methodize his memoranda until he gets home. To be brief,
—*there proves to be no asterisk at all,—either in Cod.* 756,
or in Cod. 757.

On the contrary. After ἐφοβοῦντο γάρ, the former Codex
has, in the text of S. Mark xvi. 9 (*fol.* 150 *b*), a plain cross,
—(*not* an asterisk, thus ⁜ or ⁕ or ⁜ or ⁜, but a cross,
thus +),—the intention of which is to refer the reader to
an annotation on *fol.* 151 *b*, (marked, of course, with a cross
also,) *to the effect that S. Mark xvi.* 9—20 *is undoubtedly*

---

[h] In Cod. 264 (= Paris 65) for instance, besides at S. Mk. xvi. 9, ⁕ occurs
at xi. 12, xii. 38, and xiv. 12. On the other hand, no such sign occurs at the
pericope de adulterâ.   * Further obligations to the same
friend are acknowledged in the Appendix (D).

genuine[1]. The evidence, therefore, not only breaks hopelessly down; but it is discovered that this witness has been
by accident put into the wrong box. This is, in fact, a witness
not for the plaintiff, but *for the defendant !*—As for the other
Codex, it exhibits neither asterisk nor cross; but contains
the same note or scholion attesting the genuineness of the
last twelve verses of S. Mark.

I suppose I may now pass on: but I venture to point
out that unless the Witnesses which remain to be examined
are able to produce very different testimony from that borne
by the last two, the present inquiry cannot be brought to
a close too soon. ("I took thee to curse mine enemies, and,
behold, thou hast blessed them altogether.")

(2.) In Codd. 20 and 300 (Scholz proceeds) we read as
follows:—" From here to the end forms no part of the text
in some of the copies. *In the ancient copies, however, it all
forms part of the text*[k]." Scholz (who was the first to adduce
this important testimony to the genuineness of the verses
now under consideration) takes no notice of the singular circumstance that the two MSS. he mentions have been *exactly*
assimilated in ancient times to a common model; and that
they correspond one with the other so entirely[1] that the
foregoing rubrical annotation appears *in the wrong place* in
both of them, viz. *at the close of ver.* 15, where it interrupts
the text. This was, therefore, once a scholion written in
the margin of some very ancient Codex, which has lost its
way in the process of transcription; (for there can be no
doubt that it was originally written against ver. 8.) And
let it be noted that its testimony is express; and that it
avouches for the fact that "*in the ancient copies*," S. Mark
xvi. 9—20 "*formed part of the text.*"

---

[1] Similarly, in Cod. Coisl. 20, in the Paris Library, (which = our 36,)
against S. Mark xvi. 9, is this sign ☒. It is intended (like an asterisk in a
modern book) to refer the reader to the self-same annotation which is spoken
of in the text as occurring in Cod. Vat. 756, and which is observed to occur
in the margin of the Paris MS. also.

[k] ἐντεῦθεν ἕως τοῦ τέλους ἕν τισι τῶν ἀντιγράφων οὐ
κεῖται· ἐν δε τοῖς ἀρχαίοις, πάντα ἀπαράλειπτα κεῖται.
—(Codd. 20 and 300 = Paris 188, 186.)

[1] See more concerning this matter in the Appendix (D), *ad fin.*

(3.) Yet more important is the record contained in the same two MSS., (of which also Scholz says nothing,) viz. that they exhibit a text which had been "collated with the ancient and approved copies at Jerusalem[m]." What need to point out that so remarkable a statement, taken in conjunction with the express voucher that "although some copies of the Gospels are without the verses under discussion, yet that *in the ancient copies* all the verses are found," is a *critical attestation to the genuineness* of S. Mark xvi. 9 to 20, far outweighing the bare statement (next to be noticed) of the undeniable historical fact that, "*in some copies,*" S. Mark ends at ver. 8,—but "in many *does not*"?

(4.) Scholz proceeds:—"In Cod. 22, after εφοβοῦντο γάρ + τέλος is read the following rubric:"—

ἔν τισι τῶν ἀντιγράφων ἕως ὦδε πληροῦται ὁ εὐαγγελιστής· ἐν πολλοῖς δὲ καὶ ταῦτα φέρεται[n].

And the whole of this statement is complacently copied by *all* subsequent Critics and Editors,—cross, and "τέλος," and all,—as an additional ancient attestation to the fact that "*The End*" (τέλος) *of S. Mark's Gospel* is indeed at ch. xvi. 8. Strange,—incredible rather,—that among so many learned persons, not one should have perceived that "τέλος" in this place merely denotes that here *a well-known Ecclesiastical section comes to an end!* . . . As far, therefore, as the present discussion is concerned, the circumstance is purely irrelevant[o];

---

[m] At the end of S. Matthew's Gospel in Cod. 300 (at fol. 89) is found,—

εὐαγγέλιον κατὰ Ματθαῖον ἐγράφη καὶ ἀντεβλήθη ἐκ τῶν Ἱεροσολύμοις παλαιῶν ἀντιγράφων, ἐν στίχοις βφιδ

and at the end of S. Mark's, (at fol. 147 *b*)—

εὐαγγέλιον κατὰ Μάρκον ἐγράφη καὶ ἀντεβλήθη ὁμοίως ἐκ τῶν ἐσπουδασμένων στίχοις αφς κεφαλαίοις σλε

This second colophon (though not the first) is found in Cod. 20. *Both* reappear in Cod. 262 (= Paris 53), and (with an interesting variety in the former of the two) in [what I suppose is the first half of] the uncial Codex Λ. See Scrivener's *Introduction*, p. 125.

[n] = Paris 72, *fol.* 107 *b*. He might have added, (for Wetstein had pointed it out 79 years before,) that *the same note precisely* is found between verses 8 and 9 in Cod. 15 (= Paris 64,) *fol.* 98 *b*.

[o] See more at the very end of Chap. XI.

and, (as I propose to shew in Chapter XI,) the less said
about it by the opposite party, the better.

(5.) Scholz further states that in four, (he means three,)
other Codices very nearly the same colophon as the preceding recurs, with an important additional clause. In Codd. 1,
199, 206, 209, (he says) is read,—

"In certain of the copies, the Evangelist finishes here;
up to which place Eusebius the friend of Pamphilus canonized.
In other copies, however, is found as follows ᵖ." And then
comes the rest of S. Mark's Gospel.

I shall have more to say about this reference to Eusebius,
and what he "canonized," by-and-by. But what is there in
all this, (let me in the meantime ask), to recommend the
opinion that the Gospel of S. Mark was published by its
Author in an incomplete state; or that the last twelve
verses of it are of spurious origin ?

(6.) The reader's attention is specially invited to the imposing statement which follows. Codd. 23, 34, 39, 41, (says
Scholz,) "contain these words of Severus of Antioch :—

"In the more accurate copies, the Gospel according to
Mark has its end at 'for they were afraid.' In some copies,
however, this also is added,—'Now when He was risen,'
&c. This, however, seems to contradict to some extent
what was before delivered," &c.

It may sound fabulous, but it is strictly true, that every
word of this, (unsuspiciously adopted as it has been by *every
Critic* who has since gone over the same ground,) is a mere
tissue of mistakes. For first, — Cod. 23 contains *nothing
whatever pertinent to the present inquiry.* (Scholz, evidently
through haste and inadvertence, has confounded *his own*

ᵖ Cod. 1. (at Basle), and Codd. 206, 209 (which = Venet. 6 and 10) contain
as follows :—

ἔν τισι μὲν τῶν ἀντιγράφων ἕως ὧδε πληροῦται ὁ Εὐαγγελιστής, ἕως οὗ καὶ ᾿Ευσέβιος ὁ Παμφίλου ἐκανόνισεν· ἐν
ἄλλοις δὲ ταῦτα φέρεται· ἀναστάς, κ.τ.λ.

But Cod. 199 (which = S. Mariae Benedict. Flor. Cod. IV. [*lege* 5], according to Birch (p. 226) who supplies the quotation, has only this :—

ἔν τισι τῶν ἀντιγράφων οὐ κεῖνται [?] ταῦτα.

"23" with " *Coisl.* 23," but " Coisl. 23" is his " 39,"—of
which by-and-by. This reference therefore has to be cancelled.)—Cod. 41 contains a scholion of *precisely the opposite
tendency:* I mean, a scholion which avers that *the accurate
copies of S. Mark's Gospel contain these last twelve verses.*
(Scholz borrowed this wrong reference from Wetstein,—who,
by an oversight, quotes Cod. 41 three times instead of twice.)
—There remain but Codd. 34 and 39 ; and in neither of
those two manuscripts, from the first page of S. Mark's Gospel to the last, does there exist *any " scholion of Severus
of Antioch" whatever.* Scholz, in a word, has inadvertently
made a gross misstatement[q]; and every Critic who has since
written on this subject has adopted his words,—without
acknowledgment and without examination. . . . . Such is the
evidence on which it is proposed to prove that S. Mark did
not write the last twelve verses of his Gospel !

(7.) Scholz proceeds to enumerate the following twenty-
two Codices:—24, 34, 36, 37, 38, 39, 40, 41, 108, 129, 137,
138, 143, 181, 186, 195, 199, 206, 209, 210, 221, 222. And
this imposing catalogue is what has misled Tischendorf,
Tregelles and the rest. They have not perceived that it is
a mere transcript of Griesbach's list ; which Scholz interrupts
only to give from Cod. 24, (imperfectly and at second-hand,)
the weighty scholion, (Wetstein had given it from Cod. 41,)
which relates, on the authority of an eye-witness, that
S. Mark xvi. 9—20 existed in the ancient Palestinian Copy.
(About that Scholion enough has been offered already[r].)
Scholz adds that very nearly the same words are found in
374.—What he says concerning 206 and 209 (and he might
have added 199,) has been explained above.

But when the twenty MSS. which remain[s] undisposed of
have been scrutinized, their testimony is found to be quite

---

[q] It originated in this way. At the end of S. Matthew's Gospel, in both
Codices, are found those large extracts from the "2nd Hom. on the Resurrection " which Montfaucon published in the *Bibl. Coisl.* (pp. 68—75), and which
Cramer has since reprinted at the end of his *Catena in S. Matth.* (i. 243—
251.) In Codd. 34 and 39 they are ascribed to " Severus of Antioch." See
above (p. 40.) See also pp. 39 and 57.

[r] See above, pp. 64, 65.   [s] 22—3 (199, 206, 209) = 19 + 1 (374) = 20.

different from what is commonly supposed. One of them (Nº. 38) has been cited in error : while the remaining nineteen are nothing else but copies of *Victor of Antioch's commentary on S. Mark*,—no less than *sixteen* of which contain the famous attestation that in *most of the accurate copies, and in particular the authentic Palestinian Codex, the last twelve verses of S. Mark's Gospel* WERE FOUND. (See above, pp. 64 and 65.) . . . . And this exhausts the evidence.

(8.) So far, therefore, as "Notes" and "Scholia" in MSS. are concerned, the sum of the matter proves to be simply this :—(*a*) Nine Codices [t] are observed to contain a note to the effect that the end of S. Mark's Gospel, though wanting "in some," was yet found "in others,"—"in many,"—"*in the ancient copies.*"

(*b*) Next, four Codices [*] contain subscriptions vouching for the genuineness of this portion of the Gospel by declaring that those four Codices had been *collated with approved copies preserved at Jerusalem.*

(*c*) Lastly, sixteen Codices, — (to which, besides that already mentioned by Scholz [u], I am able to add at least five others, making twenty-two in all [x],)—contain a weighty critical scholion asserting categorically that in "very many" and "accurate copies," specially in the "true Palestinian exemplar," *these verses had been found by one who seems to have verified the fact of their existence there for himself.*

(9.) And now, shall I be thought unfair if, on a review of the premisses, I assert that I do not see a shadow of reason for the imposing statement which has been adopted by Tischendorf, Tregelles, and the rest, that "there exist about thirty Codices which state that from the more ancient and more accurate copies of the Gospel, the last twelve verses of S. Mark were absent ?" I repeat, there is not so much as *one single Codex* which contains such a scholion;

---

[t] viz. Codd. L, 1, 199, 206, 209 :—20, 300 :—15, 22.

[*] Cod. Λ, 20, 262, 300.

[u] Evan. 374.

[x] viz. Evan. 24, 36, 37, 40, 41 (Wetstein.)　Add Evan. 108, 129, 137, 138, 143, 181, 186, 195, 210, 221, 222. (Birch *Varr. Lectt.* p. 225.)　Add Evan. 374 (Scholz.)　Add Evan. 12, 129, 299, 329, and the Moscow Codex (qu. Evan. 253 ?) employed by Matthaei.

while twenty-four [y] of those commonly enumerated state
the exact reverse.—We may now advance a step: but the
candid reader is invited to admit that hitherto the supposed hostile evidence is on the contrary entirely *in favour*
of the verses under discussion. ("I called thee to curse
mine enemies, and, behold, thou hast altogether blessed them
these three times.")

II. Nothing has been hitherto said about Cod. L.[*] This
is the designation of an uncial MS. of the viii[th] or ix[th]
century, in the Library at Paris, chiefly remarkable for the
correspondence of its readings with those of Cod. B and
with certain of the citations in Origen; a peculiarity which
recommends Cod. L, (as it recommends three cursive Codices
of the Gospels, 1, 33, 69,) to the especial favour of a school
with which whatever is found in Cod. B is necessarily
right. It is described as the work of an ignorant foreign
copyist, who probably wrote with several MSS. before him;
but who is found to have been wholly incompetent to determine which reading to adopt and which to reject. Certain
it is that he interrupts himself, at the end of ver. 8, to
write as follows:—

" *SOMETHING TO THIS EFFECT*
IS ALSO MET WITH:

"All that was commanded them they immediately rehearsed
unto Peter and the rest. And after these things, from East
even unto West, did JESUS Himself send forth by their means
the holy and incorruptible message of eternal Salvation.

" *BUT THIS ALSO IS MET WITH AFTER*
THE WORDS, 'FOR THEY WERE AFRAID:'

"Now, when He was risen early, the first day of the
week [z]," &c.

[y] 2 (viz. Evan. 20, 200) + 16 + 1 + 5 (enumerated in the preceding note)
= 24.   [*] Paris 62, *olim*, 2861 and 1558.

[z] See the facsimile.—The original, (which knows nothing of Tischendorf's
crosses,) reads as follows:—

ΦΕΡΕΤΕ ΠΟΥ
ΚΑΙ ΤΑΥΤΑ .

ΠΑΝΤΑ ΔΕ ΤΑ ΠΑΡΗ
ΓΓΕΛΜΕΝΑ ΤΟῖΣ
ΠΕΡΙ ΤΟΝ ΠΕΤΡΟΝ

It cannot be needful that I should delay the reader with any remarks on such a termination of the Gospel as the foregoing. It was evidently the production of some one who desired to remedy the conspicuous incompleteness of his own copy of S. Mark's Gospel, but who had imbibed so little of the spirit of the Evangelical narrative that he could not in the least imitate the Evangelist's manner. As for the scribe who executed Codex L, he was evidently incapable of distinguishing the grossest fabrication from the genuine text. The same worthless supplement is found in the margin of the Hharklensian Syriac (A.D. 616), and in a few other quarters of less importance [a].—I pass on, with the single remark that I am utterly at a loss to understand on what principle Cod. L,—a solitary MS. of the viii[th] or ix[th] century which exhibits an exceedingly vicious text,—is to

> CΥΝΤΟΜѠC ЄΞΗ
> ΓΓΙΛΑΝ · ΜЄΤΑ
> ΔЀ ΤΑῦΤΑ ΚΑῚ ΑῦΤΟC
> Ὁ ΙC̄, ἈΠΟ ἈΝΑΤΟΛΗC
> ΚΑῚ ἈΧΡΙ ΔΤCЄѠC
> ἘΞΑΠЄCΤΙΛЄΝ ΔΙ
> ΑῦΤѠΝ ΤΟ ῙЄΡΟΝ
> ΚΑῚ ἌΦΘΑΡΤΟΝ ΚΗ
> ΡΓΜΑ · ΤΗC ΑΙῶ
> ΝΙΟΤ CѠΤΗΡΙΑC ·

> ЄCΤΗΝ ΔЄ ΚΑΙ
> ΤΑῦΤΑ ΦЄΡΟ
> ΜЄΝΑ ΜЄΤΑ ΤΟ
> ἐΦΟΒΟΤΝΤΟ
> ΓΑΡ ·

> Ａ ΝΑCΤᾺC ΔЀ ΠΡѠΪ
> ΠΡѠΤΗ CΑΒΒΑΤῸ ·

i.e :—φέρεταί που καὶ ταῦτα.

Πάντα δὲ τὰ παρηγγελμένα τοῖς περὶ τὸν Πέτρον συντόμως ἐξήγγειλαν· μετὰ δὲ ταῦτα καὶ αὐτὸς ὁ Ἰησοῦς ἀπὸ ἀνατολῆς καὶ ἄχρι δύσεως ἐξαπέστειλεν δι' αὐτῶν τὸ ἱερὸν καὶ ἄφθαρτον κήρυγμα τῆς αἰωνίου σωτηρίας.

Ἔστιν δὲ καὶ ταῦτα φερόμενα μετὰ τὸ ἐφοβοῦντο γάρ.

Ἀναστὰς δὲ πρωῒ πρώτῃ σαββάτου.

[a] As, the Codex Bobbiensis (k) of the old Latin, and the margin of two Æthiopic MSS.—I am unable to understand what Scholz and his copyists have said concerning Cod. 274. I was assured again and again at Paris that they knew of no such codex as "Reg, 79ª," which is Scholz' designation (*Prolegg.* p. lxxx.) of the Cod. Evan. which, after him, we number "274."

be thought entitled to so much respectful attention on the present occasion, rebuked as it is for the fallacious evidence it bears concerning the last twelve verses of the second Gospel by all the seventeen remaining Uncials, (three of which are from 300 to 400 years more ancient than itself;) and by *every cursive copy of the Gospels in existence.* Quite certain at least is it that not the faintest additional probability is established by Cod. L that S. Mark's Gospel when it left the hands of its inspired Author was in a mutilated condition. The copyist shews that he was as well acquainted as his neighbours with our actual concluding Verses : while he betrays his own incapacity, by seeming to view with equal favour the worthless alternative which he deliberately transcribes as well, and to which he gives the foremost place. *Not* S. Mark's Gospel, *but Codex L* is the sufferer by this appeal.

III. I go back now to the statements found in certain Codices of the xth century, (derived probably from one of older date,) to the effect that "the marginal references to the Eusebian Canons extend no further than ver. 8 :"—for so, I presume, may be paraphrased the words, (see p. 120,) ἕως οὗ Εὐσέβιος ὁ Παμφίλου ἐκανόνισεν, which are found at the end of ver. 8 in Codd. 1, 206, 209.

(1.) Now this statement need not have delayed us for many minutes. But then, therewith, recent Critics have seen fit to connect another and an entirely distinct proposition : viz. that

AMMONIUS

also, a contemporary of Origen, conspires with Eusebius in disallowing the genuineness of the conclusion of S. Mark's Gospel. This is in fact a piece of evidence to which recently special prominence has been given : every Editor of the Gospels in turn, since Wetstein, having reproduced it; but no one more emphatically than Tischendorf. "Neither by *the sections of Ammonius* nor yet by the canons of Eusebius are these last verses recognised[b]." "Thus it is seen,"

---

[b] Nec AMMONII Sectionibus, nec EUSEBII Canonibus, agnoscuntur ultimi versus.—Tisch. *Nov. Test.* (*ed. 8va*), p. 406.

μηεκθαμβεισθαι·
ιηνζητειτετον
ναζαρηνοντο
εσταυρωμενον·
ηγερθηουκεστιν
ωδε· ιδεοτοπος
οπουεθηκαναυ
τον· αλλαυπαγε
τεειπατετοιςμα
θηταιςαυτουκαι
τωπετρω· οτι
προαγειυμασεις
τηνγαλιλαιαν·
εκειαυτονοψεσ
θε· καθωςειπεν
υμιν·

καιεξελθουσαιε
φυγοναποτου
μνημειου· ει
χενδεαυταςτρο
μοςκαιεκστασις
καιουδενιουδεν
ειπον· εφοβουν
τογαρ·

ΠΑΝΤΑΔΕΤΑΠΑΡΗ
ΓΓΕΛΜΕΝΑΤΟΙΣ
ΠΕΡΙΤΟΝΠΕΤΡΟΝ
ΣΥΝΤΟΜΩΣΕΞΗ
ΓΓΙΛΑΝ· ΜΕΤΑ
ΔΕΤΑΥΤΑΚΑΙΑΥΤΟC
ΟΙΣΑΠΟΑΝΑΤΟΛΗC
ΚΑΙΑΧΡΙΔΥCΕΩC
ΕΞΑΠΕΣΤΙΛΕΝΔΙ
ΑΥΤΩΝΤΟΙΕΡΟΝ
ΚΑΙΑΦΘΑΡΤΟΝΚΗ
ΡΥΓΜΑ· ΤΗCΑΙΩ
ΝΙΟΥCΩΤΗΡΙΑC·

ΤΑΥΤΑΦΟΒΟ
ΜΕΝΑΜΕΤΑΤΟ
ΕΦΟΒΟΥΝΤΟ
ΓΑΡ·

ΑΝΑΣΤΑΣΔΕΠΡΩΙ
ΠΡΩΤΗΣΑΒΒΑΤΟΥ·

THE opposite page exhibits an *exact Fac-simile*, obtained by Photography, of fol. 113 of EVAN. COD. L, ("Codex Regius," No. 62,) at Paris; containing S. Mark xvi. 6 to 9;—as explained at pp. 123-4. The Text of that MS. has been published by Dr. Tischendorf in his "Monumenta Sacra Inedita," (1846, pp. 57—399.) See p. 206.

The original Photograph was executed (Oct. 1869) by the obliging permission of M. de Wailly, who presides over the Manuscript Department of the "Bibliothèque." He has my best thanks for the kindness with which he promoted my wishes and facilitated my researches.

It should perhaps be stated that *the margin* of "Codex L" is somewhat ampler than can be represented in an octavo volume; each folio measuring very nearly nine inches, by very nearly six inches and a half.

proceeds Dr. Tregelles, "that just as Eusebius found these
verses absent in his day from the best and most numerous copies (*sic*), *so was also the case with Ammonius* when
he formed his Harmony in the preceding century [c]."

A new and independent authority therefore is appealed
to,—one of high antiquity and evidently very great importance,—Ammonius of Alexandria, A.D. 220. But Ammonius has left behind him *no known writings whatsoever.* What
then do these men mean when they appeal in this confident
way to the testimony of "Ammonius?"

To make this matter intelligible to the ordinary English
reader, I must needs introduce in this place some account
of what are popularly called the "Ammonian Sections" and
the "Eusebian Canons:" concerning both of which, however, it cannot be too plainly laid down that nothing whatever is known beyond what is discoverable from a careful
study of the "Sections" and "Canons" themselves; added
to what Eusebius has told us in that short Epistle of his
"to Carpianus,"—which I suppose has been transcribed
and reprinted more often than any other uninspired Epistle
in the world.

Eusebius there explains that Ammonius of Alexandria
constructed with great industry and labour a kind of Evangelical Harmony; the peculiarity of which was, that, retaining S. Matthew's Gospel in its integrity, it exhibited
the corresponding sections of the other three Evangelists
by the side of S. Matthew's text. There resulted this inevitable inconvenience; that the sequence of the narrative,
in the case of the three last Gospels, was interrupted
throughout; and their context hopelessly destroyed [d].

The "Diatessaron" of Ammonius, (so Eusebius styles it),
has long since disappeared; but it is plain from the foregoing account of it by a competent witness that it must

---

[c] *Printed Text,* p. 248.

[d] The reader is invited to test the accuracy of what precedes for himself:—
Ἀμμώνιος μὲν ὁ Ἀλεξανδρεὺς, πολλὴν, ὡς εἰκὸς, φιλοπονίαν καὶ σπουδὴν εἰσαγηο-
χὼς, τὸ διὰ τεσσάρων ἡμῖν καταλέλοιπεν εὐαγγέλιον, τῷ κατὰ Ματθαῖον τὰς
ὁμοφώνους τῶν λοιπῶν εὐαγγελιστῶν περικοπὰς παραθείς, ὡς ἐξ ἀνάγκης συμβῆναι
τὸν τῆς ἀκολουθίας εἱρμὸν τῶν τριῶν διαφθαρῆναι, ὅσον ἐπὶ τῷ ὕφει τῆς ἀνα-
γνώσεως.

have been a most unsatisfactory performance. It is not
easy to see how room can have been found in such a scheme
for entire chapters of S. Luke's Gospel; as well as for the
larger part of the Gospel according to S. John: in short, for
anything which was not capable of being brought into some
kind of agreement, harmony, or correspondence with something in S. Matthew's Gospel.

How it may have fared with the other Gospels in the
work of Ammonius is not in fact known, and it is profitless
to conjecture. What we know for certain is that Eusebius,
availing himself of the hint supplied by the very imperfect
labours of his predecessor, devised an entirely different expedient, whereby he extended to the Gospels of S. Mark,
S. Luke and S. John all the advantages, (and more than all,)
which Ammonius had made the distinctive property of the
first Gospel[e]. His plan was to retain the Four Gospels in
their integrity; and, besides enabling a reader to ascertain
at a glance the places which S. Matthew has in common
with the other three Evangelists, or with any two, or with
any one of them, (which, I suppose, was the sum of what
had been exhibited by the work of Ammonius,)—to shew
which places S. Luke has in common with S. Mark,—which
with S. John only; as well as which places are peculiar to
each of the four Evangelists in turn. It is abundantly clear
therefore what Eusebius means by saying that the labours of Ammonius had "*suggested to him*" his own[*]. The
sight of that Harmony of the other three Evangelists with
S. Matthew's Gospel had suggested to him the advantage
of establishing a series of parallels throughout *all the Four
Gospels.* But then, whereas Ammonius had placed alongside of S. Matthew *the dislocated sections themselves* of the

---

[e] Ἵνα δὲ σωζομένου καὶ τοῦ τῶν λοιπῶν δι' ὅλου σώματός τε καὶ εἱρμοῦ, εἰδέναι
ἔχοις τοὺς οἰκείους ἑκάστου εὐαγγελιστοῦ τό πους, ἐν οἷς κατὰ τῶν αὐτῶν ἠνέχθησαν φιλαληθῶς εἰπεῖν, ἐκ τοῦ πονήματος τοῦ προειρημένου ἀνδρὸς εἰληφὼς ἀφορ-
μὰς, καθ' ἑτέραν μέθοδον κανόνας δέκα τὸν ἀριθμὸν διεχάραξά σοι τοὺς ὑποτεταγμένους.

[*] This seems to represent *exactly* what Eusebius means in this place. The
nearest English equivalent to ἀφορμή is "a hint." Consider Euseb. *Hist. Eccl.*
v. 27. Also the following :—πολλὰς λαβόντες ἀφορμάς. (Andreas, *Proleg. in
Apocalyps.*).—λαβόντες τὰς ἀφορμάς. (Anastasius Sin., *Routh's Rell.* i. 15.)

other three Evangelists which are of corresponding purport,
Eusebius conceived the idea of accomplishing the same
object by means of a system of double numerical *references*.
He invented X Canons, or Tables : he subdivided each of the
Four Gospels into a multitude of short Sections. These he
numbered ; (a fresh series of numbers appearing in each
Gospel, and extending from the beginning right on to the
end ;) and immediately under every number, he inserted,
in vermillion, another numeral (I to X) ; whose office it was
to indicate in which of his X Canons, or Tables, the reader
would find the corresponding places in any of the other
Gospels [f]. (If the section was unique, it belonged to his last
or X[th] Canon.) Thus, against S. Matthew's account of the
Title on the Cross, is written $\frac{335}{I}$: but in the I[st] Canon
(which contains the places common to all four Evangelists)
parallel with 335, is found,—214, 324, 199 : and the Sections of S. Mark, S. Luke, and S. John thereby designated,
(which are discoverable by merely casting one's eye down
the margin of each of those several Gospels in turn, until
the required number has been reached,) will be found to
contain the parallel record in the other three Gospels.

All this is so purely elementary, that its very introduction in this place calls for apology. The extraordinary
method of the opposite party constrains me however to
establish thus clearly the true relation in which the familiar labours of Eusebius stand to the unknown work of
Ammonius.

---

[f] κανόνας . . . . διεχάραξά σοι τοὺς ὑποτεταγμένους. This at least is decisive
as to the authorship of the Canons. When therefore Jerome says of Ammonius,—"*Evangelicos canones excogitavit* quos postea secutus est Eusebius
Cæsariensis," (*De Viris Illust.* c. lv. vol. ii. p. 881,) we learn the amount of
attention to which such off-hand gain statements of this Father are entitled.

What else can be inferred from the account which Eusebius gives of the
present sectional division of the Gospels but that it was also his own ?—Αὕτη
μὲν οὖν ἡ τῶν ὑποτεταγμένων κανόνων ὑπόθεσις· ἡ δὲ σαφὴς αὐτῶν διήγησις,
ἔστιν ἥδε. Ἐφ' ἑκάστῳ τῶν τεσσάρων εὐαγγελίων ἀριθμός τις πρόκειται κατὰ
μέρος, ἀρχόμενος ἀπὸ τοῦ πρώτου, εἶτα δευτέρου, καὶ τρίτου, καὶ καθεξῆς προϊὼν
δι' ὅλου μέχρι τοῦ τέλους τοῦ βιβλίου. He proceeds to explain how the sections
thus numbered are to be referred to his X Canons :—καθ' ἕκαστον δὲ ἀριθμὸν
ὑποσημείωσις διὰ κινναβάρεως πρόκειται, δηλοῦσα ἐν ποίῳ τῶν δέκα κανόνων κεί-
μενος ὁ ἀριθμὸς τυγχάνει.

For if that earlier production be lost indeed [g],—if its precise contents, if the very details of its construction, can at this distance of time be only conjecturally ascertained,— what right has any one to appeal to *" the Sections of Ammonius,"* as to a known document ? Why above all do Tischendorf, Tregelles, and the rest deliberately claim " Ammonius" for their ally on an occasion like the present ; seeing that they must needs be perfectly well aware that they have no means whatever of knowing (except from the precarious evidence of Catenæ) what Ammonius thought about any single verse in any of the four Gospels ? At every stage of this discussion, I am constrained to ask myself,— Do then the recent Editors of the Text of the New Testament really suppose that their statements will *never* be examined ? their references *never* verified ? or is it thought that they enjoy a monopoly of the learning (such as it is) which enables a man to form an opinion in this department of sacred Science ? For,

(1st.) *Where* then and *what* are those "Sections of Ammonius" to which Tischendorf and Tregelles so confidently appeal ? It is even notorious that when they *say* the " Sections of Ammonius," what they *mean* are the "Sections of *Eusebius*."—But, (2dly.) Where is the proof,—where is even the probability,—that these two are identical ? The Critics cannot require to be reminded by me that we are absolutely

---

[g] " Frustra ad Ammonium aut Tatianum in Harmoniis provocant. Quæ supersunt vix quicquam cum Ammonio aut Tatiano commune habent." (Tischendorf *on S. Mark* xvi. 8).—Dr. Mill (1707),—because he assumed that the anonymous work which Victor of Capua brought to light in the vi[th] century, and conjecturally assigned to Tatian, was the lost work of Ammonius, (*Proleg.* p. 63, § 660,)—was of course warranted in appealing to the authority of Ammonius *in support* of the last twelve verses of S. Mark's Gospel. But in truth Mill's assumption cannot be maintained for a moment, as Wetstein has convincingly shewn. (*Proleg.* p. 68.) Any one may easily satisfy himself of the fact who will be at the pains to examine a few of the chapters with attention, bearing in mind what Eusebius has said concerning the work of Ammonius. Cap. lxxiv, for instance, contains as follows :—Mtt. xiii. 33, 34. Mk. iv. 33. Mtt. xiii. 34, 35 : 10, 11. Mk. iv. 34. Mtt. xiii. 13 to 17. But here it is *S. Matthew's* Gospel which is dislocated,—for verses 10, 11, and 13 to 17 of ch. xiii. come *after* verses 33—35 ; while ver. 12 has altogether disappeared.

The most convenient edition for reference is Schmeller's,—*Ammonii Alexandrini quæ et Tatiani dicitur Harmonia Evangeliorum.* (Vienna, 1841.)

K

without proof that so much as *one* of the Sections of Ammonius corresponded with *one* of those of Eusebius; and yet,
(3dly.) Who sees not that unless the Sections of Ammonius
and those of Eusebius can be proved to have corresponded
throughout, the name of Ammonius has no business whatever to be introduced into such a discussion as the present?
They must at least be told that in the entire absence of
proof of any kind,—(and certainly nothing that Eusebius
says warrants any such inference [h],)—to reason from the
one to the other as if they were identical, is what no sincere
inquirer after Truth is permitted to do.

It is time, however, that I should plainly declare that it
happens to be no matter of opinion at all whether the lost
Sections of Ammonius were identical with those of Eusebius
or not. It is demonstrable that they *cannot* have been so;
and the proof is supplied by the Sections themselves. It is
discovered, by a careful inspection of them, that they *imply*
and *presuppose the Ten Canons;* being in many places even
meaningless,—nugatory, in fact, (I do not of course say
that they are *practically* without *use*,)—except on the theory
that those Canons were already in existence [i]. Now the
Canons are confessedly the invention of Eusebius. He distinctly claims them [j]. Thus much then concerning the supposed testimony of Ammonius. It is *nil.*—And now for
what is alleged concerning the evidence of Eusebius.

The starting-point of this discussion, (as I began by remarking), is the following memorandum found in certain
ancient MSS.:—"Thus far did Eusebius canonize [k];" which

[h] Only by the merest license of interpretation can εἰληφὼς ἀφορμάς be
assumed to mean that Eusebius had found the four Gospels ready divided to
his hand by Ammonius into exactly 1165 sections,—every one of which he had
simply adopted for his own. Mill, (who nevertheless held this strange opinion,)
was obliged to invent the wild hypothesis that Eusebius, *besides* the work of
Ammonius which he describes, must have found in the library at Cæsarea the
private copy of the Gospels which belonged to Ammonius,—an unique volume,
in which the last-named Father (as he assumes) will have numbered the Sections
and made them exactly 1165. It is not necessary to discuss such a notion.
We are dealing with facts,—not with fictions.

[i] For proofs of what is stated above, as well as for several remarks on the
(so-called) "Ammonian" Sections, the reader is referred to the Appendix (G).

[j] See above, p. 128, note (f).   [k] See above, p. 125.

means either: (1) That his Canons recognise no section of
S. Mark's Gospel subsequent to § 233, (which number is
commonly set over against ver. 8 :) or else, (which comes to
the same thing,)—(2) That no sections of the same Gospel,
after § 233, are referred to any of his X Canons.

On this slender foundation has been raised the following
precarious superstructure. It is assumed,

(1st.) That the Section of S. Mark's Gospel which Eusebius
numbers "233," and which begins at our ver. 8, *cannot have
extended beyond* ver. 8;—whereas it may have extended, and
probably did extend, down to the end of ver. 11.

(2dly.) That because no notice is taken in the Eusebian
Canons of any sectional *number* in S. Mark's Gospel subsequent to § 233, no *Section* (with, or without, such a subsequent number) can have existed :—whereas there may
have existed one or more subsequent Sections all duly numbered[1]. This notwithstanding, Eusebius, (according to the
memorandum found in certain ancient MSS.), may have
canonized no further than § 233.

I am not disposed, however, to contest the point as far as
Eusebius is concerned. I have only said so much in order
to shew how unsatisfactory is the argumentation on the
other side. Let it be assumed, for argument sake, that the
statement "Eusebius canonized no further than ver. 8" is
equivalent to this,—"*Eusebius numbered no Sections after
ver. 8 :*" (and more it cannot mean :)—What *then ?* I am at
a loss to see what it is that the Critics propose to themselves
by insisting on the circumstance. For we knew before,—
it was in fact Eusebius himself who told us,—that Copies
of the Gospel ending abruptly at ver. 8, were anciently of
frequent occurrence. Nay, we heard the same Eusebius remark that one way of shelving a certain awkward problem would be, to plead that the subsequent portion of
S. Mark's Gospel is frequently wanting. What *more* have we
learned when we have ascertained that the same Eusebius
allowed no place to that subsequent portion in his Canons ?
The new fact, (supposing it to be a fact,) is but the correla-

[1] As a matter of fact, Codices abound in which the Sections are noted *without* the Canons, throughout. See more on this subject in the Appendix (G).

tive of the old one; and since it was Eusebius who was the
voucher for *that*, what additional probability do we establish that the inspired autograph of S. Mark ended abruptly
at ver. 8, by discovering that Eusebius is consistent with
himself, and omits to " canonize" (or even to " sectionize")
what he had already hypothetically hinted might as well be
left out altogether ?   (See above, pp. 44-6.)

So that really I am at a loss to see that one atom of progress is made in this discussion by the further discovery
that, (in a work written about A.D. 373,)

EPIPHANIUS

states casually that " the four Gospels contain 1162 sections[m]." From this it is argued[n] that since 355 of these
are commonly assigned to S. Matthew, 342 to S. Luke, and
232 to S. John, there do but remain for S. Mark 233 ; and
the 233rd section of S. Mark's Gospel confessedly begins at
ch. xvi. 8.—The probability may be thought to be thereby
slightly increased that the sectional numbers of Eusebius
extended no further than ver. 8 : but—Has it been rendered
one atom more probable that the inspired Evangelist himself ended his Gospel abruptly at the 8th verse ?   *That* fact
—(the *only* thing which our opponents have to establish)—
remains exactly where it was ; entirely unproved, and in the
highest degree improbable.

To conclude, therefore. When I read as follows in the
pages of Tischendorf:—" These verses are not recognised by
the Sections of Ammonius, nor by the Canons of Eusebius :
Epiphanius and Cæsarius bear witness to the fact ;"— I am
constrained to remark that the illustrious Critic has drawn
upon his imagination for three of his statements, and that
the fourth is of no manner of importance.

(1.) About the " Sections of Ammonius," he really knows
no more than about the lost Books of Livy. He is, therefore,
without excuse for adducing them in the way of evidence.

---

[m] τέσσαρά εἰσιν εὐαγγέλια κεφαλαίων χιλίων ἑκατὸν ἑξηκονταδύο. The words
are most unexpectedly, (may I not say *suspiciously?*), found in Epiphanius,
Ancor. 50, (*Opp.* ii. 54 B.)

[n] By Tischendorf, copying Mill's *Proleg.* p. 63, § 662 :—the foutal source,
by the way, of the twin references to " Epiphanius and Cæsarius."

(2.) That Epiphanius bears no witness whatever either as to the "Sections of Ammonius" or to "Canons of Eusebius," Tischendorf is perfectly well aware. So is my reader.

(3.) His appeal to

CÆSARIUS

is worse than infelicitous. He intends thereby to designate the younger brother of Gregory of Nazianzus ; an eminent physician of Constantinople, who died A.D. 368; and who, (as far as is known,) *never wrote anything.* A work called Πεύσεις, (which in the xth century was attributed to Cæsarius, but concerning which nothing is certainly known except that Cæsarius was certainly *not* its author,) is the composition to which Tischendorf refers. Even the approximate date of this performance, however, has never been ascertained. And yet, if Tischendorf had condescended to refer to it, (instead of taking his reference at second-hand,) he would have seen at a glance that the entire context in which the supposed testimony is found, is *nothing else but a condensed paraphrase of that part of Epiphanius,* in which the original statement occurs [o].

Thus much, then, for the supposed evidence of AMMONIUS, of EPIPHANIUS, and of CÆSARIUS on the subject of the last Twelve Verses of S. Mark's Gospel. It is exactly *nil.* In fact Pseudo-Cæsarius, so far from "bearing witness to the fact" that the concluding verses of S. Mark's Gospel are spurious, *actually quotes the 16th verse as genuine*[p].

(4.) As for Eusebius, nothing whatever has been added to what we knew before concerning his probable estimate of these verses.

IV. We are now at liberty to proceed to the only head of external testimony which remains undiscussed. I allude to the evidence of

THE CATENÆ.

"In the Catenæ on Mark," (crisply declares Dr. Davidson,) "there is no explanation of this section [q]."

---

[o] Comp. Epiph. (*Ancor.* 50,) *Opp.* ii. 53 c to 55 A, with Galland. *Bibl.* vi. 26 c to 27 A.   [p] Galland. *Bibl.* vi. 147 A.

[q] Vol. i. 165 (ii. 112).—It is only fair to add that Davidson is not alone in this statement. In substance, it has become one of the common-places of those who undertake to prove that the end of S. Mark's Gospel is spurious.

"The Catenæ on Mark :" as if they were quite common
things,—"plenty, as blackberries !" But,—*Which* of "the
Catenœ" may the learned Critic be supposed to have examined ?

1. Not the Catena which Possinus found in the library of
Charles de Montchal, Abp. of Toulouse, and which forms
the basis of his Catena published at Rome in 1673 ; because
that Codex is expressly declared by the learned Editor to be
defective from ver. 8 to the end [r].

2. Not the Catena which Corderius transcribed from the
Vatican Library and communicated to Possinus; because
in *that* Catena the 9th and 12th verses are distinctly commented on [s].

3. Still less can Dr. Davidson be thought to have inspected
the Catena commonly ascribed to Victor of Antioch,—which
Peltanus published in Latin in 1580, but which Possinus
was the first to publish in Greek (1673). Dr. Davidson,
I say, cannot certainly have examined *that* Catena; inasmuch as it contains, (as I have already largely shewn, and,
in fact, as every one may see,) a long and elaborate dissertation on the best way of reconciling the language of S. Mark
in ver. 9 with the language of the other Evangelists [t].

4. Least of all is it to be supposed that the learned Critic
has inspected either of the last two editions of the same

----

[r] See Possini *Cat.* p. 363.

[s] Ἐφάνη πρῶτον Μαρίᾳ τῇ Μαγδαληνῇ. [= ver. 9.] ταύτην Εὐσέβιος ἐν τοῖς
πρὸς Μαρῖνον ἑτέραν λέγει Μαρίαν παρὰ τὴν θεασαμένην τὸν νεανίσκον. ἢ καὶ
ἀμφότεραι ἐκ τῆς Μαγδαληνῆς ἦσαν. μετὰ δὲ ταῦτα δυσὶν ἐξ αὐτῶν περιπατοῦσι.
καὶ τὰ ἑξῆς [= ver. 12.] τοὺς ἀμφὶ τὸν Κλέοπαν, καθὼς ὁ Λουκᾶς ἱστορεῖ, (Possini *Cat.* p. 364) :—Where it will be seen that *Text* (κείμενον) and *Interpretation* (ἑρμηνεία) are confusedly thrown together. "Anonymus [Vaticanus]"
also quotes S. Mark xvi. 9 at p. 109, *ad fin.*—Matthaei (N. T. ii. 269),—overlooking the fact that "*Anonymus Vaticanus*" (or simply "*Anonymus*") and
"*Anonymus Tolosanus*" (or simply "*Tolosanus*") denote two distinct Codices,
—falls into a mistake himself while contradicting our learned countryman Mill,
who says,—"Certe Victor Antioch. ac Anonymus Tolosanus huc usque [sc.
ver. 8] nec ultra commentantur."—Scholz' dictum is,—"Commentatorum qui
in catenis SS. Patrum ad Marcum laudantur, nulla explicatio hujus pericopæ
exhibetur."

[t] See above pp. 62-3. The Latin of Peltanus may be seen in such Collections
as the *Magna Bibliotheca Vett. PP.* (1618,) vol. iv. p. 330, col. 2 E, F.—For
the Greek, see Possini *Catena*, pp. 359—61.

Catena: viz. that of Matthaei, (Moscow 1775,) or that of Cramer, (Oxford 1844,) from MSS. in the Royal Library at Paris and in the Bodleian. This is simply impossible, because (as we have seen), in *these* is contained the famous passage which categorically asserts the genuineness of the last Twelve Verses of S. Mark's Gospel [u].

Now this exhausts the subject.

To *which*, then, of "the Catenæ on Mark," I must again inquire, does this learned writer allude?—I will venture to answer the question myself; and to assert that this is only one more instance of the careless, second-hand (and third-rate) criticism which is to be met with in every part of Dr. Davidson's book : one proof more of the alacrity with which worn-out objections and worthless arguments are furbished up afresh, and paraded before an impatient generation and an unlearned age, whenever (*tanquam vile corpus*) the writings of Apostles or Evangelists are to be assailed, or the Faith of the Church of CHRIST is to be unsettled and undermined.

V. If the Reader will have the goodness to refer back to p. 39, he will perceive that I have now disposed of every witness whom I originally undertook to examine. He will also, in fairness, admit that there has not been elicited one particle of evidence, from first to last, which renders it in the slightest degree probable that the Gospel of S. Mark, as it originally came from the hands of its inspired Author, was either an imperfect or an unfinished work. Whether there have not emerged certain considerations which render such a supposition in the highest degree *un*likely,—I am quite content that my Reader shall decide.

Dismissing the external testimony, therefore, proceed we now to review those internal evidences, which are confidently appealed to as proving that the concluding Verses of S. Mark's Gospel cannot be regarded as really the work of the Evangelist.

---

[u] See above, pp. 64-5, and Appendix (E).

CHAPTER IX.

INTERNAL EVIDENCE DEMONSTRATED TO BE THE VERY REVERSE OF UNFAVOURABLE TO THESE VERSES.

The " Style" and " Phraseology" of these Verses declared by Critics to be not S. Mark's.—Insecurity of such Criticism (p. 140).—The " Style" of chap. xvi. 9—20 shewn to be the same as the style of chap. i. 9—20 (p. 142).—The " Phraseology" examined in twenty-seven particulars, and shewn to be suspicious in none (p. 145),— but in twenty-seven particulars shewn to be the reverse (p. 170).— Such Remarks fallacious (p. 173).—Judged of by a truer, a more delicate and philosophical Test, these Verses proved to be most probably genuine (p. 175).

A DISTINCT class of objections remains to be considered. An argument much relied on by those who deny or doubt the genuineness of this portion of S. Mark's Gospel, is derived from considerations of internal evidence. In the judgment of a recent Editor of the New Testament,—These twelve verses "bear traces of *another hand* from that which has shaped the *diction* and *construction* of the rest of the Gospel[a]." They are therefore "an addition to the narrative,"—of which "the internal evidence will be found to preponderate vastly against the authorship of Mark."—"A difference," (says Dr. Tregelles,) "has been remarked, and truly remarked, between *the phraseology* of this section and the rest of this Gospel."—According to Dr. Davidson,— "The *phraseology and style* of the section are unfavourable to its authenticity." "The characteristic peculiarities which pervade Mark's Gospel do not appear in it; but, on the contrary, terms and expressions," "phrases and words, are introduced which Mark never uses; or terms for which he employs others[b]."—So Meyer,—"With ver. 9, we suddenly come upon an excerpting process totally different from the previous mode of narration. The passage contains none of Mark's peculiarities (no εὐθέως, no πάλιν, &c., but the bald-

---

[a] Alford on S. Mark xvi. 9—20. [b] *Introduction, &c.* ii. p. 113.

ness and lack of clearness which mark a compiler ;) while in single expressions, it is altogether contrary to Mark's manner."—"There is" (says Professor Norton) " a difference so great between the use of language in this passage, and its use in the undisputed portion of Mark's Gospel, as to furnish strong reasons for believing the passage not genuine."—No one, however, has expressed himself more strongly on this subject than Tischendorf." " Singula" (he says) " multifariam a Marci ratione abhorrent[c]." . . . Here, then, is something very like a consensus of hostile opinion : although the terms of the indictment are somewhat vague. Difference of " Diction and Construction,"—difference of "Phraseology and Style,"—difference of "Terms and Expressions,"—difference of "Words and Phrases ;"—the absence of S. Mark's " characteristic peculiarities." I suppose, however, that all may be brought under two heads,—(I.) STYLE, and (II.) PHRASEOLOGY : meaning by "Style" whatever belongs to the Evangelist's manner ; and by " Phraseology" whatever relates to the words and expressions he has employed. It remains, therefore, that we now examine the proofs by which it is proposed to substantiate these confident assertions, and ascertain exactly what they are worth by constant appeals to the Gospel. Throughout this inquiry, we have to do not with Opinion but with Fact. The unsupported dicta of Critics, however distinguished, are entitled to no manner of attention.

1. In the meantime, as might have been expected, these confident and often-repeated asseverations have been by no means unproductive of mischievous results :

> Like ceaseless droppings, which at last are known
> To leave their dint upon the solid stone.

I observe that Scholars and Divines of the best type (as the Rev. T. S. Green[d]) at last put up with them. The wisest however reproduce them under protest, and with apology. The names of Tischendorf and Tregelles, Meyer and Davidson, command attention. It seems to be thought incredible that they can *all* be *entirely* in the wrong. They impose upon learned and unlearned readers alike. " Even Barnabas

---

[c] *Nov. Test.* Ed. 8ᵗᵃ i. p. 406. [d] *Developed Crit.* pp. 51-2.

has been carried away with their dissimulation." He has (to my surprise and regret) two suggestions:—

(*a*) The one,—That this entire section of the second Gospel may possibly have been written long after the rest; and that therefore its verbal peculiarities need not perplex or trouble us. It was, I suppose, (according to this learned and pious writer,) a kind of after-thought, or supplement, or Appendix to S. Mark's Gospel. In this way I have seen the last Chapter of S. John once and again accounted for.— To which, it ought to be a sufficient answer to point out that there is *no appearance whatever* of any such interval having been interposed between S. Mark xvi. 8 and 9 : that it is highly improbable that any such interval occurred: and that until the "verbal peculiarities" have been ascertained to exist, it is, to say the least, a gratuitous exercise of the inventive faculty to discover reasons for their existence. Whether there be not something radically unsound and wrong in all such conjectures about "after-thoughts," "supplements," "appendices," and "second editions" when the everlasting Gospel of JESUS CHRIST is the thing spoken of,— a confusing of things heavenly with things earthly which must make the Angels weep,—I forbear to press on the present occasion. It had better perhaps be discussed at another opportunity. But φίλοι ἄνδρες[e] will forgive my freedom in having already made my personal sentiment on the subject sufficiently plain.

(*b*) His other suggestion is,—That this portion may not have been penned by S. Mark himself after all. By which he clearly means no more than this,—that as we are content not to know *who* wrote the conclusion of the Books of Deuteronomy and Joshua, so, if needful, we may well be content not to know who wrote the end of the Gospel of S. Mark.—In reply to which, I have but to say, that after cause has been shewn why we should indeed believe that not S. Mark but some one else wrote the end of S. Mark's Gospel, we shall be perfectly willing to acquiesce in the new fact:—but *not till then.*

[e] ἀμφοῖν γὰρ ὄντων φίλοιν, ὅσιον προτιμᾶν τὴν ἀλήθειαν.—Arist. *Eth. Nic.* I. iii.

2. True indeed it is that here and there a voice has been lifted up in the way of protest[f] against the proposed inference from the familiar premises; (for the self-same statements have now been so often reproduced, that the eye grows weary at last of the ever-recurring string of offending vocables:)—but, with *one* honorable exception[g], men do not seem to have ever thought of calling the premises themselves in question: examining the statements one by one: contesting the ground inch by inch: refusing absolutely to submit to any dictation whatever in this behalf: insisting on bringing the whole matter to the test of severe inquiry, and making every detail the subject of strict judicial investigation. This is what I propose to do in the course of the present Chapter. I altogether deny the validity of the inference which has been drawn from "the style," "the phraseology," "the diction" of the present section of the Gospel. But I do more. I entirely deny the accuracy of almost *every individual statement* from which the unfavourable induction is made, and the hostile inference drawn. Even *this* will not nearly satisfy

[f] To the honour of the Rev. F. H. Scrivener be it said, that *he* at least absolutely refuses to pay any attention at all "to the argument against these twelve verses arising from their alleged difference in style from the rest of the Gospel." See by all means his remarks on this subject. (*Introduction*, pp. 431-2.)—One would have thought that a recent controversy concerning a short English Poem,—which some able men were confident *might* have been written by Milton, while others were just as confident that it could not possibly be his,—ought to have opened the eyes of all to the precarious nature of such Criticism.

[g] Allusion is made to the Rev. John A. Broadus, D.D.,—"Professor of Interpretation of the New Testament in the Southern Baptist Theological Seminary, Greenville, S.C.,"—the author of an able and convincing paper entitled "Exegetical Studies" in "*The Baptist Quarterly*" for July, 1869 (Philadelphia), pp. 355—62: in which "the words and phrases" contained in S. Mark xvi. 9—20 are exclusively examined.

If the present volume should ever reach the learned Professor's hands, he will perceive that I must have written the present Chapter *before* I knew of his labours: (an advantage which I owe to Mr. Scrivener's kindness:) my treatment of the subject and his own being so entirely different. But it is only due to Professor Broadus to acknowledge the interest and advantage with which I have compared my lucubrations with his, and the sincere satisfaction with which I have discovered that we have everywhere independently arrived at precisely the same result.

me. I insist that one only result can attend the exact analysis of this portion of the Gospel into its elements; namely, a profound conviction that S. Mark is most certainly its Author.

3. Let me however distinctly declare beforehand that remarks on "the style" of an Evangelist are singularly apt to be fallacious, especially when (as here) it is proposed to apply them to a very limited portion of the sacred narrative. Altogether to be mistrusted moreover are they, when (as on the present occasion) it is proposed to make them the ground for possibly rejecting such a portion of Scripture as spurious. It becomes a fatal objection to such reasoning that *the style* may indeed be exceedingly diverse, and yet *the Author* be confessedly one and the same. How exceedingly dissimilar in style are the Revelation of S. John and the Gospel of S. John! Moreover, practically, the promised remarks on "style," when the Authorship of some portion of Scripture is to be discussed, are commonly observed to degenerate at once into what is really quite a different thing. Single words, perhaps some short phrase, is appealed to, which (it is said) does not recur in any part of the same book; and thence it is argued that the Author can no longer be the same. "According to this argument, *the recurrence of the same words* constitutes identity of style; the want of such recurrence implies difference of style;—difference of style in such a sense as compels us to infer diversity of authorship. Each writer is supposed to have at his disposal a limited number of 'formulæ' within the range of which he must work. He must in each chapter employ these formulæ, and these only. He must be content with one small portion of his mother-tongue, and not dare to venture across the limits of that portion,—on pain of losing his identity [h]."

4. How utterly insecure must be every approximation to

---

[h] Dr. Kay's *Crisis Hupfeldiana*, p. 34,—the most masterly and instructive exposure of Bp. Colenso's incompetence and presumption which has ever appeared. Intended specially of *his* handling of the writings of Moses, the remarks in the text are equally applicable to much which has been put forth concerning the authorship of the end of S. Mark's Gospel.

such a method of judging about the Authorship of any twelve verses of Scripture which can be named, scarcely requires illustration. The attentive reader of S. Matthew's Gospel is aware that a mode of expression which is *six times repeated* in his viii[th] and ix[th] chapters is perhaps only once met with besides in his Gospel,—viz. in his xxi[st] chapter[i]. The "style" of the 17th verse of his i[st] chapter may be thought unlike anything else in S. Matthew. S. Luke's five opening verses are unique, both in respect of manner and of matter. S. John also in his five opening verses seems to me to have adopted a method which is not recognisable anywhere else in his writings; "rising strangely by degrees," (as Bp. Pearson expresses it[k],) "making the last word of the former sentence the first of that which followeth."—"*He* knoweth that he saith true," is the language of the same Evangelist concerning himself in chap. xix. 35. But, "*we* know that his testimony is true," is his phrase in chap. xxi. 24. Twice, and twice only throughout his Gospel, (viz. in chap. xix. 35 : xx. 31), is he observed to address his readers, and on both occasions in the same words: ("that *ye* may believe.") But what of all this? Is it to be supposed that S. Matthew, S. Luke, S. John are not the authors of those several places? From facts like these no inference whatever is to be drawn as to the genuineness or the spuriousness of a writing. It is quite to mistake the Critic's vocation to imagine that he is qualified, or called upon, to pass any judgment of the sort.

5. I have not said all this, of course, as declining the proposed investigation. I approach it on the contrary right willingly, being confident that it can be attended by only one result. With what is true, endless are the harmonies which evolve themselves: from what is false, the true is equally certain to stand out divergent[l]. And we all desire nothing but the Truth.

---

[i] S. Matth. viii. 1 (καταβάντι αὐτῷ):—5 (εἰσελθόντι τῷ 'Ι.) :—23 (ἐμβάντι αὐτῷ):—28 (ἐλθόντι αὐτῷ):—ix. 27 (παράγοντι τῷ 'Ι.):—28 (ἐλθόντι):—xxi. 23 (ἐλθόντι αὐτῷ).

[k] *On the Creed,* Art. ii. (vol. i. p. 155.)

[l] τῷ μὲν γὰρ ἀληθεῖ πάντα συνᾴδει τὰ ὑπάρχοντα, τῷ δὲ ψευδεῖ ταχὺ διαφωνεῖ τἀληθές. Aristot. *Eth. Nic.* I. c. vi.

I. To begin then with the "STYLE AND MANNER" of
S. Mark in this place.

1. We are assured that "instead of the *graphic, detailed*
description by which this Evangelist is distinguished, we
meet with an abrupt, sententious manner, resembling that
of brief notices extracted from larger accounts and loosely
linked together [m]." Surely if this be so, the only lawful
inference would be that S. Mark, in this place, *has* "extracted brief notices from larger accounts, and loosely linked
them together:" and unless such a proceeding on the part
of the Evangelist be judged incredible, it is hard to see
what is the force of the adverse criticism, as directed against
the *genuineness* of the passage now under consideration.

2. But in truth, (when divested of what is merely a gratuitous assumption,) the preceding account of the matter
is probably not far from the correct one. Of S. Mark's
practice of making "*extracts,*" I know nothing: nor Dr.
Davidson either. That there existed *any* "larger accounts"
which would have been available for such a purpose, (except
the Gospel according to S. Matthew,) there is neither a particle of evidence, nor a shadow of probability. On the other
hand, that, notwithstanding the abundant oral information
to which confessedly he had access, S. Mark has been divinely guided in this place to handle, in the briefest manner,
some of the chiefest things which took place after our LORD's
Resurrection,—is simply undeniable. And without at all
admitting that the style of the Evangelist is in consequence
either "abrupt" or "sententious [n]," I yet recognise the

---

[m] Davidson's *Introduction*, &c. i. 170.

[n] And yet, if it were ever so "sententious," ever so "abrupt;" and if his
"brief notices" were ever so "loosely linked together;"—these, *according to
Dr. Davidson,* would only be indications that S. Mark actually *was* their
Author. Hear him discussing S. Mark's "characteristics," at p. 151:—"In
the consecution of his narrations, Mark *puts them together very loosely.*"
"Mark is also characterised by a *conciseness* and apparent incompleteness of
delineation which are allied to the obscure." "The *abrupt* introduction"
of many of his details is again and again appealed to by Dr. Davidson, and
illustrated by references to the Gospel. What, in the name of common sense,
is the value of such criticism as this? What is to be thought of a gentleman
who blows hot and cold in the same breath: denying at p. 170 the genuineness

inevitable consequence of relating many dissimilar things
within very narrow limits ; namely, that the transition from
one to the other forces itself on the attention. What wonder
that the same phenomenon should *not* be discoverable in
other parts of the Gospel where the Evangelist is *not* observed to be doing the same thing ?

3. But wherever in his Gospel S. Mark *is* doing the same
thing, he is observed to adopt the style and manner which
Dr. Davidson is pleased to call "sententious" and "abrupt."
Take twelve verses in his first chapter, as an example.
Between S. Mark xvi. 9—20 and S. Mark i. 9—20, I profess
myself unable to discern any real difference of style. I proceed to transcribe the passage which I deliberately propose
for comparison ; *the twelve corresponding verses,* namely, in
S. Mark's *first* chapter, which are to be compared with the
twelve verses already under discussion, from his *last ;* and
they may be just as conveniently exhibited in English as
in Greek :—

(*S. Mark* i. 9—20.)

(ver. 9.) "And it came to pass in those days, that Jesus
" came from Nazareth of Galilee, and was baptized of John
" in Jordan.   (10.) And straightway coming up out of the
" water, He saw the heavens opened, and the Spirit like
" a dove descending upon Him : (11.) and there came a
" voice from heaven saying, Thou art My beloved Son, in
" whom I am well pleased.   (12.) And immediately the
" Spirit driveth Him into the wilderness.   (13.) And He
" was there in the wilderness forty days, tempted of Satan ;
" and was with the wild beasts ; and the Angels ministered
" unto Him.   (14.) Now after that John was put in prison,
" Jesus came into Galilee, preaching the gospel of the
" kingdom of God, (15.) and saying, The time is fulfilled,
" and the Kingdom of God is at hand : repent ye, and be-
" lieve the Gospel.   (16.) Now, as He walked by the sea
" of Galilee, He saw Simon and Andrew his brother casting
" a net into the sea : for they were fishers.   (17.) And Jesus

---

of a certain portion of Scripture *because* it exhibits the very peculiarities
which at p. 151 he had volunteered the information are *characteristic* of
its reputed Author ?

" said unto them, Come ye after Me, and I will make you
" to become fishers of men. (18.) And straightway they
" forsook their nets, and followed Him. (19.) And when
" He had gone a little farther thence, He saw James the
" son of Zebedee, and John his brother, who also were in
" the ship mending their nets. (20.) And straightway He
" called them; and they left their father Zebedee in the
" ship with the hired servants, and went after Him."

4. The candid reader must needs admit that precisely the
self-same manner is recognisable in this first chapter of
S. Mark's Gospel which is asserted to be peculiar to the last.
Note, that from our SAVIOUR's Baptism (which occupies
the first three verses) the Evangelist passes to His Temptation, which is dismissed in two. Six months elapse. The
commencement of the Ministry is dismissed in the next two
verses. The last five describe the call of four of the Apostles,—without any distinct allusion to the miracle which
was the occasion of it. . . . How was it *possible* that when
incidents considerable as these had to be condensed within
the narrow compass of twelve verses, the same " graphic,
detailed description" could reappear which renders S. Mark's
description of the miracle performed in the country of the
Gadarenes (for example) so very interesting; where a single
incident is spread over twenty verses, although the action
did not perhaps occupy an hour? I rejoice to observe that
" the *abrupt transitions* of this section" (ver. 1—13) have
also been noticed by Dean' Alford: who very justly accounts
for the phenomenon by pointing out that here " Mark
appears as *an abridger of previously well-known facts*[o]." But
then, I want to know what there is in this to induce us to
suspect *the genuineness* of either the beginning or the end of
S. Mark's Gospel?

5. For it is a mistake to speak as if " graphic, detailed description" *invariably* characterise the second Gospel.
S. Mark is quite as remarkable for his practice of occasionally exhibiting a considerable transaction in a highly
abridged form. The opening of his Gospel is singularly
concise, and altogether *sudden*. His account of John's preach-

[o] N. T. vol. i. *Prolegg.* p. 38.

ing (i. 1—8) is the shortest of all. Very concise is his account of our Saviour's Baptism (ver. 9—11). The brevity
of his description of our Lord's Temptation is even extraordinary (ver. 12, 13.)—I pass on ; premising that I shall
have occasion to remind the reader by-and-by of certain
peculiarities in these same Twelve Verses, which seem to
have been hitherto generally overlooked.

II. Nothing more true, therefore, than Dr. Tregelles' admission "that arguments on *style* are often very fallacious, and
that *by themselves* they prove very little. But" (he proceeds)
" when there does exist external evidence ; and when internal proofs as to style, manner, verbal expression, and connection, are in accordance with such independent grounds of
forming a judgment ; then, these internal considerations possess very great weight."

I have already shewn that there exists *no* such external
evidence as Dr. Tregelles supposes. And in the absence of
it, I am bold to assert that since nothing in the "Style" or
the "Phraseology" of these verses ever aroused suspicion in
times past, we have rather to be *on our guard* against suffer-
ing our judgment to be warped by arguments drawn from
such precarious considerations now. As for determining
from such data the authorship of an isolated passage ; asserting or denying its genuineness for no other reason but
because it contains certain words and expressions which do
or do not occur elsewhere in the Gospel of which it forms
part ;—let me again declare plainly that the proceeding is
in the highest degree uncritical. We are not competent
judges of what words an Evangelist was likely on any given
occasion to employ. We have no positive knowledge of the
circumstances under which any part of any one of the four
Gospels was written ; nor the influences which determined
an Evangelist's choice of certain expressions in preference to
others. We are learners,—we *can* be only learners here.
But having said all this, I proceed (as already declared)
without reluctance or misgiving to investigate the several
charges which have been brought against this section of the
Gospel ; charges derived from its Phraseology ; and which
will be found to be nothing else but repeated assertions that

L

a certain Word or Phrase,—(there are about twenty-four
such words and phrases in all P,)—"occurs nowhere in the
Gospel of Mark;" with probably the alarming asseveration
that it is "abhorrent to Mark's manner.". . . . The result of
the inquiry which follows will perhaps be not exactly what
is commonly imagined.

The first difficulty of this class is very fairly stated by
one whose name I cannot write without a pang,—the late
Dean Alford :—

(I.) The expression πρώτη σαββάτου, for the "first day of
the week" (in ver. 9) "is remarkable" (he says) "as occurring so soon after" μία σαββάτων (a precisely equivalent
expression) in ver. 2.—Yes, it is remarkable.

Scarcely more remarkable, perhaps, than that S. Luke
in the course of one and the same chapter should four times
designate the Sabbath τὸ σάββατον, and twice τὰ σάββατα :
again, twice, τὸ σάββατον,—twice, ἡ ἡμέρα τοῦ σαββάτου,—

P It may be convenient, in this place, to enumerate the several words and
expressions about to be considered :—

(i.) πρώτη σαββάτου (*ver.* 9.)—See above.

(ii.) ἀφ' ἧς ἐκβεβλήκει ἑπτὰ δαιμόνια (*ver.* 9.)—See p. 152.

(iii.) ἐκβάλλειν ἀπό (*ver.* 9.)—See p. 153.

(iv.) πορεύεσθαι (*vers.* 10, 12, 15.)—*Ibid.*

(v.) οἱ μετ' αὐτοῦ γενόμενοι (*ver.* 10.)—See p. 155.

(vi.) θεᾶσθαι (*ver.* 11 and 14.)—See p. 156.

(vii.) θεαθῆναι ὑπό (*ver.* 11.)—See p. 158.

(viii.) ἀπιστεῖν (*ver.* 11 and 16.)—*Ibid.*

(ix.) μετὰ ταῦτα (*ver.* 12.)—See p. 159.

(x.) ἕτερος (*ver.* 12.)—See p. 160.

(xi.) ὕστερον (*ver.* 14.)—*Ibid.*

(xii.) βλάπτειν (*ver.* 18.)—*Ibid.*

(xiii.) πανταχοῦ (*ver.* 20.)—See p. 161.

(xiv. and xv.) συνεργεῖν—βεβαιοῦν (*ver.* 20.)—*Ibid.*

(xvi.) πᾶσα ἡ κτίσις (*ver.* 15.)—*Ibid.*

(xvii.) ἐν τῷ ὀνόματί μου (*ver.* 17.)—See p. 162.

(xviii. and xix.) παρακολουθεῖν—ἐπακολουθεῖν (*ver.* 17 and 19.)—See p. 163.

(xx.) χεῖρας ἐπιθεῖναι ἐπί τινα (*ver.* 18.)—See p. 164.

(xxi. and xxii.) μὲν οὖν—ὁ Κύριος (*ver.* 19 and 20.)—*Ibid.*

(xxiii.) ἀναληφθῆναι (*ver.* 19.)—See p. 166.

(xxiv.) ἐκεῖνος used in a peculiar way (*verses* 10, 11 [and 13 ?].)—*Ibid.*

(xxv.) " Verses without a copulative," (*verses* 10 and 14.)—*Ibid.*

(xxvi. and xxvii.) Absence of εὐθέως and πάλιν.—See p. 168.

and once, τὰ σάββατα ^q. Or again, that S. Matthew should
in one and the same chapter five times call the Sabbath, τὰ
σάββατα, and three times, τὸ σάββατον ^r. Attentive readers
will have observed that the Evangelists seem to have been
fond in this way of varying their phrase ; suddenly introducing a new expression for something which they had designated differently just before. Often, I doubt not, this is
done with the profoundest purpose, and sometimes even with
manifest design ; but the phenomenon, however we may
explain it, still remains. Thus, S. Matthew, (in his account
of our Lord's Temptation,—chap. iv.,) has ὁ διάβολος in
ver. 1, and ὁ πειράζων in ver. 3, for him whom our Saviour
calls Σατανᾶς in ver. 10.—S. Mark, in chap. v. 2, has τὰ
μνημεῖα,—but in ver. 5, τὰ μνήματα.—S. Luke, in xxiv. 1, has
τὸ μνῆμα ; but in the next verse, τὸ μνημεῖον.—'Επί with an
accusative twice in S. Matth. xxv. 21, 23, is twice exchanged
for ἐπί with a genitive in the same two verses : and ἔριφοι
(in ver. 32) is exchanged for ἐρίφια in ver. 33.—Instead of
ἄρχων τῆς συναγωγῆς (in S. Luke viii. 41) we read, in ver. 49,
ἀρχισυνάγωγος : and for οἱ ἀπόστολοι (in ix. 10) we find
οἱ δώδεκα in ver. 12.—Οὖς in S. Luke xxii. 50 is exchanged for
ὠτίον in the next verse.—In like manner, those whom S. Luke
calls οἱ νεώτεροι in Acts v. 6, he calls νεανίσκοι in ver. 10. . . .
All such matters strike me as highly interesting, but not in
the least as suspicious. It surprises me a little, of course,
that S. Mark should present me with πρώτη σαββάτου (in
ver. 9) instead of the phrase μία σαββάτων, which he had
employed just above (in ver. 2.) But it does not surprise me
much,—when I observe that *μία σαββάτων occurs only once
in each of the Four Gospels* ^s. Whether surprised much or
little, however, — Am I constrained in consequence, (with
Tischendorf and the rest,) to regard this expression (πρώτη
σαββάτου) as a note of *spuriousness ?* That is the only thing

q S. Luke vi. 1, 2, 5, 6, 7, 9 : xiii. 10, 14, 15, 16.   S. Luke has, in fact, all
the four different designations for the Sabbath which are found in the Septuagint version of the O. T. Scriptures : for, in the Acts (xiii. 14 : xvi. 13), he
twice calls it ἡ ἡμέρα τῶν σαββάτων.

r S. Matth. xii. 1, 2, 5, 8, 10, 11, 12.

s It occurs in S. Matth. xxviii. 1. S. Mark xvi. 2. S. Luke xxiv. 1. S. John
xx. i. 19. Besides, only in Acts xx. 7.

I have to consider. Am I, with Dr. Davidson, to reason as follows :—"πρώτη, Mark would scarcely have used. It should have been μία, &c. as is proved by Mark xvi. 2, &c. The expression could scarcely have proceeded from a Jew. It betrays a Gentile author[t]." Am I to reason thus ? . . . I propose to answer this question somewhat in detail.

(1.) That among the Greek-speaking Jews of Palestine, in the days of the Gospel, ἡ μία τῶν σαββάτων was the established method of indicating "the first day of the week," is plain, not only from the fact that the day of the Resurrection is so designated by each of the Four Evangelists in turn[u]; (S. John has the expression twice;) but also from S. Paul's use of the phrase in 1 Cor. xvi. 2. It proves, indeed, to have been the ordinary Hellenistic way of exhibiting the vernacular idiom of Palestine[x]. The cardinal (μία) for the ordinal (πρώτη) in this phrase was a known Talmudic expression, which obtained also in Syriac [y]. Σάββατον and σάββατα,—designations in strictness of the *Sabbath-day*,—had come to be *also* used as designations of the *week*. A reference to S. Mark xvi. 9 and S. Luke xviii. 12 establishes this concerning σάββατον : a reference to the six places cited just now in note (*) establishes it concerning σάββατα. To see how indifferently the two forms (σάββατον and σάββατα) were employed, one has but to notice that S. Matthew, *in the course of one and the same chapter,* five times designates the Sabbath as τὰ σάββατα, and three times as τὸ σάββατον[z]. The origin and history of both words will be found explained in a note at the foot of the page[a].

[t] *Introduction, &c.* i. 169.   [u] See the foregoing note (s).

[x] See Buxtorf's *Lexicon Talmudicum,* p. 2323.

[y] Lightfoot (on 1 Cor. xvi. 2) remarks concerning S. Paul's phrase κατὰ μίαν σαββάτων,— "בחד בשבת [*b'had b'shabbath,*] ' *In the first* [lit. *one*] *of the Sabbath,*' would the Talmudists say."—Professor Gandell writes,—"in Syriac, the days of the week are similarly named. See Bernstein s. v. ܚܰܕ . ܚܰܕ ܒܫܰܒܐ , ܬܪܶܝܢ ܒܫܰܒܐ , ܬܠܳܬܐ ܒܫܰܒܐ [lit. *one in the Sabbath, two in the Sabbath, three in the Sabbath.*]"

[z] S. Mark xii. 1, 2, 5, 8, 10, 11, 12.

[a] The Sabbath-day, in the Old Testament, is invariably שַׁבָּת (*shabbath*) : a word which the Greeks could not exhibit more nearly than by the word σάββατον. The Chaldee form of this word is שַׁבְּתָא (*shabbatha :*) the

(2.) Confessedly, then, a double Hebraism is before us, which must have been simply unintelligible to Gentile readers. Μία τῶν σαββάτων sounded as enigmatical to an ordinary Greek ear, as "*una sabbatorum*" to a Roman. A convincing proof, (if proof were needed,) how abhorrent to a Latin reader was the last-named expression, is afforded by the old Latin versions of S. Matthew xxviii. 1 ; where ὄψε σαββάτων, τῇ ἐπιφωσκούσῃ εἰς μίαν σαββάτων is invariably rendered, "Vespere *sabbati*, quæ lucescit in *prima sabbati*."

(3.) The reader will now be prepared for the suggestion, that when S. Mark, (who is traditionally related to have written his Gospel *at Rome*[b],) varies, in ver. 9, the phrase

final א (*a*) being added for emphasis, as in Abba, Aceldam*a*, Bethesd*a*, Ceph*a*, Pasch*a*, &c. : and this form,—(I owe the information to my friend Professor Gandell,)—because it was so familiar to the people of Palestine, (who spoke Aramaic,) *gave rise to another form of the Greek name for the Sabbath,* —viz. σάββατα : which, naturally enough, attracted the article (τό) into agreement with its own (apparently) plural form. By the Greek-speaking population of Judæa, the Sabbath day was therefore indifferently called τὸ σάββατον and τὰ σάββατα : sometimes again, ἡ ἡμέρα τοῦ σαββάτου, and sometimes ἡ ἡμέρα τῶν σαββάτων.

Σάββατα, although plural in sound, was strictly singular in sense. (Accordingly, it is *invariably* rendered "*Sabbatum*" in the Vulgate.) Thus, in Exod. xvi. 23,—σάββατα ἀνάπαυσις ἁγία τῷ Κυρίῳ : and 25,—ἔστι γὰρ σάββατα ἀνάπαυσις τῷ Κυρίῳ. Again,—τῇ δὲ ἡμέρᾳ τῇ ἑβδόμῃ σάββατα. (Exod. xvi. 26 : xxxi. 14. Levit. xxiii. 3.) And in the Gospel, what took place on *one definite Sabbath-day,* is said to have occurred ἐν τοῖς σάββασι (S. Luke xiii. 10. S. Mark xii. 1.)

It will, I believe, be invariably found that the form ἐν τοῖς σάββασι is strictly equivalent to ἐν τῷ σαββάτῳ ; and was adopted for convenience in contradistinction to ἐν τοῖς σαββάτοις (1 Chron. xxiii. 31 and 2 Chron. ii. 4) where Sabbath *days* are spoken of.

It is not correct to say that in Levit. xxiii. 15 שַׁבָּתוֹת is put for "weeks;" though the Septuagint translators have (reasonably enough) there rendered the word ἑβδομάδας. In Levit. xxv. 8, (where the same word occurs twice,) it is once rendered ἀναπαύσεις ; once, ἑβδομάδες. Quite distinct is שָׁבוּעַ (*shavooa*) i.e. ἑβδομάς ; nor is there any substitution of the one word for the other. But inasmuch as the recurrence of the *Sabbath-day* was what constituted *a week ;* in other words, since the essential feature of a week, as a Jewish division of time, was the recurrence of the Jewish day of rest ;—τὸ σάββατον or τὰ σάββατα, the Hebrew name for *the day of rest,* became transferred to *the week.* The former designation, (as explained in the text,) is used once by S. Mark, once by S. Luke ; while the phrase μία τῶν σαββάτων occurs in the N.T., in all, six times.

[b] So Eusebius (*Eccl. Hist.* ii. 15), and Jerome (*De Viris Illust.* ii. 827), on

he had employed in ver. 2, he does so for an excellent and
indeed for an obvious reason.   In ver. 2, he had conformed
to the prevailing usage of Palestine, and followed the example set him by S. Matthew (xxviii. 1) in adopting the enigmatical expression, ἡ μία σαββάτων.   That this would be
idiomatically represented *in Latin* by the phrase "prima
sabbati," we have already seen.   In ver. 9, therefore, he is
solicitous to record the fact of the Resurrection afresh ; and
this time, his phrase is observed to be *the Greek equivalent
for the Latin "prima sabbati ;"* viz. πρώτη σαββάτου.   How
strictly equivalent the two modes of expression were felt to
be by those who were best qualified to judge, is singularly
illustrated by the fact that the *Syriac* rendering of both
places is *identical.*

(4.) But I take leave to point out that this substituted
phrase, instead of being a suspicious circumstance, is on the
contrary a striking note of genuineness.   For do we not
recognise here, in the last chapter of the Gospel, the very
same hand which, in the first chapter of it, was careful to
inform us, just for once, that " Judæa," is "a *country*,"
(ἡ Ἰουδαία χώρα,)—and "Jordan," "a *river*," (ὁ Ἰορδάνης
ποταμός)?—Is not this the very man who explained to his
readers (in chap. xv. 42) that the familiar Jewish designation for " Friday," ἡ παρασκευή, denotes *" the day before
the Sabbath*[c] *?"*—and who was so minute in informing us (in
chap. vii. 3, 4) about certain ceremonial practices of " the
Pharisees and all the Jews ?"   Yet more,—Is not the self-
same writer clearly recognisable in this xvi[th] chapter, who
in chap. vi. 37 presented us with σπεκουλάτωρ (the Latin
spiculator) for " an executioner ?" and who, in chap. xv. 39,
for "a *centurion*," wrote—not ἑκατόνταρχος, but—κεντυ-
ρίων ?—and, in chap. xii. 42, explained that the two λεπτά

the authority of Clemens Alex. and of Papias.   See also Euseb. *Hist. Eccl.* vi.
14.—The colophon in the Syriac Version shews that the same traditional
belief prevailed in the Eastern Church.   It also finds record in the *Synopsis
Scripturæ* (wrongly) ascribed to Athanasius.

  [c] παρασκευὴ, δ ἐστι προσάββατον.—Our E. V. "preparation" is from Augustine,—" Parasceue Latine præparatio est."—See Pearson's interesting note
on the word.

which the poor widow cast into the Treasury were equivalent to κοδράντης, the Latin *quadrans?*—and in chap. vii.
4, 8, introduced the Roman measure *sextarius,* (ξέστης)?
—and who volunteered the information (in chap. xv. 16) that
αὐλή is only another designation of πραιτώριον (*Prato-
rium)?*—Yes. S. Mark,—who, alone of the four Evangelists,
(in chap. xv. 21,) records the fact that Simon the Cyrenian
was "*the father of Alexander and Rufus,*" evidently for the
sake of his *Latin* readers*: S. Mark,—who alone ventures
to write in Greek letters (οὐά,—chap. xv. 29,) the Latin in-
terjection "*Vah !*"—obviously because he was writing where
that exclamation was most familiar, and the force of it best
understood [d]: S. Mark,—who attends to the Roman division
of the day, in relating our LORD's prophecy to S. Peter [e]:—
S. Mark, I say, no doubt it was who,—having conformed
himself to the precedent set him by S. Matthew and the
familiar usage of Palestine; and having written τῆς μιᾶς
σαββάτων, (which he knew would sound like "*una sabbatorum [f],*") in ver. 2;—introduced, also for the benefit of his
Latin readers, the Greek equivalent for "*prima sabbati,*"
(viz. πρώτη σαββάτου,) in ver. 9.—This, therefore, I repeat,
so far from being a circumstance "*unfavourable* to its authenticity," (by which, I presume, the learned writer means
its *genuineness*), is rather corroborative of the Church's constant belief that the present section of S. Mark's Gospel is,
equally with the rest of it, the production of S. Mark.   "Not
only was the document intended for Gentile converts :"
(remarks Dr. Davidson, p. 149,) "but there are also appearances of its adaptation to the use of Roman Christians in
particular." Just so.   And I venture to say that in the
whole of "the document" Dr. Davidson will not find a more
striking " appearance of its adaptation to the use of Roman
Christians,"—*and therefore of its genuineness,*—than this.
I shall have to request my reader by-and-by to accept it as
one of the most striking notes of Divine origin which these
verses contain.—For the moment, I pass on.

* Consider Rom. xvi. 13.   [d] Townson's *Discourses,* i. 172.   [e] *Ibid.*
[f] See the Vulgate transl. of S. Mark xvi. 2 and of S. John xx. 19. In the
same version, S. Luke xxiv. 1 and S. John xx. 1 are rendered "*una sabbati.*"

(II.) Less excusable is the coarseness of critical perception betrayed by the next remark. It has been pointed out as a suspicious circumstance that in ver. 9, "the phrase ἀφ' ἧς ἐκβεβλήκει ἑπτὰ δαιμόνια is attached to the name of Mary Magdalene, although she had been mentioned three times before without such appendix. It seems to have been taken from Luke viii. 2 *ᵍ*."—Strange perversity, and yet stranger blindness !

(1.) The phrase *cannot* have been taken from S. Luke; because S. Luke's Gospel was written after S. Mark's. It *was* not taken from S. Luke ; because *there* ἀφ' ἧς δαιμόνια ἑπτὰ ἐξεληλύθει,—here, ἀφ' ἧς ἐκβεβλήκει ἑπτὰ δαιμόνια is read.

(2.) More important is it to expose the shallowness and futility of the entire objection. — Mary Magdalene "had been mentioned three times before, *without such appendix.*" Well but,—What *then ?* After twice (ch. xiv. 54, 66) using the word αὐλή without any "appendix," in the very next chapter (xv. 16) S. Mark adds, ὅ ἐστι πραιτώριον.—The beloved Disciple having mentioned himself without any "appendix" in S. John xx. 7, mentions himself with a very elaborate "appendix" in ver. 20. But what of it?—The sister of the Blessed Virgin, having been designated in chap. xv. 40, as Μαρία ἡ 'Ιακώβου τοῦ μικροῦ καὶ 'Ιωσῆ μήτηρ; is mentioned with one half of that "appendix," (Μαρία ἡ 'Ιωσῆ) in ver. 47, and *in the very next verse,* with the other half (Μαρία ἡ τοῦ 'Ιακώβου.)—I see no reason why the Traitor, who, in S. Luke vi. 16, is called 'Ιούδας 'Ισκαριώτης, should be designated as 'Ιούδαν τὸν ἐπικαλούμενον 'Ισκαριώτην in S. Luke xxii. 3.—I am not saying that such "appendices" are either uninteresting or unimportant. That I attend to them habitually, these pages will best evince. I am only insisting that to infer from such varieties of expression that a different author is recognisable, is abhorrent to the spirit of intelligent Criticism.

(3.) But in the case before us, the hostile suggestion is peculiarly infelicitous. There is even inexpressible tenderness and beauty, the deepest Gospel significancy, in the reserva-

---

ᵍ Davidson's *Introduction,* &c. i. 169, *ed.* 1848 : (ii. 113, *ed.* 1868.)

tion of the clause "out of whom He had cast seven devils,"
for this place.   The reason, I say, is even obvious why an
"appendix," which would have been meaningless before, is
introduced in connexion with Mary Magdalene's august
privilege of being the first of the human race to behold
the risen SAVIOUR.   Jerome (I rejoice to find) has been
beforehand with me in suggesting that it was done, in order
to convey by an example the tacit assurance that " where
Sin had abounded, there did Grace much more abound [h]."
Are we to be cheated of our birthright by Critics [i] who,
entirely overlooking a solution of the difficulty (*if* difficulty
it be) Divine as this, can see in the circumstance grounds
only for suspicion and cavil ?   Ἄπαγε.

(III.) Take the next example.—The very form of the
"appendix" which we have been considering (ἀφ᾽ ἧς ἐκβεβλήκει ἑπτὰ δαιμόνια) breeds offence.   " Instead of ἐκβάλλειν
ἀπό," (oracularly remarks Dr. Davidson,) " Mark has ἐκβάλλειν ἐκ [k]."

Nothing of the sort, I answer.   S. Mark *once* has ἐκβάλλειν ἐκ [l], and *once* ἐκβάλλειν ἀπό.   So has S. Matthew,
(viz. in chap. vii. 4 and 5): and so has S. Luke, (viz. in
chap. vi. 42, and in Acts xiii. 50.)—But what of all this ?
Who sees not that such Criticism is simply nugatory ?

(IV.) We are next favoured with the notable piece of
information that the word πορεύεσθαι, "never used by
S. Mark, is three times contained in this passage;" (viz. in
verses 10, 12 and 15.)

(1.) Yes.   The uncompounded verb, never used *elsewhere*
by S. Mark, is found here three times.   But what then ?
The *compounds* of πορεύεσθαι are common enough in his
Gospel.   Thus, short as his Gospel is, he alone has εἰσ-
πορεύεσθαι, ἐκ-πορεύεσθαι, συμ-πορεύεσθαι, παρα-πορεύεσθαι,
oftener than all the other three Evangelists put together,—viz.
twenty-four times against their nineteen : while the com-

---

[h] "Maria Magdalene ipsa est ʻa quâ septem dæmonia expulerat': *ut ubi
abundaverat peccatum, superabundaret gratiæ.*" (Hieron. *Opp.* i. 327.)

[i] So Tischendorf,—"Collatis prioribus, parum apte adduntur verba ἀφ᾽ ἧς
ἐκβεβλήκει ἑ. δ." (p. 822.)   I am astonished to find the same remark reiterated
by most of the Critics : e.g. Rev. T. S. Green, p. 52.

[k] *Introduction, &c.* vol. i. p. 169.   [l] viz. in chap. vii. 26.

pound προσπορεύεσθαι is *peculiar to his Gospel.*—I am therefore inclined to suggest that the presence of the verb πορεύεσθαι in these Twelve suspected Verses, instead of being an
additional element of suspicion, is rather a circumstance
slightly corroborative of their genuineness.

(2.) But suppose that the facts had been different. The
phenomenon appealed to is of even perpetual recurrence,
and may on no account be represented as *suspicious.* Thus,
παρουσία, a word used only by S. Matthew among the Evangelists, is by him used four times; yet are all those four
instances found *in one and the same chapter.* S. Luke alone
has χαρίζεσθαι, and he has it three times: but all three
cases are met with *in one and the same chapter.* S. John
alone has λύπη, and he has it four times: but all the four
instances occur *in one and the same chapter.*

(3.) Such instances might be multiplied to almost any
extent. Out of the fifteen occasions when S. Matthew uses
the word τάλαντον, no less than fourteen occur in one
chapter. The nine occasions when S. Luke uses the word
μνᾶ all occur in one chapter. S. John uses the verb ἀνιστάναι transitively only four times: but all four instances
of it are found in one chapter.—Now, these three words
(be it observed) are *peculiar to the Gospels* in which they
severally occur.

(4.) I shall of course be reminded that τάλαντον and μνᾶ
are unusual words,—admitting of no substitute in the places
where they respectively occur. But I reply,—Unless the
Critics are able to shew me *which* of the ordinary compounds
of πορεύομαι S. Mark could *possibly* have employed for the
uncompounded verb, in the three places which have suggested the present inquiry, viz. :—

ver. 10 :—ἐκείνη πορευθεῖσα ἀπήγγειλε τοῖς μετ᾽ αὐτοῦ
γενομένοις.

ver. 12 :—δυσὶν ἐξ αὐτῶν . . . πορευομένοις εἰς ἀγρόν.

ver. 13 :—πορευθέντες εἰς τὸν κόσμον ἅπαντα, κηρύξατε
τὸ εὐαγγέλιον ;—

their objection is simply frivolous, and the proposed adverse
reasoning, worthless. Such, in fact, it most certainly is; for
it will be found that πορευθεῖσα in ver. 10,—πορευομένοις in

ver. 12,—πορευθέντες in ver. 15,—*also* "admit of no substitute in the places where they severally occur;" and therefore, since the verb itself is one of S. Mark's favourite verbs,
not only are these three places above suspicion, but they
may be fairly adduced as indications that *the same* hand was
at work here which wrote all the rest of his Gospel [m].

(V.) Then further,—the phrase τοῖς μετ' αὐτοῦ γενομένοις (in ver. 10) is noted as suspicious. "Though found in
the Acts (xx. 18) it *never occurs in the Gospels:* nor does the
word μαθηταί in this passage."

(1.) The phrase οἱ μετ' αὐτοῦ γενόμενοι occurs nowhere
in the Acts or in the Gospels, *except here.* But,—Why
should it appear elsewhere? or rather,—How *could* it? Now,
if the expression be (as it is) an ordinary, easy, and obvious
one,—*wanted* in this place, where it *is* met with; but *not*
met with elsewhere, simply because elsewhere it is *not*
wanted;—surely it is unworthy of any one calling himself
a Critic to pretend that there attaches to it the faintest
shadow of suspicion!

(2.) The essence of the phrase is clearly the expression
οἱ μετ' αὐτοῦ. (The aorist participle of γίνομαι is added of
necessity to mark the persons spoken of. In no other, (certainly in no simpler, more obvious, or more precise) way
could the followers of the risen SAVIOUR have been designated at such a time. For had He not just now "overcome
the sharpness of Death"?) But this expression, which occurs
four times in S. Matthew and four times in S. Luke, occurs
also four times in S. Mark: viz. in chap. i. 36; ii. 25; v. 40,
and here. This, therefore, is a slightly corroborative circumstance,—not at all a ground of suspicion.

(3.) But it seems to be implied that S. Mark, because he
mentions τοὺς μαθητάς often elsewhere in his Gospel, ought
to have mentioned them here.

(*a*) I answer:—He does not mention τοὺς μαθητάς nearly
so often as S. Matthew; while S. John notices them twice
as often as he does.

(*b*) Suppose, however, that he elsewhere mentioned them
five hundred times, because he had occasion five hundred

---

[m] Professor Broadus has some very good remarks on this subject.

times to speak of them;—what reason would *that* be for his mentioning them here, where he is *not* speaking of them?

(c) It must be evident to any one reading the Gospel with attention that besides οἱ μαθηταί,—(by which expression S. Mark always designates *the Twelve Apostles,*)—there was a considerable company of believers assembled together throughout the first Easter Day[n]. S. Luke notices this circumstance when he relates how the Women, on their return from the Sepulchre, "told all these things unto the Eleven, and *to all the rest*," (xxiv. 9): and again when he describes how Cleopas and his companion (δύο ἐξ αὐτῶν as S. Luke and S. Mark call them) on their return to Jerusalem, "found the Eleven gathered together, *and them that were with them.*" (xxiv. 33.) But this was at least as well known to S. Mark as it was to S. Luke. Instead, therefore, of regarding the designation "*them that had been with Him*" with suspicion,—are we not rather to recognise in it one token more that the narrative in which it occurs is unmistakably genuine? What else is this but one of those delicate discriminating touches which indicate the hand of a great Master; one of those evidences of minute accuracy which stamp on a narrative the impress of unquestionable Truth?

(VI.) We are next assured by our Critic that θεᾶσθαι "is unknown to Mark;" but it occurs twice in this section, (viz. in ver. 11 and ver. 14.) *Another* suspicious circumstance!

(1.) A strange way (as before) of stating an ordinary fact, certainly! What else is it but to assume the thing which has to be proved? If the learned writer had said instead, that the verb θεᾶσθαι, here twice employed by S. Mark, occurs *nowhere else* in his Gospel, — he would have acted more loyally, not to say more fairly by the record: but then he would have been stating a strictly ordinary phenomenon,—of no significancy, or relevancy to the matter in hand. He is probably aware that παραβαίνειν in like manner is to be found in two consecutive verses of S. Matthew's Gospel; παρακούειν, twice in the course of one

---

[n] Consider the little society which was assembled on the occasion alluded to, in Acts i. 13, 14. Note also what is clearly implied by ver. 21—6, as to the persons who were *habitually* present at such gatherings.

verse: neither word being used on any other occasion *either by S. Matthew, or by any other Evangelist. The same thing precisely* is to be said of ἀναζητεῖν and ἀνταποδιδόναι, of ἀντιπαρέρχεσθαι and διατίθεσθαι, in S. Luke: of ἀνιστάναι and ζωννύναι in S. John. But who ever dreamed of insinuating that the circumstance is suspicious?

(2.) As for θεᾶσθαι, we should have reminded our Critic that this verb, which is used seven times by S. John, and four times by S. Matthew, is used only three times by S. Luke, and only twice by S. Mark. And we should have respectfully inquired,—What possible suspicion does θεᾶσθαι throw upon the last twelve verses of S. Mark's Gospel?

(3.) None whatever, would have been the reply. But in the meantime Dr. Davidson hints that the verb *ought* to have been employed by S. Mark in chap. ii. 14 °.—It is, I presume, sufficient to point out that S. Matthew, at all events, was not of Dr. Davidson's opinion ᵖ: and I respectfully submit that the Evangelist, inasmuch as he happens to be here *writing about himself*, must be allowed, just for once, to be the better judge.

(4.) In the meantime,—Is it not perceived that θεᾶσθαι is the very word specially required in these two places,— though *nowhere else in S. Mark's Gospel* �q? The occasion is *one*,—viz. the 'beholding' of the person of the risen SAVIOUR. Does not even natural piety suggest that the uniqueness of such a 'spectacle' as *that* might well set an Evangelist on casting about for a word of somewhat less ordinary occurrence? The occasion cries aloud for this very verb θεᾶσθαι; and I can hardly conceive a more apt illustration of a darkened eye,—a spiritual faculty perverted from its lawful purpose,—than that which only discovers "a stumbling-block and occasion of falling" in expressions like the present which "should have been only for their wealth," being so manifestly designed for their edification.

° S. Luke (v. 27) has ἐθεάσατο τελώνην. S. Matthew (ix. 9) and S. Mark (ii. 14) have preferred εἶδεν ἄνθρωπον (Λευὶν τὸν τοῦ Ἀλφαίου) καθήμενον ἐπὶ τὸ τελώνιον.   ᵖ See S. Matth. ix. 9.

�q One is reminded that S. Matthew, in like manner, carefully *reserves* the verb θεωρεῖν (xxvii. 55: xxviii. 1) for the contemplation of the SAVIOUR'S Cross and of the SAVIOUR'S Sepulchre.

(VII.) But,—(it is urged by a Critic of a very different stamp,)—ἐθεάθη ὑπ' αὐτῆς (ver. 11) " is a construction only found here in the New Testament."

(1.) Very likely; but what then? The learned writer has evidently overlooked the fact that the passive θεᾶσθαι occurs but *three times* in the New Testament *in all* [q]. S. Matthew, on the *two* occasions when he employs the word, connects it with a dative [r]. What is there *suspicious* in the circumstance that θεᾶσθαι ὑπό should be the construction preferred by S. Mark? The phenomenon is not nearly so remarkable as that S. Luke, on one solitary occasion, exhibits the phrase μὴ φοβεῖσθε ἀπό [s],—instead of making the verb govern the accusative, as he does three times *in the very next verse;* and, indeed, eleven times in the course of his Gospel. To be sure, S. Luke in this instance is but copying S. Matthew, who *also* has μὴ φοβεῖσθε ἀπό once [t]; and seven times makes the verb govern an accusative. This, nevertheless, constitutes no reason whatever for suspecting the genuineness either of S. Matth. x. 28 or of S. Luke xii. 4.

(2.) In like manner, the phrase ἐφοβήθησαν φόβον μέγαν will be found to occur once, and once *only,* in S. Mark,—once, and once only, in S. Luke [u]; although S. Mark and S. Luke use the verb φοβεῖσθαι upwards of forty times. Such facts are interesting. They may prove important. But no one who is ever so little conversant with such inquiries will pretend that they are in the least degree *suspicious.*—I pass on.

(VIII.) It is next noted as a suspicious circumstance that ἀπιστεῖν occurs in ver. 11 and in ver. 16; but nowhere else in the Gospels,—except in S. Luke xxiv. 11, 14.

But really, such a remark is wholly without force, as an argument against the genuineness of the passage in which the word is found: for,

(1.) Where else in the course of this Gospel *could* ἀπιστεῖν have occurred? Now, unless some reason can be shewn why the word *should,* or at least *might* have been employed elsewhere, to remark upon its introduction in this place, *where it*

---

[q] S. Matth. vi. 1: xxiii. 5.　S. Mark xvi. 11.
[r] Πρὸς τὸ θεαθῆναι αὐτοῖς, (vi. 1); and τοῖς ἀνθρώποις, xxiii. 5).
[s] S. Luke xii. 4.　[t] S. Matth. x. 28.　[u] S. Mark iv. 41.　S. Luke ii. 9.

could scarcely be dispensed with, as a ground of suspicion, is
simply irrational. It might just as well be held to be a suspicious circumstance, in respect of verses 3 and 4, that the
verb ἀποκυλίζειν occurs there, *and there only,* in this Gospel.
Nothing whatever follows from the circumstance. It is, in
fact, a point scarcely deserving of attention.

(2.) To be sure, if the case of a verb exclusively used by
the two Evangelists, S. Mark and S. Luke, were an unique,
or even an exceedingly rare phenomenon, it might have been
held to be a somewhat suspicious circumstance that the phenomenon presented itself in the present section. But nothing
of the sort is the fact. There are no fewer than forty-five
verbs *exclusively used by S. Mark and S. Luke.* And why
should not ἀπιστεῖν be, (as it is,) one of them?

(3.) Note, next, that this word *is used twice,* and in the
course of his last chapter too, also *by S. Luke.* Nowhere
else does it occur in the Gospels. It is at least as strange
that the word ἀπιστεῖν should be found twice in the last
chapter of the Gospel according to S. Luke, as in the last
chapter of the Gospel according to S. Mark. And if no
shadow of suspicion is supposed to result from this circumstance in the case of the third Evangelist, why should it in
the case of the second ?

(4.) But, lastly, *the noun* ἀπιστία (which occurs in S. Mark
xvi. 14) occurs in two other places of the same Gospel. And
this word (which S. Matthew uses twice,) is employed by
none of the other Evangelists.—What need to add another
word ? Do not many of these supposed suspicious circumstances,—*this* one for example,—prove rather, on closer inspection, to be confirmatory facts ?

(IX.) We are next assured that μετὰ ταῦτα (ver. 12) "*is
not found in Mark,* though many opportunities occurred for
using it."

(1.) I suppose that what this learned writer means, is this ;
that if S. Mark had coveted an opportunity for introducing
the phrase μετὰ ταῦτα earlier in his Gospel, he might have
found one. (More than this cannot be meant : for *nowhere
before does* S. Mark employ *any other phrase* to express
"after these things," or "after this," or "afterwards.")

But what is the obvious inference from the facts of the case, as stated by the learned Critic, except that the blessed Evangelist *must be presumed to have been unconscious of any desire to introduce the expression under consideration on any other occasion except the present?*

(2.) Then, further, it is worth observing that while the phrase μετὰ ταῦτα occurs five times in S. Luke's Gospel, it is found only twice in the Acts; while S. Matthew *never employs it at all.* Why, then,—I would respectfully inquire—*why* need S. Mark introduce the phrase *more than once?* Why, especially, is his solitary use of the expression to be represented as a suspicious circumstance; and even perverted into an article of indictment against the genuineness of the last twelve verses of his Gospel? " Would any one argue that S. Luke was not the author of the Acts, because the author of the Acts has employed this phrase only twice,—' often as he *could* have used it?' (Meyer's phrase here[x].)"

(X.) Another objection awaits us.—"Ἕτερος also " is unknown to Mark," says Dr. Davidson;—which only means that the word occurs in chap. xvi. 12, but not elsewhere in his Gospel.

It so happens, however, that ἕτερος also occurs once only in the Gospel of S. John. Does it therefore throw suspicion on S. John xix. 37?

(XI.) The same thing is said of ὕστερον (in ver. 14) viz. that it " occurs nowhere" in the second Gospel.

But why not state the case thus?—"Ὕστερον, a word which is twice employed by S. Luke, occurs only *once* in S. Mark and *once* in S. John.—*That* would be the true way of stating the facts of the case. But it would be attended with this inconvenient result,—that it would make it plain that the word in question has no kind of bearing on the matter in hand.

(XII.) The same thing he says of βλάπτειν (in ver. 18).

But what is the fact? The word occurs *only twice in the Gospels,*—viz. in S. Mark xvi. 18 and S. Luke iv. 35. It is one of the eighty-four words which are peculiar to S. Mark

---

[x] Professor Broadus, *ubi suprà.*

and S. Luke. What possible significancy would Dr. Davidson attach to the circumstance ?

(XIII.) Once more.—"πανταχοῦ" (proceeds Dr. Davidson) "is unknown to Mark;" which (as we begin to be
aware) is the learned gentleman's way of stating that it is
only found in chap. xvi. 20.

Tischendorf, Tregelles, and Alford insist that it *also* occurs
in S. Mark i. 28. I respectfully differ from them in opinion :
but when it has been pointed out that the word *is only used
besides in S. Luke* ix. 6, what *can* be said of such Criticism but
that it is simply frivolous ?

(XIV. and XV.) Yet again :—συνεργεῖν and βεβαιοῦν are
also said by the same learned Critic to be "unknown to
Mark."

S. Mark certainly uses these two words only once,—viz. in
the last verse of the present Chapter : but what there is suspicious in this circumstance, I am at a loss even to divine.
He *could* not have used them oftener ; and since one hundred
and fifty-six words are peculiar to his Gospel, why should
not συνεργεῖν and βεβαιοῦν be two of them ?

(XVI.) "Πᾶσα κτίσις is Pauline," proceeds Dr. Davidson,
(referring to a famous expression which is found in ver. 15.)

(1.) All very oracular,—to be sure : but *why* πᾶσα κτίσις
should be thought "Pauline" rather than "Petrine," I really,
once more, cannot discover ; seeing that S. Peter has the expression as well as S. Paul['].

(2.) In this place, however, the phrase is πᾶσα ἡ κτίσις.
But even this expression is no more to be called "Pauline"
than "Marcine ;" seeing that as S. Mark uses it once and
once only, so does S. Paul use it once and once only, viz.
in Rom. viii. 22.

(3.) In the meantime, how does it come to pass that the
learned Critic has overlooked the significant fact that the
word κτίσις occurs besides in S. Mark x. 6 and xiii. 19 ; and
that it is a word which *S. Mark alone of the Evangelists uses ?*
Its occurrence, therefore, in this place is a circumstance the
very reverse of suspicious.

(4.) But lastly, inasmuch as the opening words of our

['] Col. i. 15, 23. 1 S. Pet. ii. 13.

M

LORD's Ministerial Commission to the Apostles are these,—
κηρύξατε τὸ εὐαγγέλιον πάσῃ τῇ κτίσει (ver. 15):
inasmuch, too, as S. Paul in his Epistle to the Colossians
(i. 23) almost reproduces those very words; speaking of the
Hope τοῦ εὐαγγελίου . . . τοῦ κηρυχθέντος ἐν πάσῃ
[τῇ] κτίσει τῇ ὑπὸ τὸν οὐρανόν:"—Is it not an allowable
conjecture that *a direct reference* to *that* place in S. Mark's
Gospel is contained in *this* place of S. Paul's Epistle? that
the inspired Apostle "beholding the universal tendency of
Christianity already realized," announces (and from imperial
Rome!) the fulfilment of his LORD's commands in his LORD's
own words as recorded by the Evangelist S. Mark?

I desire to be understood to deliver this only as a conjecture. But seeing that S. Mark's Gospel is commonly thought
to have been written at Rome, and under the eye of S. Peter;
and that S. Peter (and therefore S. Mark) must have been at
Rome before S. Paul visited that city in A.D. 61;—seeing,
too, that it was in A.D. 61-2 (as Wordsworth and Alford are
agreed) that S. Paul wrote his Epistle to the Colossians, and
wrote it from *Rome;*—I really can discover nothing unreasonable in the speculation. If, however, it be well founded,
—(and it is impossible to deny that the coincidence of expression *may* be such as I have suggested,)—then, what an
august corroboration would *this* be of "the last Twelve
Verses of the Gospel according to S. Mark!" . . . If, indeed,
the great Apostle on reaching Rome inspected S. Mark's
Gospel for the first time, with what awe will he have recognised in his own recent experience the fulfilment of his
SAVIOUR's great announcement concerning the "signs which
should follow them that believe!" Had he not himself "cast
out devils?"—"spoken with tongues more than they all?"—
and at Melita, not only "shaken off the serpent into the fire
and felt no harm," but also "laid hands on the sick" father
of Publius, "and he had recovered?" . . . To return, however,
to matters of fact; with an apology (if it be thought necessary) for what immediately goes before.

(XVII.) Next,—ἐν τῷ ὀνόματί μου (ver. 17) is noticed as
another suspicious peculiarity. The phrase is supposed to occur
only in this place of S. Mark's Gospel; the Evangelist else-

where employing the preposition ἐπί:—(viz. in ix. 37 : ix. 39 : xiii. 6.)

(1.) Now really, if it were so, the reasoning would be nugatory. *S. Luke* also once, and once only, has ἐν τῷ ὀνόματί σου : his usage elsewhere being, (like S. Mark's) to use ἐπί. Nay, in two consecutive verses of ch. ix, ἐπὶ τῷ ὀνόματί μου —σου is read : and yet, in the very next chapter, his Gospel exhibits an unique instance of the usage of ἐν. Was it ever thought that suspicion is thereby cast on S. Luke x. 17 ?

(2.) But, in fact, the objection is an oversight of the learned (and generally accurate) objector. The phrase recurs in S. Mark ix. 38,—as the text of that place has been revised by Tischendorf, by Tregelles and by himself. This is therefore a slightly *corroborative*, not a suspicious circumstance.

(XVIII. and XIX.) We are further assured that παρακολουθεῖν (in ver. 17) and ἐπακολουθεῖν (in ver. 20) " are both *foreign to the diction of Mark.*"

(1.) But what can the learned author of this statement possibly mean ? He is not speaking of the uncompounded verb ἀκολουθεῖν, of course ; for S. Mark employs it at least twenty times. He cannot be speaking of the compounded verb ; for συνακολουθεῖν occurs in S. Mark v. 37. He cannot mean that παρακολουθεῖν, because the Evangelist uses it only once, is suspicious ; for that would be to cast a slur on S. Luke i. 3. He cannot mean generally that verbs compounded with prepositions are " foreign to the diction of Mark ;" for there are no less than *forty-two* such verbs which are even *peculiar to S. Mark's short Gospel,*—against thirty which are peculiar to S. Matthew, and seventeen which are peculiar to S. John. He cannot mean that verbs compounded with παρά and ἐπί have a suspicious look ; for at least *thirty-three* such compounds, (besides the two before us,) occur in his sixteen chapters [z]. What, then, I must

---

[z] παραβάλλειν [I quote from the Textus Receptus of S. Mark iv. 30,—confirmed as it is by the Peshito and the Philoxenian, the Vetus and the Vulgate, the Gothic and the Armenian versions,—besides Codd. A and D, and all the other uncials (except B, L, Δ, א,) and almost every cursive Codex. The evidence of Cod. C and of Origen is doubtful. *Who* would subscribe to the different reading adopted on countless similar occasions by the most recent Editors of the N. T. ?] : παραγγέλλειν : παράγειν : παραγίνεσθαι : παραδιδόναι : παραλαμβάνειν :

really ask, can the learned Critic possibly mean ?—I respectfully pause for an answer.

(2.) In the meantime, I claim that as far as such evidence goes,—(and it certainly goes a very little way, yet, *as far as it goes*,)—it is a note of S. Mark's authorship, that within the compass of the last twelve verses of his Gospel these two compounded verbs should be met with.

(XX.) Dr. Davidson points out, as another suspicious circumstance, that (in ver. 18) the phrase χεῖρας ἐπιτιθέναι ἐπί τινα occurs ; "instead of χεῖρας ἐπιτιθέναι τινι."

(1.) But on the contrary, the phrase "*is in Mark's manner*," says Dean Alford: the plain fact being that it occurs no less than three times in his Gospel,—viz. in chap. viii. 25 : x. 16 : xvi. 18. (The other idiom, he has four times [a].) Behold, then, one and the same phrase is appealed to as a note of genuineness *and* as an indication of spurious origin. What *can* be the value of such Criticism as this ?

(2.) Indeed, the phrase before us supplies no unapt illustration of the precariousness of the style of remark which is just now engaging our attention. Within the space of three verses, S. Mark has *both* expressions,—viz. ἐπιθεὶς τὰς χεῖρας αὐτῷ (viii. 23) and also ἐπέθηκε τὰς χεῖρας ἐπί (ver. 25.) S. Matthew has the latter phrase once ; the former, twice [b]. *Who* will not admit that all this (so-called) Criticism is the veriest trifling ; and that to pretend to argue about the genuineness of a passage of Scripture from such evidence as the present is an act of rashness bordering on folly ? . . . The reader is referred to what was offered above on Art. VII.

(XXI. and XXII.) Again: the words μὲν οὖν—ὁ Κύριος (ver. 19 and ver. 20) are also declared to be "*foreign to the diction of Mark.*" I ask leave to examine these two charges separately.

παρατηρεῖν : παρατιθέναι : παραφέρειν : παρέρχεσθαι : παρέχειν : παριστάναι.—
ἐπαγγέλλεσθαι : ἐπαισχύνεσθαι : ἐπανίστασθαι : ἐπερωτᾶν : ἐπιβάλλειν : ἐπιγινώ-
σκειν : ἐπιγράφειν : ἐπιζητεῖν : ἐπιλαμβάνεσθαι : ἐπιλανθάνεσθαι : ἐπιλύειν : ἐπι-
πίπτειν : ἐπιρράπτειν : ἐπισκιάζειν : ἐπιστρέφειν : ἐπισυνάγειν : ἐπισυντρέχειν :
ἐπιτάσσειν : ἐπιτιθέναι : ἐπιτιμᾶν : ἐπιτρέπειν.

[a] S. Mark v. 23 : vi. 5 : vii. 32 : viii. 23.

[b] S. Matth. ix. 18 :—xix. 13, 15.

(1.) *μὲν οὖν* occurs only once in S. Mark's Gospel, truly : but then *it occurs only once in S. Luke* (iii. 18) ;—only twice in S. John (xix. 24 : xx. 30) :—in S. Matthew, never at all. What imaginable plea can be made out of such evidence as this, for or against the genuineness of the last Twelve Verses of S. Mark's Gospel ?—Once more, I pause for an answer.

(2.) As for *ὁ Κύριος* being "*foreign to the diction of Mark* in speaking of the LORD,"—I really do not know what the learned Critic can possibly mean ; except that he finds our LORD *nowhere called ὁ Κύριος by S. Mark, except in this place.*

But then, he is respectfully reminded that neither does he find our LORD anywhere called by S. Mark "JESUS CHRIST," except in chap. i. 1. Are we, therefore, to suspect the beginning of S. Mark's Gospel as well as the end of it ? By no means, (I shall perhaps be told :) a reason is assignable for the use of *that* expression in chap. i. 1. And so, I venture to reply, there is a fully sufficient reason assignable for the use of *this* expression in chap. xvi. 19 [c].

(3.) By S. Matthew, by S. Mark, by S. John, our LORD is called *Ἰησοῦς Χριστός,*—but *only in the first Chapter* of their respective Gospels. By S. Luke nowhere. The appellation may,—or may not,—be thought "foreign to the diction" of those Evangelists. But surely it constitutes no reason whatever why we should suspect the genuineness of the beginning of the first, or the second, or the fourth Gospel.

(4.) S. John *three times in the first verse of his first Chapter* designates the Eternal SON by the extraordinary title *ὁ Λόγος* ; but *nowhere else in his Gospel,* (except once in ver. 14,) does that Name recur. Would it be reasonable to represent *this* as a suspicious circumstance ? Is not the Divine fitness of that sublime appellation generally recognised and admitted [d] ?—Surely, we come to Scripture to be learners only : not to teach the blessed Writers how they ought to have spoken about GOD ! When will men learn that "the

---

[c] See below, pp. 184-6.

[d] See Pearson *on the Creed,* (ed. Burton), vol. i. p. 151.

Scripture-phrase, or *language of the Holy Ghost* [e]" is as much above them as Heaven is above Earth?

(XXIII.) Another complaint:—ἀναληφθῆναι, which is found in ver. 19, occurs nowhere else in the Gospels.

(1.) True. S. Mark has no fewer than seventy-four verbs which "occur nowhere else in the Gospels:" and this happens to be one of them? What possible inconvenience can be supposed to follow from that circumstance?

(2.) But the remark is unreasonable. 'Αναληφθῆναι and ἀνάληψις are words *proper to the Ascension of our LORD into Heaven.* The two Evangelists who do *not* describe that event, are *without* these words: the two Evangelists who *do* describe it, *have* them [f]. Surely, these are marks of genuineness, not grounds for suspicion!

It is high time to conclude this discussion.—Much has been said about two other minute points:—

(XXIV.) It is declared that ἐκεῖνος " is nowhere found absolutely used by S. Mark:" (the same thing may be said of S. Matthew and of S. Luke also:) " but always emphatically: whereas in verses 10 and 11, it is absolutely used [g]." Another writer says,—"The use of ἐκεῖνος in verses 10, 11, and 13 (twice) in a manner synonymous with ὁ δέ, is peculiar [h]."

(1.) Slightly peculiar it is, no doubt, but not very, that an Evangelist who employs an ordinary word in the ordinary way about thirty times in all, should use it "absolutely" in two consecutive verses.

(2.) But really, until the Critics can agree among themselves as to *which* are precisely the offending instances,— (for it is evidently a moot point whether ἐκεῖνος be emphatic in ver. 13, or not,)—we may be excused from a prolonged discussion of such a question. I shall recur to the subject in the consideration of the next Article (XXV.)

(XXV.) So again, it may be freely admitted that " in the 10th and 14th verses there are sentences without a copula-

---

[e] *Ibid.* p. 183,—at the beginning of the exposition of " *Our LORD.*"

[f] S. Mark xvi. 19. S. Luke ix. 51. Acts i. 2.

[g] Alford.   [h] Davidson.

tive : whereas Mark always has the copulative in such cases,
particularly καί." But then,—

(1.) Unless we can be shewn at least two or three other
sections of S. Mark's Gospel *resembling the present*,—(I mean,
passages in which S. Mark summarizes many disconnected
incidents, as he does here,)—is it not plain that such an
objection is wholly without point ?

(2.) Two instances are cited. In the latter, (ver. 14),
Lachmann and Tregelles read ὕστερον δέ : and the reading
is not impossible. So that the complaint is really reduced to this,—That in ver. 10 the Evangelist begins
Ἐκείνη πορευθεῖσα, instead of saying Καὶ ἐκείνη πορευθεῖσα. And (it is implied) there is something so abhorrent
to probability in this, as slightly to strengthen the suspicion
that the entire context is not the work of the Evangelist.

(3.) Now, suppose we had S. Mark back among us : and
suppose that he, on being shewn this objection, were to be
heard delivering himself somewhat to the following effect :—
"Aye. But men may not find fault with *that* turn of phrase.
I derived it from Simon Peter's lips. I have always suspected that it was a kind of echo, so to say, of what he
and 'the other Disciple' had many a time rehearsed in the
hearing of the wondering Church concerning the Magdalene on the morning of the Resurrection." And then we
should have remembered the familiar place in the fourth
Gospel :—

γύναι τί κλαίεις ; τίνα ζητεῖς ; ΕΚΕΊΝΗ δοκοῦσα κ. τ. λ.

After which, the sentence would not have seemed at all
strange, even though it *be* "without a copulative :"—

ἀφ' ἧς ἐκβεβλήκει ἑπτὰ δαιμόνια. ΕΚΕΊΝΗ πορευθεῖσα κ. τ. λ.

(4.) For after all, the *only* question to be asked is,—Will
any one pretend that such a circumstance as this is *suspicious ?* Unless *that* be asserted, I see not what is gained by
raking together,—(*as one easily might do in any section of any
of the Gospels*,)—every minute peculiarity of form or expression which can possibly be found within the space of these
twelve verses. It is an evidence of nothing so much as
an incorrigible coarseness of critical fibre, that every slight
variety of manner or language should be thus pounced upon

and represented as a note of spuriousness,—in the face of
(*a*) the unfaltering tradition of the Church universal that
the document has *never* been hitherto suspected: and
(*b*) the known proclivity of all writers, as free moral and
intellectual agents, sometimes to deviate from their else
invariable practice.—May I not here close the discussion?

There will perhaps be some to remark, that however successfully the foregoing objections may seem to have been
severally disposed of, yet that the combined force of such
a multitude of slightly suspicious circumstances must be not
only appreciable, but even remain an inconvenient, not to
say a formidable fact.   Let me point out that the supposed
remark is nothing else but a fallacy; which is detected the
instant it is steadily looked at.

For if there really had remained after the discussion of
each of the foregoing XXV Articles, a slight residuum of
suspiciousness, *then* of course the aggregate of so many frac-
tions would have amounted to something in the end.

But since it has been proved that there is absolutely
nothing at all suspicious in *any* of the alleged circumstances
which have been hitherto examined, the case becomes altogether different.   The sum of ten thousand nothings is still
nothing[1].   This may be conveniently illustrated by an appeal
to the only charge which remains to be examined.

(XXVI. and XXVII.)   The absence from these twelve
verses of the adverbs εὐθέως and πάλιν,—(both of them
favourite words with the second Evangelist,)—has been
pointed out as one more suspicious circumstance.   Let us
take the words singly:—

(*a*) The adverb εὐθέως (or εὐθύς) is indeed of *very* frequent
occurrence in S. Mark's Gospel.   And yet its absence from

---

[1] Exactly so Professor Broadus:—"Now it will not do to say that while
no one of these peculiarities would itself prove the style to be foreign to Mark,
the whole of them combined will do so.   It is very true that the multiplication
of *littles* may amount to much; but not so the multiplication of *nothings.*
And how many of the expressions which are cited, appear, in the light of our
examination, to retain the slightest real force as proving difference of authorship?   Is it not true that most of them, and those the most important, are
reduced to absolutely nothing, while the remainder possess scarcely any appreciable significance?"—p. 360, (see above, p. 139, note g.)

chap. xvi is *proved* to be in no degree a suspicious circumstance, from the discovery ⁻that though it occurs as many as

12 times in chap. i ;

and 6   „   chap. v ;

and 5   „   chap. iv, vi ;

and 3   „   chap. ii, ix, xiv ;

and 2   „   chap. vii, xi ;

it yet occurs only 1   „   chap. iii, viii, x, xv ;

while it occurs 0   „   chap. xii, xiii, xvi.

(*b*) In like manner, πάλιν, which occurs as often as

6 times in chap. xiv ;

and 5   „   chap. x ;

and 3   „   chap. viii, xv ;

and 2   „   chap. ii, iii, vii, xi, xii ;

and 1   „   chap. iv, v ;

occurs 0   „   chap. i, vi, ix, xiii. xvi. [k]

(1.) Now,—How can it possibly be more suspicious that
πάλιν should be absent from *the last twelve* verses of S. Mark,
than that it should be away from *the first forty-five ?*

(2.) Again. Since εὐθέως is not found in the xii[th] or the
xiii[th] chapters of this same Gospel,—nor πάλιν in the i[st], vi[th],
ix[th], or xiii[th] chapter,—(for the sufficient reason that *neither
word is wanted in any of those places,*)—what possible "suspiciousness" can be supposed to result from the absence of
both words from the xvi[th] chapter also, where *also* neither
of them is wanted? *Why* is the xvi[th] chapter of S. Mark's
Gospel,—or rather, why are "the last twelve verses" of it,
—to labour under such special disfavor and discredit ?

(3.) Dr. Tregelles makes answer,—"I am well aware that
arguments on *style* are often very fallacious, and that *by themselves* they prove very little : but when there does exist external evidence, and when internal proofs as to style, manner,
verbal expression, and connection, are in accordance with
such independent grounds of forming a judgment ; then these
internal considerations possess very great weight [l]."—For all

---

[k] S. John has πάλιν (47 times) much oftener than S. Mark (29 times). And
yet, πάλιν is not met with in the ii[nd], or the iii[rd], or the vth, or the vii[th], or
the xv[th], or the xvii[th] chapter of S. John's Gospel.

[l] *Printed Text,* p. 256.

rejoinder, the respected writer is asked, — (a) But when
there *does not* exist any such external evidence: what then?
Next, he is reminded (b) That whether there does, or does
not, it is at least certain that *not one* of those " proofs as to
style," &c., of which he speaks, has been able to stand
the test of strict examination. Not only is the precariousness of all such Criticism as has been brought to bear against
the genuineness of S. Mark xvi. 9—20 excessive, but the
supposed facts adduced in evidence have been found out to
be every one of them *mistakes;*—being either, (1) demonstrably without argumentative cogency of any kind;—or
else, (2) distinctly corroborative and confirmatory circumstances: indications that this part of the Gospel is indeed by
S. Mark,—*not* that it is probably the work of another hand.

And thus the formidable enumeration of twenty-seven
grounds of suspicion vanishes out of sight: fourteen of them
proving to be frivolous and nugatory ; and *thirteen*, more or
less clearly witnessing *in favour* of the section [m].

III. Of these thirteen expressions, some are even eloquent
in their witness. I am saying that it is impossible not to be
exceedingly struck by the discovery that this portion of the
Gospel contains (as I have explained already) so many indications of S. Mark's undoubted manner. Such is the reference to ἡ κτίσις (in ver. 15) :—the mention of ἀπιστία (in
ver. 14) :—the occurrence of the verb πορεύεσθαι (in ver. 10
and 12),—of the phrase ἐν τῷ ὀνόματί μου (in ver. 17),—and
of the phrase χεῖρας ἐπιτιθέναι ἐπί τινα (in ver. 18) :—of the
Evangelical term for our LORD's Ascension, viz. ἀνελήφθη
(in ver. 19) :—and lastly, of the compounds παρακολουθεῖν
and ἐπακολουθεῖν (in verses 17 and 20.)

To these Thirteen, will have to be added all those other
notes of identity of authorship,—such as they are,—which
result from recurring identity of phrase, and of which the
assailants of this portion of the Gospel have prudently said
nothing. Such are the following :—

(xiv.) 'Ανίστανai, for rising *from the dead;* which is one

---

[m] It will be found that of the former class (1) are the following :—Article iii:
vii: ix: x: xi: xii: xiii: xiv: xv: xxi: xxiv: xxv: xxvi: xxvii. Of the
latter (2) :—Art. i: ii: iv: v: vi: viii: xvi: xvii: xviii: xix: xx: xxii: xxiii.

of S. Mark's words. Taking into account the shortness of his Gospel, he has it thrice as often as S. Luke; *twelve times* as often as S. Matthew or S. John.

(xv.) The idiomatic expression πορευομένοις εἰς ἀγρόν, of which S. Matthew does not present a single specimen; but which occurs three times in the short Gospel of S. Mark[n], —of which ver. 12 is one.

(xvi.) The expression πρωΐ (in ver. 9,)—of which S. Mark avails himself six times: i.e. (if the length of the present Gospel be taken into account) almost five times as often as either S. Matthew or S. John,—S. Luke never using the word at all. In his first chapter (ver. 35), and here in his last (ver. 2), S. Mark uses λίαν in connexion with πρωΐ.

(xvii.) The *phrase* κηρύσσειν τὸ εὐαγγέλιον (in ver. 15) is another of S. Mark's phrases. Like S. Matthew, he employs it four times (i. 14: xiii. 10: xiv. 9: xvi. 15): but it occurs neither in S. Luke's nor in S. John's Gospel.

(xviii.) The same *words* singly are characteristic of his Gospel. Taking the length of their several narratives into account, S. Mark has the word κηρύσσειν more than twice as often as S. Matthew: three times as often as S. Luke.

(xix.) εὐαγγέλιον,—a word which occurs only in the first two Gospels,—is found twice as often in S. Mark's as in S. Matthew's Gospel: and if the respective length of their Gospels be considered, the proportion will be as three to one. It occurs, as above stated, in ver. 15.

(xx.) If such Critics as Dr. Davidson had been concerned to vindicate *the genuineness* of this section of the Gospel, we should have been assured that φανερουσθαι is another of S. Mark's words: by which they would have meant no more than this,—that though employed neither by S. Matthew nor by S. Luke it is used thrice by S. Mark,—being found twice in this section (verses 12, 14), as well as in ch. iv. 22.

(xxi.) They would have also pointed out that σκληροκαρδία is another of S. Mark's words: being employed neither by S. Luke nor by S. John,—by S. Matthew only once,—but by S. Mark on *two* occasions; of which ch. xvi. 14 is one.

---

[n] Ch. xiii. 16,—ὁ εἰς τὸν ἀγρὸν ὤν: and ch. xv. 21,—ἐρχόμενον ἀπ' ἀγροῦ,—an expression which S. Luke religiously reproduces in the corresponding place of his Gospel, viz. in ch. xxiii. 26.

(xxii.) In the same spirit, they would have bade us observe that πανταχοῦ (ver. 20)—unknown to S. Matthew and
S. John, and employed only once by S. Luke,—is *twice* used
by S. Mark; one instance occurring in the present section.

Nor would it have been altogether unfair if they had
added that the precisely similar word πανταχόθεν (or πάν-
τοθεν) is only found in this same Gospel,—viz. in ch. i. 45.

(xxiii.) They would further have insisted (and this time
with a greater show of reason) that the adverb καλῶς (which
is found in ver. 18) is another favorite word with S. Mark:
occurring as it does, (when the length of these several narratives is taken into account,) more than twice as often in
S. Mark's as in S. John's Gospel,—just three times as often
as in the Gospel of S. Matthew and S. Luke.

(xxiv.) A more interesting (because a more just) observation would have been that ἔχειν, in the sense of "to be," (as
in the phrase καλῶς ἔχειν, ver. 18,) is characteristic of
S. Mark. He has it oftener than any of the Evangelists,
viz. six times in all (ch. i. 32; 34: ii. 17: v. 23: vi. 55:
xvi. 18.) Taking the shortness of his Gospel into account,
he employs this idiom twice as often as S. Matthew;—three
times as often as S. John;—four times as often as S. Luke.

(xxv.) They would have told us further that ἄῤῥωστος is
another of S. Mark's favorite words: for that he has it *three*
times,—viz. in ch. vi. 5, 13, and here in ver. 18. S. Matthew
has it only once. S. Luke and S. John not at all.

(xxvi.) And we should have been certainly reminded by
them that the conjunction of. πενθοῦσι καὶ κλαίουσι (in
ver. 10) is characteristic of S. Mark,—who has κλαίοντας καὶ
ἀλαλάζοντας in ch. v. 38: θορυβεῖσθε καὶ κλαίετε in the
very next verse. As for πενθεῖν, it is one of the 123 words
common to S. Matthew and S. Mark, and peculiar to their
two Gospels.

(xxvii.) Lastly, "κατακρίνω (in ver. 16), instead of κρίνω,
is Mark's word, (comp. x. 33: xiv. 64)." The simple verb
which is used four times by S. Matthew, five times by
S. Luke, nineteen times by S. John, is never at all employed
by S. Mark: whereas the compound verb he has oftener in
proportion than S. Matthew,—more than twice as often as
either S. Luke or S. John.

Strange,—that there should be exactly "xxvii" notes of genuineness discoverable in these twelve verses, instead of "XXVII" grounds of suspicion!

But enough of all this. Here, we may with advantage review the progress hitherto made in this inquiry.

I claim to have demonstrated long since that all those imposing assertions respecting the "Style" and "Phraseology" of this section of the Gospel which were rehearsed at the outset [o],—are destitute of foundation. But from this discovery alone there results a settled conviction which it will be found difficult henceforth to disturb. A page of Scripture which has been able to endure so severe an ordeal of hostile inquiry, has been *proved* to be above suspicion. *That* character is rightly accounted *blameless* which comes out unsullied after Calumny has done her worst; done it systematically; done it with a will; done it for a hundred years.

But this is not an adequate statement of the facts of the case in respect of the conclusion of S. Mark's Gospel. Something *more* is certain than that the charges which have been so industriously brought against this portion of the Gospel are without foundation. It has been also proved that instead of there being discovered twenty-seven suspicious words and phrases scattered up and down these twelve verses of the Gospel, there actually exist exactly as many words and phrases which attest with more or less certainty that those verses are nothing else but the work of the Evangelist.

IV. And now it is high time to explain that though I have hitherto condescended to adopt the method of my opponents, I have only done so in order to shew that it proves fatal to *themselves.* I am, to say the truth, ashamed of what has last been written,—so untrustworthy do I deem the method which, (following the example of those who have preceded me in this inquiry,) I have hitherto pursued. The ".Concordance test,"—(for *that* is probably as apt and intelligible a designation as can be devised for the purely *mechanical* process whereby it is proposed by a certain school of Critics to judge of the authorship of Scripture,)—is about the coarsest as well as about the most delusive that could be

o See above, p. 146.

devised. By means of this clumsy and vulgar instrument, especially when applied, (as in the case before us,) without skill and discrimination, it would be just as easy to prove that *the first* twelve verses of S. Mark's Gospel are of a suspicious character as *the last* [P]. In truth, except in very skilful hands, it is no test at all, and can only mislead.

Thus, (in ver. 1,) we should be informed (i.) that "Mark nowhere uses the appellation JESUS CHRIST:" and (ii.) that "εὐαγγέλιον Ἰησοῦ Χριστοῦ" is "*Pauline.*"—We should be reminded (iii.) that this Evangelist nowhere introduces any of the Prophets by name, and that therefore the mention of "Isaiah[*]" (in ver. 2) is a suspicious circumstance :—(iv.) that a quotation from the Old Testament is "foreign to his manner,"—(for writers of this class would not hesitate to assume that S. Mark xv. 28 is no part of the Gospel ;)—and (v.) that the fact that here are quotations from *two* different prophets, betrays an unskilful hand.—(vi.) Because S. Mark three times calls Judæa by its usual name (Ἰουδαία, viz. in iii. 7: x. 1: xiii. 14), the *unique* designation, ἡ Ἰουδαία χώρα (in ver. 5) would be pronounced decisive against "the authorship of Mark."—(vii.) The same thing would be said of the *unique*

[P] The reader will be perhaps interested with the following passage in the pages of Professor Broadus already (p. 139 note g) alluded to :—" It occurred to me to examine the twelve just preceding verses, (xv. 44 to xvi. 8,) and by a curious coincidence, the words and expressions not elsewhere employed by Mark, footed up precisely the same number, seventeen. Those noticed are the following (text of Tregelles) :—ver. 44, τέθνηκεν (elsewhere ἀποθνήσκω) :—ver. 45, γνοὺς ἀπό, a construction found nowhere else in the New Testament : also ἐδωρήσατο and πτῶμα : ver. 46, ἐνείλησεν, λελατομημένον, πέτρας, προσεκύλισεν :—chap. xvi. ver. 1, διαγενομένου, and ἀρώματα : ver. 2, μιᾷ τῶν σαββάτων :—ver. 3, ἀποκυλίσει :—ver. 4, ἀνεκεκύλισται. Also, σφόδρα, (Mark's word is λίαν.) Ver. 5, ἐν τοῖς δεξιοῖς is a construction not found in Mark, or the other Gospels, though the word δεξιός occurs frequently :—ver. 8, εἶχεν, in this particular sense, not elsewhere in the New Testament : τρόμος.

"This list is perhaps not complete, for it was prepared in a few hours—about as much time, it may be said, without disrespect, as Fritsche and Meyer appear to have given to their collections of examples from the other passage. It is not proposed to discuss the list, though some of the instances are curious. It is not claimed that they are all important, but that they are all real. And as regards the single question of the *number* of peculiarities, they certainly form quite an offset to the number upon which Dean Alford has laid stress.'' —p. 361.   [*] Tischendorf, Tregelles, Alford.

expression, ἐν Ἰορδάνῃ ποταμῷ, which is found in ver. 5,—
seeing that this Evangelist three times designates Jordan
simply as Ἰορδάνης (i. 9 : iii. 8 : x. 1).—(viii.) *That* entire
expression in ver. 7 (*unique*, it must be confessed, in the Gospel,) οὗ οὐκ εἰμὶ ἱκανός—ὑποδημάτων αὐτοῦ, would be pronounced "abhorrent to the style of Mark."—(ix.) τὸ Πνεῦμα
twice, (viz. in ver. 10 and ver. 12) we should be told is never
used by the Evangelist absolutely for the HOLY GHOST : but
always τὸ Πνεῦμα τὸ Ἅγιον (as in ch. iii. 29 : xii. 36 :
xiii. 11).—(x.) The same would be said of οἱ Ἱεροσολυμῖται
(in ver. 5) for "the inhabitants of Jerusalem :" we should
be assured that S. Mark's phrase would rather be οἱ ἀπὸ
Ἱεροσολύμων,—as in ch. iii. 8 and 22.—And (xi.) the expression πιστεύειν ἐν τῷ εὐαγγελίῳ (ver. 15), we should be
informed "cannot be Mark's ;"—who either employs εἰς and
the accusative (as in ch. ix. 92), or else makes the verb take
a dative (as in ch. xi. 31 : xvi. 13, 14.)—We should also probably be told that the ten following words are all "unknown
to Mark :"—(xii.) τρίχες,—(xiii.) δερματίνη,—(xiv.) ὀσφύς,—
(xv.) ἀκρίδες,—(xvi.) μέλι,—(xvii.) ἄγριος, (six instances in
a single verse (ver. 6) : a highly suspicious circumstance !),—
(xviii.) κύπτειν,—(xix.) ἱμάς,—(xx.) ὑποδήματα, (all three
instances in ver. 7 !) — (xxi.) εὐδοκεῖν,—(xxii.) καὶ ἐγένετο . .
ἦλθεν (ver. 9),—unique in S. Mark !—(xxiii.) βαπτίζεσθαι
εἰς (ver 9), another unique phrase !—(xxiv.) οἱ οὐρανοί *twice*,
(viz. in verses 10, 11) yet elsewhere, when *S. Mark* speaks
of Heaven, (ch. vi. 41: vii. 34: viii. 11: xvi. 19) he always
uses the singular.—Lastly, (xxv.) the same sorry objection
which was brought against the "last twelve verses," (that
πάλιν, a favourite adverb with S. Mark, is not found there,)
is here even more conspicuous.

Turning away from all this,—(not, however, without an
apology for having lingered over such frivolous details so
long,)—I desire to point out that we have reverently to look
below the surface, if we would ascertain how far it is to be
presumed from internal considerations whether S. Mark was
indeed the author of this portion of his Gospel, or not.

V. We must devise, I say, some more delicate, more philosophical, more *real* test than the coarse, uncritical expedient

which has been hitherto considered of ascertaining by reference to the pages of a Greek Concordance whether a certain
word which is found in this section of the Gospel is, or is
not, used elsewhere by S. Mark. And I suppose it will be
generally allowed to be deserving of attention,—in fact, to
be a singularly corroborative circumstance,—that within the
narrow compass of these Twelve Verses we meet with *every
principal characteristic of S. Mark's manner :*—Thus,

(i.) Though he is the Author of the shortest of the Gospels, and though to all appearance he often merely reproduces what S. Matthew has said before him, or else anticipates something, which is afterwards delivered by S. Luke,—
it is surprising how often we are indebted to S. Mark for
precious pieces of information which we look for in vain
elsewhere. Now, this is a feature of the Evangelist's manner which is susceptible of memorable illustration from the
section before us.

How many and how considerable are the *new circumstances*
which S. Mark here delivers!—(1) That Mary Magdalene
was *the first* to behold the risen Saviour: (2) That it was
He who had cast out from her the "seven devils :" (3) *How
the men were engaged* to whom she brought her joyful message,—(4) who not only did not believe *her* story, but when
Cleopas and his companion declared what had happened to
themselves, "*neither believed they them.*" (5) The terms of
the Ministerial Commission, as set down in verses 15 and 16,
are unique. (6) The announcement of the "signs which
should follow them that believe" is even extraordinary.
Lastly, (7) this is the only place in the Gospel where *The
Session at the right Hand of God* is recorded. . . . So many,
and such precious incidents, showered into the Gospel Treasury at the last moment, and with such a lavish hand, must
needs have proceeded if not from an Apostle at least from
a companion of Apostles. O, if we had no other token to
go by, there could not be a reasonable doubt that this entire
section is by no other than S. Mark himself!

(ii.) A second striking characteristic of the second Evangelist is his love of picturesque, or at least of striking details,
—his proneness to introduce exceedingly minute particulars,

often of the profoundest significancy, and always of considerable interest. Not to look beyond the Twelve Verses (chap. i. 9—20) which were originally proposed for comparison,—We are reminded (*a*) that in describing our SAVIOUR's Baptism, it is only S. Mark who relates that "He came *from Nazareth*" to be baptized.—(*b*) In his highly elliptical account of our LORD's Temptation, it is only he who relates that "He was *with the wild beasts.*"—(*c*) In his description of the Call of the four Disciples, S. Mark alone it is who, (notwithstanding the close resemblance of his account to what is found in S. Matthew,) records that the father of S. James and S. John was left "in the ship *with the hired servants* q."—Now, of this characteristic, we have also within these twelve verses, at least four illustrations:—

(*a*) Note in ver. 10, that life-like touch which evidently proceeded from an eye-witness,—"πενθοῦσι καὶ κλαίουσι." S. Mark relates that when Mary conveyed to the Disciples the joyous tidings of the LORD's Resurrection, *she found them overwhelmed with sorrow,*—"mourning and weeping."

(*b*) Note also that the unbelief recorded in ver. 13 *is recorded only there.*

(*c*) Again. S. Mark not only says that as the two Disciples were "going into the country," (πορευόμενοι εἰς ἀγρόν ʳ, ver. 12,) JESUS also "went with them"—(συν-επορεύετο, as S. Luke relates;)—but that it was *as they actually "walked"* along (περιπατοῦσιν) that this manifestation took place.

(*d*) Among the marvellous predictions made concerning "them that believe;" what can be imagined more striking than the promise that they should "*take up serpents;*" and suffer no harm even if they should "*drink any deadly thing*"?

(iii) Next,—all have been struck, I suppose, with S. Mark's proneness to substitute some expression of his own for what he found in the Gospel of his predecessor S. Matthew: or, when he anticipates something which is afterwards met with in the Gospel of S. Luke, his aptness to deliver it in language entirely independent of the later Evangelist. I allude, for instance, to his substitution of ἐπιβαλὼν ἔκλαιε (xiv. 72)

ᑫ S. Mark i. 9: 14: 20.   ʳ The same word is found also in S. Luke's narrative of the same event, ch. xxiv. 13.

for S. Matthew's ἔκλαυσε πικρῶς (xxvi. 75) ;—and of ὁ τέκτων
(vi. 3) for ὁ τοῦ τέκτονος υἱός (S. Matth. xiii. 55).—The
" woman of Canaan" in S. Matthew's Gospel (γυνὴ Χανα-
ναία, ch. xv. 22), is called " a Greek, a Syrophenician by
nation" in S. Mark's (Ἑλληνὶς, Συροφοίνισσα τῷ γένει,
ch. vii. 26).—At the Baptism, "instead of the "*opened*"
heavens of S. Matthew (ἀνεῴχθησαν, ch. iii. 16) and S. Luke
(ἀνεῳχθῆναι, ch. iii. 22), we are presented by S. Mark with
the striking image of the heavens "*cleaving*" or " *being rent
asunder* " (σχιζομένους *, ch. i. 10).—What S. Matthew calls
τὰ ὅρια Μαγδαλά (ch. xv. 39), S. Mark designates as τὰ
μέρη Δαλμανουθά (ch. viii. 10.)—In place of S. Matthew's
ζύμη Σαδδουκαίων (ch. xvi. 6), S. Mark has ζύμη Ἡρώδου
(ch. viii. 15.)—In describing the visit to Jericho, for the δύο
τυφλοί of S. Matthew (ch. xx. 29), S. Mark gives υἱὸς Τιμαίου
Βαρτίμαιος ὁ τυφλὸς . . . . προσαιτῶν (ch. x. 46.)—For the
κλάδους of S. Matth. xxi. 8, S. Mark (ch. xi. 8) has στοι-
βάδας; and for the other's πρὶν ἀλέκτορα φωνῆσαι (xxvi.
34), he has πρὶν ἢ δίς (xiv. 30.)—It is so throughout.

Accordingly,—(as we have already more than once had occasion to remark,)—whereas the rest say only ἡ μία τῶν σαββάτων, S. Mark says πρώτη σαββάτου (in ver. 9).—Whereas
S. Luke (viii. 2) says ἀφ' ἧς δαιμόνια ἑπτὰ ἐξεληλύθει,—
S. Mark records that from her ἐκβεβλήκει ἑπτὰ δαιμόνια.—
Very different is the great ministerial Commission as set
down by S. Mark in ver. 15, 16, from what is found in
S. Matthew xxviii. 19, 20.—And whereas S. Luke says "*their
eyes were holden* that they should not know Him," S. Mark
says that " He appeared to them *in another form.*" . . . Is it
credible that any one fabricating a conclusion to S. Mark's
narrative after S. Luke's Gospel had appeared, would have
ventured so to paraphrase S. Luke's statement? And yet,
let the consistent truthfulness of either expression be carefully noted. *Both* are historically accurate, but they proceed from opposite points of view. Viewed on the heavenly
side, (GOD's side), the Disciples' "eyes" (of course) "*were*

---

* On which, Victor of Antioch (if inded it be he) finely remarks,—Σχίζονται
δὲ οἱ οὐρανοί, ἢ κατὰ Ματθαῖον ἀνοίγονται, ἵνα τοῖς ἀνθρώποις ἀποδοθῇ ἐξ οὐρανοῦ
ὁ ἁγιασμὸς, καὶ συναφθῇ τοῖς ἐπιγείοις τὰ οὐράνια.—(Cramer i. p. 271.)

holden :"—viewed on the earthly side, (Man's side), the risen SAVIOUR (no doubt) "*appeared in another form.*"

(iv.) Then further, S. Mark is observed to introduce many expressions into his Gospel which confirm the prevalent tradition that it was *at Rome* he wrote it; and that it was with an immediate view to *Latin* readers that it was published. Twelve such expressions were enumerated above (at p. 150-1); and such, it was also there shewn, most unmistakably is the phrase πρώτη σαββάτου in ver. 9.—It is simply incredible that any one but an Evangelist writing under the peculiar conditions traditionally assigned to S. Mark, would have hit upon such an expression as this,—the strict equivalent, to Latin ears, for ἡ μία σαββάτων, which has occurred just above, in ver. 2. Now this, it will be remembered, is one of the hacknied objections to the genuineness of this entire portion of the Gospel;—quite proof enough, if proof were needed, of the exceeding *improbability* which attaches to the phrase, in the judgment of those who have considered this question the most.

(v.) The last peculiarity of S. Mark to which I propose to invite attention is supplied by those expressions which connect his Gospel with S. Peter, and remind us of the constant traditional belief of the ancient Church that S. Mark was the companion of the chief of the Apostles.

That the second Gospel contains many such hints has often been pointed out; never more interestingly or more convincingly than by Townson[a] in a work which deserves to be in the hands of every student of Sacred Science. Instead of reproducing any of the familiar cases in order to illustrate my meaning, I will mention one which has perhaps never been mentioned in this connexion before.

(*a*) Reference is made to our LORD's sayings in S. Mark vii, and specially to what is found in ver. 19. *That* expression, "purging all meats" (καθαρίζων[t] πάντα τὰ βρώματα), does really seem to be no part of the Divine discourse; but the Evangelist's inspired comment on the SAVIOUR's words[u].

---

[a] Disc. v. Sect. ii.   [t] This appears to be the true reading.

[u] So Chrysostom :—ὁ δὲ Μάρκος φησὶν, ὅτι "καθαρίζων τὰ βρώματα," ταῦτα ἔλεγεν. [vii. 526 A].—He seems to have derived that remark from Origen [*in*

Our SAVIOUR (he explains) by that discourse of His—ipso facto—"*made all meats clean.*" How doubly striking a statement, when it is remembered that probably Simon Peter himself was the actual author of it;—the same who, on the house-top at Joppa, had been shewn in a vision that "GOD *had made clean*" (ὁ Θεὸς ἐκαθάρισε *) all His creatures !

(b) Now, let a few words spoken by the same S. Peter on a memorable occasion be considered :—" Wherefore of these men which have companied with us all the time that the LORD JESUS went in and out among us, *beginning from the Baptism of John*, unto that same day that *He was taken up* (ἀνελήφθη) from us, must one be ordained to be a witness with us of His Resurrection ʸ." Does not S. Peter thereby define the precise limits of our SAVIOUR's Ministry,—shewing it to have "begun" (ἀρξάμενος) "from the Baptism of John,"—and closed with the Day of our LORD's Ascension? And what else are those but the exact bounds of S. Mark's Gospel, — of which the ἀρχή (ch. i. 1) is signally declared to have been *the Baptism of John*,—and the utmost limit, the day when (as S. Mark says) " *He was taken up* (ἀνελήφθη) into Heaven,"—(ch. xvi. 19)?

(c) I will only further remind the reader, in connexion with the phrase, πάσῃ τῇ κτίσει, in ver. 15,—(concerning which, the reader is referred back to page 162-3,)—that both S. Peter and S. Mark (but no other of the sacred writers) conspire to use the expression ἀπ' ἀρχῆς κτίσεως ᶻ. S. Mark has besides κτίσεως ἧς ἔκτισε ὁ Θεός (ch. xiii. 19) ; while S. Peter alone styles the ALMIGHTY, from His work of Creation, ὁ κτίστης (1 S. Pet. iv. 19).

VI. But besides, and over and above such considerations

Matth. ed. Huet. i. 249 D] :—κατὰ τὸν Μάρκον ἔλεγε ταῦτα ὁ Σωτὴρ " καθαρίζων πάντα τὰ βρώματα."—From the same source, I suspect, Gregory Thaumaturgus (Origen's disciple), Bp. of Neocæsarea in Pontus, A.D. 261, [*Routh*, iii. 257] derived the following :—καὶ ὁ Σωτὴρ ὁ " πάντα καθαρίζων τὰ βρώματα" οὐ τὸ εἰσπορευόμενον, φησί, κοινοῖ τὸν ἄνθρωπον, ἀλλὰ τὸ ἐκπορευόμενον.—See, by all means, Field's most interesting *Adnotationes in Chrys.*, vol. iii. p. 112 . . . . . Ἐντεῦθεν (finely says Victor of Antioch) ὁ καινὸς ἄρχεται νόμος ὁ κατὰ τὸ πνεῦμα. (*Cramer* i. 335.)   ˣ Acts x. 15.

ʸ Acts i. 22, 23. Cf. ver. 2,—ἄχρι ἧς ἡμέρας . . . ἀνελήφθη.

ᶻ S. Mark x. 6 : xiii. 19.—2 S. Pet. iii. 4 (Cf. 1 S. Pet. ii. 13.)

as those which precede,—(some of which, I am aware, might be considerably evacuated of their cogency; while others, I am just as firmly convinced, will remain forcible witnesses of God's Truth to the end of Time,)—I hesitate not to avow my personal conviction that abundant and striking evidence is garnered up within the brief compass of these Twelve Verses that they are identical in respect of fabric with the rest of the Gospel; were clearly manufactured out of the same Divine materials,—wrought in the same heavenly loom.

It was even to have been expected, from what is found to have been universally the method in other parts of Scripture,—(for it was of course foreseen by ALMIGHTY GOD from the beginning that this portion of His Word would be, like its Divine Author, in these last days cavilled at, reviled, hated, rejected, denied,)—that the SPIRIT would not leave Himself without witness in this place. It was to have been anticipated, I say, that Eternal Wisdom would carefully—(I trust there is no irreverence in so speaking of GOD and His ways!)—would carefully make provision: meet the coming unbelief (as His Angel met Balaam) with a drawn sword: plant up and down throughout these Twelve Verses of the Gospel, sure indications of their Divine Original,—unmistakable notes of purpose and design,—mysterious traces and tokens of Himself; not visible indeed to the scornful and arrogant, the impatient and irreverent; yet clear as if written with a sunbeam to the patient and humble student, the man who "trembleth at GOD's Word[a]." Or, (if the Reader prefers the image,) the indications of a Divine Original to be met with in these verses shall be likened rather to those cryptic characters, invisible so long as they remain unsuspected, but which shine forth clear and strong when exposed to the Light or to the Heat; (Light and Heat, both emblems of Himself!) so that even he that gropeth in darkness must now see them, and admit that of a truth "the LORD is in this place" although he "knew it not!"

(i.) I propose then that in the first instance we compare the conclusion of S. Mark's Gospel with the beginning of it. We did this before, when our object was to ascertain whether

---

[a] Is. lxvi. 2.

the *Style* of S. Mark xvi. 9—20 be indeed as utterly dis-
cordant from that of the rest of the Gospel as is commonly
represented. We found, instead, the most striking resemblance[b]. We also instituted a brief comparison between
the two in order to discover whether the *Diction* of the one
might not possibly be found as suggestive of *verbal* doubts
as the diction of the other: and so we found it[c].—Let us
for the third time draw the two extremities of this precious
fabric into close proximity in order again to compare them.
Nothing I presume can be fairer than to elect that, once
more, our attention be chiefly directed to what is contained
within the twelve verses (ver. 9—20) of S. Mark's *first* chapter
which exactly correspond with the twelve verses of his *last*
chapter (ver. 9—20) which are the subject of the present
volume.

Now between these two sections of the Gospel, besides
(1) the obvious *verbal* resemblance, I detect (2) a singular
parallelism of *essential structure*. And this does not strike
me the less forcibly because nothing of the kind was to have
been *expected*.

(1.) On the verbal coincidences I do not propose to lay
much stress. Yet are they certainly not without argumentative weight and significancy. I allude to the following:—

(*a*) [βαπτίζων, βάπτισμα (i. 4)— καὶ ἐβαπτίζοντο (i. 5)—ἐβάπ- τισα, βαπτίσει (i. 8)]—καὶ ἐβ- απτίσθη (i. 9)	(*a*) βαπτισθείς (xvi. 16)
(*b*) [κηρύσσων, ἐκήρυσσε (i. 7)]	(*b*) ἐκήρυξαν (xvi. 20)
(*b* and *c*) κηρύσσων τὸ εὐαγγέλιον (i. 14)—[ἀρχὴ τοῦ εὐαγγελίου (i. 1)]	(*c*) κηρύξατε τὸ εὐαγγέλιον (xvi. 15)
(*c* and *d*) πιστεύετε ἐν τῷ εὐαγ- γελίῳ (i. 15)	(*d*) ἠπίστησαν (xvi. 11)—οὐδὲ ἐπίστευσαν (xvi. 13) — τὴν ἀπιστίαν, οὐκ ἐπίστευσαν (xvi. 14)—ὁ πιστεύσας, ὁ ἀπιστήσας (xvi. 16) — τοῖς πιστεύσασι (xvi. 17.)

Now this, to say the least, shews that there exists an
unmistakable relation of sympathy between the first page of

S. Mark's Gospel and the last. The same doctrinal phraseology *,—the same indications of Divine purpose,—the same prevailing cast of thought is observed to occur in both. (i.) *A Gospel* to be everywhere *preached;*—(ii.) *Faith,* to be of all required;—(iii.) *Baptism* to be universally administered; ("one LORD, one Faith, one Baptism:")—Is not *this* the theme of the beginning of S. Mark's Gospel as well as of the end of it? Surely it is as if on comparing the two extremities of a chain, with a view to ascertaining whether the fabric be identical or not, it were discovered that those extremities are even meant *to clasp !*

(2.) But the *essential* parallelism between S. Mark xvi. 9 —20 and S. Mark i. 9—20 is a profounder phenomenon and deserves even more attention. I proceed to set down side by side, as before, what ought to require neither comment nor explanation of mine. Thus we find,—

(ᴀ) *in ch.* i. 9 *to* 11:—Our LORD's Manifestation to the World (ἐπιφανεία) on His "coming up (ἀναβαίνων) out of the water" of Jordan: (having been "buried by Baptism," as the Apostle speaks:) when the Voice from Heaven proclaimed,—"Thou art My beloved SON in whom I am well pleased."

(ᴀ) *in ch.* xvi. 9 *to* 11:—Our LORD's appearance to Mary Magdalene (ἐφάνη) after His Resurrection (ἀναστάς) from Death: (of which GOD had said, "Thou art My SON, this day have I begotten Thee."

———— 12 *to* 14:—Two other Manifestations (ἐφανερώθη) to Disciples.

(ʙ) ———— 12, 13:—Christ's victory over Satan; (whereby is fulfilled the promise "Thou shalt tread upon the lion and adder: the young lion and the dragon shalt Thou trample under feet.")

(ʙ) ———— 17, 18:—CHRIST's promise that "they that believe" "shall cast out devils" and "shall take up serpents:" (as [in S. Luke x. 19] He had given the Seventy "power to tread on serpents and scorpions, and over all the power of the Enemy.")

[(c) ———— 8:—The Pentecostal Gift foretold: "He shall baptize you with the HOLY GHOST."]

(c) ———— 17:— The chief Pentecostal Gift specified: "They shall speak with new tongues."

* My attention was first drawn to this by my friend, the Rev. W. Kay, D.D.

(D) *in ch.* i. 14, 15 :— CHRIST " comes into Galilee, preaching the Gospel . . . . and saying . . . . Repent ye, and believe the Gospel."

(E) ———— 15 : His announcement, that "The time is fulfilled, and the Kingdom of GOD is at hand."

(F) ———— 16 *to* 20 :—The four Apostles' Call to the Ministry : (which [S. Luke v. 8, 9] is miraculously attested.)

(D) *in ch.* xvi. 15, 16 :—He commands His Apostles to " go into all the world and preach the Gospel to every creature. He that believeth and is baptized shall be saved."

(E) ———— 19 :—S. Mark's record concerning Him, that " He was received up into Heaven, and sat on the right hand of GOD :" (where He must reign till He hath put all enemies under His feet.")

(F) ———— 20:—The Apostles' Ministry, which is everywhere miraculously attested, —"The LORD working with them, and confirming the word by the signs that followed."

It is surely not an unmeaning circumstance, a mere accident, that the Evangelist should at the very outset and at the very conclusion of his Gospel, so express himself! If, however, it should seem to the Reader a mere matter of course, a phenomenon without interest or significancy,—nothing which I could add would probably bring him to a different mind.

(3.) Then, further : when I scrutinize attentively the two portions of Scripture thus proposed for critical survey, I am not a little struck by the discovery that the VIth Article of the ancient Creed of Jerusalem (A.D. 348) is found in the one : the Xth Article, in the other [d]. If it be a purely for-

---

[d] The Creed itself, ("ex variis Cyrillianarum Catacheseon locis collectum,") may be seen at p. 84 of De Touttée's ed. of Cyril. Let the following be compared :—

ἀνελήφθη εἰς τὸν οὐρανόν, καὶ ἐκάθισεν ἐκ δεξιῶν τοῦ Θεοῦ (ch. xvi. 19.)
'ΑΝΕΛΘΌΝΤΑ ΕἸΣ ΤΟῪΣ ΟὐΡΑΝΟῪΣ, ΚΑῚ ΚΑΘΊΣΑΝΤΑ 'ΕΚ ΔΕΞΙῶΝ ΤΟῪ ΠΑΤΡΌΣ (ART. VI.) This may be seen *in situ* at p. 224 o of Cyril.

βάπτισμα μετανοίας εἰς ἄφεσιν ἁμαρτιῶν (ch. i. 4.)
ΒΆΠΤΙΣΜΑ ΜΕΤΑΝΟΊΑΣ ΕἸΣ ᾽ΆΦΕΣΙΝ ᾽ΑΜΑΡΤΙῶΝ (ART. X.) This may be seen at p. 295 o of Cyril.

The point will be most intelligently and instructively studied in Professor Heurtley's little work *De Fide et Symbolo*, 1869, p. 9.

tuitous circumstance, that two cardinal verities like these,—
(viz. "*He ascended into Heaven, and sat down at the Right
Hand of God*,"—and "*One Baptism for the Remission of sins*,")
should be found at either extremity of one short Gospel,—
I will but point out that it is certainly one of a very remarkable series of fortuitous circumstances.—But in the
thing to be mentioned next, there neither is, nor can be,
any talk of fortuitousness at all.

(4.) Allusion is made to the diversity of Name whereby
the Son of Man is indicated in these two several places of
the Gospel; which constitutes a most Divine circumstance,
and is profoundly significant. He who in *the first* verse
(S. Mark i. 1) was designated by the joint title "'Ιησοῦς"
and "Χριστός,"—here, in the last two verses (S. Mark xvi.
19, 20) is styled for the first and for the last time, "'Ο ΚΎΡΙΟΣ"
—the LORD*.

And why? Because He who at His Circumcision was
named "JESUS," (a Name which was given Him from *His
Birth*, yea, and before His Birth); He who at His Baptism
became "the CHRIST," (a Title which belonged to *His Office*,
and which betokens His sacred *Unction*) ;—the same, on the
occasion of His Ascension into Heaven and Session at the
Right Hand of GOD,—when (as we know) "all power had
been given unto Him in Heaven and in Earth" (S. Matth.
xxviii. 18),—is designated by His Name of *Dominion ;* "the
LORD" JEHOVAH . . . "Magnifica et opportuna appellatio !"
—as Bengel well remarks.

But I take leave to point out that all this is what never
either would or could have entered into the mind of a fabricator of a conclusion to S. Mark's unfinished Gospel. No
inventor of a supplement, I say, *could* have planted his foot
in this way in exactly the right place. The proof of my
assertion is twofold :—

(*a*) First, because the present indication that the HOLY
GHOST was indeed the Author of these last Twelve Verses
is even appealed to by Dr. Davidson and his School, *as
a proof of a spurious original.* Verily, such Critics do not
recognise the token of the Divine Finger even when they
see it !

* See above,—p. 165-6.

(*b*) Next, as a matter of fact, we *have* a spurious Supplement to the Gospel,—the same which was exhibited above at p. 123-4 ; and which may here be with advantage reproduced in its Latin form :—" Omnia autem quaecumque praecepta erant illis qui cum Petro erant, breviter exposuerunt. Post haec et ipse IESUS adparuit, et ab oriente usque in occidentem misit per illos sanctam et incorruptam praedicationem salutis aeternae. Amen [l]."—Another apocryphal termination is found in certain copies of the Thebaic version. It occupies the place of ver. 20, and is as follows :—" Exeuntes terni in quatuor climata caeli praedicarunt Evangelium in mundo toto, CHRISTO operante cum iis in verbo confirmationem cum signis sequentibus eos et miraculis. Atque hoc modo cognitum est regnum Dei in terra tota et in mundo toto Israelis in testimonium gentium omnium harum quae exsistunt ab oriente ad occasum." It will be seen that the Title of *Dominion* (ὁ Κύριος—the LORD) is found in neither of these fabricated passages; but the Names of *Nativity* and of *Baptism* ('Iησοῦς and Χριστός – JESUS and CHRIST) occur instead.

(ii.) Then further : — It is an extraordinary note of genuineness that such a vast number of minute but important facts should be found accumulated within the narrow compass of these twelve verses ; and should be met with *nowhere else.* The writer,—supposing that he had only S. Matthew's Gospel before him,—traverses (except in one single instance) *wholly new ground ;* moves forward with unmistakable boldness and a rare sense of security ; and wherever he plants his foot, it is to enrich the soil with fertility and beauty. But on the supposition that he wrote after S. Luke's and S. John's Gospel had appeared,—the marvel becomes increased an hundred-fold : for how then does it come to pass that he evidently draws his information from quite independent sources? is not bound by any of their statements? even seems *purposely* to break away from their guidance, and to adventure some extraordinary state-

---

[l] *Cod. Bobbiensis* (k) : which however for "illis" has "et :" for "Petro," "puero:" and for "occidentem," "orientem." It also repeats "usque." I have ventured to alter "ab orientem" into "ab oriente."—Compare what is found in the Philoxenian margin, as given by White and Adler.

ment of his own,—which nevertheless carries the true Gospel savour with it; and is felt to be authentic from the very circumstance that no one would have ever dared to invent such a detail and put it forth on his own responsibility?

(iii.) Second to no indication that this entire section of the Gospel has a Divine original, I hold to be a famous expression which (like πρώτη σαββάτου) has occasioned general offence: I mean, the designation of Mary Magdalene as one "out of whom" the LORD "had cast seven devils;" and *that*, in immediate connexion with the record of her august privilege of being the first of the Human Race to behold His risen form.   There is such profound Gospel significancy, — such sublime improbability, — such exquisite pathos in this record,—that I would defy any fabricator, be he who he might, to have achieved it.   This has been to some extent pointed out already [g].

(iv.) It has also been pointed out, (but the circumstance must be by all means here insisted upon afresh,) that the designation (found in ver. 10) of the little company of our LORD's followers,—" τοῖς μετ᾽ αὐτοῦ γενομένοις,"— is another rare note of veracious origin.   No one but S. Mark,—or just such an one as he,— would or could have so accurately designated the little band of Christian men and women who, unconscious of their bliss, were "mourning and weeping" till after sunrise on the first Easter Day.   The reader is reminded of what has been already offered on this subject, at p. 155-6.

(v.) I venture further to point out that no writer but S. Mark, (or such an one as he [h]), would have familiarly designated the Apostolic body as " αὐτοῖς τοῖς ἕνδεκα," in ver. 14. The phrase οἱ δώδεκα, he uses in proportion *far* oftener than any other two of the Evangelists [i].   And it is evident that the phrase οἱ ἕνδεκα soon became an equally recognised designation of the Apostolic body,—"from which Judas by transgression fell."   Its familiar introduction into this place by the second Evangelist is exactly what one might have

[g] See above (Art. II.) p. 152-3.

[h] Consider S. Luke xxiv. 9: 33. Acts ii. 14.

[i] S. Matth. xxvi. 14, 20, 47.—S. Mark iv. 10 : vi. 7 : ix. 35 : x. 32 : xi. 11 : xiv. 10, 17, 20, 43.—S. Luke viii. 1: ix. 1, 12: xviii. 31: xxii. 3, 47.— S. John vi. 37, 70, 71 : xx. 24.

looked for, or at least what one is fully prepared to meet with, *in him.*

(vi.) I will close this enumeration by calling attention to an unobtrusive and unobserved verb in the last of these verses which (I venture to say) it would never have entered into the mind of any ordinary writer to employ in that particular place. I allude to the familiar word ἐξελθόντες.

The precise meaning of the expression,—depending on the known force of the preposition with which the verb is compounded,—can scarcely be missed by any one who, on the one hand, is familiar with the Evangelical method; on the other, is sufficiently acquainted with the Gospel History. Reference is certainly made to the final departure of the Apostolic body *out of the city of Jerusalem* [k]. And tacitly, beyond a question, there is herein contained a re-collection of our SAVIOUR's command to His Apostles, twice expressly recorded by S. Luke, " that they should *not depart from Jerusalem*, but wait for the promise of the FATHER." "Behold," (said He,) " I send the promise of My FATHER upon you: but *tarry ye in the city of Jerusalem*, until ye be endued with power from on high [l]." ... After many days "*they went forth,*" or " *out.*" S. Mark, (or perhaps it is rather S. Peter,) expressly says so,—ἐξελθόντες. Aye, and *that* was a memorable " outgoing," truly ! What else was its purpose but the evangelization of the World ?

VII. Let this suffice, then, concerning the evidence de-rived from Internal considerations. But lest it should here-after be reckoned as an omission, and imputed to me as a fault, that I have said nothing about the alleged *Incon-sistency* of certain statements contained in these "Twelve Verses" with the larger notices contained in the parallel narratives of S. Luke and S. John, — I proceed briefly to explain *why* I am silent on this head.

1. I cannot see for whom I should be writing; in other

---

[k] Compare S. Luke xxii. 39; and especially S. John xviii. 1,—where the moment of departure *from the city* is marked: (for observe, they had left the house and the upper chamber at ch. xiv. 31). See also ch. xix. 17,—where the going *without the gate* is indicated : (for ἔξω τῆς πύλης ἔπαθε [Heb. xiii. 12.]) So Matth. xxvii. 32. Consider S. Luke xxi. 37.

[l] S. Luke xxiv. 49. Acts i. 4.

words,—what I should propose to myself as the end to be attained by what I wrote. For,

2. What would be gained by demonstrating,—(as I am of course prepared to do,)—that there is really *no inconsistency whatever* between anything which S. Mark here says, and what the other Evangelists deliver? I should have proved that,—(assuming the *other* Evangelical narratives to be authentic, i.e. historically true,)—the narrative before us cannot be objected to on the score of its not being authentic also. But *by whom* is such proof required?

(*a*) Not by the men who insist that errors are occasionally to be met with in the Evangelical narratives. In *their* estimation, *the genuineness of an inspired writing* is a thing not in the least degree rendered suspicious by the erroneousness of its statements. According to them, the narrative may exhibit inaccuracies and inconsistencies, and may yet be the work of S. Mark. If the inconsistencies be but "trifling," and the inaccuracies "minute,"—these "sound Theologians," (for so they style themselves [m],) "have no dread whatever of acknowledging" their existence. Be it so. Then would it be a gratuitous task to set about convincing *them* that no inconsistency, no inaccuracy is discoverable within the compass of these Twelve concluding Verses.

(*b*) But neither is such proof required by faithful Readers; who, for want of the requisite Scientific knowledge, are unable to discern the perfect Harmony of the Evangelical narratives in this place. It is only one of many places where a primâ facie discrepancy, though it does not fail to strike, — yet (happily) altogether fails to distress them. Consciously or unconsciously, such readers reason with themselves somewhat as follows :—"GOD's Word, like all GOD's other Works, (and I am taught to regard GOD's Word as a very masterpiece of creative skill;)—the blessed Gospel, I say, is *full* of difficulties. And yet those difficulties are observed invariably to disappear under competent investigation. Can I seriously doubt that if sufficient critical skill were brought to bear on the highly elliptical portion of narrative contained in these Twelve Verses, it would present no

---

[m] See above, p. 2.

exception to a rule which is observed to be else universal; and that any apparent inconsistency between S. Mark's statements in this place, and those of S. Luke and S. John, would also be found to be imaginary only?"

This then is the reason why I abstain from entering upon a prolonged Inquiry, which would in fact necessitate a discussion of *the Principles of Gospel Harmony,*—for which the present would clearly not be the proper place.

VIII. Let it suffice that, in the foregoing pages,—

1. I have shewn that the supposed argument from "Style," (in itself a highly fallacious test,) disappears under investigation.

It has been proved (pp. 142-5) that, on the contrary, the style of S. Mark xvi. 9—20 is exceedingly like the style of S. Mark i. 9—20; and therefore, that *it is rendered probable by the Style* that the Author of the beginning of this Gospel was also the Author of the end of it.

2. I have further shewn that the supposed argument from "Phraseology,"—(in itself, a most unsatisfactory test; and as it has been applied to the matter in hand, a very coarse and clumsy one;)—breaks down hopelessly under severe analysis.

Instead of there being twenty-seven suspicious circumstances in the Phraseology of these Twelve Verses, it has been proved (pp. 170-3) that in twenty-seven particulars there emerge *corroborative considerations.*

3. Lastly, I have shewn that a loftier method of Criticism is at hand; and that, tested by this truer, more judicious, and more philosophical standard, *a presumption* of the highest order is created *that these Verses must needs be the work of S. Mark.*

CHAPTER X.

THE TESTIMONY OF THE LECTIONARIES SHEWN TO BE
ABSOLUTELY DECISIVE AS TO THE GENUINENESS OF
THESE VERSES.

The Lectionary of the East shewn to be a work of extraordinary an-
tiquity (p. 195).—*Proved to be older than any extant MS. of the*
Gospels, by an appeal to the Fathers (p. 198).—*In this Lectionary,*
(and also in the Lectionary of the West,) the last Twelve Verses of
S. Mark's Gospel have, from the first, occupied a most conspicuous,
as well as most honourable place, (p. 204.)—*Now, this becomes the*
testimony of ante-Nicene Christendom in their favour (p. 209.)

I HAVE reserved for the last the testimony of THE LEC-
TIONARIES, which has been hitherto all but entirely overlooked [a];—passed by without so much as a word of comment,
by those who have preceded me in this inquiry. Yet is it,
when rightly understood, altogether decisive of the question
at issue. And why? Because it is not the testimony rendered by a solitary Father or by a solitary MS.; no, nor
even the testimony yielded by a single Church, or by
a single family of MSS. But it is *the united testimony of all*
the Churches. It is therefore the evidence borne by a 'goodly
fellowship of Prophets,' a 'noble army of Martyrs' indeed; as well as by *MSS. innumerable which have long since*
perished, but which must of necessity once have been. And
so, it comes to us like the voice of many waters: dates, (as
I shall shew by-and-by,) from a period of altogether immemorial antiquity: is endorsed by the sanction of all the succeeding ages: admits of neither doubt nor evasion. This
subject, in order that it may be intelligibly handled, will be

---

[a] The one memorable exception, which I have only lately met with, is supplied by the following remark of the thoughtful and accurate Matthaei, made
in a place where it was almost safe to escape attention; viz. in a footnote
at the very end of his *Nov. Test.* (ed. 1803), vol. i. p. 748.—" Haec lectio in
Evangeliariis et Synaxariis omnibus ter notatur tribus maxime notabilibus
temporibus. Secundum ordinem temporum Ecclesiae Graecae primo legitur
κυριακῇ τῶν μυροφόρων, εἰς τὸν ὄρθρον. Secundo, τῷ ὄρθρῳ τῆς ἀναλήψεως.
Tertio, ut ἑωθινὸν ἀναστάσιμον γ'. De hoc loco ergo vetustissimis temporibus
nullo modo dubitavit Ecclesia."—Matthaei had slightly anticipated this in
his ed. of 1788, vol. ii. 267.

most conveniently approached by some remarks which shall
rehearse the matter from the beginning.

The Christian Church succeeded to the Jewish. The
younger society inherited the traditions of the elder, not less
as a measure of necessity than as a matter of right; and by
a kind of sacred instinct conformed itself from the very beginning in countless particulars to its divinely-appointed
model. The same general Order of Service went on unbroken,—conducted by a Priesthood whose spiritual succession was at least as jealously guarded as had been the natural
descent from Aaron in the Church of the Circumcision [b]. It
was found that "the Sacraments of the Jews are [but] types
of ours [c]." Still were David's Psalms antiphonally recited,
and the voices of "Moses and the Prophets" were heard in
the sacred assemblies of GOD's people "every Sabbath day."
Canticle succeeded to Canticle; while many a Versicle simply
held its ground. The congenial utterances of the chosen
race passed readily into the service of the family of the re-
deemed. Unconsciously perhaps, the very method of the
one became adopted by the other: as, for example, the method of beginning a festival from the "Eve" of the preceding Day. The Synagogue-worship became transfigured;
but it did not part with one of its characteristic features.
Above all, the same three great Festivals were still retained
which declare "the rock whence we are hewn and the hole
of the pit whence we are digged:" only was it made a question, a controversy rather, whether Easter should or should
not be celebrated *with the Jews* [d].

But it is the faithful handing on to the Christian commu-
nity of *the Lectionary practice* of the Synagogue to which the
reader's attention is now exclusively invited. That the Christian Church inherited from the Jewish the practice of reading a first and a second Lesson in its public assemblies, is
demonstrable. What the Synagogue practice was in the
time of the Apostles is known from Acts xiii. 15, 27. Justin

---

[b] Τὰς τῶν ἱερῶν ἀποστόλων διαδοχάς,—are *the first words* of the Ecclesiastical History of Eusebius.

[c] See the heading of 1 Cor. x. in our Authorized Version.

[d] See Bingham's *Origines*, Book xx. ch. v. §§ 2, 3, 4.

Martyr, (A.D. 150) describes the Christian practice in his
time as precisely similar[e]: only that for "the Law," there
is found to have been at once substituted "the Gospel." He
speaks of the writings of "*the Apostles*" and of "the Prophets." Chrysostom has the same expression (for the two
Lessons) in one of his Homilies[f]. Cassian (A.D. 400) says that
in Egypt, after the Twelve Prayers at Vespers and at Matins,
two Lessons were read, one out of the Old Testament and
the other out of the New. But *on Saturdays and Sundays,*
and the fifty days of Pentecost, both Lessons were from the
New Testament,—one from the Epistles or the Acts of the
Apostles; the other, from the Gospels[g]. Our own actual
practice seems to bear a striking resemblance to that of the
Christian Church at the earliest period: for we hear of (1)
"Moses and the Prophets," (which will have been the car-
rying on of the old synagogue-method, represented by our
first and second Lesson,)—(2) a lesson out of the "Epistles
or Acts," together with a lesson out of the "Gospels[h]."
It is, in fact, universally received that the Eastern Church
has, from a period of even Apostolic antiquity, enjoyed a Lectionary,—or established system of Scripture lessons,—of her
own. In its conception, this Lectionary is discovered to
have been fashioned (as was natural) upon the model of the
Lectionary of GOD's ancient people, the Jews: for it commences, as theirs did, *in the autumn,* (in September[i]); and

[e] Τῇ τοῦ ἡλίου λεγομένῃ ἡμέρᾳ, πάντων κατὰ πόλεις ἢ ἀγροὺς μενόντων ἐπὶ τὸ
αὐτὸ συνέλευσις γίνεται, καὶ τὰ ἀπομνημονεύματα τῶν ἀποστόλων, ἢ τὰ συγγράμ-
ματα τῶν προφητῶν ἀναγινώσκεται, μέχρις ἐγχωρεῖ. Then came the Sermon,—
then, all stood and prayed,—then followed Holy Communion.—*Apol.* i. c. 67,
(*ed.* Otto, i. 158.)

[f] ὁ μάτην ἐνταῦθα εἰσελθὼν, εἰπὲ, τίς προφήτης, ποῖος ἀπόστολος ἡμῖν σήμερον
διελέχθη, καὶ περὶ τίνων ;—(*Opp.* ix. p. 697 E. Field's text.)

[g] Cassian writes,—"Venerabilis Patrum senatus .... decrevit hunc numerum [*sc.* duodecim Orationum] tam in Vespertinis quam in Nocturnis conven-
ticulis custodiri; quibus lectiones geminas adjungentes, id est, unam Veteris
et aliam Novi Testamenti .... In die vero Sabbati vel Dominico utrasque
de Novo recitant Testamento; id est, unam de Apostolo vel Actibus Apos-
tolorum, et aliam de Evangeliis. Quod etiam totis Quinquagesimae diebus
faciunt hi, quibus lectio curae est, seu memoria Scripturarum."—*Instit.* lib. ii.
c. 6. (*ed.* 1733, p. 18.)

[h] *Constitutiones Apostolicae,* lib. ii. c. 57, 59: v. 19: viii. 5.

[i] See Scrivener's *Introduction,* p. 74, and the reff. in note (k) overleaf.

prescribes two immovable "Lections" for every *Saturday* (as well as for every Sunday) in the year: differing chiefly in this,—that the prominent place which had been hitherto assigned to "the Law and the Prophets [k]," was henceforth enjoyed by the Gospels and the Apostolic writings. "Saturday-Sunday" lections—(σαββατοκυριακαί, for so these Lections were called,)—retain their place in the "Synaxarium" of the East to the present hour. It seems also a singular note of antiquity that the Sabbath and the Sunday succeeding it do as it were cohere, and bear one appellation; so that the week takes its name—*not* from the Sunday with which it commences [l], but—from the Sabbath-and-Sunday with which *it concludes.* To mention only one out of a hundred minute traits of identity which the public Service of the sanctuary retained:—Easter Eve, which from the earliest period to this day has been called "μέγα σάββατον [m]," is discovered to have borne the self-same appellation in the Church of the Circumcision [n].—If I do not enter more minutely into the structure of the Oriental Lectionary,—(some will perhaps think I have said too much, but the interest of the subject ought to be a sufficient apology,)—it is because further details would be irrelevant to my present purpose; which is only to call attention to the three following facts:

(I.) That the practice in the Christian Church of reading publicly before the congregation certain fixed portions of Holy Writ, according to an established and generally received rule, must have existed from a period long anterior to the date of any known Greek copy of the New Testament Scriptures.

(II.) That although there happens to be extant neither "Synaxarium," (i.e. Table of Proper Lessons of the Greek

---

[k] English readers may be referred to Horne's *Introduction*, &c. (*ed.* 1856.) vol. iii. p. 281-2. The learned reader is perhaps aware of the importance of the preface to Van der Hooght's *Hebrew Bible*, (*ed.* 1705) § 35: in connexion with which, see vol. ii. p. 352 *b.*

[l] Thus, the κυριακή τῆς τυροφάγου is "Quinquagesima Sunday;" but *the week* of "the cheese-eater" is the week *previous.*

[m] See Suicer's *Thesaurus*, vol. ii. 920.

[n] "Apud Rabbinos, שַׁבָּת הַגָּדוֹל‎ *Sabbathum Magnum.* Sic vocatur Sabbathum proximum ante Pascha."—Buxtorf, *Lexicon Talmud.* p. 2323.

Church), nor " Evangelistarium," (i.e. Book containing the Ecclesiastical Lections *in extenso*), of higher antiquity than the viii[th] century,—yet that the scheme itself, as exhibited by those monuments,—certainly in every essential particular,—is older than any known Greek MS. which contains it, by *at least* four, in fact by full *five* hundred years.

(III.) Lastly,—That in the said Lectionaries of the Greek and of the Syrian Churches, the twelve concluding verses of S. Mark which are the subject of discussion throughout the present pages are observed *invariably* to occupy the same singularly conspicuous, as well as most honourable place.

I. The first of the foregoing propositions is an established fact. It is at least quite certain that in the iv[th] century (if not long before) there existed a known Lectionary system, alike in the Church of the East and of the West. Cyril of Jerusalem (A.D. 348,) having to speak about our LORD's Ascension, remarks that by a providential coincidence, on the previous day, which was Sunday, the event had formed the subject of the appointed lessons[o]; and that he had availed himself of the occasion to discourse largely on the subject.— Chrysostom, preaching at Antioch, makes it plain that, in

---

[o] Καὶ ἡ μὲν ἀκολουθία τῆς διδασκαλίας [cf. Cyril, p. 4, lines 16-7] τῆς πίστεως προέτρεπεν εἰπεῖν καὶ τὰ περὶ τῆς Ἀναλήψεως· ἀλλ' ἡ τοῦ Θεοῦ χάρις ᾠκονόμησε πληρέστατά σε ἀκοῦσαι, κατὰ τὴν ἡμετέραν ἀσθένειαν, τῇ χθὲς ἡμέρᾳ κατὰ τὴν Κυριακήν· κατ' οἰκονομίαν τῆς θείας χάριτος, ἐν τῇ Συνάξει τῆς τῶν ἀναγνωσμάτων ἀκολουθίας τὰ περὶ τῆς εἰς οὐρανοὺς ἀνόδου τοῦ Σωτῆρος ἡμῶν περιεχούσης· ἐλέγετο δὲ τὰ λεγόμενα, μάλιστα μὲν διὰ πάντας, καὶ διὰ τὸ τῶν πιστῶν ὁμοῦ πλῆθος· ἐξαιρέτως δὲ διά σε· ζητεῖται δὲ εἰ προσέσχες τοῖς λεγομένοις. Οἶδας γὰρ ὅτι ἡ ἀκολουθία τῆς Πίστεως διδάσκει σε πιστεύειν εἰς ΤΟΝ ΑΝΑΣΤΑΝΤΑ ΤΗ ΤΡΙΤΗ ΗΜΕΡΑ ΚΑΙ ΑΝΕΛΘΟΝΤΑ ΕΙΣ ΤΟΥΣ ΟΥΡΑΝΟΥΣ, ΚΑΙ ΚΑΘΙΣΑΝΤΑ ᾽ΕΚ ΔΕΞΙΩΝ ΤΟΥ ΠΑΤΡΟΣ—μάλιστα μὲν οὖν μνημονεύειν σε νομίζω τῆς ἐξηγήσεως. πλὴν ἐν παραδρομῇ καὶ νῦν ὑπομιμνήσκω σε τῶν εἰρημένων. (Cyril. Hier. *Cat.* xiv. c. 24. *Opp.* p. 217 C, D.)—Of that Sermon of his, Cyril again and again reminds his auditory. Μέμνησο δὲ καὶ τῶν εἰρημένων μοι πολλάκις περὶ τοῦ, ἐκ δεξιῶν τοῦ Πατρὸς καθέζεσθαι τὸν Υἱόν,—he says, *ibid.* p. 219 B. A little lower down, Νῦν δὲ ὑμᾶς ὑπομνηστέον ὀλίγων, τῶν ἐκ πολλῶν εἰρημένων περὶ τοῦ, ἐκ δεξιῶν τοῦ Πατρὸς καθέζεσθαι τὸν Υἱόν.—*Ibid.* D.

From this it becomes plain *why Cyril nowhere quotes S. Mark* xvi. 19,—or *S. Luke* xxiv. 51,—or *Acts* i. 9. He must needs have enlarged upon those three *inevitable* places of Scripture, the day before.

the latter part of the iv[th] century, the order of the lessons
which were publicly read in the Church *on Saturdays and
Sundays* [p] was familiarly known to the congregation : for he
invites them to sit down, and study attentively beforehand,
at home, the Sections (περικοπάς) of the Gospel which they
were about to hear in Church [q].—Augustine is express in
recording that in his time proper lessons were appointed for
Festival days [r]; and that an innovation which he had attempted on Good Friday had given general offence [s].—Now
by these few notices, to look no further, it is rendered certain that a Lectionary system of *some* sort must have been
in existence at a period long anterior to the date of any copy
of the New Testament Scriptures extant. I shall shew
by-and-by that the fact is established by the Codices (B,
ℵ, A, C, D) themselves.

But we may go back further yet ; for not only Eusebius,
but Origen and Clemens Alexandrinus, by their habitual
use of the technical term for an Ecclesiastical Lection (περικοπή, ἀνάγνωσις, ἀνάγνωσμα,) remind us that the Lectionary practice of the East was already established in
their days [t].

II. The Oriental Lectionary consists of " Synaxarion"
and "Eclogadion," (or Tables of Proper Lessons from the
Gospels and Apostolic writings daily throughout the year ;)

[p] See above, p. 193 and p. 194.

[q] Ὥστε δὲ εὐμαθέστερον γενέσθαι τὸν λόγον, δεόμεθα καὶ παρακαλοῦμεν, ὅπερ
καὶ ἐπὶ τῶν ἄλλων γραφῶν πεποιήκαμεν, προλαμβάνειν, τὴν περικοπὴν τῆς
γραφῆς ἣν ἂν μέλλωμεν ἐξηνεῖσθαι. — In Matth. *Hom.* i. (*Opp.* vii. 13 B.)—
Κατὰ μίαν σαββάτων, ἢ καὶ κατὰ σάββατον, τὴν μέλλουσαν ἐν ὑμῖν ἀναγνωσθήσεσθαι
τῶν εὐαγγελίων περικοπὴν, ταύτην πρὸ τούτων τῶν ἡμερῶν μετὰ χεῖρας λαμ-
βάνων ἕκαστος οἴκοι καθήμενος ἀναγινωσκέτω." — In Joann. *Hom.* ix, (*Opp.*
viii. 62 B.)

[r] It caused him (he says) to interrupt his teaching. " Sed quia nunc inter-
posita est sollemnitas sanctorum dierum, quibus certas ex Evangelio lectiones
oportet in Ecclesiâ recitari, quae ita sunt annuae ut aliae esse non possint ; ordo
ille quem susceperamus necessitate paullulum intermissus est, non amissus."—
(*Opp.* vol. iii. P. ii. p. 825, *Prol.*)

[s] The place will be found quoted below, p. 202, note (o).

[t] See Suicer, (i. 247 and 9 : ii. 673). He is much more full and satisfactory
than Scholz, whose remarks, nevertheless, deserve attention, (*Nov. Test.* vol. i,
Prolegg. p. xxxi.) See also above, p. 45, notes (r) and (s).

together with "Menologion," (or Calendar of immovable Festivals and Saints' Days.) That we are thoroughly acquainted with all of these, as exhibited in Codices of the viii[th], ix[th] and x[th] centuries,—is a familiar fact; in illustration of which it is enough to refer the reader to the works cited at the foot of the page [u]. But it is no less certain that the scheme of Proper Lessons itself is of much higher antiquity.

1. The proof of this, if it could only be established by an induction of particular instances, would not only be very tedious, but also very difficult indeed. It will be perceived, on reflection, that even when the occasion of a Homily (suppose) is actually recorded, the Scripture references which it contains, apart from the Author's statement that what he quotes *had* formed part of that day's Service, creates scarcely so much as a presumption of the fact: while the correspondence, however striking, between such references to Scripture and the Lectionary as we have it, is of course no proof whatever that we are so far in possession of the Lectionary of the Patristic age. Nay, on famous Festivals,

---

[u] At the beginning of every volume of the first ed. of his *Nov. Test.* (Riga, 1788) Matthaei has laboriously *edited* the "Lectiones Ecclesiasticæ" of the Greek Church. See also his Appendices,—viz. vol. ii. pp. 272—318 and 322—363. His 2nd ed. (Wittenberg, 1803,) is distinguished by the valuable peculiarity of indicating the Ecclesiastical sections throughout, in the manner of an ancient MS.; and that, with extraordinary fulness and accuracy. His Συναξάρια (i. 723—68 and iii. 1—24) though not intelligible perhaps to ordinary readers, are very important. He derived them from MSS. which he designates "B" and "H," but which are *our* "Evstt. 47 and 50,"—uncial Evangelistaria of the viii[th] century (See Scrivener's *Introd.* p. 214.)

Scholz, at the end of vol. i. of his N. T. p. 453—93, gives in full the "Synaxarium" and "Menologium" of Codd. K .and M, (viii[th] or ix[th] century.) See also his vol. ii. pp. 456—69. Unfortunately, (as Scrivener recognises, p. 110,) all here is carelessly done,—as usual with this Editor; and therefore to a great extent useless. His slovenliness is extraordinary. The "Gospels of the Passion" (τῶν ἁγίων παθῶν), he entitles τῶν ἁγίων πάντων (p. 472); and so throughout.

Mr. Scrivener (*Introduction*, pp. 68—75,) has given by far the most intelligible account of this matter, by exhibiting *in English* the Lectionary of the Eastern Church, ("gathered chiefly from Evangelist. Arund. 547, Parham 18, Harl. 5598, Burney 22, and Christ's Coll. Camb.") ; and supplying the references to Scripture in the ordinary way. See, by all means, his *Introduction*, pp. 62—65: also, pp. 211—225.

the employment of certain passages of Scripture is, in a manner, inevitable[x], and may on no account be pressed.

2. Thus, when Chrysostom[y] and when Epiphanius[z], preaching on Ascension Day, refer to Acts i. 10, 11,—we do not feel ourselves warranted to press the coincidence of such a quotation with the Liturgical section of the day.—So, again, when Chrysostom preaches on Christmas Day, and quotes from S. Matthew ii. 1, 2[a]; or on Whitsunday, and quotes from S. John vii. 38 and Acts ii. 3 and 13;—though both places form part of the Liturgical sections for the day, no *proof* results therefrom that either chapter was actually used.

3. But we are not reduced to this method. It is discovered that nearly three-fourths of Chrysostom's Homilies on S. Matthew either begin at the first verse of *a known Ecclesiastical Lection;* or else at the first ensuing verse after the close of one. Thirteen of those Homilies in succession (the 63rd to the 75th inclusive) begin with *the first words of as many known Lections.* "Let us attend to this delightful section (περικοπή) which we never cease turning to,"—are the opening words of Chrysostom's 79th Homily, of which "the text" is S. Matth. xxv. 31, i.e. the beginning of the Gospel for Sexagesima Sunday.—Cyril of Alexandria's (so called) "Commentary on S. Luke" is nothing else but a series of short Sermons, for the most part delivered on *known Ecclesiastical Lections;* which does not seem to have been as yet observed.—Augustine (A.D. 416) says expressly that he had handled S. John's Gospel in precisely the same way[b]. —All this is significant in a high degree.

---

[x] Consider the following :—Ἐν τῇ ἡμέρᾳ τοῦ σταυροῦ τὰ περὶ τοῦ σταυροῦ πάντα ἀναγινώσκομεν. ἐν τῷ σαββάτῳ τῷ μεγάλῳ πάλιν, ὅτι παρεδόθη ἡμῶν ὁ Κύριος, ὅτι ἐσταυρώθη, ὅτι ἀπέθανε τὸ κατὰ σάρκα, ὅτι ἐτάφη· τίνος οὖν ἕνεκεν καὶ τὰς πράξεις τῶν ἀποστόλων οὐ μετὰ τὴν πεντηκοστὴν ἀναγινώσκομεν, ὅτε καὶ ἐγένοντο, καὶ ἀρχὴν ἔλαβον ;—Chrys. *Opp.* iii. 88.

Again :—εἰ γὰρ τότε ἤρξαντο ποιεῖν τὰ σημεῖα οἱ ἀπόστολοι, ἤγουν μετὰ τὴν κυρίου ἀνάστασιν, τότε ἔδει καὶ τὸ βιβλίον ἀναγινώσκεσθαι τοῦτο. ὥσπερ γὰρ τὰ περὶ τοῦ σταυροῦ ἐν τῇ ἡμέρᾳ σταυροῦ ἀναγινώσκομεν, καὶ τὰ ἐν τῇ ἀναστάσει ὁμοίως, καὶ τὰ ἐν ἑκάστῃ ἑορτῇ γεγονότα τῇ αὐτῇ πάλιν ἀναγινώσκομεν, οὕτως ἔδει καὶ τὰ θαύματα τὰ ἀποστολικὰ ἐν ταῖς ἡμέραις τῶν ἀποστολικῶν σημείων ἀναγινώσκεσθαι.—*Ibid.* p. 89 D.

[y] *Opp.* ii. 454 B, D.   [z] *Opp.* ii. 290 B.   [a] *Opp.* ii. 357 E.

[b] "Meminit sanctitas vestra Evangelium secundum Joannem ex ordine lectionum nos solere tractare." (*Opp.* iii. P. ii. 825 *Prol.*)

4. I proceed, however, to adduce a few distinct proofs that the existing Lectionary of the great Eastern Church,—as it is exhibited by Matthaei, by Scholz, and by Scrivener from MSS. of the viii[th] century,—and which is contained in Syriac MSS. of the vi[th] and vii[th] — must needs be in the main a work of extraordinary antiquity. And if I do not begin by insisting that at least one century more may be claimed for it by a mere appeal to the Hierosolymitan Version, it is only because I will never knowingly admit what may prove to be untrustworthy materials[c] into my foundations.

(*a*) "Every one is aware," (says Chrysostom in a sermon on our SAVIOUR'S Baptism, preached at Antioch, A.D. 387,) "that this is called the Festival of the Epiphany. Two manifestations are thereby intended: concerning both of which *you have heard this day S. Paul discourse in his Epistle to Titus* [d]*.*" Then follows a quotation from ch. ii. 11 to 13, —which proves to be the beginning of the lection for the day in the Greek Menology. In the time of Chrysostom, therefore, Titus ii. 11, 12, 13 formed part of one of the Epiphany lessons,—as it does to this hour in the Eastern Church. What is scarcely less interesting, it is also found to have been part of the Epistle for the Epiphany in the old Gallican Liturgy[e], the affinities of which with the East are well known.

(*b*) Epiphanius (speaking of the Feasts of the Church) says, that at the Nativity, a Star shewed that the WORD had become incarnate: at the "Theophania" (*our* "Epiphany") John cried, "Behold the Lamb of GOD," &c., and a Voice from Heaven proclaimed Him at His Baptism. Accordingly, S. Matth. ii. 1—12 is found to be the ancient lection for Christmas Day: S. Mark i. 9—11 and S. Matth. iii. 13—17 the lections for Epiphany. On the morrow, was read S. John i. 29—34.

(*c*) In another of his Homilies, Chrysostom explains with considerable emphasis the reason why the Book of the Acts was read publicly in Church during the interval between Easter and Pentecost; remarking, that it had been the

---

[c] See Scrivener's *Introduction*, p. 240.

[d] Chrysostom *Opp.* ii. 369 B, C.—Compare Scrivener, *ubi supra,* p. 75.

[e] *Ed.* Mabillon, p. 116.

liturgical arrangement of a yet earlier age [f].—After such an announcement, it becomes a very striking circumstance that Augustine also (A.D. 412) should be found to bear witness to the prevalence of the same liturgical arrangement in the African Church [g]. In the old Gallican Lectionary, as might have been expected, the same rule is recognisable. It ought to be needless to add that the same arrangement is observed universally to prevail in the Lectionaries both of the East and of the West to the present hour; although the fact must have been lost sight of by the individuals who recently, under pretence of "*making some advantageous alterations*" in our Lectionary, have constructed an entirely new one, —vicious in principle and liable to the gravest objections throughout,—whereby *this* link also which bound the Church of England to the practice of Primitive Christendom, has been unhappily broken; *this* note of Catholicity also has been effaced [h].

---

[f] *Opp.* vol. iii. p. 85 B : 88 A :—τίνος ἕνεκεν οἱ πατέρες ἡμῶν ἐν τῇ πεντη-κοστῇ τὸ βιβλίον τῶν πράξεων ἀναγινώσκεσθαι ἐνομοθέτησαν.—τίνος ἕνεκεν τὸ βιβλίον τῶν πράξεων τῶν ἀποστόλων ἐν τῷ καιρῷ τῆς πεντηκοστῆς ἀναγινώ-σκεται.

[g] "Anniversariâ sollemnitate post passionem Domini nostis illum librum recitari." *Opp.* iii. (P. ii.) p. 337 Θ.

[h] I desire to leave in this place the permanent record of my deliberate con-viction that the Lectionary which, last year, was hurried with such indecent haste through Convocation,—passed in a half-empty House by the casting vote of the Prolocutor,—and rudely pressed upon the Church's acceptance by the Legislature in the course of its present session,—is the gravest calamity which has befallen the Church of England for a long time past.

Let the history of this Lectionary be remembered.

Appointed (in 1867) for an *entirely* different purpose, (viz. the Ornaments and Vestments question,) 29 Commissioners (14 Clerical and 15 Lay) found themselves further instructed "to suggest and report *whether any and what alterations and amendments may be advantageously made* in the selection of Lessons to be read at the time of Divine Service."

Thereupon, these individuals,—(the Liturgical attainments of nine-tenths of whom it would be unbecoming in such an one as myself to characterise truthfully,)—at once imposed upon themselves the duty of inventing *an en-tirely new Lectionary* for the Church of England.

So to mutilate the Word of GOD that it shall henceforth be quite impossible to understand a single Bible story, or discover the sequence of a single con-nected portion of narrative,—seems to have been the guiding principle of their deliberations. With reckless eclecticism,—entire forgetfulness of the require-ments of the poor brother,—strange disregard for Catholic Tradition and the (*d*) The purely arbitrary arrangement, (as Mr. Scrivener phrases it), by which the Book of Genesis, instead of the Gospel, is appointed to be read[i] on the *week* days of Lent, is discovered to have been fully recognised in the time of Chrysostom. Accordingly, the two series of Homilies on the Book of Genesis which that Father preached, he preached in Lent[k].

(*e*) It will be seen in the next chapter that it was from a very remote period the practice of the Eastern Church to introduce into the lesson for Thursday in Holy-week, S. Luke's account (ch. xxii. 43, 44) of our LORD's "Agony and bloody Sweat," *immediately after S. Matth.* xxvi. 39. *That* is, no doubt, the reason why Chrysostom,—who has been suspected, (I think unreasonably,) of employing an Evangelistarium instead of a copy of the Gospels in the preparation of his Homilies, is observed to quote those same two verses in that very place in his Homily on S. Matthew[l]; which shews that the Lectionary system of the Eastern Church in this respect is at least as old as the iv[th] century.

(*f*) The same two verses used to be *left out* on the Tuesday after Sexagesima ($\tau\hat{\eta}$ $\acute{\eta}$ $\tau\hat{\eta}s$ $\tau\upsilon\rho o\phi\acute{a}\gamma o\upsilon$) for which day S. Luke xxii. 39—xxiii. 1, is the appointed lection. And *this* explains why Cyril (A.D. 425) in his Homilies on S. Luke, passes them by in silence[m].

But we can carry back the witness to the Lectionary practice of omitting these verses, at least a hundred years; for

claims of immemorial antiquity;—these Commissioners, (evidently unconscious of their own unfitness for their self-imposed task,) have given us a Lectionary which will recommend itself to none but the lovers of novelty,—the impatient, —and the enemies of Divine Truth.

That the blame, *the guilt* lies at the door of *our Bishops*, is certain; but the Church has no one but herself to thank for the injury which has been thus deliberately inflicted upon her. She has suffered herself to be robbed of her ancient birthright without resistance; without remonstrance; without (in her corporate capacity) so much as a word of audible dissatisfaction. *Can* it be right in this way to defraud those who are to come after us of their lawful inheritance? ... I am amazed and grieved beyond measure at what is taking place. At least, (as on other occasions,) *liberavi animam meam.*

[i] A trace of this remains in the old Gallican Liturgy,—pp. 137-8.

[k] Bingham, XIV. iii. 3.   [l] *Opp.* vol. vii. p. 701 B.

[m] See Dean Payne Smith's Translation, p. 863.

Cod. B, (evidently for that same reason,) *also* omits them, as was stated above, in p. 79. They are wanting also in the Thebaic version, which is of the iii^rd century.

(*g*) It will be found suggested in the next chapter (page 218) that the piercing of our LORD's side, (S. John xix. 34), —thrust into Codd. B and ℵ immediately after S. Matth. xxvii. 49,—is probably indebted for its place in those two MSS. to the Eastern Lectionary practice. If this suggestion be well founded, a fresh proof is obtained that the Lectionary of the East was fully established in the beginning of the iv^th century. But see Appendix (H).

(*h*) It is a remarkable note of the antiquity of that Oriental Lectionary system with which we are acquainted, that S. Matthew's account of the Passion (ch. xxvii. 1—61,) should be there appointed to be read *alone* on the evening of Good Friday. Chrysostom clearly alludes to this practice[n]; which Augustine expressly states was also the practice in his own day[o]. Traces of the same method are discoverable in the old Gallican Lectionary[p].

(*i*) Epiphanius, (or the namesake of his who was the author of a well-known Homily on Palm Sunday,) remarks that "yesterday" had been read the history of the rising of Lazarus[q]. Now S. John xi. 1—45 is the lection for the antecedent Sabbath, in all the Lectionaries.

(*k*) In conclusion, I may be allowed so far to anticipate what will be found fully established in the next chapter, as to point out here that since in countless places the text of our oldest Evangelia as well as the readings of the primitive Fathers exhibit unmistakable traces of the corrupting influence of the Lectionary practice, *that* very fact becomes irrefragable evidence of the antiquity of the Lectionary which is the occasion of it. Not only must it be more

---

[n] κατὰ τὴν μεγάλην τοῦ Πάσχα ἑσπέραν ταῦτα πάντα ἀναγινώσκεται.—Chrys. *Opp.* vii. 818 c.

[o] "Passio autem, quia uno die legitur, non solet legi nisi secundum Matthæum. Volueram aliquando ut per singulos annos secundum omnes Evangelistas etiam Passio legeretur. Factum est. Non audierunt homines quod consueverant, et perturbati sunt."—*Opp.* vol. v. p. 980 E.

[p] *Ed.* Mabillon, pp. 130-5.   [q] Epiph. *Opp.* ii. 152-3.

ancient than Cod. B or Cod. ℵ, (which are referred to the
beginning of the iv[th] century), but it must be older than
Origen in the iii[rd] century, or the Vetus Itala and the Syriac
in the ii[nd]. And thus it is demonstrated, (1st) That fixed
Lessons were read in the Churches of the East in the immediately post-Apostolic age; and (2ndly) That, wherever
we are able to test it, the Lectionary of that remote period
corresponded with the Lectionary which has come down to
us in documents of the vi[th] and vii[th] century, and was in
fact constructed in precisely the same way.

I am content in fact to dismiss the preceding instances
with this general remark :—that a System which is found
to have been fully recognised throughout the East and
throughout the West in the beginning of the fourth century,
must of necessity have been established very long before. It is
as when we read of three British Bishops attending the
Council at Arles, A.D. 314. The Church (we say) which
could send out those three Bishops must have been *fully
organized* at a greatly antecedent period.

4. Let us attend, however, to the great Festivals of the
Church. These are declared by Chrysostom (in a Homily
delivered at Antioch 20 Dec. A.D. 386) to be the five following :—(1) Nativity: (2) the Theophania: (3) Pascha: (4)
Ascension: (5) Pentecost[r]. Epiphanius, his contemporary,
(Bishop of Constantia in the island of Cyprus,) makes the
same enumeration[s], in a Homily on the Ascension[t]. In
the Apostolical Constitutions, the same five Festivals are
enumerated[u]. Let me state a few Liturgical facts in connexion with each of these.

---

[r] Chrys. *Opp.* i. 497 c.   [s] Epiph. *Opp.* ii. 285-6.

[t] The learned reader will be delighted and instructed too by the perusal of
both passages. Chrysostom declares that Christmas-Day is the greatest
of Festivals; since all the others are but consequences of the Incarnation.

Epiphanius remarks with truth that Ascension-Day is the crowning so-
lemnity of all : being to the others what a beautiful head is to the human body.

[u] *Constt. Apostt.* lib. viii. c. 33. After the week of the Passion and the
week of (1) the Resurrection,—(2) Ascension-Day is mentioned ;—(3) Pentecost ;—(4) Nativity ;—(5) Epiphany. [Note this clear indication that this
viii[th] Book of the Constitutions was written or interpolated at a subsequent
date to that commonly assigned to the work.]

It is plain that the preceding enumeration could not have
been made at any earlier period : for the Epiphany of our
SAVIOUR and His Nativity were originally but one Festival [y].
Moreover, the circumstances are well known under which
Chrysostom (A.D. 386) announced to his Eastern auditory
that in conformity with what had been correctly ascertained
at Rome, the ancient Festival was henceforth to be disin-
tegrated [z]. But this is not material to the present inquiry.
We know that, as a matter of fact, "the Epiphanies" (for
τὰ ἐπιφανία is the name of the Festival) became in consequence distributed over Dec. 25 and Jan. 5 : our LORD's
Baptism being the event chiefly commemorated on the latter
anniversary [a],—which used to be chiefly observed in honour
of His *Birth* [b].—Concerning the Lessons for Passion-tide and
Easter, as well as concerning those for the Nativity and Epiphany, something has been offered already; to which may
be added that Hesychius, in the opening sentences of that
"Homily" which has already engaged so much of our attention [c], testifies that the conclusion of S. Mark's Gospel was
in his days, as it has been ever since, one of the lections for
Easter. He begins by saying that the Evangelical narratives
of the Resurrection were read on the Sunday night; and
proceeds to reconcile *S. Mark's* with the rest.—Chrysostom
once and again adverts to the practice of discontinuing the
reading of the Acts after Pentecost [d],—which is observed to
be also the method of the Lectionaries.

III. I speak separately of the Festival of the Ascension,
for an obvious reason. It ranked, as we have seen, in the
estimation of Primitive Christendom, with the greatest Festivals of the Church. Augustine, in a well-known passage,
hints that it may have been of Apostolical origin [e]; so ex-

---

[y] Bingham's *Origines*, B. xx. c. iv. § 2.

[z] Chrys. *Opp.* ii. 355. (See the *Monitum*, p. 352.)

[a] Chrys. *Opp.* ii. 369 D.   [b] Epiphanius, Adv. Haer. LI, c. xvi.
(*Opp.* i. 439 A.)   [c] See above, pp. 58-9 and 67.

[d] *Opp.* iii. 102 B. See Bingham on this entire subject,—B. xiv, c. iii.

[e] " Illa quae non scripta, sed tradita custodimus, quae quidem toto terrarum
orbe observantur, datur intelligi vel ab ipsis Apostolis, vel plenariis Conciliis
quorum in Ecclesia saluberrima authoritas, commendata atque statuta reti-
neri. Sicut quod Domini Passio, et Resurrectio, et Ascensio in cœlis, ut Adven-

ceedingly remote was its institution accounted in the days of
the great African Father, as well as so entirely forgotten by
that time was its first beginning.   I have to shew that in
the Great Oriental Lectionary (whether of the Greek or of
the Syrian Church) the last Twelve Verses of S. Mark's
Gospel occupy a conspicuous as well as a most honourable
place.   And this is easily done : for,

(*a*) The Lesson for Matins *on Ascension-Day* in the East,
in the oldest documents to which we have access, consisted
(as now it does) of *the last Twelve Verses,*—neither more nor
less,—of S. Mark's Gospel.   At the Liturgy on Ascension was
read S. Luke xxiv. 36—53 : but at Matins, S. Mark xvi. 9—20.
The witness of the "Synaxaria" is constant to this effect.

(*b*) The same lection precisely was adopted among the
Syrians by the Melchite Churches [f],—(the party, viz. which
maintained the decrees of the Council of Chalcedon): and it
is found appointed also in the "Evangeliarium Hierosolymitanum [g]."   In the Evangelistarium used in the Jacobite, (i.e.
the Monophysite) Churches of Syria, a striking difference
of arrangement is discoverable.   While S. Luke xxiv. 36—
53 was read at Vespers and at Matins on Ascension Day,
the last seven verses of S. Mark's Gospel (ch. xvi. 14—20)
were read *at the Liturgy* [h].   Strange, that the self-same Gospel should have been adopted at a remote age by some of
the Churches of the West [i], and should survive in our own
Book of Common Prayer to this hour !

(*c*) But S. Mark xvi. 9—20 was not only appointed by the
Greek Church to be read upon Ascension Day.   Those same
twelve verses constitute the third of the xi "*Matin Gospels
of the Resurrection,*" which were universally held in high

tus de cœlo Spiritus Sancti anniversaria sollemnitate celebrantur."—*Ep.* ad
Januarium, (*Opp.* ii. 124 B, c).

[f] "Lect. fer. quint., quae etiam Festum Adscensionis Dnī in caelos, ad mat.
eadem ac lect. tert. Resurrect.; in Euchar. lect. sext. Resurrect."—But "Lect.
γ Resurrectionis" is "Marc. xvi. 9—20 :" "Lect. ς," "Luc. xxiv. 36—53."
—See Dean Payne Smith's *Catalogus Codd. Syrr.* (1864) pp. 116, 127.

[g] See above, p. 34, note (e).   [h] R. Payne Smith's *Catal.* p. 148.

[i] *Hieronymi Comes,* (*ed.* Pamel. ii. 31.)—But it is not the Gallican. (*ed.*
Mabillon, p. 155.) . . . It strikes me as just possible that a clue may be in this
way supplied to the singular phenomenon noted above at p. 118, line 22-8.

esteem by the Eastern Churches (Greek and Syrian [k]), and
were read successively on Sundays at Matins throughout the
year; as well as daily throughout Easter week.

(*d*) A rubricated copy of S. Mark's Gospel in Syriac [*], *certainly older than* A.D. 583, attests that S. Mark xvi. 9—20 was
the "Lection for the great First Day of the week," (μεγάλη
κυριακή, i.e. Easter Day). Other copies almost as ancient [†]
add that it was used "at the end of the Service at the dawn."

(*e*) Further, these same "Twelve Verses" constituted the
Lesson at Matins for *the 2nd Sunday after Easter*,—a Sunday
which by the Greeks is called κυριακή τῶν μυροφόρων, but
with the Syrians bore the names of "Joseph and Nicodemus [l]." So also in the "Evangeliarium Hierosolymitanum."

(*f*) Next, in the Monophysite Churches of Syria, S. Mark
xvi. 9—18 (or 9—20 [m]) was also read at Matins on *Easter-
Tuesday* [n]. In the Gallican Church, the third lection for
Easter-Monday extended from S. Mark xv. 47 to xvi. 11: for
Easter-Tuesday, from xvi. 12 to the end of the Gospel [o].
Augustine says that in Africa also these concluding verses
of S. Mark's Gospel used to be publicly read *at Easter tide* [p].
The same verses (beginning with ver. 9) are indicated in the
oldest extant Lectionary of the Roman Church [q].

(*g*) Lastly, it may be stated that S. Mark xvi. 9—20 was
with the Greeks the Gospel for the Festival of S. Mary
Magdalene (ἡ μυροφόρος), July 22 [r].

[k] Εὐαγγέλια ἀναστασιμὰ ἑωθινά. See Scrivener's *Introduction*, p. 72, and
R. P. Smith's *Catal.* p. 127. See by all means, Suicer's *Thes. Eccl.* i. 1229.

[*] Dr. Wright's *Catal.* p. 70, N°. CX. (Addit. 14,464: *fol.* 61 *b*.)

[†] *Ibid.* N°. LXX (*fol.* 92 *b*), and LXXII (*fol.* 87 *b*).

[l] "Quae titulo Josephi et Nicodemi insignitur." (R. Payne Smith's *Catal.*
p. 116.)—In the "Synaxarium" of Matthaei (*Nov. Test.* 1803, i. p. 731) it
is styled Κ. τῶν μ. καὶ Ἰωσὴφ τοῦ δικαίου. [m] Adler's *N. T. Verss. Syrr.* p. 71.
[n] Dean Payne Smith's *Catal.* p. 146.   [o] *Ed.* Mabillon, pp. 144-5.

[p] "Resurrectio Domini nostri I. C. ex more legitur bis diebus [Paschalibus]
ex omnibus libris sancti Evangelii." (*Opp.* v. 977 o)—"Quoniam hoc moris est
.... *Marci Evangelium* est quod modo, cum legeretur, audivimus." "Quid
ergo audivimus Marcum dicentem?" And he subjoins a quotation from
S. Mark xvi. 12.—*Ibid.* 997 F, 998 B.   [q] *Hieron. Comes* (ed. Pamel. ii. 27.)

[r] So Scrivener's *Introduction*, p. 75.—Little stress, however, is to be laid on
Saint's Day lessons. In Matthaei's "Menologium" (*Nov. Test.* 1803, i. p. 765),
I find that S. Luke viii. 1—4, or else S. John xx. 11—18 was the appointed
Lection. See his note ([6]) at p. 750.

He knows wondrous little about this department of Sacred Science who can require to be informed that such a weight of *public* testimony as this to the last Twelve Verses of a Gospel is simply overwhelming. The single discovery that in the age of Augustine [385—430] this portion of S. Mark's Gospel was unquestionably read at Easter in the Churches of Africa, added to the express testimony of the Author of the 2nd Homily on the Resurrection, and of the oldest Syriac MSS., that they were also read by the Orientals at Easter in the public services of the Church, must be held to be in a manner decisive of the question.

Let the evidence, then, which is borne by Ecclesiastical usage to the genuineness of S. Mark xvi. 9—20, be summed up, and the entire case caused again to pass under review.

(1.) That Lessons from the New Testament were publicly read in the assemblies of the faithful according to a definite scheme, and on an established system, *at least* as early as the fourth century,—has been shewn to be a plain historical fact. Cyril, at Jerusalem,—(and by implication, his name-sake at Alexandria,)—Chrysostom, at Antioch and at Constantinople,—Augustine, in Africa,—all four expressly witness to the circumstance. In other words, there is found to have been *at least at that time* fully established throughout the Churches of Christendom a Lectionary, which seems to have been essentially one and the same in the West[s] and in the East. That it must have been of even Apostolic antiquity may be inferred from several considerations. But that it dates its beginning from a period *anterior to the age of*

---

[s] Note, (in addition to all that has gone before,) that the Festivals are actually designated by their *Greek* names in the earliest Latin Service Books : not only "Theophania," "Epiphania," "Pascha," "Pentecostes," (the second, third and fourth of which appellations survive in the Church of the West, *in memoriam,* to the present hour ;) but "Hypapante," which was the title bestowed by the Orientals in the time of Justinian, on Candlemas Day, (our Feast of the Purification, or Presentation of CHRIST in the Temple,) from the "Meeting" of Symeon on that occasion. Friday, or παρασκευή, was called "Parasceve" in the West. (Mab. *Lit. Gall.* p. 129.) So entire was the sympathy of the East with the West in such matters in very early times, that when Rome decided to celebrate the Nativity on the 25th December, Chrysostom (as we have been reminded) publicly announced the fact at Constantinople ; and it was determined that in this matter East and West would walk by the same rule.

Eusebius,—which is the age of Codices B and א,—at least admits of *no* controversy.

(2.) Next,—Documents of the vi[th] century put us in possession of the great Oriental Lectionary as it is found at that time to have universally prevailed throughout the vast unchanging East.   In other words, several of the actual Service Books, in Greek and in Syriac [t], have survived the accidents of full a thousand years : and rubricated copies of the Gospels carry us back three centuries further.   The entire agreement which is observed to prevail among these several documents,—added to the fact that when tested by the allusions incidentally made by Greek Fathers of the iv[th] century to what was the Ecclesiastical practice of their own time, there are found to emerge countless as well as highly significant notes of correspondence,—warrants us in believing, (in the absence of testimony of any sort to the contrary,) that the Lectionary we speak of differs in no essential respect from that system of Lections with which the Church of the iv[th] century was universally acquainted.

Nothing scarcely is more forcibly impressed upon us in the course of the present inquiry than the fact, that documents alone are wanting to make *that* altogether demonstrable which, in default of such evidence, must remain a matter of inevitable inference only.   The forms we are pursuing at last disappear from our sight : but it is only the mist of the early morning which shrouds them.   We still hear their voices : still track their footsteps : know that others still see them, although we ourselves see them no longer.   We are sure that *there they still are.*   Moreover they may yet reappear at any moment.   Thus, there exist Syriac MSS. of the Gospels of the vii[th] and even of the vi[th] century, in which the Lessons are rubricated in the text or on the margin.   A Syriac MS. (of part of the Old T.) is actually *dated* A.D. 464 [u].   Should an Evangelium of similar date

---

[t] From Professor Wright's *Catalogue of Syriac MSS. in the British Museum* (1870) it appears that the oldest Jacobite Lectionary is dated A.D. 824; the oldest Nestorian, A.D. 862; the oldest Malkite, A.D. 1023. The respective numbers of the MSS. are 14,485; 14,492; and 14,488.—See his *Catalogue*, Part I. pp. 146, 178, 194.

[u] It is exhibited in the same glass-case with the Cod. Alexandrinus (A.)

ever come to light of which the rubrication was evidently by
the original Scribe, the evidence of the Lectionaries would
at once be carried back full three hundred years.

But in fact we stand in need of no such testimony. Acceptable as it would be, it is plain that it would add no
strength to the argument whatever. We are already able
to plant our footsteps securely in the ivth and even in the
iiird. century. It is not enough to insist that inasmuch as
the Liturgical method of Christendom was at least fully
established in the East and in the West at the close of the
ivth century, it therefore must have had its beginning at
a far remoter period. Our two oldest Codices (B and ℵ)
bear witness throughout to the corrupting influence of a system which was evidently in full operation before the time
of Eusebius. And even this is not all. The readings in
Origen, and of the earliest versions of the Gospel, (the old
Latin, the Syriac, the Egyptian versions,) carry back our
evidence on this subject unmistakably to *the age immediately
succeeding that of the Apostles.* This will be found established
in the course of the ensuing Chapter.

Beginning our survey of the problem at the opposite end,
we arrive at the same result; with even a deepened conviction that in its essential structure, the Lectionary of
the Eastern Church must be of truly primitive antiquity :
indeed that many of its leading provisions must date back
almost,—nay *quite,*—to the Apostolic age. From whichever
side we approach this question,—whatever test we are able
to apply to our premisses,—our conclusion remains still the
very same.

(3.) Into this Lectionary then,—so universal in its extent,
so consistent in its witness, so Apostolic in its antiquity,
—"*the* Last Twelve Verses *of the Gospel according to
S. Mark*" from the very first are found to have won for
themselves not only an entrance, a lodgment, an established
place ; but, *the place of highest honour,*—an audience on two
of the Church's chiefest Festivals.

The circumstance is far too important, far too significant
to be passed by without a few words of comment.

For it is not here, (be it carefully observed,) as when

we appeal to some Patristic citation, that the recognition of
a phrase, or a verse, or a couple of verses, must be accepted
as a proof that the same ancient Father recognised the
context also in which those words are found. Not so. *All
the Twelve Verses in dispute are found in every known copy*
of the venerable Lectionary of the East. *Those same Twelve
Verses,*—neither more nor less,—*are observed to constitute
one integral Lection.*

But even this is not all. The most important fact seems
to be that to these Verses has been assigned a place of the
highest possible distinction. It is found that, from the very
first, S. Mark xvi. 9—20 has been everywhere, and by all
branches of the Church Catholic, claimed for *two* of the
Church's greatest Festivals,—Easter and Ascension. A more
weighty or a more significant circumstance can scarcely be
imagined. To suppose that a portion of Scripture singled
out for such extraordinary honour by the Church universal
is a spurious addition to the Gospel, is purely irrational; is
simply monstrous. No unauthorized "fragment," however
" remarkable," could by possibility have so established itself
in the regards of the East and of the West, from the very
first. No suspected "addition, placed here in very early
times," would have been tolerated in the Church's solemn
public Service six or seven times a-year. No. *It is impossible.* Had it been one short clause which we were invited
to surrender: a verse: two verses: even three or four:—
the plea being that (as in the case of the celebrated *pericopa
de adulterâ*) the Lectionaries knew nothing of them:—the
case would have been entirely different. But for any one
to seek to persuade us that these Twelve Verses, which
exactly constitute one of the Church's most famous Lections,
are every one of them spurious:—that the fatal taint begins
with the first verse, and only ends with the last:—*this* is
a demand on our simplicity which, in a less solemn subject,
would only provoke a smile. We are constrained to testify
astonishment and even some measure of concern. Have the
Critics then, (supposing them to be familiar with the evidence which has now been set forth so much in detail;)—
Have the Critics then, (we ask) utterly taken leave of their

senses? or do they really suppose that we have taken leave of ours?

It is time to close this discussion. It was declared at the outset that the witness of the Lectionaries to the genuineness of these Verses, though it has been generally overlooked, is the most important of any: admitting, as it does, of no evasion: being simply, as it is, decisive. I have now fully explained the grounds of that assertion. I have set the Verses, which I undertook to vindicate and establish, on a basis from which it will be found impossible any more to dislodge them. Whatever Griesbach, and Tischendorf, and Tregelles, and the rest, may think about the matter,— the Holy Eastern Church in her corporate capacity, has never been of their opinion. *They* may doubt. *The ante-Nicene Fathers* at least never doubted. If "the last Twelve Verses" of S. Mark were *deservedly* omitted from certain Copies of his Gospel in the iv[th] century, utterly incredible is it that these same TWELVE VERSES should have been disseminated, by their authority, throughout Christendom;— read, by their command, in all the Churches;—selected, by their collective judgment, from the whole body of Scripture for the special honour of being listened to once and again at EASTER time, as well as on ASCENSION-DAY.

CHAPTER XI.

THE OMISSION OF THESE TWELVE VERSES IN CERTAIN ANCIENT COPIES OF THE GOSPELS, EXPLAINED AND ACCOUNTED FOR.

The Text of our five oldest Uncials proved, by an induction of instances, to have suffered depravation throughout by the operation of the ancient Lectionary system of the Church (p. 217).—*The omission of S. Mark's "last Twelve Verses," (constituting an integral Ecclesiastical Lection,) shewn to be probably only one more example of the same depraving influence* (p. 224).

This solution of the problem corroborated by the language of Eusebius and of Hesychius (p. 232) ; *as well as favoured by the " Western" order of the Gospels* (p. 239).

I AM much mistaken if the suggestion which I am about to offer has not already presented itself to every reader of ordinary intelligence who has taken the trouble to follow the course of my argument thus far with attention. It requires no acuteness whatever,—it is, as it seems to me, the merest instinct of mother-wit,—on reaching the present stage of the discussion, to debate with oneself somewhat as follows :—

1. So then, the last Twelve Verses of S. Mark's Gospel were anciently often observed to be missing from the copies. Eusebius expressly says so. I observe that he nowhere says that *their genuineness* was anciently *suspected*. As for himself, his elaborate discussion of their contents convinces me that individually, he regarded them with favour. The mere fact,—(it is best to keep to his actual statement,)—that "the entire passage [a]" was "not met with in all the copies," is the sum of his evidence : and two Greek manuscripts, yet extant, supposed to be of the iv[th] century (Codd. B and ℵ), mutilated in this precise way, testify to the truth of his statement.

2. But then it is found that these self-same Twelve Verses, —neither more nor less,—anciently constituted *an integral*

---

[a] The reader is requested to refer back to p. 45, and the note there.—The actual words of Eusebius are given in Appendix (B).

Ecclesiastical Lection; which lection,—inasmuch as it is found
to have established itself in every part of Christendom at
the earliest period to which liturgical evidence reaches back,
and to have been assigned from the very first to two of the
chiefest Church Festivals,—must needs be a lection of almost
Apostolic antiquity. Eusebius, I observe, (see p. 45), designates the portion of Scripture in dispute by its technical
name,—κεφάλαιον or περικοπή; (for so an Ecclesiastical lection was anciently called). Here then is a rare coincidence
indeed. It is in fact simply unique. Surely, I may add
that it is in the highest degree suggestive also. It inevitably
provokes the inquiry,—Must not these two facts be not only
connected, but even *interdependent?* Will not the omission
of the Twelve concluding Verses of S. Mark from certain
ancient copies of his Gospel, have been in some way *occasioned by the fact* that those same twelve verses constituted an
integral Church Lection? How is it possible to avoid suspecting that the phenomenon to which Eusebius invites
attention, (viz. that certain copies of S. Mark's Gospel in very
ancient times had been mutilated from the end of the 8th
verse onwards,) ought to be capable of illustration,—will
have in fact *to be explained,* and in a word *accounted for,*—
by the circumstance that at the 8th verse of S. Mark's xvi[th]
chapter, one ancient Lection *came to an end,* and another
ancient Lection *began?*

Somewhat thus, (I venture to think,) must every unprejudiced Reader of intelligence hold parley with himself on
reaching the close of the preceding chapter. I need hardly
add that I am thoroughly convinced he would be reasoning
rightly. I am going to shew that the Lectionary practice
of the ancient Church does indeed furnish a sufficient clue
for the unravelment of this now famous problem: in other
words, enables us satisfactorily to account for the omission
of these Twelve Verses from ancient copies of the collected
Gospels. But I mean to do more. I propose to make my
appeal to documents which shall be observed to bear no
faltering witness in my favour. More yet. I propose that
Eusebius himself, the chief author of all this trouble, shall
be brought back into Court and invited to resyllable his

Evidence; and I am much mistaken if even *he* will not be
observed to let fall a hint that we have at last got on the
right scent;—have accurately divined how this mistake
took its first beginning;—and, (what is not least to the
purpose,) have correctly apprehended what was his own real
meaning in what he himself has said.

The proposed solution of the difficulty,—if not the evidence on which it immediately rests,—might no doubt be
exhibited within exceedingly narrow limits. Set down
abruptly, however, its weight and value would inevitably
fail to be recognised, even by those who already enjoy some
familiarity with these studies. Very few of the considerations which I shall have to rehearse are in fact unknown
to Critics: yet is it evident that their bearing on the problem before us has hitherto altogether escaped their notice.
On the other hand, by one entirely a novice to this department of sacred Science, I could scarcely hope to be so much
as understood. Let me be allowed, therefore, to preface what
I have to say with a few explanatory details which I promise shall not be tedious, and which I trust will not be
found altogether without interest either. If they are anywhere else to be met with, it is my misfortune, not my fault,
that I have been hitherto unsuccessful in discovering the place.

I. From the earliest ages of the Church, (as I shewed
at page 192-5,) it has been customary to read certain
definite portions of Holy Scripture, determined by Ecclesiastical authority, publicly before the Congregation. In
process of time, as was natural, the sections so required for
public use were collected into separate volumes: Lections
from the Gospels being written out in a Book which was
called "*Evangelistarium,*" (εὐαγγελιστάριον,)—from the Acts
and Epistles, in a book called "*Praxapostolus,*" (πραξαπό-
στολος). These Lectionary-books, both Greek and Syriac,
are yet extant in great numbers [b], and (I may remark in

---

[b] See the enumeration of Greek Service-Books in Scrivener's *Introduction,*
&c. pp. 211—25. For the Syriac Lectionaries, see Dean Payne Smith's *Catalogue,* (1864) pp. 114-29-31-4-5-8: also Professor Wright's *Catalogue,* (1870)
pp. 146 to 203.—I avail myself of this opportunity to thank both those learned
Scholars for their valuable assistance, always most obligingly rendered.

passing) deserve a far greater amount of attention than has hitherto been bestowed upon them[c].

When the Lectionary first took the form of a separate book, has not been ascertained. That no copy is known to exist (whether in Greek or in Syriac) older than the viii[th] century, proves nothing. Codices in daily use, (like the Bibles used in our Churches,) must of necessity have been of exceptionally brief duration; and Lectionaries, more even than Biblical MSS. were liable to injury and decay.

II. But it is to be observed,—(and to explain this, is much more to my present purpose,)—that besides transcribing the Ecclesiastical lections into separate books, it became the practice at a very early period *to adapt copies of the Gospels to lectionary purposes.* I suspect that this practice began in the Churches of Syria; for *Syriac* copies of the Gospels (*at least* of the vii[th] century) abound, which have the Lections more or less systematically rubricated in the Text[d]. There is in the British Museum a copy of S. Mark's Gospel according to the Peshito version, *certainly written previous to A.D. 583*, which has at least five or six rubrics so inserted by the original scribe[e]. As a rule, in all later cursive Greek MSS., (I mean those of the xii[th] to the xv[th] century,) the Ecclesiastical lections are indicated throughout: while either at the summit, or else at the foot of the page, the formula with which the Lection was to be introduced is elaborately inserted; prefaced probably by a rubricated statement (not always very easy to decipher) of the occasion *when* the ensuing portion of Scripture was to be read. The ancients, to a far greater extent than ourselves[f], were accustomed,—

[c] " Evangelistariorum codices literis uncialibus scripti nondum sic ut decet in usum criticum conversi sunt." Tischendorf, quoted by Scrivener, [*Introduction to Cod. Augiensis*,—80 pages which have been separately published and are *well* deserving of study,—p. 48,] who adds,—" I cannot even conjecture why an Evangelistarium should be thought of less value than another MS. of the same age."—See also Scrivener's *Introduction*, &c. p. 211.

[d] e.g. *Addit. MSS.* 12,141: 14,449: 14,450-2-4-5-6-7-8: 14,461-3: 17,113-4-5-6:—(= 15 Codd. in all:) from p. 45 to p. 66 of Professor Wright's *Catalogue.*

[e] *Addit. MS.* 14,464. (See Dr. Wright's *Catalogue*, p. 70.)

[f] Add to the eight examples adduced by Mr. Scrivener from our Book of C. P., (*Introduction*, p. 11), the following:—Gospels for Quinquagesima,

(in fact, they made it *a rule*,)—to prefix unauthorized formulæ to their public Lections; and these are sometimes found
to have established themselves so firmly, that at last they
became as it were ineradicable; and later copyists of the
fourfold Gospel are observed to introduce them unsuspiciously into the inspired text[g].   All that belongs to this
subject deserves particular attention; because it is *this* which
explains not a few of the perturbations (so to express oneself) which the text of the New Testament has experienced.
We are made to understand how, what was originally intended only as a *liturgical note*, became mistaken, through
the inadvertence or the stupidity of copyists, for a *critical
suggestion;* and thus, besides transpositions without number,
there has arisen, at one time, the insertion of something unauthorized into the text of Scripture,—at another, the omission of certain inspired words, to the manifest detriment of
the sacred deposit.   For although the *systematic* rubrication of
the Gospels for liturgical purposes is a comparatively recent
invention,—(I question if it be older in Greek MSS. than
the xth century,)—yet will persons engaged in the public
Services of GOD's House have been prone, from the very
earliest age, to insert memoranda of the kind referred to,
into the margin of their copies.   In this way, in fact, it may
be regarded as certain that in countless minute particulars

2nd S. after Easter, 9th, 12th, 22nd after Trinity, Whitsunday, Ascension
Day, SS. Philip and James (see below, p. 220), All Saints.

[g] Thus the words εἶπε δὲ ὁ Κύριος (S. Luke vii. 31) which *introduce an
Ecclesiastical Lection* (Friday in the iii[rd] week of S. Luke,) inasmuch as the
words are found in *no* uncial MS., and are omitted besides by the Syriac, Vulgate, Gothic and Coptic Versions, must needs be regarded as a liturgical interpolation.—The same is to be said of ὁ Ἰησοῦς in S. Matth. xiv. 22,—words
which Origen and Chrysostom, as well as the Syriac versions, omit; and which
clearly owe their place in twelve of the uncials, in the Textus Receptus, in the
Vulgate and some copies of the old Latin, to the fact that the Gospel for the
ix[th] Sunday after Pentecost *begins at that place.*—It will be kindred to the
present inquiry that I should point out that in S. Mark xvi. 9, Ἀναστάς ὁ
Ἰησοῦς is constantly met with in Greek MSS., and even in some copies of the
Vulgate; and yet there can be *no* doubt that here also the Holy Name is an
interpolation which has originated from the same cause as the preceding. The
fact is singularly illustrated by the insertion of " ὁ ι̅σ̅ " in Cod. 267
(= Reg. 69,) *rubro* above *the same contraction* (for ὁ Ἰησοῦς) in the text.

the text of Scripture has been depraved.   Let me not fail to
add, that by a judicious, and above all by an *unprejudiced*
use of the materials at our disposal, it may, even at this
distance of time, in every such particular, be successfully
restored [h].

III. I now proceed to shew, by an induction of instances,
that *even in the oldest copies in existence*, I mean in Codd. B,
א, A, C, and D, the Lectionary system of the early Church
has left abiding traces of its operation.   When a few such
undeniable cases have been adduced, all objections grounded
on *primâ facie* improbability will have been satisfactorily
disposed of.   The activity, as well as the existence of such
a disturbing force and depraving influence, *at least* as far
back as the beginning of the iv[th] century, (but it is in fact
more ancient by full two hundred years,)' will have been
established : of which I shall only have to shew, in conclusion, that the omission of " the last Twelve Verses " of
S. Mark's Gospel is probably but one more instance,—
though confessedly by far the most extraordinary of any.

(1.) From Codex B then, as well as from Cod. A, the two
grand verses which describe our LORD's "Agony and Bloody
Sweat," (S. Luke xxii. 43, 44,) are missing.   The same two
verses are absent also from a few other important MSS., as
well as from both the Egyptian versions ; but I desire to fas-
ten attention on the confessedly erring testimony in this place
of Codex B.   " Confessedly erring," I say ; for the genuineness of those two verses is no longer disputed.   Now, in
every known Evangelistarium, the two verses here omitted
by Cod. B follow, (the Church so willed it,) S. Matth. xxvi.
39, and are read as a regular part of the lesson for the
Thursday in Holy Week [i].   Of course they are also *omitted*
in the same Evangelistaria from the lesson for the Tuesday

[h] Not, of course, so long as the present senseless fashion prevails of regarding Codex B, (to which, if Cod. L. and Codd. 1, 33 and 69 are added, it is *only
because they agree with B*), as an all but infallible guide in settling the text of
Scripture ; and quietly taking it for granted that *all the other MSS. in existence* have entered into a grand conspiracy to deceive mankind.   Until this
most uncritical method, this most unphilosophical theory, is unconditionally
abandoned, progress in this department of sacred Science is simply impossible.

[i] See Matthaei's note on S. Luke xxii. 43, (*Nov. Test. ed.* 1803.)

after Sexagesima, (τῇ γ́ τῆς τυροφάγου, as the Easterns call
that day,) when S. Luke xxii. 39—xxiii. 1 used to be read.
Moreover, in all ancient copies of the Gospels which have
been accommodated to ecclesiastical use, *the reader of S. Luke*
xxii. *is invariably directed by a marginal note to leave out those
two verses,* and to proceed *per saltum* from ver. 42 to ver. 45 [k].
What more obvious therefore than that the removal of the
paragraph from its proper place in S. Luke's Gospel is to be
attributed to nothing else but the Lectionary practice of the
primitive Church? Quite unreasonable is it to impute heretical motives, or to invent any other unsupported theory,
while this plain solution of the difficulty is at hand.

(2.) The same Cod. B., (with which Codd. א, C, L, U and Γ
are observed here to conspire,) introduces the piercing of the
Saviour's side (S. John xix. 34) at the end of S. Matth.
xxvii. 49. Now, I only do not insist that this must needs
be the result of the singular Lectionary practice already described at p. 202, because a scholion in Cod. 72 records the
singular fact that in the Diatessaron of Tatian, after S. Matth.
xxvii. 48, was read ἄλλος δὲ λαβὼν λόγχην ἔνυξεν αὐτοῦ τὴν

[k] This will be best understood by actual reference to a manuscript. In
Cod. Evan. 436 (Meerman 117) which lies before me, these directions are
given as follows. After τὸ σὸν γενέσθω (i.e. the last words of ver. 42), is written ὑπέρβα εἰς τὸ τῆς γ́. Then, at the end of ver. 44, is written—ἄρξου τῆς γ́,
after which follows the text καὶ ἀναστάς, &c.

In S. Matthew's Gospel, at chap. xxvi, which contains the Liturgical section
for Thursday in Holy Week (τῇ ἁγίᾳ καὶ μεγάλῃ ἐ), my Codex has been
only imperfectly rubricated. Let me therefore be allowed to quote from Harl.
MS. 1810, (our Cod. Evan. 113) which, at fol. 84, at the end of S. Matth.
xxvi. 39, reads as follows, immediately after the words,—ἀλλ' ὡς σύ :-- ⊹/Υ ✕
(i.e. ὑπάντα.) But in order to explain what is meant, the above rubricated
word and sign are repeated at foot, as follows :—✕ ὑπάντα εἰς τὸ κατὰ Λουκᾶν
ἐν κεφαλαίῳ ρθ. ὤφθη δὲ αὐτῷ ἄγγελος : εἶτα στραφεὶς ἐνταῦθα πάλιν, λέγε· καὶ
ἔρχεται πρὸς τοὺς μαθητάς—which are the first words of S. Matth. xxvi. 40.

Accordingly, my Codex (No. 436, above referred to) immediately after
S. Luke xxii. 42, *besides* the rubric already quoted, has the following: ἄρξου
τῆς μεγάλης ἐ. Then come the two famous verses (ver. 43, 44); and, after the
words ἀναστὰς ἀπὸ τῆς προσευχῆς, the following rubric occurs : ὑπάντα εἰς τὸ
τῆς μεγάλης ἐ Ματθ. ἔρχεται πρὸς τοὺς μαθητάς.

[With the help of my nephew, (Rev. W. F. Rose, Curate of Holy Trinity,
Windsor,) I have collated every syllable of Cod. 436. Its text most nearly
resembles the Rev. F. H. Scrivener's l, m, n.]

πλευράν· καὶ ἐξῆλθεν ὕδωρ καὶ αἷμα. (Chrysostom's codex was evidently vitiated in *precisely* the same way.) This interpolation therefore *may* have resulted from the corrupting influence of Tatian's (so-called) "Harmony." See Appendix (H).

(3.) To keep on safe ground. Codd. B and D concur in what Alford justly calls the "grave error" of simply omitting from S. Luke xxiii. 34, our Lord's supplication on behalf of His murderers, (ὁ δὲ Ἰησοῦς ἔλεγε, Πάτερ, ἄφες αὐτοῖς· οὐ γὰρ οἴδασι τί ποιοῦσι). They are not quite singular in so doing; being, as usual, kept in countenance by certain copies of the old Latin, as well as by both the Egyptian versions. How is this "grave error" in so many ancient MSS. to be accounted for? (for a "grave error," or rather "a fatal omission" it certainly is). Simply by the fact that in the Eastern Church the Lection for the Thursday after Sexagesima *breaks off abruptly, immediately before these very words,*—to recommence at ver. 44 [1].

(4.) Note, that at ver. 32, *the eighth " Gospel of the Passion" begins,*—which is the reason why Codd. B and ℵ (with the Egyptian versions) exhibit a singular irregularity in that place; and why the Jerusalem Syriac introduces the established formula of the Lectionaries (σὺν τῷ Ἰησοῦ) at the same juncture.

(If I do not here insist that the absence of the famous *pericopa de adulterâ* (S. John vii. 53—viii. 11,) from so many MSS., is to be explained in precisely the same way, it is only because the genuineness of that portion of the Gospel is generally denied; and I propose, in this enumeration of instances, not to set foot on disputed ground. I am convinced, nevertheless, that the first occasion of the omission of those memorable verses was the lectionary practice of the primitive Church, which, on Whitsunday, read from S. John vii. 37 to viii. 12, *leaving out the twelve verses* in question. Those verses, from the nature of their contents, (as Augustine declares,) easily came to be viewed with dislike or suspicion. The passage, however, is as old as the second century, for it is found in certain copies of the old Latin. Moreover Jerome deliberately gave it a place in the Vulgate. I pass on.)

---

[1] See by all means Matthaei's *Nov. Test.* (ed. 1803,) i. p. 491, and 492.

(5.) The two oldest Codices in existence,—B and ℵ,—
stand all but alone in omitting from S. Luke vi. 1 the unique
and indubitably genuine word δευτεροπρώτῳ; which is also
omitted by the Peshito, Italic and Coptic versions. And
yet, when it is observed that *an Ecclesiastical lection begins
here*, and that the Evangelistaria (which *invariably* leave out
such notes of time) simply drop the word,—only substituting
for ἐν σαββάτῳ the more familiar τοῖς σάββασι,—every one
will be ready to admit that if the omission of this word be
not due to the inattention of the copyist, (which, however,
seems to me not at all unlikely[m],) it is sufficiently explained
by the Lectionary practice of the Church,—which may well
date back even to the immediately post-Apostolic age.

(6.) In S. Luke xvi. 19, Cod. D introduces the Parable of
Lazarus with the formula,—εἶπεν δὲ καὶ ἑτέραν παραβολήν;
which is nothing else but a marginal note which has found
its way into the text from the margin; being *the liturgical
introduction of a Church-lesson*[n] which afterwards began εἶπεν
ὁ Κύριος τὴν παραβολὴν ταύτην[o].

(7.) In like manner, the same Codex makes S. John xiv.
begin with *the liturgical formula*,—(it survives in our Book of
Common Prayer[*] to this very hour!)—καὶ εἶπεν τοῖς μαθηταῖς
αὐτοῦ: in which it is countenanced by certain MSS. of the
Vulgate and of the old Latin Version. Indeed, it may be
stated generally concerning the text of Cod. D, that it bears
marks *throughout* of the depraving influence of the ancient
Lectionary practice. Instances of this, (in addition to those
elsewhere cited in these pages,) will be discovered in S. Luke
iii. 23: iv. 16 (and xix. 45): v. 1 and 17: vi. 37 (and xviii.
15): vii. 1: x. 1 and 25: xx. 1: in all but three of which,
Cod. D is kept in countenance by the old Latin, often by the
Syriac, and by other versions of the greatest antiquity. But
to proceed.

(8.) Cod. A, (supported by Athanasius, the Vulgate,
Gothic, and Philoxenian versions,) for καί, in S. Luke ix. 57,

---

[m] See above, p. 75, note (h).   [n] For the 5th Sunday of S. Luke.

[o] Such variations are quite common. Matthaei, with his usual accuracy,
points out several: e.g. *Nov. Test.* (1788) vol. i. p. 19 (*note* 26), p. 23: vol. ii.
p. 10 (*note* 12), p. 14 (*notes* 14 and 15), &c.   [*] SS. Philip and James.

reads ἐγένετο δέ,—which is the reading of the Textus Receptus. Cod. D, (with some copies of the old Latin,) exhibits καὶ ἐγένετο. All the diversity which is observable in this place, (and it is considerable,) is owing to the fact that *an Ecclesiastical lection begins here* [p]. In different Churches, the formula with which the lection was introduced slightly differed.

(9.) Cod. C is supported by Chrysostom and Jerome, as well as by the Peshito, Cureton's and the Philoxenian Syriac, and some MSS. of the old Latin, in reading ὁ Ἰησοῦς at the beginning of S. Matth. xi. 20. That the words have no business there, is universally admitted. So also is the cause of their interpolation generally recognized. *The Ecclesiastical lection* for Wednesday in the iv[th] week after Pentecost *begins at that place;* and begins with the formula,—ἐν τῷ καίρῳ ἐκείνῳ, ἤρξατο ὁ Ἰησοῦς ὀνειδίζειν.

(10.) Similarly, in S. Matth. xii. 9, xiii. 36, and xiv. 14, Cod. C inserts ὁ Ἰησοῦς; a reading which on all three occasions is countenanced by the Syriac and some copies of the old Latin, and on the last of the three, by Origen also. And yet there can be no doubt that it is only because *Ecclesiastical lections begin at those places* [q], that the Holy Name is introduced there.

(11.) Let me add that the Sacred Name is confessedly an interpolation in the six places indicated at foot,—its presence being accounted for by the fact that, in each, *an Ecclesiastical lection begins* [r]. Cod. D in one of these places, Cod. A in four, is kept in countenance by the old Latin, the Syriac, the Coptic and other early versions;—convincing indications of the extent to which the Lectionary practice of the Church had established itself so early as the second century of our æra.

Cod. D, and copies of the old Latin and Egyptian versions also read τοῦ Ἰησοῦ, (instead of αὐτοῦ,) in S. Mark xiv. 3; which is only because *a Church lesson begins there.*

---

[p] viz. σαββάτῳ θ: i.e. the ix[th] Saturday in S. Luke.—Note that Cod. A also reads ἐγένετο δέ in S. Lu. xi. 1.

[q] viz. Monday in the vth, Thursday in the vi[th] week after Pentecost, and the viii[th] Sunday after Pentecost.

[r] viz. S. Luke xiii. 2 : xxiv. 36. S. John i. 29 (ὁ Ἰωάννης) : 44 : vi. 14 : xiii. 3,

(12.) The same Cod. D is all but unique in leaving out
that memorable verse in S. Luke's Gospel (xxiv. 12), in
which S. Peter's visit to the Sepulchre of our risen LORD
finds particular mention. It is only because that verse was
claimed both as the *conclusion* of the iv[th] and also as the
beginning of the vth Gospel of the Resurrection: so that the
liturgical note ἀρχή stands at the beginning,—τέλος at the
end of it. Accordingly, D is kept in countenance here only
by the Jerusalem Lectionary and some copies of the old
Latin. But what is to be thought of the editorial judgment
which (with Tregelles) encloses this verse within brackets;
and (with Tischendorf) *rejects it from the text altogether?*

(13.) Codices B, ℵ, and D are *alone* among MSS. in omitting the clause διελθὼν διὰ μέσου αὐτῶν· καὶ παρῆγεν οὕτως,
at the end of the 59th verse of S. John viii. The omission
is to be accounted for by the fact that just *there* the Church-
lesson for Tuesday in the vth week after Easter *came to
an end.*

(14.) Again. It is not at all an unusual thing to find
in cursive MSS., at the end of S. Matth. viii. 13, (with several varieties), the spurious and tasteless appendix,—καὶ
ὑποστρέψας ὁ ἑκατόνταρχος εἰς τὸν οἶκον αὐτοῦ ἐν αὐτῇ τῇ
ὥρᾳ εὗρεν τὸν παῖδα ὑγιαίνοντα: a clause which owes its
existence solely to the practice of ending the lection for the
iv[th] Sunday after Pentecost in that unauthorized manner[s].
But it is not only in cursive MSS. that these words are
found. *They are met with also in the Codex Sinaiticus* (ℵ):
a witness at once to the inveteracy of Liturgical usage in
the iv[th] century of our æra, and to the corruptions which
the "Codex omnium antiquissimus" will no doubt have inherited from a yet older copy than itself.

—to which should perhaps be added xxi. 1, where B, ℵ, A, C (not D) read
Ἰησοῦς.

[s] See by all means Matthaei's interesting note on the place,—*Nov. Test.*
(1788) vol. i. p. 113-4. It should be mentioned that Cod. C (and four other
uncials), together with the Philoxenian and Hierosolymitan versions, concur
in exhibiting the same spurious clause. Matthaei remarks, — "Origenes
(iv. 171 D) hunc pericopam haud adeo diligenter recensens terminat eum in
γεννηθήτω σοι." Will not the disturbing *Lectionary-practice* of his day sufficiently explain Origen's omission?

(15.) In conclusion, I may remark generally that there occur instances, again and again, of perturbations of the Text in our oldest MSS., (corresponding sometimes with readings vouched for by the most ancient of the Fathers,) which admit of no more intelligible or inoffensive solution than by referring them to the Lectionary practice of the primitive Church[t].

Thus when instead of καὶ ἀναβαίνων ὁ Ἰησοῦς εἰς Ἱεροσόλυμα (S. Matth. xx. 17), Cod. B reads, (and, is almost unique in reading,) Μέλλων δὲ ἀναβαίνειν ὁ Ἰησοῦς; and when Origen sometimes quotes the place in the same way, but sometimes is observed to transpose the position of the Holy Name in the sentence; when again six of Matthaei's MSS., (and Origen once,) are observed to put the same Name *after* Ἱεροσόλυμα: when, lastly, two of Field's MSS.[u], and one of Matthaei's, (and I dare say a great many more, if the truth were known,) omit the words ὁ Ἰησοῦς entirely:—*who* sees not that the true disturbing force in this place, from the ii[nd] century of our æra downwards, has been *the Lectionary practice of the primitive Church?*—the fact that *there* the lection for the Thursday after the viii[th] Sunday after Pentecost began?—And this may suffice.

IV. It has been proved then, in what goes before, more effectually even than in a preceding page[w], not only that Ecclesiastical Lections corresponding with those indicated in the "Synaxaria" were fully established in the immediately post-Apostolic age, but also that at that early period the Lectionary system of primitive Christendom had already exercised a depraving influence of a peculiar kind on the text of Scripture. Further yet, (and *this* is the only point I am now concerned to establish), that *our five oldest Copies of the Gospels,*—B and א as well as A, C and D,—exhibit

---

[t] I recal S. John x. 29: xix. 13: xxi. 1;—but the attentive student will be able to multiply such references almost indefinitely. In these and similar places, while the phraseology is exceedingly simple, the variations which the text exhibits are so exceeding numerous,—that when it is discovered that *a Church Lesson begins in those places,* we may be sure that we have been put in possession of the name of the disturbing force.

[u] Viz. K and M. (Field's *Chrys.* p. 251.)—How is it that the readings of Chrysostom are made so little account of? By Tregelles, for example, why are they overlooked entirely?   [w] See above, p. 197 to 204.

not a few traces of the mischievous agency alluded to; errors, and especially *omissions*, which sometimes seriously affect the character of those Codices as witnesses to the Truth of Scripture.—I proceed now to consider the case of S. Mark xvi. 9—20; only prefacing my remarks with a few necessary words of explanation.

V. He who takes into his hands an ordinary cursive MS. of the Gospels, is prepared to find the Church-lessons regularly indicated throughout, in the text or in the margin. A familiar contraction, executed probably in vermillion $\overset{\prime\chi\prime}{\alpha\rho}$, $\dot{\alpha}\rho$, indicates the "beginning" ($\dot{\alpha}\rho\chi\dot{\eta}$) of each lection : a corresponding contraction $\overset{\epsilon\prime}{\tau}, \overset{\widehat{\epsilon}}{\tau\prime}, \tau\epsilon\backslash:, \overset{\lambda}{\tau\epsilon}, \tau\epsilon\overset{o}{\chi}$, indicates its "end" ($\tau\epsilon\lambda os$.) Generally, these rubrical directions, (for they are nothing else,) are inserted for convenience into the body of the text,—from which the red pigment with which they are almost invariably executed, effectually distinguishes them. But all these particulars gradually disappear as recourse is had to older and yet older MSS. The studious in such matters have noticed that even the memorandums as to the "beginning" and the "end" of a lection are rare, almost in proportion to the antiquity of a Codex. When they do occur in the later uncials, they do not by any means always seem to have been the work of the original scribe; neither has care been always taken to indicate them in ink of a different colour. It will further be observed in such MSS. that whereas the sign where the reader is to begin is generally—(in order the better to attract his attention,)—inserted in *the margin* of the Codex, the note where he is to leave off, (in order the more effectually to arrest his progress,) is as a rule introduced *into the body of the text*[x]. In uncial MSS., however, all such symbols are not only rare, but (what is much to be noted) they are exceedingly irregular in their occurrence. Thus in Codex Γ, in the Bodleian Library, (a recently acquired uncial MS. of the Gospels, written A.D. 844), there occurs no indication of the "end" of a single lection in S. Luke's Gospel, until chap.

---

[x] e.g. in Cod. Evan. 10 and 270.

xvi. 31 is reached; after which, the sign abounds. In Codex L, the original notes of Ecclesiastical Lections occur at the following rare and irregular intervals: — S. Mark ix. 2: x. 46: xii. 40 (where the sign has lost its way; it should have stood against ver. 44): xv. 42 and xvi. 1ʸ. In the *oldest* uncials, nothing of the kind is discoverable. Even in the Codex Bezæ, (viᵗʰ century,) not a single liturgical direction *coeval with the MS.* is anywhere to be found.

VI. And yet, although the practice of thus indicating the beginning and the end of a liturgical section, does not seem to have come into general use until about the xiiᵗʰ century; and although, previous to the ixᵗʰ century, systematic liturgical directions are probably unknown ᶻ; the *need* of them must have been experienced by one standing up to read before the congregation, long before. The want of some reminder where he was to begin,—above all, of some hint where he was to leave off,—will have infallibly made itself felt from the first. Accordingly, there are not wanting indications that, occasionally, τελοϲ (or το τελοϲ) was written in the margin of Copies of the Gospels at an exceedingly remote epoch. One memorable example of this practice is supplied by the Codex Bezæ (D): where in S. Mark xiv. 41, instead of ἀπέχει. ἦλθεν ἡ ὥρα,—we meet with the unintelligible απεχει το τελοϲ και η ωρα. Now, nothing else has here happened but that a marginal note, designed originally to indicate the end (το τελοϲ) of the lesson for

---

ʸ In some cursive MSS. also, (which have been probably transcribed from ancient originals), the same phenomenon is observed. Thus, in Evan. 265 (= Reg. 66), τελ only occurs, in S. Mark, at ix. 9 and 41: xv. 32 and 41: xvi. 8. Αρχ at xvi. 1. It is striking to observe that so little were these ecclesiastical notes (embedded in the text) understood by the possessor of the MS., that in the margin, over against ch. xv. 41, (where "τελᵃ:" stands *in the text*,) a somewhat later hand has written,— τε[λοs] τ[ης] ὡρ[ας]. A similar liturgical note may be seen over against ch. ix. 9, and elsewhere. Cod. 25 (=Reg. 191), at the end of S. Mark's Gospel, has *only two* notes of liturgical endings: viz. at ch. xv. 1 and 42.

ᶻ Among the *Syriac* Evangelia, as explained above (p. 215), instances occur of far more ancient MSS. which exhibit a text rubricated by the original scribe. Even here, however, (as may be learned from Dr. Wright's *Catalogue*, pp. 46 —66,) such Rubrics have been only *irregularly* inserted in the oldest copies.

the third day of the ii[nd] week of the Carnival, has lost its
way from the end of ver. 42, and got thrust into the text
of ver. 41,—to the manifest destruction of the sense[a]. I find
D's error here is shared (a) by the Peshito Syriac, (b) by
the old Latin, and (c) by the Philoxenian : venerable part-
ners in error, truly ! for the first two probably carry back
this false reading to *the second century of our æra;* and so,
furnish one more remarkable proof, to be added to the fifteen
(or rather the forty) already enumerated (pp. 217-23), that the
lessons of the Eastern Church were settled at a period long
anterior to the date of the oldest MS. of the Gospels extant.

VII. Returning then to the problem before us, I venture
to suggest as follows:—What if, at a very remote period,
this same isolated liturgical note (το τελοc) occurring at
S. Mark xvi. 8, (which *is* "the end" of *the Church-lection*
for the ii[nd] Sunday after Easter,) should have unhappily
suggested to some copyist,—καλλιγραφίας *quam vel Criticæ
Sacræ vel rerum Liturgicarum peritior,*—the notion that *the
entire "Gospel according to S. Mark,"* came to an end at
verse 8 ? . . . . I see no more probable account of the matter,
I say, than this :—That the mutilation of the last chapter
of S. Mark has resulted from the fact, that some very ancient
scribe *misapprehended the import of the solitary liturgical note*
τελοc (or το τελοc) which he found at the close of verse 8.
True, that he will have probably beheld, further on, several
additional στίχοι. But if he did, how could he acknowledge the fact more loyally than by leaving (as the author
of Cod. B is observed to have done) one entire column blank,
before proceeding with S. Luke ? He hesitated, all the same,

---

[a] Note, that the Codex from which Cod. D was copied will have exhibited
the text thus,— απεχει το τελοc ηλθεν η ωρα.—which is the reading of Cod. 13 (= Reg. 50.) But the scribe of Cod. D, in order to im-
prove the sense, substituted for ἦλθεν the word καί. Note the scholion [*Anon.
Vat.*] in Possinus, p. 321 :—*ἀπέχει, τουτέστι, πεπλήρωται, τέλος ἔχει τὸ κατ' ἐμέ.*

Besides the said Cod. 13, the same reading is found in 47 and 54 (in the
Bodl.) : 56 (at Linc. Coll.) : 61 (i.e. Cod. Montfort.) : 69 (i.e. Cod. Leicestr.) :
124 (i.e. Cod. Vind. Lamb. 31) : c[scr] (i.e. Lambeth, 1177) : 2[pe] (i.e. the 2nd
of Muralt's S. Petersburg Codd.) ; and Cod. 439 (i.e. Addit. Brit. Mus. 5107).
All these eleven MSS. read *ἀπέχει τὸ τέλος* at S. Mark xiv. 41.

to transcribe any further, having before him, (as he thought,) an assurance that "THE END" had been reached at ver. 8.

VIII. That some were found in very early times eagerly to acquiesce in this omission: to sanction it: even to multiply copies of the Gospel so mutilated; (critics or commentators intent on nothing so much as reconciling the apparent discrepancies in the Evangelical narratives:)—appears to me not at all unlikely [b]. Eusebius almost says as much, when he puts into the mouth of one who is for getting rid of these verses altogether, the remark that "they would be in a manner superfluous *if it should appear that their testimony is at variance with that of the other Evangelists* [c]." (The ancients were giants in Divinity but children in Criticism.) On the other hand, I altogether agree with Dean Alford in thinking it highly improbable that the difficulty of harmonizing one Gospel with another in this place, (such as it is,) was the cause why these Twelve Verses were originally suppressed [d]. (1) First, because there really was no need to withhold more than three,—at the utmost, five of them,—if *this* had been the reason of the omission. (2) Next, because it would have

---

[b] So Scholz (i. 200) :—"Pericopa hæc *casu quodam* forsan exciderat a codice quodam Alexandrino; unde defectus iste in alios libros transiit. Nec mirum hunc defectum multis, immo in certis regionibus plerisque scribis arrisisse : confitentur enim ex ipsorum opinione Marcum Matthæo repugnare. Cf. maxime Eusebium ad Marinum," &c.

[c] περιττὰ ἂν εἴη, καὶ μάλιστα εἴπερ ἔχοιεν ἀντιλογίαν τῇ τῶν λοιπῶν εὐαγγελιστῶν μαρτυρίᾳ. (Mai, *Bibl. P.P. Nova*, vol. iv. p. 256.)

[d] Alford's N. T. vol. i. p. 433, (*ed.* 1868.)—And so Tischendorf, (ed. 8va. pp. 406-7.) "Talem dissentionem ad Marci librum tam misere mutilandum adduxisse quempiam, et quidem tanto cum successu, prorsus incredibile est, nec ullo probari potest exemplo."—Tregelles is of the same opinion. (*Printed Text*, pp. 255-6.)—Matthaei, a competent judge, seems to have thought differently. "Una autem causa cur hic locus omitteretur fuit quod Marcus in his repugnare ceteris videtur Evangelistis." The general observation which follows is true enough :—"Quæ ergo vel obscura, vel repugnantia, vel parum decora quorundam opinione habebantur, ea olim ab Criticis et interpretibus nonnullis vel sublata, vel in dubium vocata esse, ex aliis locis sanctorum Evangeliorum intelligitur." (*Nov. Test.* 1788, vol. ii. p. 266.) Presently, (at p. 270,)—"In summâ. Videtur unus et item alter ex interpretibus, qui hæc cæteris evangeliis repugnare opinebatur, in dubium vocasse. Hunc deinde plures temere secuti sunt, ut plerumque factum esse animadvertimus." Dr. Davidson says the same thing (ii. 116,) and, (what is of vastly more importance,) Mr. Scrivener also. (*Coll. Cod. Sin.* p. xliv.)

been easier far to introduce some critical correction of any
supposed discrepancy, than to sweep away the whole of the
unoffending context.   (3) Lastly, because nothing clearly
was gained by causing the Gospel to end so abruptly that
every one must see at a glance that it had been mutilated.
No.   The omission having originated in a mistake, was per-
petuated for a brief period (let us suppose) only through
infirmity of judgment: or, (as I prefer to believe), only in
consequence of the religious fidelity of copyists, who were
evidently always instructed to transcribe exactly what they
found in the copy set before them.   The Church meanwhile
in her corporate capacity, has never known anything at all
of the matter,—as was fully shewn above in Chap. X.

IX. When this solution of the problem first occurred to
me, (and it occurred to me long before I was aware of the
memorable reading το τελος in the Codex Bezæ, already
adverted to,) I reasoned with myself as follows :—But if the
mutilation of the second Gospel came about in this particular way, the MSS. are bound to remember *something* of the
circumstance; and in ancient MSS., if I am right, I ought
certainly to meet with *some* confirmation of my opinion.
According to my view, at the root of this whole matter lies
the fact that at S. Mark xvi. 8 a well-known Ecclesiastical
lesson comes to an end.   Is there not perhaps something
exceptional in the way that the close of that liturgical
section was anciently signified ?

X. In order to ascertain this, I proceeded to inspect every
copy of the Gospels in the Imperial Library at Paris[e]; and
devoted seventy hours exactly, with unflagging delight, to
the task.   The success of the experiment astonished me.

1. I began with *our* Cod. 24 (= Reg. 178) of the Gospels:
turned to the last page of S. Mark: and beheld, in a Codex
of the xi[th] Century wholly devoid of the Lectionary apparatus which is sometimes found in MSS. of a similar
date[f], at fol. 104, the word + τελος + conspicuously written
by the original scribe immediately after S. Mark xvi. 8, as

---

[e] I have to acknowledge very gratefully the obliging attentions of M. de
Wailly, the chief of the Manuscript department.

[f] See above, p. 224.

well as at the close of the Gospel. *It occurred besides only at ch.* ix. 9, (the end of the lesson for the Transfiguration.) And yet there are *at least seventy* occasions in the course of S. Mark's Gospel where, in MSS. which have been accommodated to Church use, it is usual to indicate the close of a Lection. This discovery, which surprised me not a little, convinced me that I was on the right scent; and every hour I met with some fresh confirmation of the fact.

2. For the intelligent reader will readily understand that three such deliberate liturgical memoranda, occurring solitary in a MS. of this date, are to be accounted for only in one way. They infallibly represent a corresponding peculiarity in some far more ancient document. The fact that the word τελος is here (*a*) set down unabbreviated, (*b*) in black ink, and (*c*) as part of the text,—points unmistakably in the same direction. But that Cod. 24 is derived from a Codex of much older date is rendered certain by a circumstance which shall be specified at foot [g].

3. The very same phenomena reappear in Cod. 36 [h]. The sign + τελος +, (which occurs punctually at S. Mark xvi. 8 and again at v. 20,) is found besides in S. Mark's Gospel only at chap. i. 8 [i]; at chap. xiv. 31; and (+ τελος του κεφαλ/) at chap. xv. 24 ;—being on every occasion incorporated with the Text. Now, when it is perceived that in the second and third of these places, τελος has clearly lost its way,—appearing where *no* Ecclesiastical lection came to an end,—it will be felt that the MS. before us (of the xi[th] century) if it was not actually transcribed from,—must at least exhibit at second hand,—a far more ancient Codex [k].

---

[g] Whereas in the course of S. Matthew's Gospel, only two examples of + τελος + occur, (viz. at ch. xxvi. 35 and xxvii. 2,)—in the former case the note has entirely lost its way in the process of transcription; standing where it has no business to appear. *No* Liturgical section ends thereabouts. I suspect that the transition (ὑπέρβασις) anciently made at ver. 39, was the thing to which the scribe desired to call attention.

[h] = Coisl. 20. This sumptuous MS., which has not been adapted for Church purposes, appears to me to be the work of the same scribe who produced Reg. 178, (the codex described above); but it exhibits a different text. Bound up with it are some leaves of the LXX of about the viii[th] century.

[i] End of the Lection for the Sunday before Epiphany.

[k] In S. Matthew's Gospel, I could find τελος so written only twice,—viz.

4. Only once more.—Codex 22 (= Reg. 72) was never prepared for Church purposes. A rough ha? d has indeed scrawled indications of the be ;innings and endings of a few of the Lessons, here and the;e; but these liturgical notes are no part of the original MS. At S. Mark xvi. 8, however, we are presented (as before) with the solitary note + τελοc +——, incorporated with the text. Immediately after which, (in writing of the same size,) comes a memorable statement[1] in red letters. The whole stands thus:—

φοβοῦντο γαρ +   τέλοc+——

�֍ ἔν τιcι τῶν ἀντιγράφων.

ἔωc ὧδε πληροῦται ὁ ἐυ

αγγελιcτήc : ἐν πολλοῖc

Δε. καὶ ταῦτα φέρεται +——

Ἀναcτὰσ δὲ. πρωὶ πρώτη σαββάτων.

And then follows the rest of the Gospel; at the end of which, the sign + τελοc + is again repeated,—which sign, however, occurs *nowhere else* in the MS. *nor at the end of any of the other three Gospels.* A more opportune piece of evidence could hardly have been invented. A statement so apt and so significant was surely a thing rather to be wished than to be hoped for. For here is the liturgical sign τελοc not only occurring in the wholly exceptional way of which we have already seen examples, but actually followed by the admission that "In certain copies, *the Evangelist proceeds no further."* The two circumstances so brought together seem exactly to bridge over the chasm between Codd. B and א on the one hand,—and Codd. 24 and 36 on the other; and to supply us with precisely the link of evidence which we require. For observe:—During the first six centuries of our æra, no single instance is known of a codex in which τελοc is written at the end of a Gospel. The subscription of

at ch. ii. 23 and xxvi. 75: in S. Luke only once,—viz. at ch. viii. 39. These, in all three instances, are the concluding verses of famous Lessons,—viz. the Sunday after Christmas Day, the iii[rd] Gospel of the Passion, the vi[th] Sunday of S. Luke.

[1] This has already come before us in a different connection: (see p. 119): but it must needs be reproduced here; and *this* time, it shall be exhibited as faithfully as my notes permit.

S. Mark for instance is *invariably* either ΚΑΤΑ ΜΑΡΚΟΝ,—
(as in B an.ₜ ℵ) : or else ΕΥΑΓΓΕΛΙΟΝ ΚΑΤΑ ΜΑΡΚΟΝ,—
(as in A and C, and the otᵢ er older uncials) : *never* ΤΕΛΟC.
But here is a Scribe who first copies the *liturgical* note ΤΕΛΟC,
—and then volunteers the *critical* observation that "in some
copies of S. Mark's Gospel the Evangelist proceeds no further !" A more extraordinary corroboration of the view
which I am endeavouring to recommend to the reader's
acceptance, I really cannot imagine. Why, the ancient
Copyist actually comes back, in order to assure me that
the suggestion which I have been already offering in explanation of the difficulty, is the true one !

5. I am not about to abuse the reader's patience with
a prolonged enumeration of the many additional conspiring
circumstances,—insignificant in themselves and confessedly
unimportant when considered singly, but of which the cu-
mulative force is unquestionably great,—which an examination of 99 MSS. of the Gospels brought to light [m]. Enough
has been said already to shew,

(1st.) That it must have been a customary thing, at
a very remote age, to write the word ΤΕΛΟC against S. Mark
xvi. 8, even when the same note was withheld from the
close of almost every other ecclesiastical lection in the
Gospel.

(2ndly.) That this word, or rather note, which no doubt

[m] (1) In Evan. 282 (written A.D. 1176),—a codex which *has been* adapted to
Lectionary purposes,—the sign τεχ⁰ and ϛ, strange to say, *is inserted into the
body of the Text, only at S. Mark* xv. 47 *and* xvi. 8.

(2) Evan. 268, (a truly superb MS., evidently left unfinished, the pictures
of the Evangelists only sketched in ink,) was never prepared for Lectionary
purposes; which makes it the more remarkable that, between ἐφοβοῦντο γάρ
and ἀναστάς, should be found inserted into the body of the text, τέ. in gold.

(3) I have often met with copies of S. Matthew's, or of S. Luke's, or of
S. John's Gospel, unfurnished with a subscription in which τέλος occurs : but
scarcely ever have I seen an instance of a Codex where the Gospel *according
to ·S. Mark* was one of two, or of three from which it was wanting; much less
where it stood alone in that respect. On the other hand, in the following
Codices,—Evan. 10: 22 : 30 : 293,—S. Mark's is *the only Gospel of the Four
which is furnished with the subscription,* + τέλος τοῦ κατὰ Μάρκον εὐαγγελίου ·.·
or simply + τέλος + ... In Evan. 282, S. Matthew's Gospel shares this
peculiarity with S. Mark's.

was originally written as a liturgical memorandum in the
margin, became at a very early period incorporated with the
text; where, retaining neither its use nor its significancy, it
was liable to misconception, and may have easily come to be
fatally misunderstood.

And although these two facts certainly prove nothing in
and by themselves, yet, when brought close alongside of the
problem which has to be solved, their significancy becomes
immediately apparent : for,

(3rdly.) As a matter of fact, there are found to have
existed before the time of Eusebius, copies of S. Mark's
Gospel which *did* come to an end at this very place.　Now,
that *the Evangelist* left off there, no one can believe[n].　*Why*,
then, did *the Scribe* leave off ?　But the Reader is already
in possession of the reason why.　A sufficient explanation of
the difficulty has been elicited from the very MSS. themselves.　And surely when, suspended to an old chest which
has been locked up for ages, a key is still hanging which
fits the lock exactly and enables men to open the chest with
ease, they are at liberty to assume that the key *belongs* to
the lock ; is, in fact, the only instrument by which the chest
may lawfully be opened.

XI. And now, in conclusion, I propose that we summon
back our original Witness, and invite him to syllable his
evidence afresh, in order that we may ascertain if perchance
it affords any countenance whatever to the view which I have
been advocating.　Possible at least it is that in the Patristic
record that copies of S. Mark's Gospel were anciently defective from the 8th verse onwards *some* vestige may be discoverable of the forgotten truth.　Now, it has been already
fully shewn that it is a mistake to introduce into this discussion any other name but that of Eusebius[o].　Do, then, the
terms in which *Eusebius* alludes to this matter lend us any
assistance ?　Let us have the original indictment read over
to us once more : and *this* time we are bound to listen to
every word of it with the utmost possible attention.

---

[n] " Nemini in mentem venire potest Marcum narrationis suae filum ineptis-
sime abrupisse verbis—ἐφοβοῦντο γάρ."—Griesbach *Comment. Crit.* (ii. 197.)
So, in fact, *uno ore* all the Critics.　　　　[o] Chap. V. See above, pp. 66-7.

1. A problem is proposed for solution. "There are two ways of solving it," (Eusebius begins) :—ὁ μὲν γὰρ [τὸ κεφά-λαιον αὐτὸ] τὴν τοῦτο φάσκουσαν περικοπὴν ἀθετῶν, εἴποι ἀν μὴ ἐν ἅπασιν αὐτὴν φέρεσθαι τοῖς ἀντιγράφοις τοῦ κατὰ Μάρκον εὐαγγελίου· τὰ γοῦν ἀκριβῆ τῶν ἀντιγράφων τὸ ΤΕΛΟΣ περιγράφει τῆς κατὰ τὸν Μάρκον ἱστορίας ἐν τοῖς λόγοις κ. τ. λ. οἷς ἐπιλέγει, "καὶ οὐδενὶ οὐδὲν εἶπον, ἐφοβοῦντο γάρ." Ἐν τούτῳ σχεδὸν ἐν ἅπασι τοῖς ἀντιγράφοις τοῦ κατά Μάρκον εὐαγγελίου περιγέγραπται τὸ ΤΕΛΟΣ [p]. . . . Let us halt here for one moment.

2. Surely, a new and unexpected light already begins to dawn upon this subject! How is it that we paid so little attention before to the terms in which this ancient Father delivers his evidence, that we overlooked the import of an expression of his which from the first must have struck us as peculiar, but which *now* we perceive to be of paramount sig-nificancy? Eusebius is pointing out that *one* way for a man (so minded) to get rid of the apparent inconsistency between S. Mark xvi. 9 and S. Matth. xxviii. 1, would be for him to reject the entire "Ecclesiastical Lection[q]" in which S. Mark xvi. 9 occurs. Any one adopting this course, (he proceeds ; and it is much to be noted that Eusebius is throughout deli-vering the imaginary sentiments of another,—not his own :) Such an one (he says) "will say that it is *not met with in all* the copies of S. Mark's Gospel. The accurate copies, at all events,"—and then follows an expression in which this ancient Critic is observed ingeniously to accommodate his language to the phenomenon which he has to describe, so as covertly to insinuate something else. Eusebius employs an idiom (it is found elsewhere in his writings) sufficiently colourless to have hitherto failed to arouse attention ; but of which it is impossible to overlook the actual design and import, after all that has gone before. He clearly *recognises the very phenomenon to which I have been calling*

---

[p] The English reader will follow the text with sufficient exactness if he will refer back, and read from the last line of p. 44 to the ninth line of p. 45 ; taking care to see, in two places, for "the end,"—"THE END" .... The entire context of the Greek is given in the Appendix (B).

[q] τὴν τοῦτο φάσκουσαν περικοπήν. The antecedent phrase, (τὸ κεφάλαιον αὐτό,) I suspect must be an explanatory gloss.

attention within the last two pages, and which I need not
further insist upon or explain : viz. that *the words* το τελοc
were in some very ancient (" *the accurate*") copies *found written after* ἐφοβοῦντο γάρ : although to an unsuspicious reader
the expression which he uses may well seem to denote
nothing more than that the second Gospel *generally came
to an end* there.

3. And now it is time to direct attention to the important
bearing of the foregoing remark on the main point at issue.
The true import of what Eusebius has delivered, and which
has at last been ascertained, will be observed really to set
his evidence in a novel and unsuspected light. From the
days of Jerome, it has been customary to assume that Eusebius roundly states that, in his time *almost all the Greek
copies* were without our "last Twelve Verses" of S. Mark's
Gospel[r] : whereas Eusebius really *does nowhere say so.* He
expresses himself enigmatically, resorting to a somewhat unusual phrase[s] which perhaps admits of no exact English counterpart : but what he says clearly amounts to no more than
this,—that "*the accurate* copies, at the words ἐφοβοῦντο γάρ,
circumscribe THE END (το τελοc) of Mark's narrative :" that
there, " in almost all the Copies of the Gospel according to
Mark, is circumscribed THE END." He says no more. He
does not say that *there* " is circumscribed *the Gospel.*" As
for the twelve verses which follow, he merely declares that
they were " *not met with in all* the copies ;" i.e. that *some*
copies did not contain them. But this, so far from being

---

[r] " This then is clear," (is Dr. Tregelles' comment,) " that the greater part
of the Greek copies had not the verses in question."—*Printed Text,* p. 247.

[s] Observe, the peculiarity of the expression in this place of Eusebius consists
entirely in his introduction of the words τὸ τέλος. Had he merely said τὰ
ἀκριβῆ τῶν ἀντιγράφων τὸ εὐαγγέλιον κατὰ Μάρκον περιγράφει ἐν τοῖς λόγοις
κ. τ. λ. . . . . Ἐν τούτῳ γὰρ σχεδὸν ἐν ἅπασι τοῖς ἀντιγράφοις περιγέγραπται τὸ
κατὰ Μάρκον εὐαγγέλιον,—there would have been nothing extraordinary in
the mode of expression. We should have been reminded of such places as the
following in the writings of Eusebius himself:—Ὁ Κλήμης . . . εἰς τὴν Κομόδου
τελευτὴν περιγράφει τοὺς χρόνους, (*Hist. Eccl.* lib. vi. c. 6.)—Ἱππόλυτος . . .
ἐπὶ τὸ πρῶτον ἔτος αὐτοκράτορος Ἀλεξάνδρου τοὺς χρόνους περιγράφει, (*Ibid.*
c. 22. See the note of Valcsius on the place.)—Or this, referred to by Stephanus (*in voce*),—Ἑνὸς δ' ἔτι μνησθεὶς περιγράψω τὸν λόγον, (*Praep. Evang.*
lib. vi. c. 10, [p. 280 c, *ed.* 1628].) But the substitution of τὸ τέλος for τὸ εὐαγγέλιον wants explaining ; and can be only satisfactorily explained in one way.

a startling statement, is no more than what Codd. B and ℵ in themselves are sufficient to establish. In other words, Eusebius, (whose testimony on this subject as it is commonly understood is so extravagant [see above, p. 48-9,] as to carry with it its own sufficient refutation,) is found to bear consistent testimony to the two following modest propositions; which, however, are not adduced by him as reasons for rejecting S. Mark xvi. 9—20, but only as samples of *what might be urged* by one desirous of shelving a difficulty suggested by their contents;—

(1st.) That from *some* ancient copies of S. Mark's Gospel these last Twelve Verses were away.

(2nd.) That in *almost all* the copies,—(whether mutilated or not, he does not state,)—the words το τελος were found immediately after ver. 8; which, (he seems to hint,) let those who please accept as evidence that there also is *the end of the Gospel.*

4. But I cannot dismiss the testimony of Eusebius until I have recorded my own entire conviction that this Father is no more an original authority here than Jerome, or Hesychius, or Victor[t]. He is evidently adopting the language of some more ancient writer than himself. I observe that he introduces the problem with the remark that what follows is one of the questions " for ever mooted by every body[u]." I suspect (with Matthaei, [*suprâ*, p. 66,]) that *Origen* is the *true* author of all this confusion. He certainly relates of himself that among his voluminous exegetical writings was *a treatise on S. Mark's Gospel*[x]. To Origen's works, Eusebius, (his

---

[t] See above, p. 66 and p. 67.   [u] Πάρειμι νῦν . . . πρὸς τῷ τέλει τῶν αὐτῶν πάντοτε τοῖς πᾶσι ζητούμενα [*sic*].—Mai, vol. iv. p. 255.

[x] " Consentit autem nobis ad *tractatum quem fecimus de scripturâ* Marci."—Origen. (*Opp.* iii. 929 B.) *Tractat.* xxxv. *in Matth.* [I owe the reference to Cave (i. 118.) It seems to have escaped the vigilance of Huet.]—This serves to explain why Victor of Antioch's Catena on S. Mark was sometimes anciently attributed to Origen: as in Paris Cod. 703, [*olim* 2330, 958, and 1048: also 18.] where is read (at fol. 247), Ὠριγένους πρόλογος εἰς τὴν ἑρμηνείαν τοῦ κατὰ Μάρκον εὐαγγελίου. Note, that Reg. 937 is but a (xvi[th] cent.) counterpart of the preceding; which has been transcribed [xviii[th] cent.] in Par. Suppl. Graec. 40.

Possevinus [*Apparat. Sac.* ii. 542,] (quoted by Huet, *Origeniana*, p. 274) states that there is in the Library of C. C. C., Oxford, a Commentary on S. Mark's Gospel by Origen. The source of this misstatement has been acutely

apologist and admirer,) is known to have habitually resorted ; and, like many others, to have derived not a few
of his notions from that fervid and acute, but most erratic
intellect. Origen's writings in short, seem to have been
the source of much, if not most of the mistaken Criticism
of Antiquity. (The reader is reminded of what has been
offered above at p. 96-7). And this would not be the first
occasion on which it would appear that when an ancient
Writer speaks of *"the accurate copies,"* what he actually
means is *the text of Scripture which was employed or approved
by Origen* [z]. The more attentively the language of Eusebius in this place is considered, the more firmly (it is
thought) will the suspicion be entertained that he is here
only reproducing the sentiments of another person. But,
however this may be, it is at least certain that the precise
meaning of what he says, has been hitherto generally overlooked. He certainly does *not* say, as Jerome, from his
loose translation of the passage [a], evidently imagined,—" om-

---

pointed out to me by the Rev. W. R. Churton. James, in his "Ecloga Oxonio-
Cantabrig.," (1600, lib. i. p. 49,) mentions *"Homiliae Origenis super Evangelio Marcae,* Stabat ad monumentum."—Read instead, (with Rev. H. O.
Coxe, "Cat. Codd. MSS. C. C. C.;" [N°. 142, 4,]) as follows :—"Origenis
presb. Hom. in istud Johannis, *Maria stabat ad monumentum,*" &c. But what
actually led Possevinus astray, I perceive, was James's consummation of his own
blunder in lib. ii. p. 49,—which Possevinus has simply appropriated.

[z] So Chrysostom, speaking of the reading Βηθαβαρά.

Origen (iv. 140) says that not only σχεδὸν ἐν πᾶσι τοῖς ἀντιγράφοις, but also
that *apud Heracleonem,* (who wrote within 50 years of S. John's death,) he
found Βηθανία written in S. John i. 28. Moved by *geographical* considerations,
however, (as he explains,) for Βηθανία, Origen proposes to read Βηθαβαρά.
—Chrysostom (viii. 96 D), after noticing the former reading, declares,—ὅσα δὲ
τῶν ἀντιγράφων ἀκριβέστερον ἔχει ἐν Βηθαβαρά φησιν : but he goes on *to reproduce Origen's reasoning ;*—thereby betraying himself.—The author of the
Catena in Matth. (Cramer, i. 190-1) simply reproduces Chrysostom :—χρὴ δὲ
γινώσκειν ὅτι τὰ ἀκριβῆ τῶν ἀντιγράφων ἐν Βηθαβαρὰ περιέχει. And so, other
Scholia ; until at last what was only due to the mistaken assiduity of Origen,
became generally received as the reading of the "more accurate copies."

A scholium on S. Luke xxiv. 13, in like manner, declares that the true reading of that place is not "60" but "160,"—οὗτως γὰρ τὰ ἀκριβῆ περιέχει, καὶ ἡ
Ὠριγένους τῆς ἀληθείας βεβαίωσις. Accordingly, *Eusebius* also reads the place
in the same erroneous way.

[a] Jerome says of himself (*Opp.* vii. 537,)—" Non digne Græca in Latinum
transfero : aut Græcos lege (si ejusdem linguae habes scientiam) aut si tantum

nibus Graeciae libris pene hoc capitulum in fine non habentibus :"
but only,—"*non in omnibus Evangelii exemplaribus hoc capitulum inveniri ;"* which is an entirely different thing. Eusebius adds,—" Accuratiora saltem exemplaria FINEM narrationis secundum Marcum circumscribunt in verbis ἐφοβοῦντο
γάρ;"—and, " In hoc, fere in omnibus exemplaribus Evangelii
secundum Marcum, FINEM circumscribi."—The point, however, of greatest interest is, that Eusebius here calls attention
to the prevalence in MSS. of his time of the very *liturgical
peculiarity* which plainly supplies the one true solution of
the problem under discussion. His testimony is a marvellous corroboration of what we learn from Cod. 22, (see
above, p. 230,) and, rightly understood, does not go a whit
beyond it.

5. What wonder that Hesychius, because he adopted
blindly what he found in Eusebius, should at once betray
his author and exactly miss the point of what his author
says? Τὸ κατὰ Μάρκον εὐαγγέλιον (so he writes) μέχρι τοῦ
" ἐφοβοῦντο γάρ," ἔχει τὸ τέλος [b].

6. This may suffice concerning the testimony of Eusebius.
—It will be understood that I suppose Origen to have fallen
in with one or more copies of S. Mark's Gospel which exhibited *the Liturgical hint*, (ΤΟ ΤΕΛΟC,) conspicuously written
against S. Mark xvi. 9. Such a copy may, or may not,
have there terminated abruptly. I suspect however that it
did. Origen at all events, (*more suo*,) will have remarked
on the phenomenon before him; and Eusebius will have
adopted his remarks,—as the heralds say, " with *a difference*,"—simply because they suited his purpose, and seemed
to him ingenious and interesting.

7. For the copy in question,—(like *that* other copy of
S. Mark from which the Peshito translation was made, and
in which ΤΟ ΤΕΛΟC most inopportunely occurs at chap. xiv.
41 [c],)—will have become the progenitor of several other
copies (as Codd. B and ℵ); and some of these, it is pretty
evident, were familiarly known to Eusebius.

Latinus es, noli de gratuito munere judicare, et, ut vulgare proverbium est :
equi dentes inspicere donati."
    [b] See above, pp. 57-9 : also Appendix (C), § 2.   [c] See above, pp. 225-6.

8. Let it however be clearly borne in mind that nothing
of all this is in the least degree essential to my argument.
Eusebius, (for aught that I know or care,) may be *solely*
responsible for every word that he has delivered concerning
S. Mark xvi. 9—20. Every link in my argument will remain undisturbed, and the conclusion will be still precisely
the same, whether the mistaken Criticism before us originated with another or with himself.

XII. But *why*, (it may reasonably be asked,)—*Why* should
there have been anything exceptional in the way of indicating the end of this particular Lection? *Why* should
τέλος be so constantly found written after S. Mark xvi. 8?

I answer,—I suppose it was because the Lections which
respectively ended and began at that place were so many,
and were Lections of such unusual importance. Thus,—
(1) On the 2nd Sunday after Easter, (κυριακή γ′ τῶν μυροφόρων, as it was called,) at the Liturgy, was read S. Mark
xv. 43 to xvi. 8; and (2) on the same day at Matins, (by
the Melchite Syrian Christians as well as by the Greeks[d],)
S. Mark xvi. 9—20. The severance, therefore, was at ver. 8.
(3) In certain of the Syrian Churches the liturgical section
for Easter Day was S. Mark xvi. 2—8[e]: in the Churches of
the Jacobite, or Monophysite Christians, the Eucharistic
lesson for Easter-Day was ver. 1—8[f]. (4) The second matin
lesson of the Resurrection (xvi. 1—8) also ends,—and (5)
the third (xvi. 9—20) begins, at the same place: and these
two Gospels (both in the Greek and in the Syrian Churches)
were in constant use not only at Easter, but throughout the
year[g]. (6) *That* same third matin lesson of the Resurrection was also the Lesson at Matins on Ascension-Day; as
well in the Syrian[h] as in the Greek[i] Churches. (7) With

---

[d] R. Payne Smith's *Catal.* p. 116.   [e] See Adler's N. T. *Verss.*
Syrr., p. 70.   [f] R. Payne Smith's *Catal.* p. 146.
[g] See p. 206, also note (k).   [h] R. Payne Smith's *Catal.* p. 117.
[i] Accordingly, in Cod. Evan. 266 (= Paris Reg. 67) is read, at S. Mark
xvi. 8 (*fol.* 125), as follows :—ἐφοβοῦντο γάρ. [then, *rubro*,] τέλος τοῦ Β′ ἑωθίνου,
καὶ τῆς κυριακῆς τῶν μυροφόρων. ἀρχή. [then the text:] Ἀναστὰς κ.τ.λ. . . .
After ver. 20, (at *fol.* 126 of the same Codex) is found the following concluding rubric :—τέλος τοῦ Γ′ ἑωθίνου εὐαγγελίου.
In the same place, (viz. at the end of S. Mark's Gospel,) is found in another

the Monophysite Christians, the lection "feriae tertiae in
albis, ad primam vesperam," (i.e. for the Tuesday in Easter-
Week) was S. Mark xv. 37—xvi. 8: and (8) on the same
day, at Matins, ch. xvi. 9—18 [k].—During eighteen weeks
after Easter therefore, *the only parts* of S. Mark's Gospel
publicly read were (*a*) the last thirteen [ch. xv. 43—xvi. 8],
and (*b*) "*the last twelve*" [ch. xvi. 9—20] verses. Can it
be deemed a strange thing that it should have been found
indispensable to mark, with altogether exceptional emphasis,
—to make it unmistakably plain,—where the former Lection
came to an end, and where the latter Lection began [1]?

XIII. One more circumstance, and but one, remains to
be adverted to in the way of evidence; and one more suggestion to be offered. The circumstance is familiar indeed
to all, but its bearing on the present discussion has never
been pointed out. I allude to the fact that anciently, in
copies of the fourfold Gospel, *the Gospel according to S. Mark
frequently stood last.*

This is memorably the case in respect of the Codex Bezae
[vi]: more memorably yet, in respect of the Gothic version
of Ulphilas (A.D. 360): in both of which MSS., the order
of the Gospels is (1) S. Matthew, (2) S. John, (3) S. Luke,
(4) S. Mark. This is in fact *the usual Western order.* Accordingly it is thus that the Gospels stand in the Codd. Vercel-
lensis (*a*), Veronensis (*b*), Palatinus (*e*), Brixianus (*f*) of the
old Latin version. But this order is not *exclusively* Western.
It is found in Cod. 309. It is also observed in Matthaei's
Codd. 13, 14, (which last is *our* Evan. 256), at Moscow. And

Codex (Evan. 7 = Paris Reg. 71,) the following rubric:—τέλος τοῦ τρίτου τοῦ
ἐωθίνου, καὶ τοῦ ὄρθρου τῆς ἀναλήψεως.   [k] R. Payne Smith's *Catal.* p. 146.

[1] Cod. 27 (xi) is not provided with any lectionary apparatus, and is written
continuously throughout: and yet at S. Mark xvi. 9 a fresh paragraph is
observed to commence.

Not dissimilar is the phenomenon recorded in respect of some copies of the
Armenian version. "The Armenian, in the edition of Zohrab, separates the
concluding 12 verses from the rest of the Gospel . . . Many of the oldest MSS.,
after the words ἐφοβοῦντο γάρ, put the final Εὐαγγέλιον κατὰ Μάρκον, and then
give the additional verses with a new superscription." (Tregelles, *Printed
Text*, p. 253)... We are now in a position to *understand* the Armenian evidence, which has been described above, at p. 36, as well as to estimate its
exact value.

in the same order Eusebius and others of the ancients [m] are
occasionally observed to refer to the four Gospels,—which
induces a suspicion that they were not unfamiliar with it.
Nor is this all. In Codd. 19 and 90 the Gospel according
to S. Mark stands last; though in the former of these the
order of the three antecedent Gospels is (1) S. John, (2) S.
Matthew, (3) S. Luke [*]; in the latter, (1) S. John, (2) S. Luke,
(3) S. Matthew.   What need of many words to explain the
bearing of these facts on the present discussion?   Of course
it will have *sometimes* happened that S. Mark xvi. 8 came to
be written *at the bottom of the left hand page* of a MS. [n] And
we have but to suppose that in the case of one such Codex
the next leaf, which would have been *the last,* was missing,
—(*the very thing which has happened in respect of one of the
Codices at Moscow* [o])—and what else *could* result when a
copyist reached the words,

ΕΦΟΒΟΥΝΤΟ ΓΑΡ. ΤΟ ΤΕΛΟΣ

but the very phenomenon which has exercised critics so sorely
and which gives rise to the whole of the present discussion?
The copyist will have brought S. Mark's Gospel to an end
there, *of course.*   What else could he possibly do? . . . .
Somewhat less excusably was our learned countryman Mill
betrayed into the statement, (inadvertently adopted by Wetstein, Griesbach, and Tischendorf,) that " the last verse of
S. John's Gospel *is omitted* in Cod. 63 :" the truth of the
matter being (as Mr. Scrivener has lately proved) that *the*

---

[m] Euseb. apud Mai, iv. p. 264 = p. 287. Again at p. 289-90.—So also the
author of the 2nd Homily on the Resurr. (Greg. Nyss. *Opp.* iii. 411-2.)—
And see the third of the fragments ascribed to Polycarp. *Patres Apostol.,*
(ed. Jacobson) ii. p. 515.

[*] I believe this will be found to be the *invariable* order of the Gospels *in
the Lectionaries.*

[n] This is the case for instance in Evan. 15 (= Reg. 64). See *fol.* 98 *b.*

[o] I allude of course to Matthaei's Cod. g. (See the note in his *N. T.* vol.
ix. p. 228.) Whether or no the learned critic was right in his conjecture
"aliquot folia excidisse," matters nothing. *The left hand page ends at the
words ἐφοβοῦντο γάρ.* Now, if τέλος had followed, how obvious would have
been the inference that the Gospel itself of S. Mark had come to an end there!

Note, that in the Codex Bezæ (D), S. Mark's Gospel ends at ver. 15: in the
Gothic Codex Argenteus, at ver. 11. The Codex Vercell. (*a*) proves to be imperfect from ch. xv. 15; Cod. Veron. (*b*) from xiii. 24; Cod. Brix. (*f*) from xiv. 70.

last leaf of Cod. 63,—on which the last verse of S. John's Gospel was demonstrably once written,—*has been lost* [q].

XIV. To sum up.

1. It will be perceived that I suppose the omission of "the last Twelve Verses" of S. Mark's Gospel to have originated in a sheer error and misconception on the part of some very ancient Copyist. He *saw* το τελος written after ver. 8: he *assumed* that it was the Subscription, or at least that it denoted "the End," *of the Gospel*.

2. Whether certain ancient Critics, because it was acceptable to them, were not found to promote this mistake,—it is useless to inquire. That there may have arisen some old harmonizer of the Gospels, who, (in the words of Eusebius,) was disposed to "regard what followed as superfluous from its seeming inconsistency with the testimony of the other Evangelists [r];"—and that in this way the error became propagated;—is likely enough. But an error it most certainly was : and to that *error*, the *accident* described in the last preceding paragraph *would have* very materially conduced, and it may have very easily done so.

3. I request however that it may be observed that the "accident" is not *needed* in order to account for the "error." The mere presence of το τελος at ver. 8, so near the end of the Gospel, would be quite enough to occasion it. And we have seen that in very ancient times the word τελος frequently *did* occur in an altogether exceptional manner in that very place. Moreover, we have ascertained that its meaning was *not understood* by the transcribers of ancient MSS.

4. And will any one venture to maintain that it is to him a thing incredible that an intelligent copyist of the iii[rd] century, because he read the words το τελος at S. Mark xvi. 8, can have been beguiled thereby into the supposition that those words indicated "the End" of *S. Mark's Gospel?*— Shall I be told that, even if *one* can have so entirely overlooked the meaning of the liturgical sign as to suffer it to insinuate itself into his text [s], it is nevertheless so im-

---

[q] Scrivener, *Coll. Cod. Sin.* p. lix.   [r] See p. 227.   [s] See above, p. 226.

probable as to pass all credence that *another* can have supposed
that it designated *the termination of the Gospel* of the second
Evangelist?—For all reply, I take leave to point out that
Scholz, and Tischendorf, and Tregelles, and Mai and the
rest of the Critics have, *one and all, without exception, misunderstood the same word occurring in the same place, and in
precisely the same way.*

Yes. The forgotten inadvertence of a solitary Scribe in
the *second* or *third* century has been, *in the nineteenth,* deliberately reproduced, adopted, and stereotyped by every Critic
and every Editor of the New Testament in turn.

What wonder,—(I propose the question deliberately,)—
What wonder that an ancient Copyist should have been misled by a phenomenon which in our own days is observed to
have imposed upon two generations of professed Biblical
Critics discussing this very textual problem, and therefore
fully on their guard against delusion[1]? To this hour, the
illustrious Editors of the text of the Gospels are clearly, one
and all, labouring under the grave error of supposing that
" ἐφοβοῦντο γάρ + τέλος,"—(for which they are so careful
to refer us to " Cod. 22,")—is an indication that *there,* by
rights, comes *the " END" of the Gospel according to S. Mark.*
They have failed to perceive that ΤΕΛΟC in that place is only
a liturgical sign,—the same with which (in its contracted
form) they are sufficiently familiar; and that it serves no
other purpose whatever, but to mark that *there* a famous
Ecclesiastical Lection comes to an end.

With a few pages of summary, we may now bring this
long disquisition to an end.

---

[1] So Scholz:—" hic [sc. 22] post γὰρ + τέλος; dein atramento rubro," &c.
—Tischendorf,—" Testantur scholia . . . *Marci Evangelium* . . . versu 9 *finem
habuisse.* Ita, ut de 30 fere Codd. certe tres videamus, 22 habet: ἐφοβουντο
γαρ + τελος. εν τισι," &c.—Tregelles appeals to copies, " sometimes with τέλος
interposed after ver. 8," (p. 254.)—Mai (iv. 256) in the same spirit remarks,—
" Codex Vaticano-palatinus [220], ex quo Eusebium producimus, post octavum
versum *habet quidem* vocem τέλος, ut alibi interdum observatum fuit; *sed
tamen* ibidem eadem manu subscribitur incrementum cum progredientibus
sectionum notis."

CHAPTER XII.

GENERAL REVIEW OF THE QUESTION: SUMMARY OF THE EVIDENCE; AND CONCLUSION OF THE WHOLE SUBJECT.

This discussion narrowed to a single issue (p. 244).—That S. Mark's Gospel was imperfect from the very first, a thing altogether incredible (p. 246):—But that at some very remote period Copies have suffered mutilation, a supposition probable in the highest degree (p. 248).—Consequences of this admission (p. 252).—Parting words (p. 254.)

THIS Inquiry has at last reached its close. The problem was fully explained at the outset [a]. All the known evidence has since been produced [b], every Witness examined [c]. Counsel has been heard on both sides. A just Sentence will assuredly follow. But it may not be improper that I should in conclusion ask leave to direct attention to the *single issue* which has to be decided, and which has been strangely thrust into the background and practically kept out of sight, by those who have preceded me in this Investigation. The case stands simply thus:—

It being freely admitted that, in the beginning of the iv[th] century, there must have existed Copies of the Gospels in which the last chapter of S. Mark extended no further than ver. 8, the Question arises,—*How is this phenomenon to be accounted for?* ... The problem is not only highly interesting and strictly legitimate, but it is even inevitable. In the immediately preceding chapter, I have endeavoured to solve it, and I believe in a wholly unsuspected way.

But the most recent Editors of the text of the New Testament, declining to entertain so much as the *possibility* that certain copies of the second Gospel *had experienced mutilation in very early times* in respect of these Twelve concluding

---

[a] Chap. I. and II.   [b] Chap. IV, VI—X.   [c] Chap. III, V, and VIII.

Verses, have chosen to occupy themselves rather with conjectures as to how it may have happened that S. Mark's
Gospel *was without a conclusion from the very first.* Persuaded
that no more probable account is to be given of the phenomenon than that *the Evangelist himself put forth a Gospel
which* (for some unexplained reason) *terminated abruptly at
the words* ἐφοβοῦντο γάρ (chap. xvi. 8),—they have unhappily seen fit to illustrate the liveliness of this conviction
of theirs, by presenting the world with his Gospel mutilated
in this particular way.   Practically, therefore, the question
has been reduced to the following single issue:—Whether
of the two suppositions which follow is the more reasonable:

First,—That the Gospel according to S. Mark, as it left the
hands of its inspired Author, *was in this imperfect or unfinished
state ;* ending abruptly at (what we call now) the 8th verse
of the last chapter:—of which solemn circumstance, at the
end of eighteen centuries, Cod. B and Cod. א are the alone
surviving Manuscript witnesses ? . . . or,

Secondly,—That certain copies of S. Mark's Gospel *having
suffered mutilation* in respect of their Twelve concluding
Verses in the post-Apostolic age, Cod. B and Cod. א are the
only examples of MSS. so mutilated which are known to
exist at the present day ?

I. Editors who adopt the former hypothesis, are observed
(*a*) to sever the Verses in question from their context [d] :—(*b*)
to introduce after ver. 8, the subscription " ΚΑΤΑ ΜΑΡΚΟΝ [e] :"
—(*c*) to shut up verses 9—20 within brackets [f].   Regarding
them as "no integral part of the Gospel [g],"—"as an authentic anonymous addition to what Mark himself wrote
down [h]," — a " remarkable Fragment," "placed as a com-
pletion of the Gospel in very early times [i] ;"—they consider
themselves at liberty to go on to suggest that "the Evangelist may have been interrupted in his work :" at any rate,

---

[d] Tischendorf, Tregelles, Alford.

[e] Tregelles, Alford.   [f] Alford.

[g] " Hæc non a Marco scripta esse argumentis probatur idoneis."—See the
rest of Tischendorf's verdict, *suprà*, p. 10; and opposite, p. 245.

[h] Tregelles' *Account of the Printed Text,* p. 259.

[i] Alford's *New Test.* vol. i. *Proleg.* [p. 38] and p. 437.

that " something may have occurred, (as the death of
S. Peter,) to cause him to leave it unfinished [k]." But " the
most probable supposition" (we are assured) " is, that *the
last leaf of the original Gospel was torn away* [l]."

We listen with astonishment; contenting ourselves with
modestly suggesting that surely it will be time to conjecture
why S. Mark's Gospel was left by its Divinely inspired
Author in an unfinished state, when the fact has been established that it probably *was* so left. In the meantime, we
request to be furnished with some evidence of *that fact.*

But not a particle of Evidence is forthcoming. It is not
even pretended that any such evidence exists. Instead, we
are magisterially informed by " the first Biblical Critic in
Europe,"—(I desire to speak of him with gratitude and respect, but S. Mark's Gospel is a vast deal more precious to
me than Dr. Tischendorf's reputation,)—that " *a healthy piety
reclaims against the endeavours of those who are for palming
off as Mark's what the Evangelist is so plainly shewn* [where?]
to have known nothing at all about [m]." In the meanwhile, it
is assumed to be a more reasonable supposition,—(*a*) That
S. Mark published an imperfect Gospel; and that the Twelve
Verses with which his Gospel concludes were the fabrication of a subsequent age; than,—(β) That some ancient
Scribe having with design or by accident left out these
Twelve concluding Verses, copies of the second Gospel so
mutilated become multiplied, and in the beginning of the
iv[th] century existed in considerable numbers.

And yet it is notorious that very soon after the Apostolic
age, liberties precisely of this kind were freely taken with
the text of the New Testament. Origen (A.D. 185—254)
complains of the licentious tampering with the Scriptures
which prevailed in his day. " Men add to them," (he says)
" or *leave out,*—as seems good to themselves [n]." Dionysius
of Corinth, yet earlier, (A.D. 168—176) remarks that it was
no wonder his own writings were added to and *taken from,*
seeing that men presumed to deprave the Word of GOD

---

[k] So Norton, Tregelles, and others.

This suggestion, which was originally Griesbach's, is found in Alford's *New
Test.* vol. i. p. 433, (*ed.* 1868.)—See above, p. 12. The italics are not mine.

[m] Vide *suprà*, p. 10.　　　　　　　　　[n] *Opp.* vol. iii. p. 671.

in the same manner[o]. Irenæus, his contemporary, (living within seventy years of S. John's death,) complains of a corrupted Text[p]. We are able to go back yet half a century, and the depravations of Holy Writ become avowed and flagrant[q]. A competent authority has declared it "no less true to fact than paradoxical in sound, that *the worst corruptions to which the New Testament has been ever subjected* originated within a hundred years after it was composed[r]." Above all, it is demonstrable that Cod. B and Cod. ℵ abound in unwarrantable omissions very like the present[*]; omissions which only do not provoke the same amount of attention because they are of less moment. One such extraordinary depravation of the Text, *in which they also stand alone among MSS.* and to which their patrons are observed to appeal with triumphant complacency, has been already made the subject of distinct investigation. I am much mistaken if it has not been shewn in my VIIth chapter, that the omission of the words ἐν Ἐφέσῳ from Ephes. i. 1, is just as unauthorized,—quite as serious a blemish,—as the suppression of S. Mark xvi. 9—20.

Now, in the face of facts like these, and in the absence of *any Evidence whatever* to prove that S. Mark's Gospel was imperfect from the first,—I submit that an hypothesis so violent and improbable, as well as so wholly uncalled for, is simply undeserving of serious attention. For,

(1st.) It is plain from internal considerations that the improbability of the hypothesis is excessive; "the contents of these Verses being such as to preclude the supposition that they were the work of a post-Apostolic period. The very difficulties which they present afford the strongest presumption of their genuineness." No fabricator of a supplement to S. Mark's Gospel would have ventured on introducing so many minute *seeming* discrepancies: and cer-

---

[o] Eusebius *Eccl. Hist.* iv. 23. Consider Rev. xxii. 18, 19.

[p] Note the remarkable adjuration of Irenæus, *Opp.* i. 821, preserved by Eusebius, *lib.* v. 20.—See Scrivener's *Introduction*, p. 383-4. Consider the attestations at the end of the account of Polycarp's martyrdom, *PP. App.* ii. 614-6.

[q] Allusion is made to the Gnostics Basilides and Valentinus; especially to the work of Marcion.

[r] Scrivener's *Introduction*, pp. 381—391.　　　　[*] See Chap. VI.

tainly "his contemporaries would not have accepted and transmitted such an addition," if he had. It has also been shewn at great length that the Internal Evidence for the genuineness of these Verses is overwhelmingly strong [s]. But,

(2nd.) Even external Evidence is not wanting. It has been acutely pointed out long since, that the absence of a vast assemblage of various Readings in this place, is, in itself, a convincing argument that we have here to do with no spurious appendage to the Gospel [t]. Were this a deservedly suspected passage, it must have shared the fate of all other deservedly (or undeservedly) suspected passages. It never could have come to pass that the various Readings which these Twelve Verses exhibit would be *considerably fewer* than those which attach to the last twelve verses of any of the other three Gospels.

(3rd.) And then surely, if the original Gospel of S. Mark had been such an incomplete work as is feigned, the fact would have been notorious from the first, and must needs have become the subject of general comment [u]. It may be regarded as certain that so extraordinary a circumstance would have been largely remarked upon by the Ancients, and that evidence of the fact would have survived in a hundred quarters. It is, I repeat, simply incredible that Tradition would have proved so utterly neglectful of her office as to remain *quite* silent on such a subject, if the facts had been such as are imagined. Either Papias, or else John the Presbyter,—Justin Martyr, or Hegesippus, or one of the "Seniores apud Irenæum,"—Clemens Alexandrinus, or Tertullian, or Hippolytus,—if not Origen, yet at least Eusebius,—if not

[s] Chap. IX.

[t] "Ad defendendum hunc locum in primis etiam valet mirus Codicum consensus in vocabulis et loquendi formulis singulis. Nam in locis παρεγγράπτοις, etiam multo brevioribus, quo plures sunt Codices, eo plures quoque sunt varietates. Comparetur modo Act. xv. 18, Matth. viii. 13, et loca similia."— C. F. Matthaei's *Nov. Test.* (1788) vol. ii. p. 271.

[u] Speaking of the abrupt termination of the second Gospel at ver. 8, Dr. Tregelles asks,—" Would this have been transmitted as a fact by good witnesses, if there had not been real grounds for regarding it to be true?"— (*Printed Text*, p. 257.) Certainly not, we answer. But *where* are the "good witnesses" of the "transmitted fact?" *There is not so much as one.*

Eusebius, yet certainly Jerome,—*some* early Writer, I say,
must *certainly* have recorded the tradition that S. Mark's
Gospel, as it came from the hands of its inspired author, was
an incomplete or unfinished work.   The silence of the
Ancients, joined to the inherent improbability of the conjecture,—(*that* silence so profound, *this* improbability so gross!)
—is enough, I submit, *in the entire absence of Evidence on the
other side*, to establish *the very contradictory* of the alternative
which recent Critics are so strenuous in recommending to
our acceptance.

(4th.) But on the contrary. We have indirect yet convincing testimony that the *oldest* copies of all *did contain* the
Verses in question[x] : while so far are any of the Writers
just now enumerated from recording that these verses were
absent from the early copies, that five out of those ten
Fathers actually quote, or else refer to the verses in question
in a way which shews that in their day they were the recognised termination of S. Mark's Gospel[y].

We consider ourselves at liberty, therefore, to turn our
attention to the rival alternative.   Our astonishment is even
excessive that it should have been seriously expected of us
that we could accept without Proof of any sort,—without
a particle of Evidence, external, internal, or even traditional,
—the extravagant hypothesis that S. Mark put forth an
unfinished Gospel ; when the obvious and easy alternative
solicits us, of supposing,

II. That, at some period *subsequent* to the time of the
Evangelist, certain copies of S. Mark's Gospel suffered that
mutilation in respect of their last Twelve Verses of which
we meet with *no trace whatever, no record of any sort, until
the beginning of the fourth century*.

(i.) And the facts which *now* meet us on the very thresh-
old, are in a manner conclusive: for if Papias and Justin
Martyr [A.D. 150] do not refer to, yet certainly Irenæus
[A.D. 185] and Hippolytus [A.D. 190—227] *distinctly quote*
Six out of the Twelve suspected Verses,—which are also met
with in the two oldest Syriac Versions, as well as in the old
Latin Translation.   Now the latest of these authorities is

[x] See above, pp. 86—90.   [y] See Chap. III.

earlier by full a hundred years than *the earliest record* that the verses in question were ever absent from ancient MSS. At the eighth Council of Carthage, (as Cyprian relates,) [A.D. 256] Vincentius a Thiberi, one of the eighty-seven African Bishops there assembled, quoted the 17th verse in the presence of the Council.

(ii.) Nor is this all[z]. Besides the Gothic and Egyptian versions in the iv[th] century; besides Ambrose, Cyril of Alexandria, Jerome, and Augustine in the vth, to say nothing of Codices A and C;—the Lectionary of the Church universal, *probably from the second century of our æra,* is found to bestow its solemn and emphatic sanction on *every one* of these Twelve Verses. They are met with *in every MS. of the Gospels in existence,* uncial and cursive,—*except two*[a]; they are found *in every Version;* and are contained besides in *every known Lectionary,* where they are appointed to be read at Easter and on Ascension Day[b].

(iii.) Early in the iv[th] century, however, we are encountered by a famous place in the writings of Eusebius [A.D. 300—340], who, (as I have elsewhere explained[c],) is the *only* Father who delivers any independent testimony on this subject at all. What he says has been strangely misrepresented. It is simply as follows:—

(*a*) One, "Marinus," is introduced *quoting this part of S. Mark's Gospel without suspicion,* and enquiring, How its opening statement is to be reconciled with S. Matth. xxviii. 1? Eusebius, in reply, points out that a man whose only object was to get rid of the difficulty, might adopt the expedient of saying that this last section of S. Mark's Gospel "*is not found in all the copies:*" (μὴ ἐν ἅπασι φέρεσθαι.) Declining, however, to act thus presumptuously in respect of anything claiming to be a part of Evangelical Scripture, (οὐδ' ὁτιοῦν τολμῶν ἀθετεῖν τῶν ὁπωσοῦν ἐν τῇ τῶν εὐαγγελίων γραφῇ φερομένων,)—he *adopts the hypothesis that the text is genuine.* Καὶ δὴ τοῦδε τοῦ μέρους συγχωρουμένου εἶναι ἀληθοῦς, he begins: and he enters at once without hesitation on an elu-

---

[z] See above, Chap. III. and IV.

[a] "Habent perlochain hanc Codices Græci, si unum B excipias, omnes." (Scholz, adopting the statement of Griesbach.) —See above, p. 70.

[b] See above, Chap. X.   [c] See above, pp. 66—68.

borate discussion to shew *how the two places may be reconciled*[d]. What there is in this to countenance the notion that in the opinion of Eusebius "the Gospel according to S. Mark originally terminated at the 8th verse of the last chapter,"— I profess myself unable to discover. I draw from his words the precisely opposite inference. It is not even clear to me that the Verses in dispute were absent from the copy which Eusebius habitually employed. He certainly quotes one of those verses once and again[e]. On the other hand, the express statement of Victor of Antioch [A.D. 450 ?] *that he knew of the mutilation, but had ascertained by Critical research the genuineness of this Section of Scripture, and had adopted the Text of the authentic "Palestinian" Copy*[f], — is more than enough to outweigh the faint presumption created (as some might think) by the words of Eusebius, that his own copy was without it. And yet, as already stated, there is nothing whatever to shew that Eusebius himself deliberately rejected the last Twelve Verses of S. Mark's Gospel. Still less does that Father anywhere say, or even hint, that in his judgment the original Text of S. Mark was without them. If he may be judged by his words, *he accepted them as genuine :* for (what is at least certain) he argues upon their contents at great length, and apparently without misgiving.

(*b*) It is high time however to point out that, after all, the question to be decided is, not *what Eusebius thought* on this subject, but what is historically probable. As a plain matter of fact, the sum of the Patristic Evidence against these Verses is the hypothetical suggestion of Eusebius already quoted; which, (after a fashion well understood by those who have given any attention to these studies), is observed to have rapidly propagated itself in the congenial soil of the vth century. And even if it could be shewn that Eusebius deliberately *rejected* this portion of Scripture, (which has never been done,)—yet, inasmuch as it may be regarded as certain that those famous codices in the library of his friend

---

[d] See above, pp. 41 to 51 : also Appendix (B).

[e] The reader is referred to Mai's *Nov. PP. Bibl.* vol. iv. p. 262, line 12 : p. 264 line 28 : p. 301, line 3—4, and 6—8.

[f] See above, p. 64-5 : also Appendix (E).

Pamphilus at Cæsarea, to which the ancients habitually referred, *recognised it as genuine*[g],—the only sufferer from such a conflict of evidence would surely be Eusebius himself : (not *S. Mark*, I say, but *Eusebius :*) who is observed to employ an incorrect text of Scripture on many other occasions; and must (in such case) be held to have been unduly partial to copies of S. Mark in the mutilated condition of Cod. B or Cod. ℵ. His words were translated by Jerome[h]; adopted by Hesychius[i]; referred to by Victor[j]; reproduced "with a difference" in more than one ancient scholion[k]. But they are found to have died away into a very faint echo when Euthymius Zigabenus[l] rehearsed them for the last time in his Commentary on the Gospels, A.D. 1116. Exaggerated and misunderstood, behold them resuscitated after an interval of seven centuries by Griesbach, and Tischendorf, and Tregelles and the rest: again destined to fall into a congenial, though very differently prepared soil; and again destined (I venture to predict) to die out and soon to be forgotten for ever.

(iv.) After all that has gone before, our two oldest Codices (Cod. B and Cod. ℵ) which alone witness to the truth of Eusebius' testimony as to the state of certain copies of the Gospels in his own day, need not detain us long. They are thought to be as old as the iv[th] century: they are certainly without the concluding section of S. Mark's Gospel. But it may not be forgotten that both Codices alike are disfigured throughout by errors, interpolations and omissions without number; that their testimony is continually divergent; and that it often happens that where they both agree they are both demonstrably in error[m]. Moreover, it is a highly significant circumstance that the Vatican Codex (B), which is the more ancient of the two, exhibits *a vacant column* at the end of S. Mark's Gospel,—*the only vacant column in the whole codex :* whereby it is shewn that the Copyist was aware of the existence of the Twelve concluding Verses of S. Mark's Gospel, even though he left them out[n]: while the

[g] P. 08 and note (d); p. 119 and note (m).   [h] P. 51-7.   [i] P. 57-9.
[j] P. 59—66.   [k] P. 114—125.   [l] P. 08-9.
[m] Chap. VI.   [n] See above, pp. 86 to 88.

original Scribe of the Codex Sinaiticus (א) is declared by
Tischendorf to have actually *omitted the concluding verse of
S. John's Gospel,*—in which unenviable peculiarity *it stands
alone among MSS.*[o]

(I.) And thus we are brought back to the point from
which we started. We are reminded that the one thing
to be accounted for is *the mutilated condition of certain copies
of S. Mark's Gospel in the beginning of the fourth century;*
of which, Cod. B and Cod. א are the two solitary surviving
specimens,—Eusebius, the one historical witness. We have
to decide, I mean, between the *evidence* for this *fact,*—(namely,
that within the first two centuries and a-half of our æra, the
Gospel according to S. Mark *suffered mutilation;*)—and the
reasonableness of the other *opinion,* namely, that S. Mark's
original autograph extended no farther than ch. xvi. 8. All
is reduced to this one issue; and unless any are prepared
to prove that the Twelve familiar Verses (ver. 9 to ver. 20)
with which S. Mark ends his Gospel *cannot* be his,—(I have
proved on the contrary that he must needs be thought to
have written them[p],)—I submit that it is simply irrational
to persist in asseverating that the reason why those verses
are not found in our two Codexes of the iv[th] century must
be because they did not exist in the original autograph of
the Evangelist. What else is this but to set unsupported
opinion, or rather unreasoning *prejudice,* before the *historical
evidence* of a *fact?* The assumption is not only gratuitous,
arbitrary, groundless; but it is discountenanced by the evidence of MSS., of Versions, of Fathers, (Versions and
Fathers much older than the iv[th] century:) is rendered
in the highest degree improbable by every internal, every

---

[o] Will it be believed that Tischendorf accordingly rejects *that* verse also as
spurious; and brings the fourth Gospel to an end at ver. 24, as he brings the
second Gospel to an end at ver. 8? For my own part,—having (through the
kindness and liberality of the Keeper of the Imperial MSS. at S. Petersburg,
aided by the good offices of my friend, the Rev. A. S. Thompson, Chaplain at
S. Petersburg,) obtained a photograph of the last page of S. John's Gospel,—I
must be allowed altogether to call in question the accuracy of Dr. Tischendorf's judgment in this particular. The utmost which can be allowed is that
the Scribe may have possibly changed his pen, or been called away from his
task, just before bringing the fourth Gospel to a close.   [p] See Chap. IX.

external consideration : is condemned by *the deliberate judgment of the universal Church,* — which, in its corporate capacity, for eighteen hundred years, in all places, has not only solemnly accepted the last Twelve Verses of S. Mark's Gospel as genuine, but has even singled them out for special honour [q].

(II.) Let it be asked in conclusion,—(for this prolonged discussion is now happily at an end,)—Are any inconveniences likely to result from a frank and loyal admission, (*in the absence of any Evidence whatever to the contrary,*) that doubtless the last Twelve Verses of S. Mark's Gospel are just as worthy of acceptance as the rest ? It might reasonably be supposed, from the strenuous earnestness with which the rejection of these Verses is generally advocated, that some considerations must surely be assignable why the opinion of their genuineness ought on no account to be entertained. Do any such reasons exist ? Are any inconveniences whatever likely to supervene ?

No reasons whatever are assignable, I reply ; neither are there *any* inconvenient consequences of any sort to be anticipated,—except indeed to the Critics : to whom, it must be confessed, the result proves damaging enough.

It will only follow,

(1st) That Cod. B and Cod. ℵ must be henceforth allowed to be *in one more serious particular* untrustworthy and erring witnesses. They have been convicted, in fact, of bearing false witness in respect of S. Mark xvi. 9—20, where their evidence had been hitherto reckoned upon with the most undoubting confidence.

(2ndly) That the critical statements of recent Editors, and indeed the remarks of Critics generally, in respect of S. Mark xvi. 9—20, will have to undergo serious revision : in every important particular, will have to be unconditionally withdrawn.

(3rdly) That, in all future critical editions of the New Testament, these "Twelve Verses" will have to be restored to their rightful honours : never more appearing disfigured with brackets, encumbered with doubts, banished from their

[q] Chapter X.

context, or molested with notes of suspicion. On the contrary. A few words of caution against the resuscitation of what has been proved to be a "vulgar error," will have henceforth to be introduced *in memoriam rei.*

(4thly) Lastly, men must be no longer taught to look with distrust on this precious part of the Deposit; and encouraged to dispute the Divine sayings which it contains on the plea that *perhaps* they may not be Divine, after all; for that *probably* the entire section is not genuine. They must be assured, on the contrary, that these Twelve Verses are wholly undistinguishable in respect of genuineness from the rest of the Gospel of S. Mark; and it may not be amiss to remind them the Creed called the "Athanasian" speaks no other language than that employed by the Divine Author of our Religion and Object of our Faith. The Church warns her children against the peril incurred by as many as wilfully reject the Truth, in no other language but that of the Great Head of the Church. No person may presume to speak disparagingly of S. Mark xvi. 16, any more.

(III.) Whether,—after the foregoing exposure of a very prevalent and highly popular, but at the same time most calamitous misapprehension,—it will not become necessary for Editors of the Text of the New Testament to reconsider their conclusions in countless other places:—whether they must not be required to review their method, and to remodel their text throughout, now that they have been shewn the insecurity of the foundation on which they have so confidently builded, and been forced to reverse their verdict in respect of a place of Scripture where at least they supposed themselves impregnable;—I forbear at this time to inquire.

Enough to have demonstrated, as I claim to have now done, that *not a particle of doubt,* that *not an atom of suspicion,* attaches to "THE LAST TWELVE VERSES OF THE GOSPEL ACCORDING TO S. MARK."

Τὸ τέλος.

APPENDIX.

CONTENTS.

APPENDIX (A).

On the importance of attending to Patristic Citations of Scripture.—
The correct Text of S. Luke ii. 14, *established.*

(Referred to at p. 22.)

In Chapter III. the importance of attending to Patristic citations of Scripture has been largely insisted upon. The controverted reading of S. Luke ii. 14 supplies an apt illustration of the position there maintained, viz. that this subject has not hitherto engaged nearly as much attention as it deserves.

I. Instead of ἐν ἀνθρώποις εὐδοκία, (which is the reading of the " Textus receptus,") Lachmann, Tischendorf, Tregelles and Alford present us with ἐν ἀνθρώποις εὐδοκίας. Their authority for this reading is the consentient testimony of THE FOUR OLDEST MSS. WHICH CONTAIN S. Luke ii. 14 (viz. B, ℵ, A, D) : THE LATIN VERSIONS generally ("*in hominibus bonae voluntatis*") ; and THE GOTHIC. Against these are to be set, COD. A (in the Hymn at the end of the Psalms) ; ALL THE OTHER UNCIALS ; together with EVERY KNOWN CURSIVE MS. ; and EVERY OTHER ANCIENT VERSION in existence.

So far, the evidence of mere Antiquity may be supposed to preponderate in favour of εὐδοκίας : though no judicious Critic, it is thought, should hesitate in deciding in favour of εὐδοκία, even upon the evidence already adduced. The advocates of the popular Theory ask,—But *why* should the four oldest MSS., together with the Latin and the Gothic Versions, conspire in reading εὐδοκίας, if εὐδοκία be right? That question shall be resolved by-and-by. Let them in the mean time tell us, if they can,—How is it credible that, in such a matter as this, *every other MS. and every other Version in the world* should read εὐδοκία, if εὐδοκία be wrong? But the evidence of Antiquity has not yet been nearly cited. I proceed to set it forth in detail.

It is found then, that whereas εὐδοκίας *is read by none*, εὐδοκία is read by all the following Fathers :—

(1) ORIGEN, in three places of his writings, [i. 374 D: ii. 714 B: iv. 15 B,—A.D. 240.]

(2) The APOSTOLICAL CONSTITUTIONS, twice, [vii. 47 : viii. 12 *ad fin.*,—IIIrd cent.]

(3) METHODIUS, [*Galland.* iii. 809 B,—A.D. 290.]

(4) EUSEBIUS, twice, [*Dem. Ev.* 163 c : 342 B,—A.D. 320.]

(5) APHRAATES THE PERSIAN, (for whose name [*suprà*, pp. 26-7] that of ' Jacobus of Nisibis' has been erroneously substituted), twice, [i. 180 and 385,—A.D. 337.]

(6) TITUS OF BOSTRA, twice, [*in loc.*, but especially in S. Luc. xix. 29 (*Cramer*, ii. 141, *line* 20),—A.D. 350.]

(7) GREGORY OF NAZIANZUS, [i. 845 c,—A.D. 360.]

(8) CYRIL OF JERUSALEM, [A.D. 370], as will be found explained below.

(9) EPIPHANIUS, [i. 154 D,—A.D. 375.]

(10) CHRYSOSTOM, four times, [vii. 311 B : 674 c : viii. 85 c : xi. 374 B expressly,—A.D. 400.]

(11) CYRIL OF ALEXANDRIA, in three places, [*Comm. on S. Luke*, pp. 12 and 16. Also *Opp.* ii. 593 A : vi. 398 c,—A.D. 420.]

(12) THEODORET, [*in Coloss.* i. 20,—A.D. 430.]

(13) THEODOTUS OF ANCYRA, [*Galland.* x. 446 B,—A.D. 430.]

(14) PROCLUS, Abp. of Constantinople, [*Gall.* x. 629 A,—A.D. 434.]

To which may be added the evidence of

(15) COSMAS INDICOPLEUSTES, four times repeated, [*Coll. Nov. PP.*, (Montfaucon,) ii. 152 A, 160 D, 247 E, 269 c,—A.D. 535.]

(16) EULOGIUS, Abp. of Alexandria, [*Gall.* xii. 308 E,—A.D. 581.]

(17) ANDREAS of Crete, twice, [*Gall.* xiii. 100 D, 123 c, —A.D. 635.]

Now, when it is considered that these seventeen Fathers of the Church[a] all concur in exhibiting the Angelic Hymn *as our own Textus Receptus exhibits it*,—(viz. ἐν ἀνθρώποις εὐδοκία,)—*who does not see that the four oldest uncial autho-*

---

[a] Pseudo-Gregory Thaumaturgus, Pseudo-Basil, Patricius, and Marius Mercator, are designedly omitted in this enumeration.

rities for εὐδοκίας are hopelessly outvoted by authorities yet older than themselves? Here is, to all intents and purposes, a record of what was once found in *two Codices of the* iii*rd century;* in *nine of the* iv*th;* in *three of the* v*th;*—added to the testimony of the two Syriac, the Egyptian, the Ethiopic, and the Armenian versions. In this instance therefore the evidence of Antiquity is even overwhelming.

Most decisive of all, perhaps, is the fact this was the form in which *the Churches of the East* preserved the Angelic Hymn in their private, as well as their solemn public Devotions.   Take it, from a document of the vth century:—

ΔΟΞΑ ϵΝ ΤΨΙCΤΟΙC ΘϵѠ
ΚΑΙ ϵΠΙ ΓΗC ϵΙΡΗΝΗ
ϵΝ ΑΝΘΡѠΠΟΙC ϵΤΔΟΚΙΑ [b].

But the text of this Hymn, as a Liturgical document, at a yet earlier period is unequivocally established by the combined testimony of the Apostolical Constitutions (already quoted,) and of Chrysostom, who says expressly:—Εὐχαρισ-τοῦντες λέγομεν, Δόξα ἐν ὑψίστοις Θεῷ, καὶ ἐπὶ γῆς εἰρήνη, ἐν ἀνθρώποις εὐδοκία. [*Opp.* xi. 347 B.]   Now this incontestably proves that *the Church's established way of reciting the Angelic Hymn in the* iv*th century* was in conformity with the reading of the Textus Receptus.   And this fact infinitely outweighs the evidence of any extant MSS. which can be named: for it is the consentient evidence of hundreds,—or rather of thousands of copies of the Gospels of a date anterior to A.D. 400, which have long since perished.

To insist upon this, however, is not at all my present purpose.   About the true reading of S. Luke ii. 14, (which is *not* the reading of Lachmann, Tischendorf, Tregelles, Alford,) there is clearly no longer any room for doubt.   It is perhaps one of the best established readings in the whole compass of the New Testament.   My sole object is to call attention to the two following facts:—

(1) That *the four oldest Codices which contain S. Luke* ii. 14 (B, ℵ, A, D, A.D. 320—520), and two of the oldest Versions, conspire in exhibiting the Angelic Hymn *incorrectly.*

(2) That we are indebted to *fourteen of the Fathers* (A.D.

[b] Codex A,—ὕμνος ἑωθινός at the end of the Psalms.

240—434), and to the rest of the ancient Versions, for the true reading of that memorable place of Scripture.

II. Against all this, it is urged (by Tischendorf) that,—

1. IRENÆUS sides with the oldest uncials.—Now, the Greek of the place referred to is lost. A Latin translation is all that survives. According to *that* evidence, Irenæus, having quoted the place in conformity with the Vulgate reading (iii. c. x. § 41,—" *Gloria in excelsis DEO et in terra pax hominibus bonae voluntatis,*") presently adds,—" In eo quod dicunt, *Gloria in altissimis DEO et in terra pax,* eum qui sit altissimorum, hoc est, supercaelestium factor et eorum, quae super terram omnium conditor, his sermonibus glorificaverunt; qui suo plasmati, hoc est hominibus suam benignitatem salutis de caelo misit." (*ed.* Stieren, i. 459).—But it must suffice to point out (1) that these words really prove nothing: and (2) that it would be very unsafe to build upon them, even if they did; since (3) it is plain that the Latin translator exhibits the place in the Latin form most familiar to himself: (consider his substitution of " excelsis" for " altissimis.")

2. Next, ORIGEN is claimed on the same side, on the strength of the following passage in (Jerome's version of) his lost Homilies on S. Luke :—" Si scriptum esset, *Super terram pax,* et hucusque esset finita sententia, recte quaestio nasceretur. Nunc vero in eo quod additum est, hoc est, quod post pacem dicitur, *In hominibus bonae voluntatis,* solvit quaestionem. Pax enim quam non dat Dominus super terram, non est pax bonae voluntatis." (*Opp.* iii. p. 946.) " From this," (says Tischendorf, who is followed by Tregelles,) " it is plain that Origen regarded εὐδοκίας as the true reading; not εὐδοκία—which is now thrice found in his Greek writings."—But,

Is one here more struck with the unfairness of the Critic, or with the feebleness of his reasoning? For,—(to say nothing of the insecurity of building on a Latin Translation [c],

---

[c] The old Latin Interpreter of Origen's Commentary on S. Matthew seems to have found in Origen's text a quotation from S. Luke ii. 14 which is *not represented in the extant Greek text of Origen.* Here also we are presented with " hominibus *bonae voluntatis.*" (*Opp.* iii. 537 c). We can say nothing to such second-hand evidence.

especially in such a matter as the present,)—How can testimony like this be considered to outweigh the three distinct places in the original writings of this Father, where he reads not εὐδοκίας but εὐδοκία? Again. Why is a doubt insinuated concerning the trustworthiness of those three places, ("ut *nunc* reperitur,") where there really is *no* doubt? How is Truth ever to be attained if investigations like the present are to be conducted in the spirit of an eager partisan, instead of with the calm gravity of an impartial judge?

But I may as well state plainly that the context of the passage above quoted shews that Tischendorf's proposed inference is inadmissible. Origen is supposing some one to ask the following question:—"Since Angels on the night when CHRIST was born proclaimed 'on earth *Peace*,'—why does our SAVIOUR say, 'I am *not* come to send Peace upon earth, but a sword? . . . . Consider," (he proceeds) "whether the answer may not be this:"—and then comes the extract given above. Origen, (to express oneself with colloquial truthfulness,) is *at his old tricks*. He is evidently acquainted with the reading εὐδοκίας : and because it enables him to offer (what appears to him) an ingenious solution of a certain problem, he adopts it for the nonce: his proposal to take the words εἰρήνη εὐδοκίας together, being simply preposterous,—as no one ever knew better than Origen himself[d].

3. Lastly, CYRIL OF JERUSALEM is invariably cited by the latest Critics as favouring the reading εὐδοκίας. Those learned persons have evidently overlooked the candid acknowledgment of De Touttée, Cyril's editor, (p. 180, cf. bottom of p. 162,) that though *the MSS. of Cyril* exhibit εὐδοκία, yet in his editorial capacity he had ventured *to print* εὐδοκίας. This therefore is one more Patristic attestation to the trustworthiness of the Textus Receptus in respect of S. Luke ii. 14, which has been hitherto unaccountably lost sight of by Critics. (May I, without offence, remind Editors of Scripture that instead of *copying*, they ought in every instance *to verify* their references?)

---

[d] Consider his exactly similar method concerning Eph. i. 1. (*Suprà*, pp. 96—99.)

III. The history of this corruption of the Text is not hard
to discover. It is interesting and instructive also.

(1.) In the immediately post-Apostolic age,—if not earlier
still,—some Copyist will have omitted the ἐν before ἀνθρώποις. The resemblance of the letters and the similarity
of the sound (ϵΝ, ΑΝ,) misled him :—

ϵΝΑΝΘΡѠΠΟΙϹ

Every one must see at a glance how easily the thing may
have happened. (It is in fact precisely what *has* happened
in Acts iv. 12 ; where, for ἐν ἀνθρώποις, D and a few cursive MSS. read ἀνθρώποις,—being countenanced therein by
the Latin Versions generally, and by them only.)

(2.) The result however—(δόξα ἐν ὑψίστοις Θεῷ καὶ
ἐπὶ γῆς εἰρήνη ἀνθρώποις εὐδοκία)—was obviously an impossible sentence. It could not be allowed to stand. And yet
it was not by any means clear what had happened to it. In
order, as it seems, to *force* a meaning into the words, some
one with the best intentions will have put the sign of the
genitive (ϲ) at the end of εὐδοκία. The copy so depraved
was destined to play an important part ; for it became the
fontal source of the Latin Version, which exhibits the place
thus :—*Gloria in altissimis Dᴇo, et in terra pax hominibus
bonae voluntatis.* . . . . It is evident, by the way, (if the quotation from Irenæus, given above, is to be depended upon,)
that Irenæus must have so read the place : (viz. εἰρήνη
ἀνθρώποις εὐδοκίας.)

(3.) To restore the preposition (ϵΝ) which had been acci-
dentally thrust out, and to obliterate the sign of the genitive (ϲ) which had been without authority thrust in, was an
obvious proceeding. Accordingly, *every Greek Evangelium
extant* exhibits ἐν ἀνθρώποις : while *all but four* (B, ℵ, A, D)
read εὐδοκία. In like manner, into some MSS. of the Vulgate (e.g. the *Cod. Amiatinus,*) the preposition ("in") has
found its way back ; but the genitive (" bonae voluntatis")
has never been rectified in a single copy of the Latin version.—The Gothic represents a copy which exhibited ἐν ἀνθρώποις εὐδοκίας [c].

---

[c] From the Rev. Professor Bosworth.

The consequence is that a well-nigh untranslatable expression retains its place in the Vulgate to the present hour. Whether (with Origen) we connect εὐδοκίας with εἰρήνη,—or (with the moderns) we propose to understand " men of good pleasure,"—the result is still the same. The harmony of the three-part Anthem which the Angels sang on the night of the Nativity is hopelessly marred, and an unintelligible discord substituted in its place. Logic, Divinity, Documents are here all at one. The reading of Stephens is unquestionably correct. The reading of the latest Editors is as certainly corrupt. This is a case therefore where the value of Patristic testimony becomes strikingly apparent. It affords also one more crucial proof of the essential hollowness of the theory on which it has been recently proposed by Lachmann, Tischendorf, Tregelles and the rest to reconstruct the text of the New Testament.

To some, it may perhaps seem unreasonable that so many words should be devoted to the establishment of the text of a single place of Scripture,—depending, as that text does, on the insertion or the omission of a single letter. I am content to ask in reply,—*What* is important, if not the utterance of Heaven, when, at the laying of the corner-stone of the New Creation, " the Morning Stars sang together, and all the Sons of GOD shouted for joy ? "

IV. Only one word in conclusion.

Whenever the time comes for the Church of England to revise her Authorized Version (1611), it will become necessary that she should in the first instance instruct some of the more judicious and learned of her sons carefully to revise the Greek Text of Stephens (1550). Men require to know precisely what it is they have to translate before they can pretend to translate it. As for supposing that Scholars who have been appointed to revise *a Translation* are competent at a moment's notice, as every fresh difficulty presents itself, to develope the skill requisite for revising *the original Text*,— it is clearly nothing else but supposing that experts in one Science can at pleasure shew themselves proficients in another.

But it so happens that, on the present occasion, that *other*

Science is one of exceeding difficulty. Revisionists *here* will find it necessary altogether to disabuse their minds of the *Theory* of Textual Criticism which is at present the dominant and the popular one,—and of which I have made it my business to expose the fallaciousness, in respect of several crucial texts, in the course of the present work.

I cannot so far forget the unhappy circumstances of the times as to close this note without the further suggestion, (sure therein of the approval of our trans-Atlantic brethren,) that, for a Revision of the Authorized Version to enjoy the confidence of the Nation, and to procure for itself acceptance at the hands of the Church,—it will be found necessary that the work should be confided to *Churchmen.* The Church may never abdicate her function of being "a Witness and a Keeper of Holy Writ." Neither can she, without flagrant inconsistency and scandalous consequence, ally herself in the work of Revision with the Sects. Least of all may she associate with herself in the sacred undertaking an Unitarian Teacher,—one who avowedly [see the letter of "One of the Revisionists, G. V. S.," in the "Times" of July 11, 1870] denies the eternal Godhead of her LORD. That the individual alluded to has shewn any peculiar aptitude for the work of a Revisionist; or that he is a famous Scholar; or that he can boast of acquaintance with any of the less familiar departments of Sacred Learning; is not even pretended. (It would matter nothing if the reverse were the case.) What else, then, is this but to offer a deliberate insult to the Majesty of Heaven in the Divine Person of Him who is alike the Object of the Everlasting Gospel, and its Author?

APPENDIX (B).

Eusebius " ad Marinum" *concerning the reconcilement of* S. Mark xvi. 9 *with* S. Matthew xxviii. 1.

(Referred to at pp. 46, 47, 54, and 233.)

Subjoined is the original text of Eusebius, taken from the " Quæstiones ad Marinum" published by Card. Mai, in his " Nova Patrum Bibliotheca" (Romae, 1847,) vol. iv. pp. 255-7.

I. Πῶς παρὰ μὲν τῷ Ματθαίῳ ὄψε σαββάτων φαίνεται ἐγεγερμένος ὁ Σωτήρ, παρὰ δὲ τῷ Μάρκῳ πρωὶ τῇ μιᾷ τῶν σαββάτων.

Τούτου διττὴ ἂν εἴη ἡ λύσις· ὁ μὲν γὰρ [τὸ κεφάλαιον αὐτὸ *del.** ?] τὴν τοῦτο φάσκουσαν περικοπὴν ἀθετῶν, εἴποι ἂν μὴ ἐν ἅπασιν αὐτὴν φέρεσθαι τοῖς ἀντιγράφοις τοῦ κατὰ Μάρκον εὐαγγελίου· τὰ γοῦν ἀκριβῆ τῶν ἀντιγράφων τὸ τέλος περιγράφει τῆς κατὰ τὸν Μάρκον ἱστορίας ἐν τοῖς λόγοις τοῦ ὀφθέντος νεανίσκου ταῖς γυναιξὶ καὶ εἰρηκότος αὐταῖς " μὴ φοβεῖσθε, Ἰησοῦν ζητεῖτε τὸν Ναζαρηνόν." καὶ τοῖς ἑξῆς, οἷς ἐπιλέγει· " καὶ ἀκούσασαι ἔφυγον, καὶ οὐδενὶ οὐδὲν εἶπον, ἐφοβοῦντο γάρ." Ἐν τούτῳ γὰρ σχεδὸν ἐν ἅπασι τοῖς ἀντιγράφοις τοῦ κατὰ Μάρκον εὐαγγελίου περιγέγραπται τὸ τέλος· τὰ δὲ ἑξῆς σπανίως ἔν τισιν ἀλλ' οὐκ ἐν πᾶσι φερόμενα περιττὰ ἂν εἴη, καὶ μάλιστα εἴπερ ἔχοιεν ἀντιλογίαν τῇ τῶν λοιπῶν εὐαγγελιστῶν μαρτυρίᾳ. ταῦτα μὲν οὖν εἴποι ἄν τις παραιτούμενος καὶ πάντη ἀναιρῶν περιττὸν ἐρώτημα. Ἄλλος δέ τις οὐδ' ὁτιοῦν τολμῶν ἀθετεῖν τῶν ὁπωσοῦν ἐν τῇ τῶν εὐαγγελίων γραφῇ φερομένων, διπλῆν εἶναί φησι τὴν ἀνάγνωσιν, ὡς καὶ ἐν ἑτέροις πολλοῖς, ἑκατέραν τε παραδεκτέαν ὑπάρχειν, τῷ μὴ μᾶλλον ταύτην ἐκείνης, ἢ ἐκείνην ταύτης, παρὰ τοῖς πιστοῖς καὶ εὐλαβέσιν ἐγκρίνεσθαι.

Καὶ δὴ τοῦδε τοῦ μέρους συγχωρουμένου εἶναι ἀληθοῦς, προσήκει τὸν νοῦν διερμηνεύειν τοῦ ἀναγνώσματος· εἰ γοῦν διέλοιμεν τὴν τοῦ λόγου διάνοιαν, οὐκ ἂν εὕροιμεν αὐτὴν ἐναντίαν τοῖς παρὰ τοῦ Ματθαίου ὀψὲ σαββάτων ἐγηγέρθαι τὸν Σωτῆρα λελεγμένοις· τὸ γὰρ " ἀναστὰς δὲ πρωὶ τῇ μιᾷ

• *Vid. supra*, p. 233.

τοῦ σαββάτου" κατὰ τὸν Μάρκον, μετὰ διαστολῆς ἀναγνω-
σόμεθα· καὶ μετὰ τὸ ἀναστὰς δὲ, ὑποστίξομεν*· καὶ τὴν διάνοιαν ἀφορίζομεν τῶν ἑξῆς ἐπιλεγομένων. εἶτα τὸ μὲν ἀναστὰς ἂν, ἐπὶ τὴν παρὰ τῷ Ματθαίῳ ὀψέ σαββάτων. τότε γὰρ
ἐγήγερτο· τὸ δὲ ἑξῆς ἑτέρας ὂν διανοίας ὑποστατικὸν, συνάψωμεν τοῖς ἐπιλεγομένοις· πρωΐ γὰρ τῇ μιᾷ τοῦ σαββάτου ἐφάνη
Μαρίᾳ τῇ Μαγδαληνῇ. τοῦτο γοῦν ἐδήλωσε καὶ ὁ Ἰωάννης
πρωΐ καὶ αὐτὸς τῇ μιᾷ τοῦ σαββάτου ὦφθαι αὐτὸν τῇ Μαγδαληνῇ μαρτυρήσας. οὕτως οὖν καὶ παρὰ τῷ Μάρκῳ πρωΐ
ἐφάνη αὐτῇ. οὐ πρωΐ ἀναστὰς, ἀλλὰ πολὺ πρότερον κατὰ τὸν
Ματθαῖον ὀψέ τοῦ σαββάτου. τότε γὰρ ἀναστὰς ἐφάνη τῇ
Μαρίᾳ, οὐ τότε ἀλλὰ πρωΐ. ὡς παρίστασθαι ἐν τούτοις
καιροὺς δύο. τὸν μὲν γὰρ τῆς ἀναστάσεως τὸν ὀψέ τοῦ σαββάτου, τὸν δὲ τῆς τοῦ Σωτῆρος ἐπιφανείας, τὸν πρωΐ, ὂν
ἔγραψεν ὁ Μάρκος εἰπὼν (ὃ καὶ μετὰ διαστολῆς ἀναγνωστέον) ἀναστὰς δέ· εἶτα ὑποστίξαντες, τὸ ἑξῆς ῥητέον, πρωΐ
τῇ μιᾷ τοῦ σαββάτου ἐφάνη Μαρίᾳ τῇ Μαγδαληνῇ, ἀφ᾽ ἧς
ἐκβεβλήκει ἑπτὰ δαιμόνια.

II. Πῶς κατὰ τὸν Ματθαῖον ὀψέ σαββάτων ἡ Μαγδαληνὴ
τεθεαμένη τὴν ἀνάστασιν, κατὰ τὸν Ἰωάννην ἡ αὐτὴ ἑστῶσα
κλαίει παρὰ τῷ μνημείῳ τῇ μιᾷ τοῦ σαββάτου.

Οὐδὲν ἂν ζητηθείη κατὰ τοὺς τόπους, εἰ τὸ ὀψέ σαββάτων
μὴ τὴν ἑσπερινὴν ὥραν τὴν μετὰ τὴν ἡμέραν τοῦ σαββάτου
λέγεσθαι ὑπολάβοιμεν, ὥς τινες ὑπειλήφασιν, ἀλλὰ τὸ βραδὺ
καὶ ὀψέ τῆς νυκτὸς τῆς μετὰ τὸ σάββατον, κ.τ.λ.

---

* P.S. I avail myself of this blank space to introduce
a passage from THEOPHYLACT (A.D. 1077) which should have
obtained notice in a much earlier page:—Ἀναστὰς δὲ ὁ
Ἰησοῦς· ἐνταῦθα στίξον, εἶτα εἰπέ· πρωΐ πρώτη σαββάτου
ἐφάνη Μαρίᾳ τῇ Μαγδαληνῇ. οὐ γὰρ ἀνέστη πρωΐ (τίς γὰρ
οἶδε πότε ἀνέστη;) ἀλλ᾽ ἐφάνη πρωΐ κυριακῇ ἡμέρᾳ (αὕτη
γὰρ ἡ πρώτη τοῦ σαββάτου, τουτέστι, τῆς ἑβδομάδος,) ἣν ἄνω
ἐκάλεσε μίαν σαββάτων· [*Opp.* vol. i. p. 263 c.]

It must be superfluous to point out that Theophylact also,
—like Victor, Jerome, and Hesychius,—is here only reproducing Eusebius. See above, p. 66, note (c).

APPENDIX (C).

Proof that HESYCHIUS *is a copyist only in what he says concerning the end of S. Mark's Gospel.*

(Referred to at pp. 57-58.)

§ 1.

IT was confidently stated above (at p. 58) that HESY-CHIUS, discussing the consistency of S. Matthew's ὀψὲ τῶν σαββάτων (chap. xxviii. 1), with the πρωὶ of S. Mark (chap. xvi. 9), is *a copyist* only ; and that he copies from the "Quaestiones ad Marinum" of EUSEBIUS. The proof of that statement is subjoined. It should perhaps be explained that the extracts in the right-hand column have been dislocated in order to shew their close resemblance to what is set down in the left-hand column from Eusebius :—

(EUSEBIUS.)

τὸ ὀψὲ σαββάτων μὴ τὴν ἑσπερινὴν ὥραν τὴν μετὰ τὴν ἡμέραν τοῦ σαββάτου λέγεσθαι ὑπολάβοιμεν . . . .

ἀλλὰ τὸ βραδὺ καὶ ὀψὲ τῆς νυκτός.

οὕτω γὰρ καὶ ὀψὲ τῆς ὥρας εἰώθαμεν λέγειν, καὶ ὀψὲ τοῦ καιροῦ, καὶ ὀψὲ τῆς χρείας· οὐ τὴν ἑσπέραν δηλοῦντες, οὐδὲ τὸν μετὰ ἡλίου δυσμὰς χρόνον, τὸ δὲ σφόδρα βράδιον τούτῳ σημαίνοντες τῷ τρόπῳ·

ὅθεν ὥσπερ διερμηνεύων αὐτὸς ἑαυτὸν ὁ Ματθαῖος μετὰ τὸ ὀψὲ σαββάτων, ἐπήγαγε τῇ ἐπιφωσκούσῃ εἰς μίαν σαββάτων.

Ἔθος δὲ ὅλην τὴν ἑβδομάδα σάββατον καλεῖν.

λέγεται γοῦν παρὰ τοῖς Εὐαγγελισταῖς τῇ μιᾷ τῶν σαββάτων·

ἐν δὲ τῇ συνηθείᾳ, δευτέρα σαββάτων, καί τρίτη σαββάτων.

(EUSEBIUS ad Marinum, *apud* Mai, vol. iv. p. 257-8.)

(HESYCHIUS, or Severus.)

τὸ δὲ ὀψὲ σαββάτων οὐ τὴν ἑσπέραν τὴν μετὰ τὴν δύσιν τοῦ ἡλίου δηλοῖ. . . .

ἀλλὰ . . . . τὸ βράδιον καὶ πολὺ διεστηκὸς. . . .

καὶ γάρ που καὶ οὕτως ἡμῖν σύνηθες λέγειν, ὀψὲ τοῦ καιροῦ παραγεγόνας· ὀψὲ τῆς ὥρας, ὀψὲ τῆς χρείας· οὐχὶ τὴν ἑσπέραν, καὶ τὸν μετὰ ἡλίου δυσμὰς χρόνον δηλοῦσιν· ἀλλὰ τὸ βράδιον, ... τὸν τρόπον τοῦτον μηνύουσι.

ὁ Ματθαῖος . . . . ὥσπερ ἑρμηνεύων ἑαυτὸν, ἐπήγαγε τῇ ἐπιφωσκούσῃ εἰς μίαν σαββάτων.

σάββατον δὲ τὴν πᾶσαν ἑβδομάδα καλεῖν Ἑβραίοις ἔθος.

αὐτίκα γοῦν οἱ εὐαγγελισταὶ τῇ μιᾷ τῶν σαββάτων φασί·

οὕτω δὴ καὶ ἐν τῇ συνηθείᾳ κεκχρήμεθα, δευτέραν σαββάτων, καὶ τρίτην σαββάτων.

(GREG. NYSS. [*vid. suprà*, p. 39 to 41.] *Opp.* vol. iii. p. 402.

§ 2. Subjoined, in the right-hand column, is the original text of the passage of Hesychius exhibited in English at p. 57. The intention of setting down the parallel passages from Eusebius, and from Victor of Antioch, is in order to shew the sources from which Hesychius obtained his materials,—as explained at p. 58 :—

(Eusebius.)

τὰ γοῦν ἀκριβῆ τῶν ἀντιγράφων τὸ τέλος περιγράφει τῆς κατὰ τὸν Μάρκον ἱστορίας ἐν τοῖς λόγοις κ.τ.λ. οἷς ἐπιλέγει· . . . " καὶ οὐδενὶ οὐδὲν, εἶπον, ἐφοβοῦντο γάρ."

(Eusebius ad Marinum, *apud* Mai, iv. p. 255.)

(Victor of Antioch.)

ἐπειδὴ δὲ ἔν τισι . . . πρόσκειται . . . " Ἀναστὰς " κ. τ. λ. δοκεῖ δὲ τοῦτο διαφωνεῖν τῷ ὑπὸ Ματθαίου εἰρημένῳ. . . .

οὕτως ἀναγνωσόμεθα· " Ἀναστὰς δὲ," καὶ ὑποστίξαντες ἐπάγωμεν, "πρωΐ τῇ μιᾷ τῶν σαββάτων ἐφάνη Μαρίᾳ τῇ Μαγδαληνῇ·" ἵνα τὸ μὲν " ἀναστὰς "—

(Victor Antioch., *ed. Cramer,* vol. i. p. 444, line 19 to line 27.)

(Hesychius, or Severus.)

ἐν μὲν οὖν τοῖς ἀκριβεστέροις ἀντιγράφοις τὸ κατὰ Μάρκον εὐαγγέλιον μεχρὶ τοῦ " ἐφοβοῦντο γὰρ," ἔχει τὸ τέλος.

ἐν δέ τισι πρόσκειται καὶ ταῦτα. " Ἀναστὰς " κ.τ.λ. τοῦτο δὲ ἐναντίωσίν τινα δοκεῖ ἔχειν πρὸς τὰ ἔμπροσθεν εἰρημένα·

[τῆς γὰρ ὥρας τῆς νυκτὸς ἀγνώστου τυγχανούσης καθ᾽ ἢν ὁ Σωτὴρ ἀνέστη, πῶς ἐνταῦθα ἀναστῆναι " πρωΐ " γέγραπται; ἀλλ᾽ οὐδὲν ἐναντίον φανήσεται τὸ ῥητὸν, εἰ]

μετ᾽ ἐπιστήμης ἀναγνωσόμεθα· καὶ γὰρ ὑποστίξαι δεῖ συνετῶς· " Ἀναστὰς δὲ," κὰι οὕτως ἐπαγάγειν, "πρωΐ πρώτῃ σαββάτων ἐφάνη πρῶτον Μαρίᾳ τῇ Μαγδαληνῇ." ἵνα τὸ μὲν " ἀναστὰς "

[ἔχῃ τὴν ἀναφορὰν συμφώνως τῷ Ματθαίῳ, πρὸς τὸν προλαβόντα καιρὸν, τὸ δὲ " πρωΐ " πρὸς τὴν τῆς Μαρίας γενομένην ἐπιφάνειαν ἀποδοθείη.]

(Greg. Nyss. *Opp.* vol. iii. p. 411, B, C, D: which may be also seen in Cramer's *Catenae,* [vol. i. p. 250, line 21· to line 33,] ascribed to " Severus, Archbishop of Antioch," [*Ibid.* p. 243.])

APPENDIX (D).

Some account of Victor of Antioch's *Commentary on S. Mark's Gospel; together with an enumeration of MSS. which contain Victor's Work.*

(Referred to at p. 60.)

"Après avoir examiné avec soin les MSS. de la Bibliothèque du Roi," (says the Père Simon in his *Hist. Crit. du N. T.* p. 79,) "j'ai réconnu que cet ouvrage" (he is speaking of the Commentary on S. Mark's Gospel popularly ascribed to Victor of Antioch,) "n'est ni d'Origéne, ni de Victor d'Antioche, ni de Cyrille, ni d'aucun autre auteur en particulier. C'est un recueil de plusieurs Pères, dont on a marqué les noms dans quelques exemplaires; et si ces noms ne se trouvent point dans d'autres, cela est assez ordinaire à ces recueils, qu'on appelle *chaînes* [a]." It will be seen from the notices of the work in question already offered, (*suprà,* p. 59 to p. 65,) that I am able to yield only a limited acquiescence in this learned writer's verdict. That the materials out of which Victor of Antioch constructed his Commentary are scarcely ever original,—is what no one will deny who examines the work with attention. But the Author of a compilation is an Author still; and to put Victor's claim to the work before us on a level with that of Origen or of Cyril, is entirely to misrepresent the case and hopelessly to perplex the question.

Concerning Victor himself, nothing whatever is known except that he was "a presbyter of Antioch." Concerning his Work, I will not here repeat what I have already stated elsewhere; but, requesting the Reader to refer to what was remarked at pp. 59 to 65, I propose to offer a few observations with which I was unwilling before to encumber the

---

[a] Kollar, (editing Lambecius,—iii. 159, 114,) expresses the same opinion.— Huet (*Origeniana,* lib. iii. c. 4, pp. 274·5,) has a brief and unsatisfactory dissertation on the same subject; but he arrives at a far shrewder conclusion.

text; holding it to be a species of duty for those who have
given any time and attention to a subject like the present to
contribute the result, (however slender and unsatisfactory it
may prove,) to the common store. Let abler men enlarge
the ensuing scanty notices, and correct me if in any respect
I shall have inadvertently fallen into error.

1. There exists a Commentary, then, on S. Mark's Gospel,
which generally claims on its front "VICTOR, PRESBYTER
OF ANTIOCH," for its Author[b].   A Latin translation of this
work, (not the original Greek,) was, in the first instance,
published at Ingolstadt in 1580[c], by Theodore Peltanus.
His Latin version found its way at once into "Bibliothecæ,"
(or Collections of Writings of the Fathers,) and has been
again and again reprinted.

2. The Greek text of Victor was first published at Rome
by Peter Possinus in 1673, from a MS. existing somewhere
in Germany; which Bathazar Corderius had transcribed and
presented to Possinus about thirty years before.   Corderius
gave Possinus at the same time his transcript of an anonymous Commentary on S. Mark preserved in the Vatican;
and Possinus had already in his possession the transcript of
a third Commentary on the same Evangelist (also anonymous) which he had obtained from the Library of Charles
de Montchal, Abp. of Toulouse.   These three transcripts Possinus published in a well-known volume.   It is to be wished
that he had kept them distinct, instead of to some extent
blending their contents confusedly into one[d].   Still, the dis-

---

[b] The copies which I have seen, are headed,—BIKTOPOC (sometimes BIK-
TωPOC) ΠΡΕΣΒΥΤΕΡΟΥ ΑΝΤΙΟΧΕΙΑΣ ΕΡΜΗΝΕΙΑ ΕΙΣ ΤΟ ΚΑΤΑ ΜΑΡΚΟΝ
ΕΥΑΓΓΕΛΙΟΝ; or with words precisely to that effect. Very often no Author's
name is given.   Rarely is the Commentary assigned to Cyril, Origen, &c.—
Vide infrà, N°. iii, xii, xiv, xix, xlviii. Also, N°. xlvii (comp. xxviii.)

[c] *Victoris Antiocheni in Marcum, et Titi Bostrorum Episcopi in Evangelium Lucae commentarii; ante hac quidem nunquam in lucem editi, nunc
vero studio et operâ Theodori Peltani luce simul et Latinitate donati.* In-
golstad. 1580, 8vo. pp. 510.

[d] "Ex hoc ego, quasi metallo triplici, una conflata massa, inde annulos for-
mavi, quos singulos Evangelici contextus articulis aptatos, inter seque morsu
ac nexu mutuo commissos, in torquem producerem, quo, si possem consequi,
sancto Evangelistae Marco decus et ornamentum adderetur."—*Præfatio :* from
which the particulars in the text are obtained.

located paragraphs of Victor of Antioch are recognisable by
the name of their author (" Victor Antiochenus") prefixed
to each : while " Tolosanus" designates the Toulouse MS. :
" Vaticanus" (or simply " Anonymus") the Vatican.

3. At the end of another century, (1775) C. F. Matthaei
put forth at Moscow, with his usual skill and accuracy,
a new and independent Edition of Victor's Commentary[e] :
the text of which is based on four of the Moscow MSS.
This work, which appeared in two parts, has become of
extraordinary rarity. I have only just ascertained (June,
1871,) that one entire Copy is preserved in this country.

4. Lastly, (in 1840,) Dr. J. A. Cramer, in the first volume
of his *Catenae* on the N. T., reproduced Victor's work from
independent MS. sources. He took for his basis two Codices
in the Paris Library, (No. 186 and No. 188), which, however,
prove to have been anciently so exactly assimilated the one to
the other [*infrà*, p. 279] as to be, in fact, but duplicates of one
and the same original. Cramer supplemented their contents
from Laud. Gr. 33, (in the Bodleian :) Coisl. 23 : and Reg.
178 at Paris. The result has been by far the fullest and
most satisfactory exhibition of the Commentary of Victor of
Antioch which has hitherto appeared. Only is it to be
regretted that the work should have been suffered to come
abroad disfigured in every page with errors so gross as to be
even scandalous, and with traces of slovenly editorship which
are simply unintelligible. I cannot bring myself to believe
that Dr. Cramer ever inspected the MSS. in the Paris
Library in person. Else would the slender advantage which
those abundant materials have proved to so learned and accomplished a scholar, be altogether unaccountable. Moreover, he is incorrect in what he says about them[f]: while
his reasons for proposing to assign the work of Victor
of Antioch to Cyril of Alexandria are undeserving of serious attention.

On a comparison of these four Editions of the same work,
it is discovered that the Latin version of Peltanus (1580),

---

[e] ΒΙΚΤΩΡΟΣ πρεσβυτέρου Ἀντιοχείας καὶ ἄλλων τινῶν ἁγίων πατέρων ἐξήσησις
εἰς τὸ κατὰ Μάρκον ἅγιον εὐαγγέλιον: *ex Codd. Mosqq. edidit* C. F. Matthæi,
Mosquae, 1775.   [f] P. xxvii—xxviii.

represents the same Greek text which Possinus gave to the
world in 1673. Peltanus translates very loosely; in fact
he paraphrases rather than translates his author, and con-
fesses that he has taken great liberties with Victor's text.
But I believe it will be found that there can have been no
considerable discrepancy between the MS. which Peltanus
employed, and that which Possinus afterwards published.—
Not so the text which Matthaei edited, which is in fact for
the most part, (though not invariably,) rather an Epitome
of Victor's Commentary. On the other hand, Cramer's
text is more full than that of Possinus. There seem to be
only a few lines in Possinus, here and there, which are not
to be met with in Cramer; whereas no less than twenty-
eight of Cramer's pages are not found in the work of Possinus. Cramer's edition, therefore, is by far the most complete
which has hitherto appeared. And though it cries aloud
for revision throughout; though many important corrections might easily be introduced into it, and the whole
brought back in countless particulars more nearly to the
state in which it is plain that Victor originally left it;—
I question whether more than a few pages of *additional
matter* could easily be anywhere recovered. I collated several
pages of Cramer (Oct. 1869) with every MS. of Victor in
the Paris Library; and all but invariably found that Cramer's text was fuller than that of the MS. which lay before
me. Seldom indeed did I meet with a few lines in any
MS. which had not already seen the light in Cramer's edition. One or other of the four Codices which he employed
seems to fill up almost every hiatus which is met with in
any of the MSS. of this Father.

For it must be stated, once for all, that an immense, and
I must add, a most unaccountable discrepancy is observable
between the several extant copies of Victor: yet not so
much in respect of various readings, or serious modifications
of his text; (though the transpositions are very frequent,
and often very mischievous [g];) as resulting from the bound-

---

[g] To understand what is alluded to, the reader should compare the upper
and the lower half of p. 442 in Cramer: noting that he has one and the same
annotation before him; but diversely exhibited. (The lower part of the page

less license which every fresh copyist seems to have allowed himself chiefly in *abridging* his author.—To skip a few lines: to omit an explanatory paragraph, quotation, or digression: to pass *per saltum* from the beginning to the end of a passage: sometimes to leave out a whole page: to transpose: to paraphrase: to begin or to end with quite a different form of words;—proves to have been the rule. Two copyists engaged on the same portion of Commentary are observed to abridge it in two quite different ways. I question whether there exist in Europe three manuscripts of Victor which correspond entirely throughout. The result is perplexing in a high degree. Not unfrequently (as might be expected) we are presented with two or even three different exhibitions of one and the same annotation [h]. Meanwhile, as if to render the work of collation (in a manner) impossible,— (1) Peltanus pleads guilty to having transposed and otherwise taken liberties with the text he translated: (2) Possinus confessedly welded three codices into one: (3) Matthaei pieced and patched his edition out of four MSS.; and (4) Cramer, out of five.

The only excuse I can invent for this strange licentiousness on the part of Victor's ancient transcribers is this:— They must have known perfectly well, (in fact it is obvious,) that the work before them was really little else but a compilation; and that Victor had already abridged in the same merciless way the writings of the Fathers (Chrysostom chiefly) from whom he obtained his materials. We are to remember also, I suppose, the labour which transcription involved, and the costliness of the skins out of which ancient books were manufactured. But when all has been said, I must candidly admit that the extent of license which the ancients evidently allowed themselves quite perplexes me [i]. *Why*, for example, remodel the struc-

is taken from Cod. 178.) Besides transposing the sentences, the author of Cod. 178 has suppressed the reference to Chrysostom, and omitted the name of Apolinarius in line 10. (Compare Field's ed. of *Chrys.* iii. 529, top of the page.)

[h] Thus the two notes on p. 440 are found substantially to agree with the note on p. 441, which = Chrys. p. 527. See also *infrà*, p. 289.

[i] Let any one, with Mai's edition of the "Quaestiones ad Marinum" of Eu-

ture of a sentence and needlessly vary its phraseology? Never I think in my life have I been more hopelessly confused than in the *Bibliothèque*, while attempting to collate certain copies of Victor of Antioch.

I dismiss this feature of the case by saying that if any person desires a sample of the process I have been describing, he cannot do better than bestow a little attention on the "Preface" (ὑπόθεσις) at the beginning of Victor's Commentary. It consists of thirty-eight lines in Cramer's edition: of which Possinus omits eleven; and Matthaei also, eleven;—but *not the same eleven*. On the other hand, Matthaei] *prolongs* the Preface by eight lines. Strange to relate, the MS. from which Cramer professes to publish, goes on differently. If I may depend on my hasty pencilling, after ἐκκλησίαις [*Cramer*, i. p. 264, line 16,] Evan. 300, [= Reg. 186, *fol.* 93, line 16 from bottom] proceeds,—Κλήμης ἐν ἕκτῳ τῶν ὑποτυπώσεων, (thirty-one lines, ending) χαρακτὴρ ἐγένετο.

On referring to the work of Possinus, "Anonymus Vaticanus" is found to exhibit so admirable a condensation (?) of the ὑπόθεσις in question, that it is difficult to divest oneself of the suspicion that it must needs be an original and independent composition; the germ out of which the longer Preface has grown . . . . We inspect the first few pages of the Commentary, and nothing but perplexity awaits us at every step. It is not till we have turned over a few pages that we begin to find something like exact correspondence.

As for the Work,—(for I must now divest myself of the perplexing recollections which the hurried collation of so many MSS. left behind; and plainly state that, in spite of all, I yet distinctly ascertained, and am fully persuaded that the original work was *one*,—the production, no doubt, of "Victor, Presbyter of Antioch," as 19 out of the 52 MSS. declare) :—For the Commentary itself, I say, Victor explains at the outset what his method had been. Having

sebius before him, note how mercilessly they are abridged, mutilated, amputated by subsequent writers. Compare for instance p. 257 with Cramer's "Catenae," i. p. 251-2; and this again with the "Catena in Joannem" of Corderius, p. 448-9.　　　　] With whom, Reg. 177 and 703 agree.

failed to discover any separate exposition of S. Mark's Gospel, he had determined to construct one, by collecting the occasional notices scattered up and down the writings of Fathers of the Church[k]. Accordingly, he presents us in the first few lines of his Commentary (p. 266) with a brief quotation from the work of Eusebius "to Marinus, on the seeming inconsistency of the Evangelical accounts of the Resurrection;" following it up with a passage from "the vi[th] [vii[th] ?] tome of Origen's Exegetics on S. John's Gospel." We are thus presented at the outset with *two* of Victor's favorite authorities. The work of Eusebius just named he was evidently thoroughly familiar with[l]. I suspect that he has many an unsuspected quotation from its pages. Towards the end of his Commentary, (as already elsewhere explained,) he quotes it once and again.

Of Origen also Victor was evidently very fond[m]: and his words on two or three occasions seem to shew that he had recourse besides habitually to the exegetical labours of Apolinarius, Theodore of Mopsuestia, and Titus of Bostra[n]. Passages from Cyril of Alexandria are occasionally met with[o]; and once at least (p. 370) he has an extract from Basil. The historian Josephus he sometimes refers to by name[p].

But the Father to whom Victor is chiefly indebted is Chrysostom,—whom he styles "the blessed John, Bishop of the Royal City;" (meaning Constantinople[q]). Not that

[k] p. 263, line 3 to 13, and in Possinus, p. 4.

[l] Eusebius is again quoted at p. 444, and referred to at p. 445 (line 23-5). See especially p. 446.

[m] What is found at p. 314 (on S. Mark v. 1,) is a famous place. (Cf. Huet's ed. ii. 131.) Compare also Victor's first note on i. 7 with the same edit. of Origen, ii. 125 C, D,—which Victor is found to have abridged. Compare the last note on p. 346 with Orig. i. 284 A. Note, that ἄλλος δέ φησι, (foot of p. 427) is also Origen. Cf. Possinus, p. 324.

[n] See pp. 408, 418, 442.

[o] e.g. the first note on p. 311; (comp. Possinus, p. 95): and the last note on p. 323; (comp. Poss. p. 123.) Compare also Cramer, p. 395 (line 16-22) with Poss. p. 249.—I observe that part of a note on p. 315 is ascribed by Possinus (p. 102) to Athanasius: while a scholium at p. 321 and p. 359, has no owner.

[p] e.g. p. 408, 411 (twice).

[q] In p. 418,—ὁ τῆς βασιλίδος πόλεως ἐπίσκοπος Ἰωάννης. For instances of

Victor, strictly speaking, *transcribes* from Chrysostom; at
least, to any extent. His general practice is slightly to
adapt his Author's language to his own purpose; sometimes,
to leave out a few words; a paragraph; half a page[r]. Then,
he proceeds to quote another Father probably; or, it may
be, to offer something of his own. But he seldom gives any
intimation of what it is he does: and if it were not for the
occasional introduction of the phrase ὁ μέν φησι or ἄλλος δέ
φησι[s], a reader of Victor's Commentary might almost mistake it for an original composition. So little pains does this
Author take to let his reader know when he is speaking in
his own person, when not, that he has not scrupled to retain
Chrysostom's phrases ἐγὼ δὲ οἶμαι[t], &c. The result is that
it is often impossible to know to *whose* sentiments we are
listening. It cannot be too clearly borne in mind that
ancient ideas concerning authorship differed entirely from
those of modern times; especially when Holy Scripture was
to be commented on.

I suspect that, occasionally, copyists of Victor's work,
as they recognised a fragment here and there, prefixed to it

quotation from Chrysostom, comp. V. A. p. 315 with Chrys. pp. 398-9 : p. 376
with Chrys. pp. 227-8 : p. 420 with Chrys. p. 447, &c.

[r] Take for example Victor's Commentary on the stilling of the storm
(pp. 312-3), which is merely an abridged version of the first part of Chrysostom's 28th Homily on S. Matthew (pp. 395-8); about 45 lines being left out.
Observe Victor's method however. Chrysostom begins as follows :—Ὁ μὲν
οὖν Λουκᾶς, ἀπαλλάττων ἑαυτὸν τοῦ ἀπαιτηθῆναι τῶν χρόνων τὴν τάξιν, οὕτως
εἶπεν. (Then follows S. Luke viii. 22.) καὶ ὁ Μάρκος ὁμοίως. Οὗτος δὲ οὐχ
οὕτως· ἀλλὰ καὶ ἀκολουθίαν ἐνταῦθα διατηρεῖ. Victor, because he had S. Mark
(not S. Matthew) to comment upon, begins thus :—Ὁ μὲν Μάρκος ἀπαλλάττων
ἑαυτὸν τοῦ ἀπαιτηθῆναι τῶν χρόνων τὴν τάξιν, οὕτως εἶπεν, ὁμοίως δὲ καὶ ὁ Λοῦκας·
ὁ δὲ Ματθαῖος οὐχ οὕτως· ἀλλὰ καὶ ἀκολουθίαν ἐνταῦθα διατηρεῖ.

[s] e.g. V. A. p. 422 (from ὁ μέν φησιν to ἄλλος δέ φησιν) = Chrys. p. 460.
Observe the next paragraph also, (p. 423,) begins, ἄλλος φησιν.—So again, V.
A. pp. 426-7 = Chrys. pp. 473-6 : where ἄλλος δέ φησι, at the foot of p. 427
introduces a quotation from Origen, as appears from Possinus, p. 324.—See
also p. 269, line 1,—which is from Chrys. p. 130,—ἢ ὡς ὁ ἄλλος being the next
words.—The first three lines in p. 316 = Chrys. p. 399. Then follows, ἄλλος δέ
φησιν. See also pp. 392 : 407 (φασί τινες—ἕτερος δέ φησιν) : pp. 415 and 433.
After quoting Eusebius by name (p. 446-7), Victor says (line 3) ἄλλος δέ
φησιν.

[t] e.g. V. A. p. 420 line 15, which = Chrys. p. 447.

the name of its author. This would account for the extremely partial and irregular occurrence of such notes of authorship; as well as explain why a name duly prefixed in one copy is often missing in another [u]. Whether Victor's Commentary can in strictness be called a " Catena," or not, must remain uncertain until some one is found willing to undertake the labour of re-editing his pages; from which, by the way, I cannot but think that some highly interesting (if not some important) results would follow.

Yet, inasmuch as Victor never, or certainly very seldom, prefixes to a passage from a Father *the name of its Author ;* —above all, seeing that sometimes, at all events, he is original, or at least speaks in his own person ;—I think the title of " Catena" inappropriate to his Commentary.

As favourable and as interesting a specimen of this work as could be found, is supplied by his annotation on S. Mark xiv. 3. He begins as follows, (quoting Chrysostom, p. 436) : —" One and the same woman seems to be spoken of by all the Evangelists. Yet is this not the case. By three of them one and the same seems to be spoken of; not however by S. John, but another famous person,—the sister of Lazarus. This is what is said by John, the Bishop of the Royal City.—Origen on the other hand says that she who, in S. Matthew and S. Mark, poured the ointment in the house of Simon the leper was a different person from the sinner whom S. Luke writes about who poured the ointment on His feet in the house of the Pharisee.—Apolinarius [x] and Theodorus say that all the Evangelists mention one and the same person; but that John rehearses the story more accurately than the others. It is plain, however, that Matthew, Mark, and John speak of the same individual; for they relate that Bethany was the scene of the transaction; and this is *a village ;* whereas Luke [viii. 37] speaks of some one else ; for, 'Behold,' (saith he) 'a woman *in the city* which was *a sinner,'* " &c., &c.

[u] e.g. Theod. Mops., (p. 414,) which name is absent from Cod. Reg. 201 :— Basil, (p. 370) whose name Possinus does not seem to have read :—Cyril's name, which Possinus found in a certain place (p. 311), is not mentioned in *Laud. Gr.* 33 *fol.* 100 *b,* at top, &c.

[x] So in the *Catena* of Corderius, *in S. Joannem,* p. 302.

But the most important instance by far of independent
and sound judgment is supplied by that concluding paragraph, already quoted and largely remarked upon, at pp.
64-5 ; in which, after rehearsing all that had been said
against the concluding verses of S. Mark's Gospel, Victor
vindicates their genuineness by appealing in his own person
to the best and the most authentic copies. The Reader is
referred to Victor's Text, which is given below, at p. 288.

It only remains to point out, that since Chrysostom, (whom
Victor speaks of as ὁ ἐν ἁγίοις, [p. 408,] and ὁ μακαριος,
[p. 442,]) died in A.D. 407, it *cannot* be right to quote " 401 "
as the date of Victor's work. Rather would A.D. 450 be
a more reasonable suggestion : seeing that extracts from
Cyril, who lived on till A.D. 444, are found here and there
in Victor's pages. We shall not perhaps materially err
if we assign A.D. 430—450 as Victor of Antioch's approximate date.

I conclude these notices of an unjustly neglected Father,
by specifying the MSS. which contain his Work. Dry
enough to ordinary readers, these pages will not prove uninteresting to the critical student. An enumeration of all
the extant Codices with which I am acquainted which contain VICTOR OF ANTIOCH'S Commentary on S. Mark's Gospel,
follows :—

(i.) EVAN. 12 (= Reg. 230) *a most beautiful MS.*
The Commentary on S. Mark is here assigned to VICTOR by
name ; being a recension very like that which Matthaei has published. S. Mark's text is given *in extenso.*

(ii.) EVAN. 19 (= Reg. 189 : anciently numbered 437 and
1880. Also 134 and 135. At back, 1603.) *A grand folio, well-
bound and splendidly written. Pictures of the Evangelists in such
marvellous condition that the very tools employed by a scribe might be
reproduced. The ground gilded. Headings, &c. and words from
Scripture all in gold.*
Here also the Commentary on S. Mark's Gospel is assigned to
VICTOR. The differences between this text and that of Cramer
(e.g. at fol. 320-3, 370,) are hopelessly numerous and complicated.
There seem to have been extraordinary liberties taken with the
text of this copy throughout.

(iii.) Evan. 20 (= Reg. 188: anciently numbered 1883.) *A splendid folio,—the work of several hands and beautifully written.*

Victor's Commentary on S. Mark's Gospel is generally considered to be claimed for Cyril of Alexandria by the following words :

ΥΠΟΘΕCΙC ΕΙC ΤΟ ΚΑΤΑ ΜΑΡΚΟΝ ΑΓΙΟΝ ΕΥΑΓΓΕΛΙΟΝ
ΕΚ ΤΗC ΕΙC ΑΥΤΟΝ ΕΡΜΗΝΕΙΑC ΤΟΥ ΕΝ ΑΓΙΟΙC
ΚΥΡΙΛΛΟΥ ΑΛΕΞΑΝΔΡΕΙΑC.

The correspondence between Evan. 20 and Evan. 300 [*infrà*, N°. xiv], (= Reg. 188 and 186), is extraordinary [y]. In S. Mark's Gospel, (which alone I examined,) *every page begins with the same syllable, both of Text and Commentary :* (i.e. Reg. 186, fol. 94 to 197 = Reg. 188, fol. 87 to 140). Not that the number of words and letters in every line corresponds : but the discrepancy is compensated for by a blank at the end of each column, and at the foot of each page. Evan. 20 and Evan. 300 seem, therefore, in some mysterious way referable to a common original. The sacred Text of these two MSS., originally very dissimilar, has been made identical throughout ; some very ancient (the original?) possessor of Reg. 188 having carefully assimilated the readings of his MS. to those of Reg. 186, the more roughly written copy ; which therefore, in the judgment of the possessor of Reg. 188, exhibits the purer text. But how then does it happen that in both Codices alike, each of the Gospels (except S. Matthew's Gospel in Reg. 188,) ends with the attestation that it has been collated with approved copies ? Are we to suppose that the colophon in question was added *after* the one text had been assimilated to the other ? This is a subject which well deserves attention. The reader is reminded that these two Codices have already come before us at pp. 118-9,—where see the notes.

I proceed to set down some of the discrepancies between the texts of these two MSS. : in every one of which, Reg. 188 has been made conformable to Reg. 186 :—

(Cod. Reg. 186.)	(Cod. Reg. 188.)
(1) Matth. xxvi. 70. αὐτῶν λέγων	αὐτῶν πάντων λέγων
(2) Mk. i. 2. ὡς	κάθως
(3) ,, 11. ᾧ	σοι
(4) ,, 16. βάλλοντας ἀμφί-βληστρον	ἀμφιβάλλοντας ἀμφίβλητρον

[y] I believe it will be found that Cod. Reg. 186 corresponds *exactly* with Cod. Reg. 188 : also that the contents of Cod. Reg. 201 correspond with those of Cod. Reg. 206 ; to which last two, I believe is to be added Cod. Reg. 187.

(Cod. Reg. 186.)   (Cod. Reg. 188.)

		(Cod. Reg. 186.)	(Cod. Reg. 188.)
(5)	Mk. ii. 21.	παλαιῷ· εἰ δὲ μή γε αἱρεῖ ἀπ' αὐτοῦ τὸ πλήρωμα	παλαιῷ· εἰ δὲ μή, αἵρει τὸ πλήρωμα αὐτοῦ
(6)	,, iii. 10.	ἐθεράπευεν	ἐθεράπευσεν
(7)	,, 17.	τοῦ Ἰακώβου	Ἰακώβου.
(8)	,, 18.	καὶ Ματθαῖον καὶ Θ.	καί Μ. τὸν τελώνην καὶ Θ.
(9)	,, vi. 9.	μὴ ἐνδύσησθε	ἐνδέδυσθαι
(10)	,, 10.	μένετε	μείνατε

In the 2nd, 3rd, and 6th of these instances, Tischendorf is found
(1869) to adopt the readings of Reg. 188: in the last four, those of
Reg. 186. In the 1st, 4th, and 5th, he follows neither.

(iv.) EVAN. 24 (= Reg. 178.) *A most beautifully written fol.*
Note, that this Codex has been mutilated at p. 70-1; from
S. Matth. xxvii. 20 to S. Mark iv. 22 being away. It cannot therefore be ascertained whether the Commentary on S. Mark was here
attributed to Victor or not. Cramer employed it largely in his
edition of Victor (*Catenae*, vol. i. p. xxix,), as I have explained
already at p. 271. Some notices of the present Codex are given
above at p. 228-9.

(v.) EVAN. 25 (= Reg. 191: anciently numbered Colb. 2259:
1880. *Folio: grandly written.*
3)
No Author's name to the Commentary on S. Mark. The text of
the Evangelist is given *in extenso.*

(vi.) EVAN. 34 (= Coisl. 195.) *A grand folio, splendidly written, and in splendid condition: the paintings as they came from the
hand of the artist.*
At fol. 172, the Commentary on S. Mark is claimed for VICTOR.
It will be found that Coisl. 23 (*infrà*, Nº. ix.) and Coisl. 195 are
derived from a common original; but Cod. 195 is the more perfect copy, and should have been employed by Cramer in preference to the other (*suprà*, p. 271.) There has been an older and
a more recent hand employed on the Commentary.

(vii.) EVAN. 36 (= Coisl. 20.) *A truly sumptuous Codex.*
Some notices of this Codex have been given already, at p. 229.
The Commentary on S. Mark is Victor's, but is without any
Author's name.

(viii.) EVAN. 37 (= Coisl. 21.) *Fol.*

The Commentary on S. Mark is claimed for VICTOR at fol. 117. It seems to be very much the same recension which is exhibited by Coisl. 19 (*infrà*, N°. xviii.) and Coisl. 24 (*infrà*, N°. xi.) The Text is given *in extenso :* the Commentary, in the margin.

(ix.) EVAN. 39 (= Coisl. 23.) *A grand large fol. The writing singularly abbreviated.*

The Commentary on S. Mark is claimed for VICTOR : but is very dissimilar in its text from that which forms the basis of Cramer's editions. (See above, on N°. vi.) It is Cramer's " P." (See his *Catenae,* vol. i. p. xxviii ; and *vide supra,* p. 271.)

(x.) EVAN. 40 (= Coisl. 22.)

No Author's name is prefixed to the Commentary (fol. 103); which is a recension resembling Matthaei's. The Text is *in extenso :* the Commentary, in the margin.

(xi.) EVAN. 41 (= Coisl. 24.) *Fol.*

This is a Commentary, not a Text. It is expressly claimed for VICTOR. The recension seems to approximate to that published by Matthaei. (See on N°. viii.) One leaf is missing. (See fol. 136 b.)

(xii.) EVAN. 50 (= Bodl. Laud. Graec. 33.) 4to. The Commentary here seems to be claimed for CYRIL OF ALEXANDRIA, but in the same unsatisfactory way as N°. iii and xiv. (See Coxe's *Cat.* i. 516.)

(xiii.) EVAN. 299 (= Reg. 177 : anciently numbered 2242³).

The Commentary on S. Mark is Victor's, but is without any Author's name. The Text of S. Mark is given *in extenso :* Victor's Commentary, in the margin.

(xiv.) EVAN. 300 (= Reg. 186 : anciently numbered 692, 750, and 1882.) *A noble Codex : but the work of different scribes. It is most beautifully written.*

At fol. 94, the Commentary on S. Mark is claimed for CYRIL OF ALEXANDRIA, in the same equivocal manner as above in N°. iii and xii. The writer states in the colophon that he had diversely found it ascribed to Cyril and to Victor. (ἐπληρώθη σὺν Θεῷ ἡ ἑρμηνεία τοῦ κατὰ Μάρκον ἁγίου εὐαγγελίου ἀπὸ φωνῆς, ἔν τισιν εὗρον Κυρίλλου 'Αλεξανδρέως, ἐν ἄλλοις δὲ Βίκτορος πρεσβυτέρου.)

See above, the note on Evan. 20 (N°. iii),—a MS. which, as already explained, has been elaborately assimilated to the present.

(xv.) EVAN. 301 (= Reg. 187 : anciently numbered 504, 537 and 1879.) *A splendid fol. beautifully written throughout.*
The Commentary on S. Mark is here claimed for VICTOR.

(xvi.) EVAN. 309 (= Reg. 201 : anciently numbered 176 and 2423.) *A very interesting little fol. : very peculiar in its style. Drawings old and curious. Beautifully written.*
The Commentary is here claimed for VICTOR. This is not properly a text of the Gospel ; but parts of the text interwoven with the Commentary. Take a specimen* : (S. Mark xvi. 8—20.)

Και εξελθουσαι εφυγον απο του μνημειου. ειχεν δε αυτας τρομος και εκστασις. εως δια των επακολουθουντων σημειων.

Over the text is written κ$\overset{M}{ε}$ι (*κειμένον* i.e. *Text*) and over the Commentary ε$\overset{M}{ρ}$ (*ἑρμηνεία*, i.e. *Interpretation.*) See the next.

(xvii.) EVAN. 312 (= Reg. 206 : anciently numbered 968, 1058, 2283 ; and behind, 1604. Also A. 67.) *A beautiful little fol.*
Contains only the Commentary, which is expressly assigned to VICTOR. This Copy of Victor's Commentary is very nearly indeed a duplicate of Cod. 309, (N°. xvi.) both in its contents and in its method ; but it is less beautifully written.

(xviii.) EVAN. 329 (= Coisl. 19.) *A very grand fol.*
The Commentary on S. Mark is Victor's, but is without any Author's name. (See above, on N°. viii.)

(xix.) REG. 703, (anciently numbered 958 : 1048, and Reg. 2330 : also No. 18.) *A grand large* 4to.
The Commentary is here claimed for ORIGEN. Such at least is probably the intention of the heading (in gold capital letters) of the Prologue :—

ΩΡΙΓΕΝΟΤC ΠΡΟΛΟΓΟC ΕΙC ΤΗΝ ΕΡΜΗΝΕΙΑΝ ΤΟΤ
ΚΑΤΑ ΜΑΡΚΟΝ ΕΤΑΓΓΕΛΙΟΤ.

See on this subject the note at foot of p. 235.

---

* Note, that this recurs at fol. 145 of a Codex at Moscow numbered 384 in the *Syr. Cat.*

(xx.) Evan. 304 (=Reg. 194. Teller 1892.)

The text of S. Mark is here interwoven with a Commentary which I do not recognise. But from the correspondence of a note at the end with what is found in Possinus, pp. 361—3, I am led to suspect that the contents of this MS. will be found to correspond with what Possinus published and designated as "Tolosanus."

(xxi.) Evan. 77 (Vind. Ness. 114, Lambec. 29.) Victor's Commentary is here anonymous.

(xxii.) Evan. 92 (which belonged to Faesch of Basle [see Wetstein's *Proleg.*], and which Haenel [p. 658 *b*] says is now in Basle Library). Wetstein's account of this Codex shews that the Commentary on S. Mark is here distinctly ascribed to Victor. He says,—"Continet Marcum et in eum *Victoris Antiocheni Commentarios*, foliis 5 mutilos. Item Scholia in Epistolas Catholicas," &c. And so Haenel.

(xxiii.) Evan. 94 (As before, precisely; except that Haenel's [inaccurate] notice is at p. 657 *b*.) This Codex contains Victor of Antioch's Commentary on S. Mark, (which is evidently here also assigned to him *by name;*) and Titus of Bostra on S. Luke. Also several Scholia: among the rest, I suspect, (from what Haenel says), the Scholia spoken of *suprà*, p. 47, note (x).

(xxiv.) In addition to the preceding, and before mentioning them, Haenel says there also exists in the Library at Basle,—"Victoris Antiocheni Scholia in Evang. Marci: chart[a]."

(xxv.) Evan. 108 (Vind. Forlos. 5. Koll. 4.) Birch (p. 225) refers to it for the Scholion given in the next article. (Append. E.)

(xxvi.) Evan. 129 (Vat. 358.) ΒΙΚΟΡΟϹ. ΠΡΤ ΑΝΤΙΟΧ ЄΡΜ ЄΙϹ ΚΑΤΑ ΜΑΡΚΟΝ. The Commentary is written along the top and bottom and down the side of each page; and there are references (α′, β′, γ′) inserted in the text to the paragraphs in the margin,—as in some of the MSS. at Paris. Prefixed is an exegetical apparatus by Eusebius, &c.

Note, that of these five MSS. in the Vatican, (358, 756, 757, 1229, 1445), the 3rd and 4th are without the prefatory section (beginning πολλῶν εἰς τὸ κατὰ Μ.)—All 5 begin, Μάρκος ὁ εὐαγγελιστής. In all but the 4th, the second paragraph begins σαφέστερον.

[a] *Catalogus Librorum MSS.* Lips. 1830, 4to, p 656 *b*.

The third passage begins in all 5, Ἰσοδυναμεῖ τοῦτο. Any one seeking to understand this by a reference to the editions of Cramer or of Possinus will recognise the truth of what was stated above, p. 274, line 24 to 27.

(xxvii.) EVAN. 137 (Vat. 756.) The Commentary is written as in Vat. 358 (N°. xxvi) : but no Author's name is given.

(xxviii.) EVAN. 138 (Vat. 757.) On a blank page or fly-leaf at the beginning are these words :—ὁ ἀντίγραφος (sic) οὗτός ἐστιν ὁ Πέτρος ὁ τῆς Λαοδικείας ὅστις προηγεῖται τῶν ἄλλων ἐξηγητῶν ἐνταῦθα. (Comp. N°. xlvii.) The Commentary and Text are not kept distinct, as in the preceding Codex. Both are written in an ill-looking, slovenly hand.

(xxix.) EVAN. 143 (Vat. 1,229.) The Commentary is written as in Vat. 358 (N°. xxvi), but without the references ; and no Author's name is given.

(xxx.) EVAN. 181 (Xavier, Cod. Zelada.) Birch was shewn this Codex of the Four Gospels in the Library of Cardinal Xavier of Zelada (*Prolegomena*, p. lviii) : " Cujus forma est in folio, pp. 596. In margine passim occurrunt scholia ex Patrum Commentariis exscripta."

(xxxi.) EVAN. 186 (Laur. vi. 18.) This Codex is minutely described by Bandini (*Cat.* i. 130), who gives the Scholion (*infra*, p. 388-9), and says that the Commentary is without any Author's name.

(xxxii.) EVAN. 194 (Laur. vi. 33.) Βίκτορος πρεσβυτέρου Ἀντιο-χείας ἑρμηνεία εἰς τὸ κατὰ Μάρκον εὐαγγέλιον. (See the description of this Codex in Bandini's *Cat.* i. 158.)

(xxxiii.) EVAN. 195 (Laur. vi. 34.) This Codex seems to correspond in its contents with N°. xxxi. *suprà :* the Commentary containing the Scholion, and being anonymous. (See Bandini, p. 161.)

(xxxiv.) EVAN. 197 (Laur. viii. 14.) The Commentary, (which is Victor's, but has no Author's name prefixed,) is defective at the end. (See Bandini, p. 355.)

(xxxv.) EVAN. 210 (Venet. 27.) " Conveniunt initio Commentarii eum iis qui Victori Antiocheno tribuuntur, progressu autem discrepant." (Theupoli *Graeca D. Marci Bibl. Codd. MSS.* Venet. 1740.) I infer that the work is anonymous.

(xxxvi.) Venet. 495. "Victoris Antiocheni Presbyteri expositio in Evangelium Marci, collecta ex diversis Patribus." (I obtain this reference from the Catalogue of Theupolus.)

(xxxvii.) Evan. 215 (Venet. 544.) I presume, from the description in the Catalogue of Theupolus, that this Codex also contains a copy of Victor's Commentary.

(xxxviii.) Evan. 221 (Vind. Ness. 117, Lambec. 38). Kollar has a long note (B) [iii. 157] on the Commentary, which has no Author's name prefixed. Birch (p. 225) refers to it for the purpose recorded under N°. xxv.

(xxxix.) Evan. 222 (Vind. Ness. 180, Lambec. 39.) The Commentary is anonymous. Birch refers to it, as before.

Add the following six MSS. at Moscow, concerning which, see Matthaei's Nov. Test. (1788) vol. ii. p. xii. :—

(xl.) Evan. 237 (This is Matthaei's d or D [described in his *N. T.* ix. 242. Also *Vict. Ant.* ii. 137.] "SS. Synod. 42 :") and is one of the MSS. employed by Matthaei in his ed. of Victor.— The Commentary on S. Mark has no Author's name prefixed.

(xli.) Evan. 238 (Matthaei's e or E [described in his *N. T.* ix. 200. Also *Vict. Ant.* ii. 141.] "SS. Synod. 48.") This Codex formed the basis of Matthaei's ed. of Victor, [See the *Not. Codd. MSS.* at the end of vol. ii. p. 123. Also *N. T.* ix. 202.] The Commentary on S. Mark is anonymous.

(xlii.) Evan. 253 (Matthaei's 10 [described in his *N. T.* ix. 234.] It was lent him by Archbishop Nicephorus.) Matthaei says (p. 236) that it corresponds with a (*our* Evan. 259). No Author's name is prefixed to the Commentary on S. Mark.

(xliii.) Evan. 255 (Matthaei's 12 [described in his *N.T.* ix. 222. Also *Vict. Ant.* ii. 133.] "SS. Synod. 139." The Scholia on S. Mark are here entitled ἐξηγητικαὶ ἐκλογαί, and (as in 14) are few in number. For some unexplained reason, in his edition of Victor of Antioch, Matthaei saw fit to designate this MS. as "B." [*N. T.* ix. 224 *note*.] . . . . See by all means, *infrà*, the "Postscript."

(xliv.) Evan. 256 (Matthaei's 14 [described in his *N. T.* ix. 220.] "Bibl. Typ. Synod. 3.") The Commentary on S. Mark is here assigned to Victor, presbyter of Antioch; but the Scholia are said to be (as in "12" [Nº. xxxix]) few in number.

(xlv.) Evan. 259 (Matthaei's a or A [described in his *N. T.* ix. 237. Also *Vict. Ant.* ii. 128.] " SS. Synod. 45.") This is one of the MSS. employed by Matthaei in his ed. of Victor. No Author's name is prefixed to the Commentary.

(xlvi.) Evan. 332 (Taurin. xx *b* iv. 20.) Victor's Commentary is here given anonymously. (See the Catalogue of Pasinus, P. i. p. 91.)

(xlvii.) Evan. 353 (Ambros. M. 93): with the same Commentary as Evan. 181, (i.e. Nº. xxx.)

(xlviii.) Evan. 374 (Vat. 1445.) Written continuously in a very minute character. The Commentary is headed (in a later Greek hand) + ἑρμηνεία Πέτρου Λαοδικείας εἰς τοὺς δ᾽ ἁγ[ίους] εὐαγγελιστάς +. This is simply a mistake. No such Work exists: and the Commentary on the second Evangelist is that of Victor. (See Nº. xxviii.)

(xlix.) Evan. 428 (Monacensis 381. Augsburg 11): said to be duplicate of Evan. 300 (i.e. of Nº. xiv.)

(l.) Evan. 432 (Monacensis 99.) The Commentary contained in this Codex is evidently assigned to Victor.

(li.) Evan. 7^pe (ix. 3. 471.) A valuable copy of the Four Gospels, dated 1062; which Edw. de Muralto (in his Catalogue of the Greek MSS. in the Imperial Library at S. Petersburg) says contains the Commentary of Victor Ant. (See Scrivener's *Introduction*, p. 178.).

(lii.) At Toledo, in the " Biblioteca de la Iglesia Mayor," Haenel [p. 885] mentions :—" Victor Antiochenus Comm. Graec. in iv. [?] Evangelia saec. xiv. membr. fol."

To this enumeration, (which could certainly be very extensively increased,) will probably have to be added the following :—

Evan. 146 (Palatino-Vat. 5.)
Evan. 233 (Escurial Y. ii. 8.)

EVAN. 373 (Vat. 1423.)
EVAN. 379 (Vat. 1769.)
EVAN. 427 (Monacensis 465, Augsburg 10.)

Middle Hill, N°. 13,975,—a MS. in the collection of Sir Thomas Phillipps.

In conclusion, it can scarcely require to be pointed out that VICTOR's Commentary,—of which the Church in her palmiest days shewed herself so careful to multiply copies, and of which there survive to this hour such a vast number of specimens,—must needs anciently have enjoyed very peculiar favour. It is evident, in fact, that an Epitome of Chrysostom's Homilies on S. Matthew, together with *VICTOR's compilation on S. Mark,*—Titus of Bostra on S. Luke,—and a work in the main derived from Chrysostom's Homilies on S. John;—that these four constituted the established Commentary of ancient Christendom on the fourfold Gospel. Individual copyists, no doubt, will have been found occasionally to abridge certain of the Annotations, and to omit others: or else, out of the multitude of Scholia by various ancient Fathers which were evidently once in circulation, and must have been held in very high esteem,—(Irenæus, Origen, Ammonius, Eusebius, Apolinarius, Cyril, Chrysostom, the Gregorys, Basil, Theodore of Mopsuestia, and Theodore of Heraclea,) they will have introduced extracts according to their individual caprice. In this way, the general sameness of the several copies is probably to be accounted for, while their endless discrepancy in matters of detail is perhaps satisfactorily explained.

These last remarks are offered in the way of partial elucidation of the difficulty pointed out above, at pp. 272—4.

APPENDIX (E).

Text of the concluding Scholion of Victor of Antioch's *Commentary on S. Mark's Gospel; in which Victor bears emphatic testimony to the genuineness of "the last Twelve Verses."*

(Referred to at p. 65.)

I have thought this very remarkable specimen of the method of an ancient and (as I think) unjustly neglected Commentator, deserving of extraordinary attention. Besides presenting the reader, therefore, with what seems to be a fair approximation to the original text of the passage, I have subjoined as many various readings as have come to my knowledge. It is hoped that they are given with tolerable exactness; but I have been too often obliged to depend on printed books and the testimony of others. I can at least rely on the readings furnished me from the Vatican.

The text chiefly followed is that of Coisl. 20, (in the Paris Library,—our Evan. 36;) supplemented by several other MSS., which, for convenience, I have arbitrarily designated by the letters of the alphabet as under [a].

Εἰ δὲ καὶ τὸ "'Αναστὰς [b] δὲ πρωὶ πρώτῃ σαββάτου ἐφάνη πρῶτον Μαρίᾳ τῇ Μαγδαληνῇ," καὶ τὰ ἑξῆς ἐπιφερόμενα, ἐν τῷ κατὰ Μάρκον εὐαγγελίῳ παρὰ [c] πλείστοις ἀντιγράφοις οὐ κεῖνται [d], (ὡς νόθα γὰρ ἐνόμισαν αὐτά τινες εἶναι [e]) ἀλλ'

---

[a] *Reg.* 177 = A : 178 = B : 230 = C.—*Coisl.* 19 = D : 20 = E : 21 = F : 22 = G : 24 = H.—*Matthaei's* d or D = I : *his* e or E = J : *his* 12 = K : *his* a or A = L.—*Vat.* 358 = M : 756 = N : 757 = O : 1229 = P : 1445 = Q.—*Vind. Koll.* 4 *Forlos.* 5 = R.—*Xav. de Zelada* = S.—*Laur.* 18 = T : 34 = U.—*Venet.* 27 = V.—*Vind. Lamb.* 38 = W : 39 = X.

[b] So B—E (which I chiefly follow) begins,—Το δε αναστας.

[c] B begins thus,—Ει δε και το αναστας δε πρωι μετα τα επιφερομενα παρα. It is at this word (παρα) that most copies of the present scholion (A, C, D, F, G, H, I, J, K, L, M, N, O, P, Q, R, S, T, U, V, W, X) begin.

[d] So far (except in its opening phrase) E. But C, D, F, H, I, J, K, L, M, N, O, P, T, begin,—Παρα πλειστοις αντιγραφοις ου κειναι [I, ου κειται : J, ουκ ην δε] ταυτα τα [M, O, T om. τα] επιφερομενα εν [D, F, H om. εν] τῳ κατα Μαρκον [B, εν τω παροντι] ευαγγελιῳ.

[e] So I, J, K, L, and H. P proceeds,—ως νοθα νομισθεντα τισιν ειναι. But

ἡμεῖς ἐξ ἀκριβῶν ἀντιγράφων, ὡς ἐν πλείστοις εὑρόντες αὐτὰ ʹ,
κατὰ τὸ Παλαιστιναῖον εὐαγγέλιον Μάρκου, ὡς ἔχει ἡ ἀλή-
θεια, συντεθείκαμεν ᵍ καὶ τὴν ἐν αὐτῷ ἐπιφερομόνην δεσπο-
τικὴν ἀνάστασιν, μετὰ τὸ " ἐφοβοῦντο γάρ ʰ." τουτέστιν ἀπὸ
τοῦ " ἀναστὰς δὲ πρωῒ πρώτῃ σαββάτου," καὶ καθ᾽ ἑξῆς μέχρι
τοῦ " διὰ τῶν ἐπακολουθούντων σημείων. Ἀμήν ⁱ."

More pains than enough (it will perhaps be thought)
have been taken to exhibit accurately this short Scholion.
And yet, it has not been without design (the reader may be
sure) that so many various readings have been laboriously
accumulated. The result, it is thought, is eminently instructive, and (to the student of Ecclesiastical Antiquity) important also.

For it will be perceived by the attentive reader that not
more than two or three of the multitude of various readings afforded by this short Scholion can have possibly resulted from careless transcription ᵏ. The rest have been unmistakably occasioned by the merest licentiousness: every
fresh Copyist evidently considering himself at liberty to take
just whatever liberties he pleased with the words before

B, C, D, E, F, G, M, N, O, T exhibit,—ως νοθα νομισαντες αυτα τινες [B om.
τινες] ειναι. On the other hand, A and Q begin and proceed as follows,—Παρα
πλειστοις αντιγραφοις ταυτα τα [Q om. τα] επιφερομενα εν [A om. εν] τῳ κατα
Μαρκον ευαγγελιῳ ως νοθα νομισαντες τινες [Q, τινας (a clerical error): A om.
τινες] ουκ εθηκαν.

ʹ So B, except that it omits ως. So also, A, D, E, F, G, H, J, M, N, O, P,
Q, T, except that they begin the sentence, ημεις δε.

ᵍ So D, E, F, G, H, J, M, N, O, P, T: also B and Q, except that they prefix
και to κατα το Π. B is peculiar in reading,—ως εχει η αληθεια Μαρκου (transposing Μαρκου): while C and P read,—ομως ημεις εξ ακριβων αντιγραφων και
πλειστων ου μην αλλα και εν τῳ Παλαιστιναιῳ ευαγγελιῳ Μαρκου ευροντες αυτα
ως εχει η αληθεια συντεθεικαμεν.

ʰ So all, apparently: except that P reads εμφερομενην for επιφερομενην; and
M, after αναστασιν inserts εδηλωσαμεν, with a point (.) before μετα: while C
and P (after αναστασιν,) proceed,—και την [C, ειτα] αναληψιν και καθεδραν εκ
δεξιων του Πατρος ῳ πρεπει η δοξα και η τιμη νυν και εις τους αιωνας. αμην. But
J [and I think, H] (after γαρ) proceeds,—διο δοξαν αναπεμψωμεν τῳ ανασταντι
εκ νεκρων Χριστῳ τῳ Θεῳ ημων αμα τῳ αναρχῳ Πατρι και ζωοποιῳ Πνευματι νυν
και αει και εις τους αιωνας των αιωνων. αμην.

ⁱ So B. All, except B, C, H, J, P seem to end at εφοβουντο γαρ.

ᵏ e.g. ουκ ην δε for ου κεινται.

him. To amputate, or otherwise to mutilate; to abridge; to amplify; to transpose; to remodel;—this has been the rule with all. The *types* (so to speak) are reducible to two, or at most to three; but the varieties are almost as numerous as the MSS. of Victor's work.

And yet it is impossible to doubt that this Scholion was originally one, and one only. Irrecoverable perhaps, in some of its minuter details, as the actual text of Victor may be, it is nevertheless self-evident that *in the main* we are in possession of what he actually wrote on this occasion. In spite of all the needless variations observable in the manner of stating a certain fact, it is still unmistakably one and the same fact which is every time stated. It is invariably declared,—

(1.) That from certain copies of S. Mark's Gospel the last Twelve Verses had been LEFT OUT; and (2) That this had been done because their genuineness had been by certain persons suspected: but, (3) That the Writer, convinced of their genuineness, had restored them to their rightful place; (4) Because he had found them in accurate copies, and in the authentic Palestinian copy, which had supplied him with his exemplar.

It is obvious to suggest that after familiarizing ourselves with this specimen of what proves to have been the licentious method of the ancient copyists in respect of the text of an early Father, we are in a position to approach more intelligently the Commentary of Victor itself; and, to some extent, to understand how it comes to pass that so many liberties have been taken with it throughout. The Reader is reminded of what has been already offered on this subject at pp. 272-3.

APPENDIX (F).

On the Relative antiquity of the CODEX VATICANUS (B), *and the* CODEX
SINAITICUS (ℵ).

(Referred to at p. 70.)

I. "VIX differt aetate a Codice Sinaitico," says Tischen-
dorf, (*ed. 8va*, 1869, p. ix,) speaking of the Codex Vaticanus
(B). Yet does he perpetually designate his own Sinaitic
Codex (ℵ) as "omnium antiquissimus." Now,

(1) The (all but unique) sectional division of the Text of
Codex B,—confessedly the oldest scheme of chapters extant,
is in itself a striking note of primitiveness. The author of
the Codex knew nothing, apparently, of the Eusebian method.
But I venture further to suggest that the following peculiarities in Codex ℵ unmistakably indicate for it a later date
than Codex B.

(2) Cod. ℵ, (like C, and other later MSS.,) is broken up
into short paragraphs throughout. The Vatican Codex, on
the contrary, has very few breaks indeed: e.g. it is without
break of any sort from S. Matth. xvii. 24 to xx. 17: whereas,
within the same limits, there are in Cod. ℵ as many as *thirty*
interruptions of the context. From S. Mark xiii. 1 to the
end of the Gospel the text is absolutely continuous in Cod. B,
except in *one* place: but in Cod. ℵ it is interrupted upwards
of *fifty* times. Again: from S. Luke xvii. 11, to the end of
the Gospel there is but *one* break in Cod. B. But it is
broken into well nigh *an hundred and fifty* short paragraphs
in Cod. ℵ.

There can be no doubt that the unbroken text of Codex B,
(resembling the style of the papyrus of *Hyperides* published
by Mr. Babington,) is the more ancient. The only places
where it approximates to the method of Cod. ℵ, is where
the Commandments are briefly recited (S. Matth. xix. 18,
&c.), and where our LORD proclaims the eight Beatitudes
(S. Matth. v.)

(3) Again; Cod. א is prone to exhibit, on extraordinary occasions, *a single word* in a line, as at—

S. Matth. xv. 30.	S. Mark x. 29.	S. Luke xiv. 13.
ΧѠΛΟΥϹ	Η ΑΔΕΛΦΑϹ	ΠΤѠΧΟΥϹ
ΤΥΦΛΟΥϹ	Η ΠΑΤΕΡΑ	ΑΝΑΠΗΡΟΥϹ
ΚΥΛΛΟΥϹ	Η ΜΗΤΕΡΑ	ΧѠΛΟΥϹ
ΚѠΦΟΥϹ	Η ΤΕΚΝΑ	ΤΥΦΛΟΥϹ
	Η ΑΓΡΟΥϹ	

This became a prevailing fashion in the vi[th] century; e.g. when the Cod. Laudianus of the Acts (E) was written. The only trace of anything of the kind in Cod. B is at the Genealogy of our Lord.

(4) At the commencement of every fresh paragraph, the initial letter in Cod. א *slightly projects into the margin,*— beyond the left hand edge of the column; as usual in all later MSS. This characteristic is only not undiscoverable in Cod. B. Instances of it there *are* in the earlier Codex; but they are of exceedingly rare occurrence.

(5) Further; Cod. א abounds in such contractions as A̅N̅O̅C̅, O̅Y̅N̅O̅C̅ (with all their cases), for ANΘΡѠΠΟϹ, ΟΥΡΑΝΟϹ, &c. Not only Π̅Ν̅Α̅, Π̅Η̅Ρ̅, Π̅Ε̅Ρ̅, Π̅Ρ̅Α̅, Μ̅Ρ̅Α̅ (for ΠΝΕΤΜΑ, ΠΑΤΗΡ-ΤΕΡ-ΤΕΡΑ, ΜΗΤΕΡΑ), but also C̅Τ̅Ρ̅Θ̅Η̅, Ι̅Η̅Λ̅, Ι̅Η̅Λ̅Η̅Μ̅, for ϹΤΑΥΡѠΘΗ, ΙϹΡΑΗΛ, ΙΕΡΟΥϹΑΛΗΜ.

But Cod. B, though familiar with ι̅c̅, and a few other of the most ordinary abbreviations, knows nothing of these compendia: which certainly *cannot* have existed in the earliest copies of all. Once more, it seems reasonable to suppose that their constant occurrence in Cod א indicates for that Codex a date subsequent to Cod. B.

(6) The very discrepancy observable between these two Codices in their method of dealing with "the last twelve verses of S. Mark's Gospel," (already adverted to at p. 88,) is a further indication, and as it seems to the present writer a very striking one, that Cod. B is the older of the two. Cod. א is evidently *familiar* with the phenomenon which *astonishes* Cod. B by its novelty and strangeness.

(7) But the most striking feature of difference, after all, is only to be recognised by one who surveys the Codices themselves with attention. It is *that* general air of primi-

tiveness in Cod. B which makes itself at once *felt.* The even
symmetry of the unbroken columns;—the work of the *prima
manus* everywhere vanishing through sheer antiquity; —
the small, even, *square* writing, which partly recals the style
of the Herculanean rolls; partly, the papyrus fragments
of the *Oration against Demosthenes* (published by Harris in
1848):—all these notes of superior antiquity infallibly set
Cod. B before Cod. א; though it may be impossible to determine whether by 50, by 75, or by 100 years.

II. It has been conjectured by one whose words are always entitled to most respectful attention, that Codex Sinaiticus may have been " one of the fifty Codices of Holy Scripture which Eusebius prepared A.D. 331, by Constantine's
direction, for the use of the new Capital." (Scrivener's
Collation of the Cod. Sin., Introd. p. xxxvii-viii.)

1. But this, which is rendered improbable by the many
instances of grave discrepancy between its readings and
those with which Eusebius proves to have been most familiar, is made impossible by the discovery that it is without S. Mark xv. 28, which constitutes the Eusebian Section
numbered "216" in S. Mark's Gospel. [Quite in vain has
Tischendorf perversely laboured to throw doubt on this circumstance. It remains altogether undeniable,—as a far less
accomplished critic than Tischendorf may see at a glance.
Tischendorf's only plea is the fact that in Cod. M, (he
might have added and in the Codex Sinaiticus, *which explains
the phenomenon* in Cod. M), *against ver.* 29 is set the number,
("216,") instead of against ver. 28. But what then? Has
not the number *demonstrably* lost its place? And is there
not *still* one of the Eusebian Sections missing? And *which*
can it *possibly* have been, if it was not S. Mark xv. 28?]
Again. Cod. א, (like B, C, L, U, Γ, and some others), gives the
piercing of the SAVIOUR's side at S. Matth. xxvii. 49: but if
Eusebius had read that incident in the same place, he would
have infallibly included S. John xix. 34, 35, with S. Matth.
xxvii. 49, in his vii[th] Canon, where matters are contained
which are common to S. Matthew and S. John, — instead
of referring S. John xix. 31—37 to his x[th] Canon, which

specifies things peculiar to each of the four Evangelists.
Eusebius, moreover, in a certain place (*Dem. Evan.* x. 8
[quoted by Tisch.]) has an allusion to the same transaction,
and expressly says that it is recorded *by S. John.*

2. No inference as to the antiquity of this Codex can be
drawn from the Eusebian notation of Sections in the margin : *that* notation having been confessedly added at a subsequent date.

3. On the other hand, the subdivision of Cod. א into paragraphs, proves to have been made without any reference to
the sectional distribution of Eusebius. Thus, there are in
the Codex thirty distinct paragraphs from S. Matthew xi. 20
to xii. 34, inclusive ; but there are comprised within the
same limits only seventeen Eusebian sections. And yet, of
those seventeen sections only nine correspond with as many
paragraphs of the Codex Sinaiticus. This, in itself, is enough
to prove that Eusebius knew nothing of the present Codex.
His record is express :—ἐφ᾽ ἑκάστῳ τῶν τεσσάρων εὐαγγελίων ἀριθμός τις πρόκειται κατὰ μέρος κ.τ.λ.

III. The supposed resemblance of the opened volume to
an Egyptian papyrus,—when eight columns (σελίδες) are
exhibited to the eye at once, side by side,—seems to be a fallacious note of high antiquity. If Cod. א has four columns
in a page,—Cod. B three,—Cod. A two,—Cod. C has only
one. But Cod. C is certainly as old as Cod. A. Again,
Cod. D, which is of the vi[th] century, is written (like Cod. C)
across the page : yet was it " copied from an older model
similarly divided in respect to the lines or verses,"—and
therefore similarly written across the page. It is almost
obvious that the size of the skins on which a Codex was
written will have decided whether the columns should be
four or only three in a page.

IV. In fine, nothing doubting the high antiquity of both
Codices, (B and א,) I am nevertheless fully persuaded that
an interval of at least half a century,—if not of a far greater
span of years, — is absolutely required to account for the
marked dissimilarity between them.

APPENDIX (G).

On the so-called "AMMONIAN SECTIONS" *and* "EUSEBIAN CANONS."
(Referred to at p. 130.)

I. THAT the Sections (popularly miscalled *"Ammonian"*) with which EUSEBIUS [A.D. 320] has made the world thoroughly familiar, and of which some account was given above (pp. 127-8), cannot be the same which AMMONIUS of Alexandria [A.D. 220] employed,—but must needs be the invention of EUSEBIUS himself,—admits of demonstration. On this subject, external testimony is altogether insecure*. The only safe appeal is to the Sections themselves.

1. The Call of the Four Apostles is described by the first three Evangelists, within the following limits of their respective Gospels:—S. Matthew iv. 18—22 : S. Mark i. 16—20 : S. Luke (with the attendant miraculous draught of fishes,) v. 1—11. Now, these three portions of narrative are observed to be dealt with in the sectional system of EUSEBIUS after the following extraordinary fashion : (the fourth column represents the Gospel according to S. John):—

(1.)	. . . .	§ 29, (v. 1—3)	
(2.) § 20, (iv. 17, 18)	§ 9, (i. 14½—16)		
(3.)	. . . .	§ 30, (v. 4—7)	§219, (xxi. 1-6)
(4.)	. . . .	§ 30 (v. 4—7)	§ 222, (xxi. 11)
(5.)	. . . .	§ 31, (v. 8—10½)	
(6.) § 21, (iv. 19, 20)	§ 10, (i. 17,18)	§ 32, (v. 10½, 11)	
(7.) § 22, (iv. 21, 22)	§ 11, (i. 19,20)		

* Jerome evidently supposed that Ammonius was the author of *the Canons* as well:—"Canones quos *Eusebius* Caesariensis Episcopus *Alexandrinum secutus Ammonium* in decem numeros ordinavit, sicut in Graeco habentur expressimus." (*Ad Papam Damasum. Epist.*) And again : "*Ammonius* . . . . *Evangelicos Canones excogitavit* quos postea secutus est Eusebius Caesariensis." (*De Viris Illustr.* c. 55 [*Opp.* ii. 881.])—See above, p. 128.

It will be perceived from this, that Eusebius subdivides these three portions of the sacred Narrative into ten Sections ("§§;")—of which three belong to S. Matthew, viz. §§ 20, 21, 22:—three to S. Mark, viz. §§ 9, 10, 11:—four to S. Luke, viz. §§ 29, 30, 31, 32: which ten Sections, Eusebius distributes over four of his Canons: referring three of them to his IInd Canon, (which exhibits what S. Matthew, S. Mark, and S. Luke have in common); four of them to his VIth Canon, (which shews what S. Matthew and S. Mark have in common); one, to his IXth, (which contains what is common to S. Luke and S. John); two, to his Xth, (in which is found what is peculiar to each Evangelist.)

Now, the design which *Eusebius* had in breaking up this portion of the sacred Text, (S. Matth. iv. 18—22, S. Mark i. 16—20, S. Luke v. 1—11,) after so arbitrary a fashion, into ten portions; divorcing three of those Sections from S. Matthew's Gospel, (viz. S. Luke's §§ 29, 30, 31); and connecting one of these last three (§ 30) *with two Sections* (§§ 219, 222) *of S. John;*—is perfectly plain. His object was, (as he himself explains,) to shew—not only (*a*) what S. Matthew has in common with S. Mark and S. Luke; but also (*b*) *what S. Luke has in common with S. John;*—as well as (*c*) what S. Luke has *peculiar to himself.* But, in the work of Ammonius, *as far as we know anything about that work,* all this would have been simply impossible. (I have already described his " Diatessaron," at pp. 126-7.) Intent on exhibiting the Sections of the other Gospels which correspond with the Sections of *S. Matthew,* Ammonius would not if he could,—(and he could not if he would,)—have dissociated from its context S. Luke's account of the first miraculous draught of fishes in the beginning of our Lord's Ministry, for the purpose of establishing its resemblance to S. John's account of the *second* miraculous draught of fishes which took place after the Resurrection, and is only found in S. John's Gospel. These Sections therefore are " Eusebian," not Ammonian. They are *necessary,* according to the scheme of Eusebius. They are not only unnecessary and even meaningless, but actually impossible, in the Ammonian scheme.

2. Let me call attention to another, and, as I think, a more convincing instance. I am content in fact to narrow the whole question to the following single issue:—Let me be shewn how it is rationally conceivable that Ammonius can have split up S. John xxi. 12, 13, into *three distinct Sections;* and S. John xxi. 15, 16, 17, into *six?* and yet, after so many injudicious disintegrations of the sacred Text, how it is credible that he can have made but *one* Section of S. John xxi. 18 to 25,—which nevertheless, from its very varied contents, confessedly requires even *repeated* subdivision? . . . . Why *Eusebius* did all this, is abundantly plain. His peculiar plan constrained him to refer the *former* half of ver. 12,—the *latter* half of verses 15, 16, 17—to his IXth Canon, where S. Luke and S. John are brought together; (ἐν ᾧ οἱ δύο τὰ παραπλήσια εἰρήκασι):—and to consign the *latter* half of ver. 12,—the *former* half of verses 15, 16, 17, —together with the whole of the *last eight verses* of S. John's Gospel, to his X^th (or last) Canon, where what is peculiar to each of the four Evangelists is set down, (ἐν ᾧ περὶ τίνων ἕκαστος αὐτῶν ἰδίως ἀνέγραψεν.)   But Ammonius, because he confessedly *recognised no such Canons*, was under no such constraint.   He had in fact *no such opportunity.*   He therefore simply *cannot* have adopted the same extraordinary sectional subdivision.

3. To state the matter somewhat differently, and perhaps to exhibit the argument in a more convincing form:—The Canons of Eusebius, and the so-called " Ammonian Sections,"—(by which, confessedly, nothing else whatever is *meant* but the Sections of *Eusebius*,)—are discovered mutually to imply one another. Those Canons are without meaning or use apart from the Sections,—for the sake of which they were clearly invented. Those Sections, whatever convenience they may possess apart from the Canons, nevertheless are discovered to presuppose the Canons throughout: to be manifestly subsequent to them in order of time: to depend upon them for their very existence: in some places to be even unaccountable in the eccentricity of their arrangement, except when explained by the requirements of the *Eusebian* Canons.   I say—*That* particular sectional sub-

division, in other words, to which the epithet " AMMONIAN "
is popularly applied,—(applied however without authority,
and in fact by the merest license,)—proves on careful inspection to have been only capable of being devised by one
who was already in possession of the Canons of EUSEBIUS.   In
plain terms, they are demonstrably *the work of EUSEBIUS
himself,*—who expressly claims *The Canons* for his own (κανόνας δέκα τὸν ἀριθμὸν διεχάραξά σοι), and leaves it to be
inferred that he is the Author of the Sections also.   Wetstein (*Proleg.* p. 70,) and Bishop Lloyd (in the " Monitum"
prefixed to his ed. of the Greek Test. p. x,) so understand
the matter ; and Mr. Scrivener (*Introduction,* p. 51) evidently
inclines to the same opinion.

II. I desire, in the next place, to point out that a careful
inspection of the Eusebian " Sections," (for Eusebius himself
calls them περικοπαί, not κεφάλαια,) leads inevitably to the
inference that they are only rightly understood when regarded in the light of " MARGINAL REFERENCES."   This has
been hitherto overlooked.   Bp. Lloyd, in the interesting
" Monitum" already quoted, remarks of the Eusebian Canons,
—" quorum haec est utilitas, ut eorum scilicet ope quivis,
nullo labore, Harmoniam sibi quatuor Evangeliorum possit
conficere."   The learned Prelate can never have made the
attempt in this way " Harmoniam sibi conficere," or he
would not have so written.   He evidently did not advert to
the fact that Eusebius refers his readers (in his IIIrd Canon)
from S. John's account of the *Healing of the Nobleman's son*
to the account given by S. Matthew and S. Luke of the
Healing of the Centurion's servant.   It is perfectly plain in fact
that to enable a reader " to construct for himself *a Harmony of the Gospels,*" was no part of Eusebius' intention ;
and quite certain that any one who shall ever attempt to
avail himself of the system of Sections and Canons before us
with that object, will speedily find himself landed in hopeless confusion [a].

* There was published at the University Press in 1805, a handsome quarto
volume (pp. 216) entitled *Harmonia quatuor Evangeliorum juxta Sectiones
Ammonianas et Eusebii Canones.*   It is merely the contents of the X Canons

But in fact there is no danger of his making much progress in his task. His first discovery would probably be that S. John's weighty doctrinal statements concerning our LORD's *Eternal Godhead* in chap. i. 1—5 : 9, 10 : 14, are represented as parallel with the *Human Genealogy* of our SAVIOUR as recorded by S. Matthew i. 1—16, and by S. Luke iii. 23—38 :—the next, that the first half of the Visit of the Magi (S. Matthew ii. 1—6) is exhibited as corresponding with S. John vii. 41, 42.—Two such facts ought to open the eyes of a reader of ordinary acuteness quite wide to the true nature of the Canons of Eusebius. They are *Tables of Reference only.*

Eusebius has in fact himself explained his object in constructing them ; which (he says) was twofold : (1st) To enable a reader to see at a glance, *" which* of the Evangelists have said *things of the same kind,"* (τίνες τὰ παραπλήσια εἰρήκασι : the phrase occurs *four times* in the course of his short Epistle) : and (2ndly), To enable him to find out *where* they have severally done so : (τοὺς οἰκείους ἑκάστου εὐαγγελιστοῦ τόπους, ἐν οἷς κατὰ τῶν αὐτῶν ἠνέχθησαν εἰπεῖν ; Eusebius uses the phrase *twice.*) But this, (as all are aware) is precisely the office of (what are called) " Marginal References." Accordingly,

(*a.*) Whether referring *from* S. Matth. x. 40 (§ 98) ; S. Mark ix. 37 (§ 96) ; or S. Luke x. 16 (§ 116) ;—we find ourselves referred *to* the following *six* places of S. John,—v. 23 : xii. 44, 45 : xiii. 20 : xiv. 21 : xiv. 24, 25 : xv. 23 [b] (= §§ 40, 111, 120, 129, 131, 144 [b].) Again,

(*b.*) Whether we refer *from* S. Matth. xi. 27 (§§ 111, 112,) or S. Luke x. 22 (§ 119),—we find ourselves referred *to* the following *eleven* places of S. John,—i. 18 : iii. 35 : v. 37 : vi. 46 : vii. 28, 29 : viii. 19 : x. 15 : xiii. 3 : xv. 21 : xvi. 15 : xvii. 25 (§§ 8, 30, 44, 61, 76, 87, 90, 114, 142, 148, 154.)

(*c.*) So also, from S. Matthew's (xvi. 13—16), S. Mark's (viii. 27—29), and S. Luke's (ix. 18—20) account of S.

---

of Eusebius printed *in extenso,*—and of course is no " Harmony " at all. It would have been a really useful book, notwithstanding ; but that the editor, strange to say, has omitted to number the sections.

[b] This last § according to *Tischendorf's* ed. of the Eusebian Canons.

Peter's Confession at Cæsarea Philippi, — we are referred
to S. John i. 42, 43,—a singular reference; and to S. John
vi. 68, 69.

(*d.*) From the mention of the last Passover by the three
earlier Evangelists, (S. Matth. xxvi. 1, 2: S. Mark xiv. 1:
S. Luke xxii. 1,) we are referred to S. John's mention of the
first Passover (ii. 13 = § 20); and of the *second* (vi. 4 =
§ 48); as well as of the fourth (xi. 55 = § 96.)

(*e.*) From the words of Consecration at the Last Supper,
as recorded by S. Matth. (xxvi. 16), S. Mark (xiv. 22), and
S. Luke (xxii. 19),—we are referred to the four following
Sections of our LORD's Discourse in the Synagogue at Caper-
naum recorded by S. John, which took place a year before,
—S. John vi. 35, 36: 48: 51: 55: (§§ 55, 63, 65, 67).

(*f.*) Nothing but the spirit in which "Marginal References" are made would warrant a critic in linking together
three incidents like the following,—similar, indeed, yet entirely distinct: viz. S. Matth. xxvii. 34: S. Mark xv. 24:
and S. John xix. 28, 29.

(*g.*) I was about to say that scarcely could such an excuse
be invented for referring a Reader from S. Luke xxii. 32,
to S. John xxi. 15, and 16, and 17 (= §§ 227, 228, 229,)—
but I perceive that the same three References stand in the
margin of our own Bibles. Not even the margin of the
English Bible, however, sends a Reader (as the IXth Canon
of Eusebius does) from our LORD's eating "broiled fish and
honeycomb," in the presence of the ten Apostles at Jerusalem on the evening of the first Easter-Day, (S. Luke xxiv.
41—43 (= § 341,)) to His feeding the seven Apostles with
bread and fish at the Sea of Galilee many days after.
(S. John xxi. 9, 10: 12: 13 = §§ 221, 223, 224.) — And
this may suffice.

It is at all events certain that the correctest notion of the
use and the value of the Eusebian Sections will be obtained
by one who will be at the pains to substitute for *the Eusebian
Numbers* in the margin of a copy of the Greek Gospels *the
References* which these numbers severally indicate. It will
then become plain that the system of Sections and Canons
which Eusebius invented,—ingenious, interesting, and useful

as it certainly is; highly important also, as being the known work of an illustrious Father of the Church, as well as most precious occasionally for critical purposes[c],—is nothing else but a clumsy substitute for what is achieved by an ordinary "Reference Bible":—participating in every inconvenience incidental to the unskilfully contrived apparatus with which English readers are familiar[d], and yet inferior in the following four respects:—

(1st.) The references of Eusebius, (except those found in Canon X.), require in every instance to be *deciphered*, before they can be verified; and they can only be deciphered by making search, (and sometimes laborious search,) in another part of the volume. They are not, in fact, (nor do they pretend to be,) references to the inspired Text at all; but only *references to the Eusebian Canons*.

(2ndly.) In their scope, they are of course strictly *confined to the Gospels*,—which most inconveniently limits their use, as well as diminishes their value. (Thus, by no possibility is Eusebius able to refer a reader from S. Luke xxii. 19, 20 to 1 Cor. xi. 23—25.)

(3rdly.) By the very nature of their constitution, reference even to *another part of the same Gospel* is impossible. (Euse-

---

[c] Thus, certain disputed passages of importance are proved to have been recognised at least *by Eusebius*. Our LORD'S Agony in the Garden for instance, (S. Luke xxii. 43, 44—wanting in Cod. B,) is by him numbered § 283: and that often rejected verse, S. Mark xv. 28, he certainly numbered § 216,—whatever Tischendorf may say to the contrary. (See p. 293.)

[d] It is obvious to suggest that, (1) whereas our Marginal References follow the order of the Sacred Books, they ought rather to stand in the order of their importance, or at least of their relevancy to the matter in hand:—and that, (2) actual Quotations, and even Allusions to other parts of Scripture when they are undeniable, should be referred to in some distinguishing way. It is also certain that, (3) to a far greater extent than at present, *sets* of References might be kept *together;* not scattered about in small parcels over the whole Book.—Above all, (as the point most pertinent to the present occasion,) (4) it is to be wished that *strictly parallel places* in the Gospels might be distinguished from those which are illustrative only, or are merely recalled by their similarity of subject or expression. All this would admit of interesting and useful illustration. While on this subject, let me ask,—Why is it no longer possible to purchase a Bible with References to the Apocrypha? *Who* does not miss the reference to "Ecclus. xliii. 11, 12" at Gen. ix. 14? *Who* can afford to do without the reference to "1 Macc. iv. 59" at S. John x. 22?

bius is unable, for example, to refer a reader from S. John xix. 39, to iii. 1 and vii. 50.)

But besides the preceding, which are disadvantages inherent in the scheme and inseparable from it, it will be found (4thly), That Eusebius, while he introduces not a few wholly undesirable references, (of which some specimens are supplied above), is observed occasionally to withhold references which cannot by any means be dispensed with. Thus, he omits to refer his reader from S. Luke's account of the visit to the Sepulchre (chap. xxiv. 12) to S. John's memorable account of the same transaction (chap. xx. 3—10) : *not* because he disallowed the verse in S. Luke's Gospel,—for in a certain place *he discusses its statements* [e].

III. It is abundantly plain from all that has gone before that the work of EUSEBIUS was entirely different in its structure and intention from the work of AMMONIUS. Enough, in fact, has been said to make it fully apparent that it is nothing short of impossible that there can have been any extensive correspondence between the two. According to EUSEBIUS, S. Mark has 21 Sections [f] *peculiar to his Gospel :* S. Luke, 72 : S. John, 97 [g]. According to the same EUSEBIUS, 14 Sections [h] are common to S. Luke and S. Mark *only :* 21, to S. Luke and S. John *only*. But those 225 Sections can have found *no place* in the work of AMMONIUS. And if, (in some unexplained way,) room *was* found for those parts of the Gospels, *with what possible motive can AMMONIUS have subdivided them into exactly 225 portions ?* It is nothing else but irrational to assume that he did so.

Not unaware am I that it has been pointed out by a most judicious living Critic as a " ground for hesitation before we ascribe the Sections as well as the Canons to Eusebius, that not a few ancient MSS. contain the former while they omit the latter [i]." He considers it to be certainly indicated thereby " that in the judgment of critics and transcribers,

---

[e] Mai, vol. iv. p. 287. See also p. 293.   [f] Tischendorf says 19 only.

[g] Tischendorf says 96 only.   [h] Tischendorf says 13 only.

[i] Scrivener specifies the following Codd. C, F, H, I, P, Q, R, W⁶, Y, Z, 54, 59, 60, 68, 440, 1ˢᶜʳ, 8ˢᶜʳ. Also D and K. (*Cod. Bezæ*, p. xx, and *Introd.* pp. 51, 2.) Add Evan. 117 : (but I think *not* 263.)

(whatever that judgment may be deemed worth,) the Ammonian Sections had a previous existence to the Eusebian Canons, as well as served for an independent purpose." But I respectfully demur to the former of the two proposed inferences. I also learn with surprise that "those who have studied them most, can the least tell what use the Ammonian Sections can serve, unless in connection with Canons of Harmony [k]."

However irregular and arbitrary these subdivisions of the Evangelical text are observed to be in their construction, their usefulness is paramount. They are observed to fulfil *exactly the same office* as our own actual division of the Text into 89 Chapters and 3780 Verses. Of course, 1165 subdivisions are (for certain purposes) somewhat less convenient than 3780;—but on the other hand, a place in the Gospels would be more easily discovered, I suspect, for the most part, by the employment of such a single set of consecutive numbers, than by requiring a Reader first to find the Chapter by its Roman numeral, and then the Verse by its Arabic figure. Be this as it may, there can be at least only one opinion as to the *supreme convenience to a Reader*, whether ancient or modern, of knowing that the copy of the Gospels which he holds in his hands is subdivided into exactly the same 1165 Sections as every other Greek copy which is likely to come in his way; and that, in every such copy, he may depend on finding every one of those sections invariably distinguished by the self-same number.

A Greek copy of the Gospels, therefore, having its margin furnished with the Eusebian *Sectional* notation, may be considered to correspond generally with an English copy merely divided into Chapters and Verses. The addition of the Eusebian *Canons* at the beginning, with numerical references thereto inserted in the margin throughout, does but superadd something analogous to the convenience of our *Marginal References*,—and may just as reasonably (or just as unreasonably) be dispensed with.

I think it not improbable, in fact, that in the preparation of a Codex, it will have been sometimes judged commercially

[k] Scrivener's *Introduction*, pp. 51 and 52 : *Cod. Bezæ*, p. xx. note [2.]

expedient to leave its purchaser to decide whether he would
or would not submit to the additional expense (which in the
case of illuminated MSS. must have been very considerable)
of having the Eusebian Tables inserted at the commencement
of his Book*,—without which *the References* thereto would
confessedly have been of no manner of avail. In this way it
will have come to pass, (as Mr. Scrivener points out,) that
" not a few ancient MSS. contain the *Sections* but omit the
Canons." Whether, however, the omission of References to
the Canons in Copies which retain in the margin the sectional numbers, is to be explained in this way, or not,—
AMMONIUS, at all events, will have had no more to do with
either the one or the other, than with our modern division
into Chapters and Verses. It is, in short, nothing else but
a " vulgar error" to designate the Eusebian Sections as the
" Sections of AMMONIUS." The expression cannot be too
soon banished from our critical terminology. Whether
banished or retained, *to reason about* the lost work of AMMO-
NIUS from the Sections of EUSEBIUS (as Tischendorf and the
rest habitually do) is an offence against ¦historical Truth
which no one who values his critical reputation will probably
hereafter venture to commit.

IV. This subject may not be dismissed until a circumstance of considerable interest has been explained which has
already attracted some notice, but which evidently is not yet
understood by Biblical Critics[1].

As already remarked, the necessity of resorting to the
Eusebian Tables of Canons in order to make any use of
a marginal reference, is a tedious and a cumbersome process ;
for which, men must have early sought to devise a remedy.
They were not slow in perceiving that a far simpler expedient would be to note at the foot of every page of a Gospel
the numbers of the Sections of that Gospel contained *in extenso* on the same page ; and, parallel with those numbers, to
exhibit the numbers of the corresponding Sections in the

---

* Evan. 263, for instance, has certainly *blank* Eusebian Tables at the beginning : the *frame* only.　　[1] See Scrivener's *Introduction*, p. 51 (note 2),
—where Tregelles (in Horne's *Introd.* iv. 200) is quoted.

other Gospels. Many Codices, furnished with such an apparatus at the foot of the page, are known to exist[m]. For instance, in Cod. 262 (= Reg. 53, at Paris), which is written in double columns, at foot of the first page (*fol.* 111) of S. Mark, is found as follows :—

The meaning of this, every one will see who,—(remembering what is signified by the monograms MP, Λο, Ιω, ΜΘ,[n])—will turn successively to the IInd, the I[st], the VIth, and the I[st] of the Eusebian Canons. Translated into expressions more familiar to English readers, it evidently amounts to this: that we are referred,

(§ 1) From S. Mark i. 1, 2,—to S. Matth. xi. 10 : S. Luke vii. 27.
(§ 2) . . . . i. 3,—to S. Matth. iii. 3 : S. Luke iii. 3—6.
(§ 3) . . . . i. 4, 5, 6,—to S. Matth. iii. 4—6.
(§ 4) . . . . i. 7, 8, —to S. Matth. iii. 11 : S. Luke iii. 16 :
                             S. John i. 15, 26-27, 30-1 : iii. 28.

(I venture to add that any one who will compare the above with the margin of S. Mark's Gospel in a common English "reference Bible," will obtain a very fair notion of the convenience, and of the inconveniences of the Eusebian system. But to proceed with our remarks on the apparatus at the foot of Cod. 262.)

The owner of such a MS. was able to refer to parallel passages, (as above,) *by merely turning over the pages of his book.* E.g. The parallel places to S. Mark's § 1 (A) being § 70 of

---

[m] e.g. Codd. M, 262 and 264. (I saw at least one other at Paris, but I have not preserved a record of the number.) To these, Tregelles adds E ; (Scrivener's *Introduction,* p. 51, note [²].) Scrivener adds W[d], and Tischendorf T[b], (Scrivener's *Cod. Bezae,* p. xx.)

[n] The *order* of these monograms requires explanation.

S. Luke (O) and § 103 of S. Matthew (Ρ Γ),—it was just as easy for him to find those two places as it is for us to turn to S. Luke vii. 27 and S. Matth. xi. 10: perhaps easier.

V. I suspect that this peculiar method of exhibiting the Eusebian references (Canons as well as Sections) at a glance, was derived to the Greek Church from the Syrian Christians. What is certain, a precisely similar expedient for enabling readers to discover *Parallel Passages* prevails extensively in the oldest Syriac Evangelia extant. There are in the British Museum about twelve Syriac Evangelia furnished with such an apparatus of reference [o]; of which a specimen is subjoined,—derived however (because it was near at hand) from a MS. in the Bodleian [p], of the vii[th] or viii[th] century.

From this MS., I select for obvious reasons the last page but one (*fol.* 82) of S. Mark's Gospel, which contains ch. xvi. 8—18. The Reader will learn with interest and surprise that in the margin of this page against ver. 8, is written in vermilion, *by the original scribe*, $\frac{281}{1}$: against ver. 9,—$\frac{282}{10}$: against ver. 10,—$\frac{283}{1}$: against ver. 11,— $\frac{284}{8}$: against ver. 12,—$\frac{285}{8}$: against ver. 13,—$\frac{286}{8}$: against ver. 14,—$\frac{287}{10}$: against ver. 15,—$\frac{288}{6}$: against ver. 16,— $\frac{289}{10}$: against ver. 19,—$\frac{290}{8}$. That these sectional numbers [q], with references to the Eusebian Canons subscribed, are no part of the (so-called) *"Ammonian"* system, will be recognised at a glance. According to *that* scheme, S. Mark xiv. 8 is numbered $\frac{233}{2}$. But to proceed.

---

[o] Addit. MSS. 14,449 : 14,450, and 1, and 2, and 4, and 5, and 7, and 8 : 14,463, and 9 : 17,113. (Dr. Wright's *Catalogue*, 4to. 1870.) Also Rich. 7,157. The reader is referred to Assemani ; and to Adler, p. 52-3 : also p. 63.

[p] "Dawkins 3." See Dean Payne Smith's *Catalogue*, p. 72.

[q] It will be observed that, according to the Syrian scheme, *every verse* of S. Mark xvi, from ver. 8 to ver. 15 inclusive, constitutes an independent section (§§ 281—288) : ver. 16—18 another (§ 289); and verr. 19—20, another (§ 290), which is the last. The Greek scheme, as a rule, makes independent sections of verr. 8, 9, 14, 19, 20; but throws together ver. 10—11 : 12—13 : 15—16 : 17—18. (*Vide infrà*, p. 311.)

At the foot of the same page, (which is written in two columns), is found the following set of rubricated references to parallel places in the other three Gospels :—

The exact English counterpart of which,—(I owe it to the kind help of M. Neubauer, of the Bodleian),—is subjoined. The Reader will scarcely require to be reminded that the reason why §§ 282, 287, 289 do not appear in this Table is because those Sections, (belonging to the tenth Canon,) have nothing parallel to them in the other Gospels.

Luke	Matthew	Mark		John	Luke	Matthew	Mark
391	. . .	286		247	390	421	281
. . .	426	288		247	390	421	283
				. . .	391	. . .	284
				. . .	393	. . .	285

The general intention of this is sufficiently obvious : but the Reader must be told that on making reference to S. MAT-THEW's Gospel, in this Syriac Codex, it is found that § 421 = chap. xxviii. 8 ; and § 426 = chap. xxviii. 19, 20 :

That, in S. LUKE's Gospel,—§ 390 = chap. xxiv. 8—10 : § 391 = chap. xxiv. 11 ; and § 393 = chap. xxiv. 13—17 [r] :

That, in S. JOHN's Gospel,—§ 247 = chap. xx. 17 ($\pi o\rho\epsilon\acute{v}ov$ down to $\Theta\epsilon\grave{o}\nu$ $\acute{v}\mu\hat{\omega}\nu$ [s].)

[r] Note that § $392 \atop 9$ = S. Luke xxiv. 12 : § $394 \atop 10$ = ver. 18—34 : § $395 \atop 8$ = ver. 35 : § $396 \atop 9$ is incomplete. [Dr. Wright supplies the lacune for me, thus : § $396 \atop 9$ = ver. 36—41 (down to $\theta av\mu a\zeta\acute{o}v\tau\omega\nu$) : § $397 \atop 9$ = $\epsilon\hat{i}\pi\epsilon\nu$ $a\mathring{v}\tauo\hat{i}s$ down to the end of ver. 41 : § $398 \atop 9$ = ver. 42 : § $399 \atop 9$ = ver. 43 : § $400 \atop 10$ = ver. 44—50 : § $401 \atop 8$ = 51 : § $402 \atop 10$ = ver. 52, 3.]

Critical readers will be interested in comparing, or rather contrasting, the Sectional system of a Syriac MS. with that which prevails in all Greek

So that, exhibited in familiar language, these Syriac *Marginal References* are intended to guide a Reader,

(§ 281) From S. Mark xvi. 8,—to S. Matth. xxviii. 8 : S. Luke
xxiv. 8—10 : S. John xx. 17 (πο-
ρεύου *to the end of the verse*).

(§ 283) . . . . xvi. 10,—to the same three places.
(§ 284) . . . . xvi. 11,—to S. Luke xxiv. 11.
(§ 285) . . . . xvi. 12,—to S. Luke xxiv. 13—17,
(§ 286) . . . . xvi. 13,—to S. Luke xxiv. 11.
(§ 288) . . . . xvi. 15,—to S. Matth. xxiv. 19, 20.

Here then, although the Ten Eusebian Canons are faithfully retained, it is much to be noted that we are presented
with *a different set of Sectional subdivisions.* This will be
best understood by attentively comparing all the details
which precede with the Eusebian references in the inner
margin of a copy of Lloyd's Greek Testament.

But the convincing *proof* that these Syriac Sections are
not those with which we have been hitherto acquainted from
Greek MSS., is supplied by the fact that they are so many

Codices. S. John's § $\frac{248}{1}$ = xx. 18 : his § $\frac{249}{9}$ = ver. 19 to εἰρήνη ὑμῖν in

ver. 21 : his § $\frac{250}{7}$ = ver. 21 (καθώς to the end of the verse) : his § $\frac{251}{10}$

= ver. 22 : his § $\frac{252}{7}$ = ver. 23 : his § $\frac{253}{[10]}$ = ver. 24-5 : his § $\frac{254}{[9]}$ = ver.

26-7 : his § $\frac{255}{10}$ = ver. 28 to the end of xxi. 4 : his § $\frac{256}{9}$ = xxi. 5 : his § $\frac{257}{9}$

= xxi. 6 (to εὑρήσετε) : his § $\frac{258}{9}$ = ver. 6, (ἔβαλον to the end) : his § $\frac{259}{[10]}$

= ver. 7, 8 : his § $\frac{260}{[9]}$ = ver. 9 : his § $\frac{261}{10}$ = ver. 10 : his § $\frac{262}{9}$ = ver. 11 :

his § $\frac{263}{9}$ = first half of ver. 12 : his § $\frac{264}{10}$ is incomplete.

[But Dr. Wright, (remarking that in his MSS., which are evidently the
correcter ones, $\frac{263}{10}$ stands opposite the middle of ver. 12 [οὐδεὶς δὲ ἐτόλμα], and
$\frac{264}{9}$ opposite ver. 13 [ἔρχεται οὖν],) proceeds to supply the lacune for me,
thus : § $\frac{264}{9}$ = ver. 13 : § $\frac{265}{10}$ = ver. 14-5 (down to φιλῶ σε· λέγει αὐτῷ) : § $\frac{266}{9}$
= βόσκε τὰ ἀρνία μου, (end of ver. 15) : § $\frac{267}{10}$ = ver. 16 (down to φιλῶ σε) : § $\frac{268}{9}$
= λέγει αὐτῷ, Ποίμαινε τὰ πρόβατά μου (end of ver. 16) : § $\frac{269}{10}$ = ver. 17
(down to φιλῶ σε) : § $\frac{270}{9}$ = λέγει αὐτῷ ὁ Ἰ., β. τὰ π. μου (end of ver. 17) : § $\frac{271}{10}$
= ver. 18 to 25.]

more *in number*. The sum of the Sections in each of the Gospels follows; for which, (the Bodleian Codex being mutilated,) I am indebted to the learning and obligingness of Dr. Wright[t]. He quotes from "the beautiful MS. Addit. 7,157, written A.D. 768[u]." From this, it appears that the Sections in the Gospel according to,—

S. MATTHEW, (instead of being from are 426: (the last Section, $\S\frac{426,}{6}$
　　　　　359 to 355,) consisting of ver. 19, 20.)

S. MARK, (. . . . . 241 to 233,) . . 290: (the last Section, $\S\frac{290,}{8}$
　　　　　consisting of ver. 19, 20.)

S. LUKE, (. . . . . 349 to 342,) . . 402: (the last Section, $\S\frac{402,}{10}$
　　　　　consisting of ver. 52, 53.)

S. JOHN, (. . . . . 232,) . . 271: (the last Section, $\S\frac{271,}{10}$
　　　　　consisting of ver. 18—25.)

The sum of the Sections therefore, in *Syriac* MSS. instead of being between 1181 and 1162[v], is found to be invariably 1389.

But here, the question arises,—Did the Syrian Christians then retain the Ten Tables, dressing their contents afresh, so as to adapt them to their own ampler system of sectional subdivision? or did they merely retain the elementary principle of referring each Section to one of Ten Canons, but substitute for the Eusebian Tables a species of harmony, or apparatus of reference, at the foot of every page?

The foregoing doubt is triumphantly resolved by a reference to Assemani's engraved representation, on xxii Copper Plates, of the X Eusebian Tables from a superb Syriac Codex (A.D. 586) in the Medicean Library[w]. The student who

---

[t] " I have examined for your purposes, Add. 14,449; 14,457; 14,458; and 7,157. The first three are N[os]. lxix, lxx, and lxxi, in my own Catalogue: the last, a Nestorian MS., is N°. xiii in the old Catalogue of Forshall and Rosen (London, 1838). All four agree in their numeration."

[u] See the preceding note.—Availing myself of the reference given me by my learned correspondent, I read as follows in the Catalogue:—" Inter ipsa textus verba, numeris viridi colore pictis, notatur Canon harmoniae Eusebianae, ad quem quaevis sectio referenda est. Sic, { [i.e. 1] indicat canonem in quo omnes Evangelistae concurrunt," &c. &c.

[v] Suidas [A.D. 980], by giving 236 to S. Mark and 348 to S. Luke, makes the sum of the Sections in Greek Evangelia 1,171.

[w] This sheet was all but out of the printer's hands when the place in vol. i.

inquires for Assemani's work will find that the numbers in
the last line of each of the X Tables is as follows:—

	Matthew	*Mark*	*Luke*	*John*
Canon i	421	283	390	247
—— ii	416	276	383	. . .
—— iii	134	. . .	145	178
—— iv	394	212	. . .	223
—— v	319	. . .	262	. . .
—— vi	426	288	. . .	. . .
—— vii	425	. . .	. . .	249
—— viii	. . .	290	401	. . .
—— ix	. . .	. . .	399	262
—— x	424	289	402	271

The Syrian Church, therefore, from a period of the re-
motest antiquity, not only subdivided the Gospels into a far
greater number of Sections than were in use among the
Greeks, but also habitually employed Eusebian Tables which
—identical as they are in *appearance* and in *the principle*
of their arrangement with those with which Greek MSS.
have made us familiar,—yet differ materially from these as
to *the numerical details* of their contents.

Let abler men follow up this inquiry to its lawful results.
When the extreme antiquity of the Syriac documents is considered, may it not almost be made a question whether
Eusebius himself put forth the larger or the smaller number
of Sections?   But however *that* may be, more palpably precarious than ever, I venture to submit, becomes the confident
assertion of the Critics that, "just as EUSEBIUS found these
Verses [S. Mark xvi. 9—20] absent in his day from the best
and most numerous [*sic*] copies, *so was also the case with AM-
MONIUS* when he formed his Harmony in the preceding century"[x].   To speak plainly, the statement is purely mythical.

VI. Birch [*Varr. Lectt.* p. 226], asserts that in the best
Codices, the Sections of S. Mark's Gospel are not numbered
beyond ch. xvi. 8.   Tischendorf prudently adds, "*or* ver. 9:"

of Assemani's *Bibliotheca Medicea*, (fol. 1742,) was shewn me by my learned
friend, P. E. Pusey, Esq., of Ch. Ch.—Dr. Wright had already most obligingly and satisfactorily resolved my inquiry from the mutilated fragments of
the Canons, as well as of the Epistle to Carpianus in Add. 17,213 and 14,450.

[x] Dr. Tregelles.   (*Vide suprà*, pp. 125-6.)   And so, Tischendorf.

but to introduce *that* alternative is to surrender everything. I subjoin the result of an appeal to 151 Greek Evangelia. There is written opposite to,

ver. 6, . . § 232, in 3 Codices, (viz. A, U, 286)
— 8, . . § 233, . . 34 . . . . . . (including L, S)[y]
— 9, (?) § 234, . . 41 . . . . . . (including Γ, Δ, Π)[z]
— 10, (?) § 235, . . 4 . . . . . . (viz. 67, 282, 331, 406)
— 12, (?) § 236, . . 7 . . . . (the number assigned by Suidas)[n]
— 14, (?) § 237, . . 12 . . . . . . (including Λ)[b]
— 15, . . § 238, . . 3 . . . . . . (viz. Add. 19,387: 27,861, Ti²)
— 17, . . § 239, . . 1 . . . . . . (viz. G)
— 19, . . § 240, . . 10 . . . . (including H, M, and the Codices from which the Hharklensian Revision, A.D. 616, was made)[c]
— 20, . . § 241, . . 36 . . . . . . (including C, E, K, V)[d]

Thus, it is found that 114 Codices sectionize the last Twelve Verses, against 37 which close the account at ver. 8, or sooner. I infer—(a) That the reckoning which would limit the sections to precisely 233, is altogether precarious; and—(b) That the sum of the Sections assigned to S. Mark's Gospel by Suidas and by Stephens (viz. 236) is arbitrary.

VII. To some, it may not be unacceptable, in conclusion, to be presented with the very words in which Eusebius explains how he would have his Sections and Canons used. His language requires attention. He says:—

Εἰ οὖν ἀναπτύξας ἔν τι τῶν τεσσάρων εὐαγγελίων ὁποιον-
δήποτε, βουληθείης ἐπιστῆναί τινι ᾧ βούλει κεφαλαίῳ, καὶ
γνῶναι τίνες τὰ παραπλήσια εἰρήκασι, καὶ τοὺς οἰκείους ἐν

---

[y] The others are 11, 14, 22, 23, 28, 32, 37, 40, 45, 52, 98, 113, 115, 127, 129, 132, 133, 134, 137, 169, 186, 188, 193, 195, 265, 269, 276, 371. Add. 18,211, Cromwell 15, Wake 12 *and* 27.

[z] The others are 5, 6, 9, 12, 13, 15, 24, 29, 54 [more §§ ?], 65, 68, 111, 112, 114, 118, 157, 183, 190, 202, 263, 268, 270, 273, 277, 278, 284, 287, 294, 414, 438, 439. Rich 7,141. Add. 17,741 *and* 17,982. Cromw. 16. Canonici 36 *and* 112. Wake 21. ᵃ Viz. 184, 192, 264, hˢᶜʳ, Add. 11,836. Ti⁴. Wake 29.

[b] The others are 10, 20, 21, 36, 49, 187, 262, 266, 300, 364. Rawl. 141.

[c] *Vide supra*, p. 33. Assemani, vol. i. p. 28. (Comp. Adler, p. 53.) The others are 8, 26, 72, 299, 447. Bodl. Miscell. 17. Wake 36.

[d] The others are 7, 27, 34, 38, 39, 46, 74, 89, 105, 116, 117, 135, 179, 185, 194, 198, 207, 212, 260, 261, 267, 275, 279, 293, 301, 445, kˢᶜʳ. Add. 22,740. Wake 22, 24, 30; *and* 31 in which, ver. 20 is numbered СМВ.

ἑκάστῳ τόπους εὑρεῖν ἐν οἷς κατὰ τῶν αὐτῶν ἠνέχθησαν, ἧς
ἐπέχεις περικοπῆς ἀναλαβὼν τὸν προκείμενον ἀριθμὸν, ἐπιζητήσας τὲ αὐτὸν ἔνδον ἐν τῷ κανόνι ὃν ἡ διὰ τοῦ κινναβάρεως
ὑποσημείωσις ὑποβέβληκεν, εἴσῃ μὲν εὐθὺς ἐκ τῶν ἐπὶ μετώ-
που τοῦ κανόνος προγραφῶν, ὁπόσοι καὶ τίνες τὰ παραπλήσια
εἰρήκασιν· ἐπιστήσας δὲ καὶ τοῖς τῶν λοιπῶν εὐαγγελίων
ἀριθμοῖς τοῖς ἐν τῷ κανόνι ᾧ ἐπέχεις ἀριθμῷ παρακειμένοις,
ἐπιζητήσας τὲ αὐτοὺς ἔνδον ἐν τοῖς οἰκείοις ἑκάστου εὐαγγελίου τόποις, τὰ παραπλήσια λέγοντας εὑρήσεις.

Jerome,—who is observed sometimes to exhibit the sense
of his author very loosely,—renders this as follows :—

"Cum igitur aperto Codice, verbi gratia, illud sive illud
Capitulum scire volueris cujus Canonis sit, statim ex sub-
jecto numero docebaris ; et recurrens ad principia, in quibus
Canonum est distincta congeries, eodemque statim Canone
ex titulo frontis invento, illum quem quærebas numerum,
ejusdem Evangelistæ, qui et ipse ex inscriptione signatur, in-
venies ; atque e vicino ceterorum tramitibus inspectis, quos
numeros e regione habeant, annotabis.   Et cum scieris, re-
curres ad volumina singulorum, et sine mora repertis numeris quos ante signaveras, reperies et loca in quibus vel
eadem, vel vicina dixerunt."

This may be a very masterly way of explaining the use
of the Eusebian Canons.   But the points of the original are
missed.   What Eusebius actually says is this :—

"If therefore, on opening any one soever of the four Gospels, thou desirest to study any given Section, and to ascertain
which of the Evangelists have said things of the same kind ;
as well as to discover the particular place where each has
been led [to speak] of the same things ;—note the number
of the Section thou art studying, and seek that number in
the Canon indicated by the numeral subscribed in vermilion.
Thou wilt be made aware, at once, from the heading of
each Canon, how many of the Evangelists, and which of
them, have said things of the same kind.   Then, by attending to the parallel numbers relating to the other Gospels in
the same Canon, and by turning to each in its proper place,
thou wilt discover the Evangelists saying things of the
same kind."

APPENDIX (H).

On the Interpolation of the text of CODEX B *and* CODEX ℵ *at*
S. MATTHEW xxvii. 48 *or* 49.

(Referred to at pp. 202 and 219.)

IT is well known that our two oldest Codices, Cod. B
and Cod. ℵ, (see above, p. 80,) exhibit S. Matthew xxvii. 49,
as follows. After σωσων [*Cod. Sinait.* σωσαι] αυτον, they
read :—

(COD. B.)	(COD. ℵ.)
	αλλος
αλλος δε λαβῶ	δε λαβων λογχη̄
λογχην ενυξεν αυτου	ενυξεν αυτου τη̄
την πλευραν και εξηλ	πλευραν και εξηλ
θεν υδωρ και αιμα	θεν υδωρ και αι
	μα

Then comes, ο δε ῑς παλιν κραξας κ.τ.λ. The same is
also the reading of Codd. C, L, U, Γ: and it is known to
recur in the following cursives,—5, 48, 67, 115, 127 [a].

Obvious is it to suspect with Matthaei, (ed. 1803, vol. i.
p. 158,) that it was the Lectionary practice of the Oriental Church which occasioned this interpolation. In S. John
xix. 34 occurs the well-known record,—ἀλλ᾽ εἷς τῶν στρατιωτῶν λόγχῃ αὐτοῦ τὴν πλευρὰν ἔνυξε, καὶ εὐθὺς ἐξῆλθεν
αἷμα καὶ ὕδωρ: and it was the established practice of the
Easterns, in the Ecclesiastical lection for Good Friday,
(viz. S. Matth. xxvii. 1—61,) *to interpose S. John* xix. 31
to 37 between the 54th and the 55th verses of S. Matthew.
This will be found alluded to above, at p. 202 and again at
pp. 218-9.

---

[a] But Cod. U inserts ευθεως before εξηλθεν; and (at least two of the other
Codices, viz.) 48, 67 read αιμα και υδωρ.

After the pages just quoted were in type, while examining Harl. MS. 5647 in the British Museum, (*our* Evan. 72,) I alighted on the following Scholion, which I have since found that Wetstein duly published; but which has certainly not attracted the attention it deserves, and which is incorrectly represented as referring to the end of S. Matth. xxvii. 49. It is *against* ver. 48 that there is written in the margin,—

(Η [b] Ὅτι εἰς τὸ καθ᾽ ἱστορίαν εὐαγγέλιον Διαδώρου καὶ Τατιανοῦ καὶ ἄλλων διαφόρων ἁγίων πατέρων· τοῦτο πρόσκειται :

(Η Ἄλλος δὲ λαβὼν· λόγχην ἔνυξεν αὐτοῦ τὴν πλευρὰν . καὶ ἐξῆλθεν ὕδωρ καὶ αἷμα : τοῦτο λέγει καὶ ὁ Χρυσόστομος.

This writer is perfectly correct in his statement. In Chrysostom's 88th Homily on S. Matthew's Gospel, (*Opp.* vii, 825 c : [vol. ii, p. 526, *ed.* Field.]) is read as follows :— Ἐνόμισαν Ἠλίαν εἶναι, φησὶ, τὸν καλούμενον, καὶ εὐθέως ἐπότισαν αὐτὸν ὄξος: (which is clearly meant to be a summary of the contents *of ver.* 48 : then follows) ἕτερος δὲ προσελθὼν λόγχῃ αὐτοῦ τὴν πλευρὰν ἔνυξε. (Chrysostom quotes no further, but proceeds,—Τί γένοιτ᾽ ἂν τούτων παρανομώτερον, τί δὲ θηριωδέστερον, κ.τ.λ.)

I find it impossible on a review of the evidence to adhere to the opinion I once held, and have partially expressed above, (viz. at p. 202,) that the Lectionary-practice of the Eastern Church was the occasion of this corrupt reading in our two oldest uncials. A corrupt reading it undeniably is; and the discredit of exhibiting it, Codd. B, ℵ, (not to say Codd.

[b] Σημείωσις is what we call an "Annotation." [On the sign in the text, see the Catalogue of MSS. in the Turin Library, P. i. p. 93.] On the word, and on σημειοῦσθαι, (consider 2 Thess. iii. 14,) see the interesting remarks of Huet, *Origeniana*, iii. § i. 4. (at the end of vol. iv. of Origen's *Opp.* p. 292-3.)—Eusebius (*Hist. Eccl.* v. 20) uses σημείωσις in this sense. (See the note of Valesius.) But it is plain from the rendering of Jerome and Rufinus (*subscriptio*), that it often denoted a "signature," or signing of the name. Eusebius so employs the word in *lib.* v. 19 *ad fin.*

C, L, U, Γ,) must continue to sustain. That Chrysostom and Cyril also employed Codices disfigured by this self-same blemish, is certain. It is an interesting and suggestive circumstance. Nor is this all. Severus[e] relates that between A.D. 496 and 511, being at Constantinople, he had known this very reading strenuously discussed : whereupon had been produced a splendid copy of S. Matthew's Gospel, traditionally said to have been found with the body of the Apostle Barnabas in the Island of Cyprus in the time of the Emperor Zeno (A.D. 474—491) ; and preserved in the palace with superstitious veneration in consequence. It contained no record of the piercing of the Saviour's side : nor (adds Severus) does any ancient Interpreter mention the transaction in that place,—except Chrysostom *and Cyril of Alexandria;* into whose Commentaries it has found its way.— Thus, to Codices B, ℵ, C and the copy familiarly employed by Chrysostom, has to be added the copy which Cyril of Alexandria [d] employed ; as well as evidently sundry other Codices extant at Constantinople about A.D. 500. That the corruption of the text of S. Matthew's Gospel under review is ancient therefore, and was once very widely spread, is certain. The question remains,—and this is the only point to be determined,—How did it *originate ?*

Now it must be candidly admitted, that if the strange method of the Lectionaries already explained, (viz. of interposing seven verses of S. John's xix[th] chapter [ver. 31—7] between the 54th and 55th verses of S. Matth. xxvii,) really were the occasion of this interpolation of S. John xix. 34 after S. Matth. xxvii. 48 or 49,—two points would seem to call for explanation which at present remain unexplained : First, (1) Why does *only that one verse* find place in the interpolated copies ? And next, (2) How does it come to pass

---

[e] He was Patriarch of Antioch, A.D. 512-9. — The extract (made by Petrus junior, Monophysite Patriarch of Antioch, A.D. 578,) purports to be derived from the 26th Epistle, (Book 9,) which Severus addressed to Thomas Bp. of Germanicia after his exile. See Assemani, *Bibl. Orient.* vol. ii. pp. 81-2.

[d] I cannot find the place in Cyril. I suppose it occurs in a lost Commentary of this Father,—whose Works by the way are miserably indexed.

that *that* one verse is exhibited in so very depraved and so peculiar a form?

For, to say nothing of the inverted order of the two principal words, (which is clearly due to 1 S. John v. 6,) let it be carefully noted that the substitution of ἄλλος δὲ λαβὼν λόγχην, for ἀλλ᾽ εἰς τῶν στρατιωτῶν λόγχῃ of the Evangelist, is a tell-tale circumstance. The turn thus licentiously given to the narrative clearly proceeded from some one who was bent on weaving incidents related by different writers into a connected narrative, and who was sometimes constrained to take liberties with his Text in consequence. (Thus, S. Matthew having supplied the fact that "ONE OF THEM ran, and *took a sponge,* and filled it with vinegar, and put it on a reed, and gave Him to drink," S. John is made to say, "AND ANOTHER—*took a spear.*") Now, this is exactly what Tatian is related by Eusebius to have done: viz. "after some fashion of his own, to have composed out of the four Gospels one connected narrative[e]."

When therefore, (as in the present Scholion,) an ancient Critic who appears to have been familiarly acquainted with the lost "Diatessaron" of Tatian, comes before us with the express declaration that in that famous monument of the primitive age (A.D. 173), S. John's record of the piercing of our SAVIOUR's side was thrust into S. Matthew's History of the Passion in this precise way and in these very terms,— (for, "Note," he says, "That into the Evangelical History of Diodorus, of Tatian, and of divers other holy Fathers, is introduced [here] the following addition: 'And another took a spear and pierced His side, and there came out Water and Blood.' This, Chrysostom also says"),—it is even unreasonable to seek for any other explanation of the vitiated text of our two oldest Codices. Not only is the testimony to the critical fact abundantly sufficient, but the proposed solution of the difficulty, in itself the reverse of improbable,

---

[e] Ὁ μέντοι γε πρότερος αὐτῶν [viz. the sect of the Severiani] ἀρχηγὸς ὁ Τατιανὸς συνάφειάν τινα καὶ συναγωγὴν οὐκ οἶδ᾽ ὅπως τῶν εὐαγγελίων συνθεὶς, τὸ διὰ τεσσάρων τοῦτο προσωνόμασεν. Ὁ καὶ παρά τισιν εἰσέτι νῦν φέρεται. The next words are every way suggestive. Τοῦ δὲ ἀποστόλου φασὶ τολμῆσαί τινας αὐτὸν μεταφράσαι φωνὰς, ὡς ἐπιδιωρθούμενον αὐτῶν τὴν τῆς φράσεως σύνταξιν.—Eusebius, *Hist. Eccl.* iv. 29, § 4.

is in the highest degree suggestive as well as important.
For,—May we not venture to opine that the same καθ' ἱστορίαν εὐαγγέλιον,—as this Writer aptly designates Tatian's
work,—is responsible for not a few of the *monstra potius
quam variae lectiones* [f] which are occasionally met with in
the earliest MSS. of all ? And,—Am I not right in suggesting that the circumstance before us is *the only thing
we know for certain* about the text of Tatian's (miscalled)
"Harmony ?"

To conclude.—That the " Diatessaron" of Tatian, (for so,
according to Eusebius and Theodoret, Tatian himself styled
it,) has long since disappeared, no one now doubts [g]. That
Eusebius himself, (who lived 150 years after the probable
date of its composition,) had never seen it, may I suppose be
inferred from the terms in which he speaks of it. Jerome
does not so much as mention its existence. Epiphanius,
who is very full and particular concerning the heresy of
Tatian, affords no indication that he was acquainted with
his work. On the contrary. "The Diatessaron Gospel,"
(he remarks in passing,) " which some call the Gospel according to the Hebrews, is said to have been the production
of this writer [h]." The most interesting notice we have of
Tatian's work is from the pen of Theodoret. After explaining that Tatian the Syrian, originally a Sophist, and next
a disciple of Justin Martyr [A.D. 150], after Justin's death
aspired to being a heretical leader,—(statements which are
first found in Irenæus,)—Theodoret enumerates his special
tenets. " This man" (he proceeds) "put together the so-
called *Diatessaron Gospel*,—from which he cut away the
genealogies, and whatever else shews that the LORD was
born of the seed of David. The book was used not only by
those who favoured Tatian's opinions, but by the orthodox
as well; who, unaware of the mischievous spirit in which
the work had been executed, in their simplicity used the
book as an epitome. *I myself found upwards of two hundred
such copies honourably preserved in the Churches of this place*,"
(Cyrus in Syria namely, of which Theodoret was made

---

[f] See, for example, the readings of B or ℵ, or both, specified from p. 80 to
p. 86.   [g] *Vid. supra*, p. 129, note (g.)   [h] *Opp.* vol. i. p. 391 D.

Bishop, A.D. 423,)—"all of which I collected together, and put aside; substituting the Gospels of the Four Evangelists in their room [1]."

The diocese of Theodoret (he says) contained eight hundred Parishes [k]. It cannot be thought surprising that a work of which copies had been multiplied to such an extraordinary extent, and which was evidently once held in high esteem, should have had *some* influence on the text of the earliest Codices; and here, side by side with a categorical statement as to one of its licentious interpolations, we are furnished with documentary proof that many an early MS. also was infected with the same taint. To assume that the two phenomena stand related to one another in the way of cause and effect, seems to be even an inevitable proceeding.

I will not prolong this note by inquiring concerning the " Diodorus" of whom the unknown author of this scholion speaks: but I suppose it was *that* Diodorus who was made Bishop of Tarsus in A.D. 378. He is related to have been the preceptor of Chrysostom; was a very voluminous writer; and, among the rest, according to Suidas, wrote a work " on the Four Gospels."

Lastly,—How about the singular introduction *into the Lection for Good-Friday* of this incident of the piercing of the REDEEMER's side? Is it allowable to conjecture that, indirectly, the Diatessaron of Tatian may have been the occasion of *that* circumstance also; as well as of certain other similar phenomena in the Evangeliaria?

---

[1] *Haeret. Fab.* lib. i. c. xx. (*Opp.* iv. 208.)

[k] Clinton, F. R. ii. *Appendix*, p. 473, quoting Theodoret's " Ep. 113, p. 1190. [*al.* vol. iii. p. 986-7]."

POSTSCRIPT.

(Promised at p. 51.)

I proceed to fulfil the promise made at p. 51.—C. F. Matthaei (*Nov. Test.*, 1788, vol. iii. p. 269) states that in one of the MSS. at Moscow occurs the following "Scholion of Eusebius:—κατὰ Μάρκον μετὰ τὴν ἀνάστασιν οὐ λέγεται ὤφθαι τοῖς μαθηταῖς." On this, Griesbach remarks (*Comm. Crit.* ii. 200),—"quod scribere non potuisset si pericopam dubiam agnovisset:" the record in S. Mark xvi. 14, being express, —Ὕστερον ἀνακειμένοις αὐτοῖς τοῖς ἕνδεκα ἐφανερώθη. The epigrammatic smartness of Griesbach's dictum has recommended it to Dr. Tregelles and others who look unfavourably on the conclusion of S. Mark's Gospel; and to this hour the Scholion of Matthaei remains unchallenged.

But to accept the proposed inference from it, is impossible. It ought to be obvious to every thoughtful person that problems of this class will not bear to be so handled. It is as if one were to apply the rigid mathematical method to the ordinary transactions of daily life, for which it is clearly unsuitable. Before we move a single step, however, we desire a few more particulars concerning this supposed evidence of Eusebius.

Accordingly, I invoked the good offices of my friend, the Rev. W. G. Penny, English Chaplain at Moscow, to obtain for me *the entire context* in which this "Scholion of Eusebius" occurs: little anticipating the trouble I was about to give him. His task would have been comparatively easy had I been able to furnish him (which I was not) with the exact designation of the Codex required. At last by sheer determination and the display of no small ability, he discovered the place, and sent me a tracing of the whole page: viz. fol. 286 (the last ten words being overleaf) of Matthaei's "12," ("Synod. 139,") our Evan. 255.

It proves to be the concluding portion of Victor's Commentary, and to correspond with what is found at p. 365 of

Possinus, and p. 446-7 of Cramer: except that after the words " ἀποκυλίσειε τὸν λίθον :· ᴖ," and before the words " ἄλλος δέ φησιν" [Possinus, *line* 12 *from bottom* : Cramer, *line* 3 *from the top*], is read as follows :—

σχὄ'
εὖσε
βίου

κατ᾿ Μάρκον· μετὰ τὴν ἀνάστασιν οὐ λέγεται ὦφθαι τοῖc μαθηταῖc: κατὰ Ματθαῖον· μετὰ τὴν ἀνάστασιν τοῖc μαθηταῖc ὦφθη ἐν τῇ Γαλιλαίᾳ :·   ᴖ

κατὰ Ἰωάννην· ἐν αὐτῇ τῇ ἡμέρᾳ τῆc ἀναστάσεωc τῶν θυρῶν κεκλεισμένων ὁ Ἰησοῦc μέσοc τῶν μαθητῶν μὴ παρόντος τοῦ Θωμᾶ ἔστη· καὶ μεθ᾿ ἡμέρας πάλιν ὀκτὼ συμπαρόντος καὶ τοῦ Θωμᾶ. μετὰ ταῦτα πάλιν ἐφάνη αὐτοῖc ἐπὶ τῆc θαλασσηc τῆc Τιβεριάδος :·   ⸴⸴

κατὰ Λουκᾶν· ὦφθη Κλεόπᾳ σὺν τῷ ἑταίρῳ αὐτοῦ αὐτῇ τῇ ἡμέρᾳ τῆc ἀναστάσεωc· καὶ πάλιν ὑποστρέψασιν εἰς Ἱερουσαλὴμ ὦφθη τῇ αὐτῇ ἡμέρᾳ συνηγμένων τῶν λοιπῶλ μαθητῶν· καὶ ὦφθη Σίμωνι· καὶ πάλιν ἐξήγαγεν αὐτοὺc εἰς Βηθανίαν καὶ διέστη ἀπ᾿ αὐτῶν.

But surely no one who considers the matter attentively, will conceive that he is warranted in drawing from this so serious an inference as that Eusebius disallowed the last Section of S. Mark's Gospel.

(1.) In the first place, we have already [*suprà*, p. 44] heard Eusebius elaborately discuss the Section in question. That he allowed it, is therefore *certain*.

(2.) But next, this σχόλιον εὐσεβίου at the utmost can only be regarded as a general summary of what Eusebius has somewhere delivered concerning our LORD's appearances after His Resurrection. *As it stands*, it clearly is not the work of Eusebius.

(3.) And because I shall be reminded that such a statement cannot be accepted on my own mere 'ipse dixit,' I proceed to subjoin the original Scholion of which the preceding is evidently only an epitome. It is found in three of the Moscow MSS., (our Evan. 239, 259, 237,) but without any Author's name :—

Δεικνὺς δὲ ὁ εὐαγγελιστὴς, ὅτι μετὰ τὴν ἀνάστασιν οὐκέτι συνεχῶς αὐτοῖς συνῆν, λέγει, τοῦτο ἤδη τρίτον τοῖς μαθηταῖς ὤφθη ὁ Κύριος μετὰ τὴν ἀνάστασιν· οὐ τοῦτο λέγων, ὅτι μόνον τρίτον, ἀλλὰ τὰ τοῖς ἄλλοις παραλελειμμένα λέγων, τοῦτο ἤδη πρὸς τοῖς ἄλλοις τρίτον ἐφανερώθη τοῖς μαθηταῖς. κατὰ μὲν γὰρ τὸν Ματθαῖον, ὤφθη αὐτοῖς ἐν τῇ Γαλιλαίᾳ μόνον· κατὰ δὲ τὸν Ἰωάννην, ἐν αὐτῇ τῇ ἡμέρᾳ τῆς ἀναστάσεως, τῶν θυρῶν κεκλεισμένων, μέσος αὐτῶν ἔστη, ὄντων ἐν Ἱερουσαλήμ, μὴ παρόντος ἐκει Θωμᾶ. καὶ πάλιν μεθ᾽ ἡμέρας ὀκτὼ, παρόντος καὶ τοῦ Θωμᾶ, ὤφθη αὐτοῖς, ἤδη κεκλεισμένων τῶν θυρῶν. μετὰ ταῦτα ἐπὶ τῆς θαλάσσης τῆς Τιβεριάδος ἐφάνη αὐτοῖς, οὐ τοῖς ιᾱ ἀλλὰ μόνοις ζ. κατὰ δὲ Λουκᾶν ὤφθη Κλεόπᾳ σὺν τῷ ἑταίρῳ αὐτοῦ, αὐτῇ τῇ ἡμέρᾳ τῆς ἀναστάσεως. καὶ πάλιν ὑποστρέψασιν εἰς Ἱερουσαλὴμ αὐτῇ τῇ ἡμέρᾳ, συνηγμένων τῶν μαθητῶν, ὤφθη Σίμωνι. καὶ πάλιν ἐξαγαγὼν αὐτοὺς εἰς Βηθανίαν, ὅτε καὶ διέστη ἀναληφθεὶς ἀπ᾽ αὐτῶν· ὡς ἐκ τούτου παρίστασθαι ζ. εἶναι τὰς εἰς τοὺς μαθητὰς μετὰ τὴν ἀνάστασιν γεγονυίας ὀπτασίας τοῦ Σωτῆρος ἡμῶν Ἰησοῦ Χριστοῦ. μίαν μὲν παρὰ τῷ Ματθαίῳ, τρεῖς δὲ παρὰ τῷ Ἰωάννῃ, καὶ τρεῖς τῷ Λουκᾷ ὁμοίως *.

(4.) Now, the chief thing deserving of attention here,—the *only* thing in fact which I am concerned to point out,—is the notable circumstance that the supposed dictum of Eusebius,—("quod scribere non potuisset si pericopam dubiam agnovisset,")—*is no longer discoverable.* To say that 'it has disappeared,' would be incorrect. In the original document *it has no existence.* In plain terms, the famous "σχόλιον εὐσεβίου" proves to be every way a figment. It is a worthless interpolation, thrust by some nameless scribe into his abridgement of a Scholion, of which Eusebius (as I shall presently shew) *cannot* have been the Author.

(5.) I may as well point out *why* the person who wrote the longer Scholion says nothing about S. Mark's Gospel. It is because there was nothing for him to say.

* *Quoted by Matthaei, N. T.* (1788) vol. ix. p. 228, *from* g, n, d.

He is enumerating our LORD's *appearances to His Disciples* after His Resurrection; and he discovers that these were exactly seven in number: *one* being peculiar to S. Matthew,—*three*, to S. John,—*three*, to S. Luke. But because, (as every one is aware), there exists *no* record of an appearance to the Disciples *peculiar* to S. Mark's Gospel, the Author of the Scholion is silent concerning S. Mark *perforce.*

.... How so acute and accomplished a Critic as Matthaei can have overlooked all this: how he can have failed to recognise the identity of his longer and his shorter Scholion: how he came to say of the latter, "conjicias ergo Eusebium hunc totum locum repudiasse;" and, of the former, "ultimam partem Evangelii Marci videtur tollere [a]:" lastly, how Tischendorf (1869) can write,—"est enim ejusmodi ut ultimam partem evangelii Marci, de quo quaeritur, excludat [b]:"—I profess myself unable to understand.

(6.) The epitomizer however, missing the point of his Author,—besides enumerating *all* the appearances of our SAVIOUR which S. Luke anywhere records,—is further convicted of having injudiciously *invented* the negative statement about S. Mark's Gospel which is occasioning us all this trouble.

(7.) And yet, by that unlucky sentence of his, he certainly did not mean what is commonly imagined. I am not concerned to defend him: but it is only fair to point out that, to suppose he intended *to disallow the end of S. Mark's Gospel*, is altogether to misapprehend the gist of his remarks, and to impute to him a purpose of which he clearly knew nothing. Note, how he throws his first two statements into a separate paragraph; contrasts, and evidently *balances* one against the other: thus,—

κατὰ Μάρκον, μετὰ τὴν ἀνάστασιν οὐ λέγεται ὢφθαι,— κατὰ Ματθαῖον μετὰ τὴν ἀνάστασιν ὢφθη,— τοῖς μαθηταῖς ἐν τῇ Γαλιλαίᾳ.

Perfectly evident is it that the 'plena locutio' so to speak, of the Writer would have been somewhat as follows:—

'[The first two Evangelists are engaged with our SAVIOUR's appearance to His Disciples *in Galilee*: but] by

---

[a] *Ibid.*, ii. 69, and ix. 228.　　　[b] *Nov. Test.* (1869), p. 404.

S. Mark, He is *not*—by S. Matthew, He *is*—related to have been actually *seen* by them there.

'[The other two Evangelists relate the appearances *in Jerusalem* : and] according to S. John, &c. &c.

'According to S. Luke,' &c. &c.

(8.) And on passing the "Quaestiones ad Marinum" of Eusebius under review, I am constrained to admit that the Scholion before us is just such a clumsy bit of writing as an unskilful person might easily be betrayed into, who should attempt to exhibit in a few short sentences the substance of more than one tedious disquisition of this ancient Father [c]. Its remote parentage would fully account for its being designated "σχόλιον εὐσεβίου," all the same.

(9.) Least of all am I concerned to say anything more about the longer Scholion ; seeing that S. Mark is not so much as mentioned in it. But I may as well point out that, *as it stands*, Eusebius cannot have been its Author: the proof being, that whereas the Scholion in question is a note on S. John xxi. 12, (as Matthaei is careful to inform us,)— its opening sentence is derived *from Chrysostom's Commentary on that same verse* in his 87th Homily on S. John [d].

(10.) And thus, one by one, every imposing statement of the Critics is observed hopelessly to collapse as soon as it is questioned, and to vanish into thin air.

So much has been offered, only because of the deliberate pledge I gave in p. 51.—Never again, I undertake to say, will the " Scholion of Eusebius" which has cost my friend at Moscow, his Archimandrites, and me, so much trouble, be introduced into any discussion of the genuineness of the last Twelve Verses of the Gospel according to S. Mark. As the oversight of one (C. F. Matthaei) who was singularly accurate, and towards whom we must all feel as towards a Benefactor, let it be freely forgiven as well as loyally forgotten !

[c] Let the reader examine his "Quaestio ix," (Mai, vol. iv. p. 293-5) : his "Quaestio x," (p. 295, last seven lines). See also p. 296, line 29—32.

[d] See Chrys. *Opp.* vol. viii. p. 522 o:—ὅτι δὲ οὐδὲ συνεχῶς ἐπεχωρίαζεν, οὐδὲ ὁμοίως, λέγει ὅτι τρίτον τοῦτο ἐφάνη αὐτοῖς, ὅτε ἐγέρθη ἐκ νεκρῶν.

L'ENVOY

As one, escaped the bustling trafficking town,
Worn out and weary, climbs his favourite hill
And thinks it Heaven to see the calm green fields
Mapped out in beautiful sunlight at his feet :
Or walks enraptured where the fitful south
Comes past the beans in blossom ; and no sight
Or scent or sound but fills his soul with glee :—
So I,—rejoicing once again to stand
Where Siloa's brook flows softly, and the meads
Are all enamell'd o'er with deathless flowers,
And Angel voices fill the dewy air.
Strife is so hateful to me ! most of all
A strife of words about the things of God.
Better by far the peasant's uncouth speech
Meant for the heart's confession of its hope.
Sweeter by far in village-school the words
But half remembered from the Book of Life,
Or scarce articulate lispings of the Creed.

And yet, three times that miracle of Spring
The grand old tree that darkens Exeter wall
Hath decked itself with blossoms as with stars,
Since I, like one that striveth unto death,
Find myself early and late and oft all day
Engaged in eager conflict for God's Truth ;
God's Truth, to be maintained against Man's lie.
And lo, my brook which widened out long since
Into a river, threatens now at length
To burst its channel and become a sea.

O Sister, who ere yet my task is done
Art lying (my loved Sister !) in thy shroud
With a calm placid smile upon thy lips
As thou wert only " taking of rest in sleep,"
Soon to wake up to ministries of love,—
Open those lips, kind Sister, for my sake
In the mysterious place of thy sojourn,
(For thou must needs be with the bless'd,—yea, where
The pure in heart draw wondrous nigh to GOD,)
And tell the Evangelist of thy brother's toil ;
Adding (be sure !) " He found it his reward,
Yet supplicates thy blessing and thy prayers,
The blessing, saintly Stranger, of thy prayers,
Sure at the least unceasingly of mine !"

One other landed on the eternal shore !
One other garnered into perfect peace !
One other hid from hearing and from sight ! . . .
O but the days go heavily, and the toil
Which used to seem so pleasant yields scant joy.
There come no tokens to us from the dead :
Save—it may be—that now and then we reap
Where not we sowed, and *that* may be from *them,*
Fruit of their prayers when we forgot to pray !
Meantime there comes no message, comes no word :
Day after day no message and no sign :
And the heart droops, and finds that it was Love
Not Fame it longed for, lived for : only Love.

CANTERBURY.

GENERAL INDEX.

Under " Codices" will be found all the Evangelia described or quoted : under " Texts" all the places of Scripture illustrated or referred to.

" Acta Pilati," p. 25.

Aᴏᴛs, p. 199-200. *See* Texts.

Addit. *See* Codices.

Adler, J. G. C., p. 33-4.

Alford, Dean, p. 8, 13, 38, 77, 103, 164, 227, 244-5, 259.

Algasia, p. 52.

Ambrose, p. 27.

" Ammonian" Sections, p. 126-32, 295—311 ; in the four Gospels, p. 309 ; in S. Mark's Gospel, p. 311.

Ammonius, p. 125—32.

ἀνάγνωσις, p. 196.

ἀνάγνωσμα, p. 45, 196.

ἀναληφθῆναι, p. 166.

Andreas of Crete, p. 258.

Angelic Hymn, p. 257—63.

ἀντεβλήθη, p. 119.

ἀπέχει, p. 225, 6.

ἀφορμή, p. 127, 137.

Aphraates the Persian, p. 26-7, 258.

ἀπιστεῖν, p. 158-9.

Apocrypha, p. 301.

Apolinarius, p. 275, 277.

" Apostolical Constitutions," p. 25, 258.

ἀρχή, p. 224-5.

Armenian Version, p. 36, 239.

Ascension, The, p. 195.

——— Lessons, p. 204-5, 238-9.

Assemani, p. 309-10, 315.

Asterisks, p. 116-8, 218.

Athanasian Creed, p. 3, 254.

Athanasius, p. 30, 275 ; how he read S. Jo. xvii. 15, 16, p. 74.

Augustine, p. 28, 198, 200.

Babington, Rev. C., p. 291.

Basil, p. 93-9, 275.

βασιλίς, p. 275.

Basle, p. 283. *See* Codices.

Bede, Ven., p. 30.

Bengel, J. A., p. 17, 101-2, 185.

Benson, Rev. Dr., p. 101.

Βηθαβαρά and Βηθανία, p. 236.

Bibliothèque at Paris, p. 228-31, 278-83.

Birch's N. T., Andr., p. 5, 116-8, 311.

βλάπτειν, p. 160.

Bobbiensis, Codex, p. 35, 124, 186.

Bodleian. *See* Codices.

Book of Common Prayer, p. 215.

Bostra, *see* Titus.

Bosworth, Rev. Prof., p. 262.

Broadus, Prof., p. 139, 155, 168, 174

Cæsarius, p. 133.

Canons, p. 127-31, 295-312. *See* Sections.

Carpian, Letter to, p. 126-8, 311-2.

Carthage. *See* Council.

Cassian, p. 193.

Catenæ, p. 133-5. *See* Corderius, Cramer, Matthaei, Peltanus, Possinus, Victor.

Chrysostom, p. 27, 85, 110, 179, 193, 198-9, 201-4, 223, 258-9, 275-7, 278, 314-6, 323.

Church, the Christian, p. 192.

——— Festivals, p. 203.

Churton, Rev. W. R., p. 236.

" Circular," A, p. 101-5.

Citations, *see* Patristic.

Clemens Alex., p. 30.

Codices, depraved, p. 80-6, 217-24. *See* Corrupt readings, Dated, Syriac.

——— 151, referred to p. 311.

CODICES.

Codex ℵ, p. 70—90, 77, 109—13, 218-22, 252, 257, 313 ; how it exhibits the end of S. Mark, 88-90 ; omissions, 73-5, 79, 80 ; Ephes. i. 1, 91—109 ; interpolations and de-

---

θεᾶσθαι, p. 156-8.

Thebaic Version, p. 35.

Theodore of Mopsuestia, p. 275, 7.

Theodoret, p. 258, 317-8.

Theodotus of Ancyra, p. 258.

Theophania, p. 207.

Theophylact, p. 30, 266.

θεωρεῖν, p. 157.

Thompson, Rev. A. S., p. ii, 252.

Thomson, Abp., p. 13.

Tischendorf, Dr., p. 8, 9, 10, 38, 77-9, 85-6, 93, 109-14, 123, 125-33, 137, 153, 222, 7, 242, 4, 251 2, 9, 260-1, 280, 293, 311, 322, viii—ix.

Titus of Bostra, p. 258, 275, 283.

Toledo, see Codices.

Townson, Rev. Dr., p. 151, 179.

Tregelles, Dr., p. 9, 10—12, 38, 9, 60, 76, 114, 126-9, 136. 145, 169, 222-3, 227, 234, 242, 4, 5, 7, 251, 9, 260, 319, viii—ix.

Turin, see Codices.

Ulphilas, p. 35, 262.

Uncial MSS. p. 20, 71. See Codices.

ὑπόθεσις, p. 274-5.

ὕστερον, p. 160.

Vatican, p. 117, 283-4, 288-9: see Codices.

Vaticanus, see Codex.

Venice, see Codices.

Vercellone, C., p. 73.

Versions, see Armenian, &c.

Vetus Itala, p. 35.

Victor of Antioch, p. 29, 59—65, 67, 122, 134, 178, 180, 235, 250, 268, 269-87; Codices, 278-87; Scholion, 288-90.

ΤΟ ΤΕΛΟϹ.

Dean John William Burgon's
Vindication
of the
Last Twelve Verses of Mark

~~~~~~~~~~

The Fatal Blow to Manuscripts 'B' and 'Aleph'

By
Rev. D. A. Waite, Th.D., Ph.D., Director
THE BIBLE FOR TODAY
900 Park Avenue, Collingswood, NJ 08108
Phone: 609-854-4452; FAX: 609-854-2464
Orders: 1-800-JOHN 10:9

the
BIBLE
FOR
TODAY

900 Park Avenue
Collingswood, N. J. 08108
Phone: 609-854-4452

B.F.T. #2506

[NOTE: This booklet is taken from a message delivered on Thursday evening, August 18, 1994, at the 16th Annual Meeting of the DEAN BURGON SOCIETY. The meetings were held in the Bible Brethren Church, Hagerstown, Maryland.]

Foreword

Though the following pages are, in some measure, technical, it is hoped by the author that the reader will be able to grasp the central thesis, that is:

> **The Vatican ("B") and the Sinai ("Aleph") manuscripts (which form the bedrock foundation of ALL modern versions and perversions) rise or fall on what they have done to Mark 16:9-20, the last twelve verses of Mark.**

If it can be shown to the reader's satisfaction, that "B" and "Aleph" fail here, then doubt is cast upon all of their other questionable readings throughout the entire New Testament. Nowhere is there any clearer application of Luke 16:10 than in this instance:

> (Luke 16:10) "He that is **faithful in that which is least is faithful also in much:** and **he that is unjust in the least is unjust also in much.**"

For truly, the Received Greek Text which contains without question Mark 16:9-20, is **"faithful in that which is least"** as well as being **"faithful also in much."** The Revised Greek Text which eliminates Mark 16:9-20, represented by the Vatican and Sinai manuscripts, is indeed **"unjust . . . in much"** as well as being **"unjust in the least."**

In no place other than the book by Dean John William Burgon entitled *The Last Twelve Verses of Mark* is there to be found such an abundance of information and data with which to vindicate once and for all Mark 16:9-20. The reader is urged to purchase a copy of this valuable book, to study it diligently, and then to share its conclusions widely!

D. a. Waite

Rev. D. A. Waite, Th.D., Ph.D.
Director, THE BIBLE FOR TODAY, INCORPORATED

TABLE OF CONTENTS

Dean John William Burgon's
Vindication
of the
Last Twelve Verses of Mark

The subject of this booklet is one that I have been asked to talk about for a number of years. It is entitled, **"Dean John William Burgon's Vindication of the Last Twelve Verses of Mark."** In the original message, I used some overhead transparencies in order to make the subject as clear and as interesting as possible. These are included here in boxes, with brief comments.

I. Mark 16:9-20 Is Part of the Greek Textual Battle We Face

We are in a battle, a Greek textual battle. We are in a fight for the very Words of God. Therefore, in accord with Jude 1:3, we must *". . . earnestly contend for the faith which was once delivered unto the saints."* Our Greek New Testament is an ESSENTIAL, BASIC, and FUNDAMENTAL part of "THE FAITH" for which we should "EARNESTLY CONTEND."

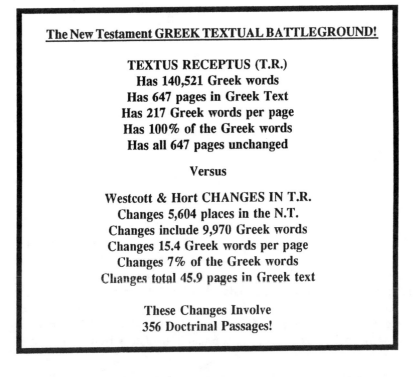

The New Testament GREEK TEXTUAL BATTLEGROUND!

TEXTUS RECEPTUS (T.R.)
Has 140,521 Greek words
Has 647 pages in Greek Text
Has 217 Greek words per page
Has 100% of the Greek words
Has all 647 pages unchanged

Versus

Westcott & Hort CHANGES IN T.R.
Changes 5,604 places in the N.T.
Changes include 9,970 Greek words
Changes 15.4 Greek words per page
Changes 7% of the Greek words
Changes total 45.9 pages in Greek text

These Changes Involve
356 Doctrinal Passages!

From this chart, we can see that the Textus Receptus has **140,521 Greek words**. This makes up **647 pages** in the Greek New Testament text. This text has 100% of the proper Greek words in our Greek New Testament.

Yes, we are fighting a Greek New Testament textual battle. Who is the enemy? The enemy is the Westcott and Hort type of Greek text of 1881, the text which changed the Textus Receptus in **5,604 places** in the Greek New Testament. That includes **9,970 Greek words**, an average of **15.4 Greek words per page**, or **7% of the whole Greek New Testament**. If you put all of these Greek words together in one place, this would total **45.9 pages in Greek text**.

II. Mark 16:9-20 Is Part of the Issue of the Doctrinal Corruption of the Greek New Testament and the New Versions Based Upon it

A. There are a Total of 356 Doctrinal Passages With Which the Westcott and Hort Type of Greek Text Has Tampered.

We must remember that these changes involve **356 doctrinal passages!** That is by actual count according to Dr. Jack Moorman's excellent work in that subject and field. The name of his book is *Early Manuscripts and the Authorized Version--A Closer Look*. It is **BFT #1825** for a **GIFT of $15.00**.

B. Doctrinal Heresy Was Present in the False Doctrines of Early Heretics on the Person and Work of the Lord Jesus Christ.

In the next chart, note how much Christian DOCTRINE was disputed in the first five centuries. All of these false doctrines could have motivated early heretics to have corrupted and altered the Greek New Testament. It is my personal belief that this is exactly what was done. The chart on the next page was compiled by Dr. J. Oliver Buswell, A Systematic Theology of the Christian Religion. Volume Two; Soteriology and Eschatology. The material presented in the chart is adapted from lectures delivered by the late Dr. Cleland B. McAfee, as sent to this writer by Dr. John C. Whitcomb.

Why is it **not presumed to be possible** for heretics such as the Docetists, the Ebionites, the Arians, the Apollinarians, the Nestorians, the Eutychians, and others to have systematically and for dogmatic purposes altered the Greek New Testament to further their own heterodox doctrines? From some of the changes that affect the doctrine of Christ (Christology) as listed in my book, *Defending the King James Bible*, Chapter V, it is clear that Christological false teachers were at work on various titles of Christ found in the Greek New Testament.

EARLY HISTORY OF THE DOCTRINE OF
THE PERSON AND THE NATURES OF CHRIST

Party	Time	Reference	Human Nature	Divine Nature
Docetist	1st Century	John 4:1-3	Denied	Affirmed
Eblonites	2nd Century	Irenaeus, etc.	Affirmed	Denied
Arians	4th Century	Condemned by Nicaea 325	Affirmed	Reduced
Apollinarians	4th Century	Condemned by Constantinople 381	Reduced	Affirmed
Nestorians	5th Century	Condemned by Ephesus, 431	Affirmed (1)	Affirmed
Eutychians	5th Century	Condemned by Chalcedon 451 and III Constantinople, 680	Reduced (2)	Reduced
Orthodox	From Beginning	Defined by Chalcedon 451	Affirmed (3)	Affirmed

(1) Nestorians held that Christ was two persons
(2) Eutychians held that Christ had one mixed nature, neither fully human or Divine
(3) Orthodox view: Christ is One Person with a fully Divine nature and a fully human nature.

Christ is One Person. *prosOpon, hypostasis*

His natures are:

without mixture *asynchutOs*

without change *atreptOs*

without division *adiairetOs*

without separation *achoristOs*

C. The False Statements by Bible Believing Leaders Regarding DOCTRINAL Changes in the Greek Texts and/or in the English Versions Based Upon them.

Some of these six heretical groups (and others) were no doubt among those who corrupted the Bible to suit their heresies. And, yet, there is a denial by Bible believing leaders that DOCTRINE is affected either by Greek texts or by English versions. That's important to see. There has been a DENIAL by Bible believing LEADERS that DOCTRINE has been altered or even "affected in any way."

1. The False statement by Dr. Arthur T. Pierson Regarding Doctrine. He wrote:

"... *it is remarkable how faithful ALL THE STANDARD TRANSLATIONS ARE, and most remarkable how, amid all the thousands of doubtful disputed renderings, even of the most perplexing passages, NOT ONE* [doubtful disputed rendering] *AFFECTS A SINGLE VITAL DOCTRINE OF THE WORD OF GOD."* [In his *Knowing The Scripture,* the chapter on "Bible Versions And Translations" as quoted in *Bible Translations* by Evangelist R. L. Sumner, p. 21, 1979].

2. The False Statement by Dr. Louis T. Talbot Regarding Doctrine. He wrote:

"Yet, to repeat for emphasis, for all practical purposes, we still cling to the King James Version, using the REVISED [that is, the ENGLISH REVISED VERSION of 1881, or the AMERICAN STANDARD VERSION of 1901] *as a kind of commentary for analytical study. And let me add that NO FUNDAMENTAL DOCTRINE HAS BEEN CHANGED IN THE LEAST BY THE LATER VERSION."* [As quoted in *Bible Translations* by Evangelist R. L. Sumner, p. 20, 1979]

Talbot Seminary is named for Dr. Talbot. There are over 356 doctrinal passages that are affected. I mention 158 of them in my book, *Defending the King James Bible.* This is available as **BFT #1594-P** for a GIFT of **$12.00** plus **$3.50** postage and handling.

3. The False Statement by Dr. John R. Rice Regarding Doctrine. He wrote:

"The DIFFERENCES IN THE TRANSLATIONS ARE SO MINOR, SO INSIGNIFICANT, THAT WE CAN BE SURE NOT A SINGLE DOCTRINE, NOT A SINGLE STATEMENT OF FACT, NOT A SINGLE COMMAND OR EXHORTATION, HAS BEEN MISSED IN OUR TRANSLATIONS." [As quoted in *Bible Translations* by Evangelist R. L. Sumner, p. 18, 1979]

I met Dr. Rice, heard him preach, and respected him in the Lord. Many of the things that he has done are fine. I don't agree with his denial of secondary separation and a number of other things. In the above statement, he is certainly wrong. It is a false statement. We'll see in Mark 16:9-20 that there **is** doctrine involved, and these men **are** denying it to be so.

4. The False Statement by Dr. Robert L. Sumner Regarding Doctrine. He wrote:

"Faithful, textual criticism by honest Christian scholars has made it

possible for us to be dead certain about the major portion of the Hebrew, Aramaic and Greek--especially the New Testament Greek--and THE RARE PARTS ABOUT WHICH THERE IS STILL UNCERTAINTY DO NOT EFFECT [sic] IN ANY WAY ANY DOCTRINE."

Mark 16:9-20 is one of the largest portions of Scripture that affects doctrine-- consisting of twelve entire verses.

5. The False Statement by Dr. Robert L. Thomas Regarding Doctrine. Dr. Thomas was writing as one of Dr. John MacArthur's Professors in his Master's Seminary in the Los Angeles area. He wrote:

"AND NO MAJOR DOCTRINE OF SCRIPTURE IS AFFECTED BY A VARIANT READING." [From *MASTERPIECE MAGAZINE*, January/February, 1990, p. 17, "The King James Controversy" article by Dr. Robert L. Thomas, as quoted in *MacArthur's Man Answered On EIGHTEEN ERRORS Concerning THE KING JAMES BIBLE* by Rev. D. A. Waite, Th.D., Ph.D., p. 3, published by BIBLE FOR TODAY, 900 Park Avenue, Collingswood, NJ 08108]

That is from the *MASTERPIECE MAGAZINE*. **But the variant readings in Greek do affect doctrine.** We definitely know that, and that is not a true statement.

6. The False Statement by Dr. H. S. Miller Regarding Doctrine. He wrote:

"These VARIATIONS include such matters as differences in spelling, transposition of letters, words, clauses, order of words, order of sentences, reduplication, etc. NO DOCTRINE IS AFFECTED, and very often not even the translation is affected." [From *General Biblical Introduction* as quoted by Dr. Ernest Pickering in "Questions And Answers About Bible Translations," pp. 7-8. Also quoted in *Refutation Of Dr. Ernest D. Pickering On Bible Translations*, by Rev. D. A. Waite, Th.D., Ph.D., p. 33, 1991].

Doctrine means teaching. Are teachings affected? Yes they are. We'll see illustrations of this in our passage in Mark 16:9-20.

7. The False Statement by Dr. Stanley Gundry Regarding Doctrine. He wrote:

"ONLY A FEW OUTSTANDING PROBLEMS REMAIN, AND THESE DO NOT AFFECT DOCTRINE OR DIVINE COMMAND TO US." ["What Happened To Those King James Verses?" *Moody Monthly*, 1990, p. 46, as quoted in "Questions And Answers About Bible Translations" by Dr. Ernest Pickering, p. 8. Also quoted in *Refutation of Dr. Ernest D. Pickering On Bible Translations* by Dr. D. A. Waite, *op. cit.*, p. 34].

There are many doctrines involved!

8. The False Statement by Dr. Ernest D. Pickering Regarding Doctrine. I know Dr. Pickering from Dallas Theological Seminary. We went to school together. He wrote:

"IMPORTANT DIFFERENCES OF TEXTUAL READINGS ARE RELA-TIVELY FEW AND ALMOST NONE WOULD AFFECT ANY MAJOR CHRISTIAN DOCTRINE." ["Questions and Answers About Bible Translations," by Dr. Ernest D. Pickering, p. 3, as quoted in *Refutation Of Dr. Ernest D. Pickering On Bible Translations* by Dr. D. A. Waite, *op. cit.*, p. 10].

We will see about some doctrines a little later.

9. The False Statement by Rev. Richard DeHaan Regarding Doctrine. Rev. DeHaan is the Teacher of The Radio Bible Class. I have talked about his position and that of the present Radio Bible Class in our thirty minute radio series. These are available on five, two-hour audio cassettes as **#BFT/87-91** for a GIFT of **$15.00.** He wrote:

"And of those 400 differences where the sense of a passage is involved, NOT ONE OF THEM INVOLVES A SINGLE BASIC DOCTRINE OF THE CHRISTIAN FAITH. NONE of the thousands of variants DENIES ONE FOUNDATIONAL CHRISTIAN TRUTH." [From his 1984 booklet, *The World's Greatest Book*, p. 29]

I would urge the reader to consult my book, *Defending the King James Bible*, Chapter V for 158 examples and illustrations of **DOCTRINAL CHANGES** both in the false Egyptian Greek texts of "B" (Vatican) and "Aleph" (Sinai) manuscripts as well as in one or more of the four versions used by Bible believing people today, that is, the NIV, NASV, NKJV-FN, and the NB. Many of these theological errors are of the utmost seriousness, and should be repudiated by all.

III. The Introduction to Mark 16:9-20

A. Mark 16:9-20 in the Textus Receptus Greek Text.

The following are the exact Greek words that we are defending:

9 Ἀναστὰς δὲ πρωῒ πρώτῃ σαββάτου ἐφάνη πρῶτον Μαρίᾳ τῇ Μαγδαληνῇ, ἀφ' ἧς ἐκβεβλήκει ἑπτὰ δαιμόνια.
10 ἐκείνη πορευθεῖσα ἀπήγγειλε τοῖς μετ' αὐτοῦ γενομένοις, πενθοῦσι καὶ κλαίουσι.
11 κἀκεῖνοι ἀκούσαντες ὅτι ζῇ καὶ ἐθεάθη ὑπ' αὐτῆς ἠπίστησαν.
12 Μετὰ δὲ ταῦτα δυσὶν ἐξ αὐτῶν περιπατοῦσιν ἐφανερώθη ἐν ἑτέρᾳ μορφῇ, πορευομένοις εἰς ἀγρόν.
13 κἀκεῖνοι ἀπελθόντες ἀπήγγειλαν τοῖς λοιποῖς· οὐδὲ ἐκείνοις ἐπίστευσαν.
14 Ὕστερον, ἀνακειμένοις αὐτοῖς τοῖς ἕνδεκα ἐφανερώθη, καὶ ὠνείδισε τὴν ἀπιστίαν αὐτῶν καὶ σκληροκαρδίαν, ὅτι τοῖς θεασαμένοις αὐτὸν ἐγηγερμένον, οὐκ ἐπίστευσαν.
15 καὶ εἶπεν αὐτοῖς, Πορευθέντες εἰς τὸν κόσμον ἅπαντα, κηρύξατε τὸ εὐαγγέλιον πάσῃ τῇ κτίσει.
16 ὁ πιστεύσας καὶ βαπτισθεὶς, σωθήσεται· ὁ δὲ ἀπιστήσας, κατακριθήσεται.
17 σημεῖα δὲ τοῖς πιστεύσασι ταῦτα παρακολουθήσει· ἐν τῷ ὀνόματί μου δαιμόνια ἐκβαλοῦσι· γλώσσαις λαλήσουσι καιναῖς,
18 ὄφεις ἀροῦσι· κἂν θανάσιμόν τι πίωσιν, οὐ μὴ αὐτοὺς βλάψει, ἐπὶ ἀρρώστους χεῖρας ἐπιθήσουσι, καὶ καλῶς ἕξουσιν.
19 Ὁ μὲν οὖν Κύριος, μετὰ τὸ λαλῆσαι αὐτοῖς, ἀνελήφθη εἰς τὸν οὐρανὸν, καὶ ἐκάθισεν ἐκ δεξιῶν τοῦ Θεοῦ.
20 ἐκεῖνοι δὲ ἐξελθόντες ἐκήρυξαν πανταχοῦ, τοῦ Κυρίου συνεργοῦντος, καὶ τὸν λόγον βεβαιοῦντος διὰ τῶν ἐπακολουθούντων σημείων. Ἀμήν.

B. The Number of Greek and English Words Involved in Mark 16:9-20.

> **THE LAST 12 VERSES OF MARK**
> **Mark 16:9-20**
>
> **Mark 16:9-20 Involves:**
> **166 Greek Words!**
> **And**
> **255 English Words!**

(Mark 8:38) WHOSOEVER THEREFORE SHALL BE ASHAMED OF ME AND OF MY WORDS in this adulterous and sinful generation; OF HIM ALSO SHALL THE SON OF MAN BE ASHAMED, WHEN HE COMETH in the glory of his Father with the holy angels.

The last twelve verses of Mark 16, verses 9 through 20, involve **166 Greek words**. That's exactly what we are fighting about. That's **255 English words** in our King James Bible. We must not be ashamed of Christ's WORDS. We believe that Mark 16:9-20 are the Lord Jesus Christ's WORDS. We've got some WORDS to defend, and Dean Burgon did that job.

C. Mark 16:9-20 in the King James English Bible.

(Mark 16:9) Now when {Jesus} was risen early the first {day} of the week, he appeared first to Mary Magdalene, out of whom he had cast seven devils. (Mark 16:10) {And} she went and told them that had been with him, as they mourned and wept. (Mark 16:11) And they, when they had heard that he was alive, and had been seen of her, believed not. (Mark 16:12) After that he appeared in another form unto two of them, as they walked, and went into the country. (Mark 16:13) And they went and told {it} unto the residue: neither believed they them. (Mark 16:14) Afterward he appeared unto the eleven as they sat at meat, and upbraided them with their unbelief and hardness of heart, because they believed not them which had seen him after he was risen. (Mark 16:15) And he said unto them, Go ye into all the world, and preach the gospel to every creature. (Mark 16:16) He that believeth and is baptized shall be saved; but he that believeth not shall be damned. (Mark 16:17) And these signs shall follow them that believe; In my name shall they cast out devils; they shall speak with new tongues; (Mark 16:18) They shall take up serpents; and if they

drink any deadly thing, it shall not hurt them; they shall lay hands on the sick, and they shall recover. (Mark 16:19) So then after the Lord had spoken unto them, he was received up into heaven, and sat on the right hand of God. (Mark 16:20) And they went forth, and preached every where, the Lord working with {them}, and confirming the word with signs following. Amen.

D. Twenty-Seven Doctrines or Teachings Contained in Mark 16:9-20. Here's Mark 16:9-20 with a listing of **at least twenty-seven DOCTRINES** that are involved:

Mark 16:9-20
The Last 12 Verses of Mark
The DOCTRINES or TEACHINGS in the Verses

Verse #1 of 12

(Mark 16:9) Now when {Jesus} was risen [#1: THE DOCTRINE OF THE BODILY RESURRECTION OF CHRIST] **early the first {day} of the week, [#2: THE TIME OF THE RESURRECTION] he appeared first [#3: THE ORDER OF CHRIST'S RESURRECTION APPEARANCES] to Mary Magdalene, [#4: THE PERSON TO WHOM CHRIST APPEARED] out of whom he had cast seven devils. [#5: A MIRACLE OF CHRIST]**

Verse #2 of 12

(Mark 16:10) {And} she went and told them that had been with him, [#6: MARY'S WITNESS TO CHRIST'S BODILY RESURRECTION TO CHRIST'S DISCIPLES] **as they mourned and wept. [#7: A DESCRIP-** TION OF CHRIST'S DISCIPLES' EMOTIONAL CONDITION]

Verse #3 of 12

(Mark 16:11) And they, when they had heard that he was alive, and had been seen of her, [#8: CONFIRMATION THAT CHRIST'S DISCIPLES RECEIVED THE TESTIMONY OF MARY ABOUT HIS BODILY RESURRECTION] **believed not. [#9: TESTIMONY TO** CHRIST'S DISCIPLES' DISBELIEF IN HIS BODILY RESUR- RECTION]

Verse #4 of 12

(Mark 16:12) After that he appeared in another form unto two of them, as they walked, and went into the country. [#10: TWO OTHERS WITNESSED CHRIST'S BODILY RESURRECTION]

Verse #5 of 12

(Mark 16:13) **And they went and told {it} unto the residue:** [#11: ANOTHER TESTIMONY TO THE BODILY RESURRECTION OF CHRIST] **neither believed they them.** [#12: ANOTHER EXAMPLE OF DISBELIEF BY CHRIST'S DISCIPLES IN HIS BODILY RESURREC- TION]

Verse #6 of 12

(Mark 16:14) **Afterward he appeared unto the eleven as they sat at meat,** [#13: ANOTHER OF CHRIST'S APPEARANCES AFTER HIS BODILY RESURRECTION] **and upbraided them with their unbelief and hardness of heart, because they believed not them which had seen him after he was risen.** [#14: CHRIST UPBRAIDED HIS DISCIPLES FOR UNBELIEF, HARD HEARTS, AND FAILING TO BELIEVE THE WITNESSES TO HIS BODILY RESURRECTION]

Verse #7 of 12

(Mark 16:15) **And he said unto them, Go ye into all the world, and preach the gospel to every creature.** [#15: CHRIST'S COMMAND TO PREACH THE GOSPEL WORLDWIDE TO EVERYONE]

Verse #8 of 12

(Mark 16:16) **He that believeth and is baptized shall be saved;** [#16: SALVATION BY BELIEF OF THE GOSPEL] **but he that believeth not shall be damned.** [#17: CONDEMNATION TO HELL BY DISBELIEF OF THE GOSPEL]

Verse #9 of 12

(Mark 16:17) **And these signs shall follow them that believe;** [#18: SPECIAL APOSTOLIC MIRACLE-SIGNS WOULD BE EVIDENT DURING THEIR LIFETIME] **In my name shall they cast out devils;** [#19: APOSTOLIC CASTING OUT OF DEMONS] **they shall speak with new tongues;** [#20 : APOSTOLIC SPEAKING THE GOSPEL IN FOREIGN LANGUAGES]

Verse #10 of 12

(Mark 16:18) **They shall take up serpents;** [#21: APOSTOLIC PROTECTION FROM DEADLY SERPENTS] **and if they drink any deadly thing, it shall not hurt them;** [#22: APOSTOLIC PROTECTION FROM POISONOUS DRINKS] **they shall lay hands on the sick, and they shall recover.** [#23: APOSTOLIC PHYSICAL HEALING OF THE SICK]

Verse #11 of 12

(Mark 16:19) **So then after the Lord had spoken unto them, he was received up into heaven,** [#24: CHRIST'S BODILY ASCENSION INTO HEAVEN] **and sat on the right hand of God.** [#25: CHRIST'S BODILY SESSION AT THE RIGHT HAND OF GOD]

Verse #12 of 12

(Mark 16:20) **And they went forth, and preached every where,** [#26: THE OBEDIENCE OF THE DISCIPLES TO CHRIST'S COMMAND TO PREACH EVERYWHERE] **the Lord working with {them}, and confirming the word with signs following. Amen.** [#27: CHRIST'S FULFILLMENT OF HIS PROMISED APOSTOLIC MIRACLE-SIGNS]

Doctrine is teaching of any kind, big or little--teaching about the **Word of God.** These preceding DOCTRINES are precious "TEACHINGS" which either have been eliminated or brought into doubt by the "B" (Vatican) and "Aleph" (Sinai) Greek manuscripts and many English versions.

IV. Statements of Doubt by Current Bible Versions as to the Genuineness of Mark 16:9-20

What are some of the statements made in four of the Bible versions? What do they say about the last twelve verses of Mark?

A. The *NEW KING JAMES VERSION'S (NKJV)* Statement of Doubt about Mark 16:9-20.

> *"Verses 9-20 are bracketed in NU* [Nestle/United Bible Society] *texts as NOT ORIGINAL. They are lacking in Codex Sinaiticus and Codex Vaticanus, though nearly all other manuscripts of Mark contain them."*

B. The *NEW AMERICAN STANDARD VERSION'S (NASV)* Statement of Doubt about Mark 16:9-20.

> *"SOME OF THE OLDEST MSS. OMIT FROM VERSE 9 THROUGH 20. A few later mss. and versions contain this paragraph, usually after verse 8; a few have it at the end of the chapter. . . ."* [Then follows two and one half lines of another alleged ending. MARK 16:9-20 IS SET OFF IN BRACKETS, SHOWING THAT THE NASV DOES NOT THINK THE VERSES

ARE GENUINE.]

C. The *NEW INTERNATIONAL VERSION'S (NIV)* Statement of Doubt about Mark 16:9-20.

"The two MOST RELIABLE EARLY MANUSCRIPTS DO NOT HAVE MARK 16:9-20." [To indicate that the NIV does not think these verses are genuine, they separate them from verse 8 with a black, unbroken line.]

D. The *RYRIE STUDY BIBLE NEW TESTAMENT'S (KING JAMES VERSION)* Statement of Doubt about Mark 16:9-20.

"THESE VERSES DO NOT APPEAR IN TWO OF THE MOST TRUSTWORTHY MANUSCRIPTS OF THE N.T., though they are part of many other manuscripts and versions. If they are not a part of the genuine text of Mark, the abrupt ending at verse 8 is probably because the original closing verses were lost. The DOUBTFUL GENUINENESS Of VERSES 9-20 MAKES IT UNWISE TO BUILD A DOCTRINE OR BASE AN EXPERIENCE ON THEM (ESPECIALLY vv. 18-20)."

From the above quotations, you can see that the NKJV, the NASV, the NIV, and the *Ryrie Study Bible* are all in favor of DOUBTING if not outright REJECTING Mark 16:9-20!

V. Dean John William Burgon's Masterful Defense of the Last Twelve Verses of Mark (Mark 16:9-20).

A. Dean Burgon's Statement of the Case Regarding Mark 16:9-20. He wrote:

"It shall be my endeavour in the ensuing pages to shew, on the contrary, [1] That MANUSCRIPT EVIDENCE is so overwhelmingly in their favour that no room is left for doubt or suspicion; [2] That there is NOT SO MUCH AS ONE OF THE FATHERS, early or late, who gives it as his opinion that these verses are spurious:--and, [3] That the argument derived from INTERNAL CONSIDERATIONS proves on inquiry to be BASELESS AND UNSUBSTANTIAL AS A DREAM." [The Last Twelve Verses of Mark, by Dean John William Burgon, Chapter I, p. 1]

B. Dean Burgon's METHOD of Vindicating and Establishing Mark 16:9-20. He wrote:

> *"This present inquiry must be conducted SOLELY on grounds of EVI-DENCE, [1] EXTERNAL and [2] INTERNAL. For the full consideration of the former, SEVEN CHAPTERS will be necessary [Chapters III--VIII & X]; for a discussion of the latter, one seventh of that space will suffice [Chapter IX]."*

C. Dean Burgon's Evaluation of the IMPORTANCE of Mark 16:9-20 Being Proved to Be GENUINE When Dealing with the Critical Methods of Tischendorf, Tregelles, Westcott & Hort, and Others of Today. He wrote:

> *"If they* [Tischendorf, Tregelles, etc.] *are right, there is no help for it but that the convictions of EIGHTEEN CENTURIES in this respect must be SURRENDERED. BUT if Tischendorf and Tregelles are WRONG in this particular, it follows of necessity that DOUBT IS THROWN OVER THE WHOLE OF THEIR CRITICAL METHOD. The case is a CRUCIAL ONE. EVERY PAGE OF THEIRS INCURS SUSPICION if their deliberate verdict in THIS instance shall prove to be MISTAKEN."* [Dean Burgon, *Last Twelve Verses of Mark*, Chapter II, p. 9]

D. Dean Burgon's MANUSCRIPT Evidence Supporting Mark 16:9-20. The manuscript evidence for and against **the last twelve verses of Mark** (Mark 16:9-20) is summarized in the following table. It was taken from *THE LAST TWELVE VERSES OF MARK* (pages 70-113) by Dean John William Burgon (**BFT #1139**, 350 pages, available for a GIFT of **$15.00**).

You will notice in the following chart the overwhelming flood of Greek manuscript authority vindicating the last twelve verses of Mark, that is, Mark 16:9-20. Even if there were no evidence from the 10 early New Testament versions, even if there were no evidence from the 19 early Church Fathers, the evidence of the Greek manuscripts alone should resolve the question for the honest, unprejudiced student of Scripture. How possibly can merely **two manuscripts** (Vatican and Sinai) stand successfully against the united testimony of 18 other uncials, about 600 cursives, and every known Lectionary of the East?! Dean Burgon has amassed decidedly **more** evidence than would be needed to restore completely Mark 16:9-20 to its rightful place in Mark's Gospel. On the contrary, this entire situation should forever taint the testimony of "B" (Vatican) and "Aleph" (Sinai) in any other part of the Greek New Testament where critical questions arise.

> ## Manuscript Evidence for Mark 16:9-20
> ## SUMMARIZED (In Burgon's Day):
>
> **a.   AGAINST Mark 16:9-20:**
>   (1) Codex "B" (Vatican) [p. 70]
>   (2) Codex "Aleph" (Sinai) [p. 70]
>
> **b.   FOR Mark 16:9-20:**
>   (1) 18 Uncials [p. 71]
>   (2) c. 600 Cursive Copies [p. 71]
>   (3) Every known Uncial or Cursive
>   in existence! [p. 71]
>   (4) Every known Lectionary of the
>   East! [p. 210]

E. Vatican ("B") and Sinai ("Aleph") Manuscripts Were Defended by Bishop Westcott and Professor Hort as Opponents of Mark 16:9-20.

1. Some of the Tenets of Westcott and Hort.

a. <u>Westcott and Hort Denied the Inerrancy of the Original Greek New Testament.</u> They wrote:

"Little is gained by speculating as to the precise point at which SUCH CORRUPTIONS CAME IN. THEY MAY BE DUE TO THE ORIGINAL WRITER, OR TO HIS AMANUENSIS if he wrote from dictation, or they may be due to one of the earliest transcribers."   [F. H. A. Hort, & B. F. Westcott, *Introduction to Their Greek New Testament*, p. 280]

b. <u>Westcott and Hort Denied There Was Any Deliberate Doctrinal Falsification of the Greek New Testament.</u> They wrote:

"It will not be out of place to add here a distinct expression of our belief that even among the numerous unquestionably spurious readings [in their point of view] **of the New Testament THERE ARE NO SIGNS OF DELIBERATE FALSIFICATION OF THE TEXT FOR DOGMATIC PURPOSES."**   [F. H. A.

Hort, & B. F. Westcott, *Introduction to Their Greek New Testament*, p. 282]

c. Westcott and Hort Thought the N.T. Was Like Any Other Book. They wrote as follows:

"The principles of criticism explained in the foregoing section hold good FOR ALL ANCIENT TEXTS preserved in a plurality of documents. In dealing with the text of the New Testament, NO NEW PRINCIPLE WHATEVER IS NEEDED OR LEGITIMATE: . . ." [F. H. A. Hort, & B. F. Westcott, *Introduction to Their Greek New Testament*, p. 73]

d. Westcott and Hort Admitted that the Traditional Greek Text That Underlies the King James Bible Was from the 4th Century. They wrote:

"THE FUNDAMENTAL TEXT OF LATE EXTANT GREEK MSS GENERALLY IS <u>BEYOND ALL QUESTION</u> IDENTICAL WITH THE DOMINANT ANTIOCHIAN OR GRAECO-SYRIAN TEXT OF THE <u>SECOND HALF OF THE FOURTH CENTURY.</u>" (350-399 A.D.) [F. H. A. Hort, & B. F. Westcott, *Introduction to Their Greek New Testament*, p. 92]

2. Some Defects of the Vatican ("B") and Sinai ("Aleph") Manuscripts. Here are some statements as to the various defects of Manuscript "B" (Vatican) and "Aleph" (Sinai). They are the only two Greek manuscripts that leave Mark 16:9-20 out. So what sort of character do they have? Dr. Branine had an excellent analysis of "B" and "Aleph" in his message to the DEAN BURGON SOCIETY (August 17, 1994). He talked about all the omissions and additions in these two spurious manuscripts. Get the Dean Burgon Society Message Book for 1994 for his message [**$27.00**] along with the others contained therein.

a. Westcott and Hort Accepted the New Testament Greek Vatican Manuscript ("B") As Superior to All Others. Westcott and Hort wrote:

"We learn next that B VERY FAR EXCEEDS ALL OTHER DOCUMENTS IN NEUTRALITY OF TEXT AS MEASURED BY THE ABOVE TESTS, BEING IN FACT ALWAYS OR NEARLY ALWAYS NEUTRAL . . ." [F. H. A. Hort, & B. F. Westcott, *Introduction to Their Greek New Testament*, p. 171]

b. <u>Westcott & Hort Believed that When the Vatican ("B") and Sinai ("Aleph") Agreed, This Was the Text of the Autographs.</u> Speaking of when "B" & "Aleph" were in agreement, they wrote:

" . . . but the fullest comparison does but increase the conviction that THEIR ["B" & "Aleph"] RELATIVE PURITY IS LIKEWISE APPROXIMATELY ABSOLUTE, A TRUE APPROXIMATE REPRODUCTION OF THE TEXT OF THE AUTOGRAPHS, . . ." [F. H. A. Hort, & B. F. Westcott, *Introduction to Their Greek New Testament*, p. 276]

c. <u>Westcott & Hort Believed That the Combination of Vatican Manuscript ("B") Plus Any Other Primary Manuscript Was Considered by them as Being Genuine.</u>

They wrote:

"Now every such BINARY GROUP [that is "B" plus another primary manuscript] containing B is found by this process to offer a LARGE PROPORTION OF READINGS WHICH on the closest scrutiny HAVE THE RING OF GENUINENESS, while IT IS DIFFICULT TO FIND ANY READINGS SO ATTESTED WHICH LOOK SUSPICIOUS after full consideration." [F. H. A. Hort, & B. F. Westcott, *Introduction to Their Greek New Testament*, p. 227]

d. <u>Various Statements as to the Defects of Manuscript "B" (Vatican) and "Aleph" (Sinai)</u>

(1) Dean Burgon Believed That the Deficiency of the Vatican ("B") and Sinai ("Aleph") Manuscripts at Mark 16:9-20 Destroys Confidence in these Two False Texts In a Thousand Other Places. He wrote:

"The omission of these twelve verses [Mark 16:9-20], I repeat, IN ITSELF, DESTROYS HIS [that is, an unprejudiced student's] CONFIDENCE in Codex B and Codex Aleph: for it is obvious that a copy of the Gospels which has been so SERIOUSLY MUTILATED IN ONE PLACE may have been slightly tampered with in another. . . . MISTRUST will no doubt have been thrown over the evidence borne to the text of Scripture IN A THOUSAND OTHER PLACES by Codex B and Codex Aleph,

after demonstration that those two Codices EXHIBIT A MUTI-LATED TEXT in this present place." [Dean Burgon, *The Last 12 Verses of Mark*, Chapter VI, pp. 71-72]

In other words the whole base, the whole foundation of the modern versions of the Bible, based as they are on "B" and "Aleph" [Vatican and Sinai Greek manuscripts], falls because they are lying witnesses in this huge section of twelve verses. That is what Burgon is saying. If you can't depend upon them in this important thing, how can you trust them anywhere?

(2) Dean Burgon Stated that the Vatican ("B") Manuscript Has Careless Transcription in Every Page. He wrote:

"Codex B comes to us WITHOUT A HISTORY: WITHOUT RECOMMENDATION OF ANY KIND, except that of its antiquity. It bears traces of CARELESS TRANSCRIPTION IN EVERY PAGE. The MISTAKES which the original transcriber made are of PERPETUAL RECURRENCE." [Dean Burgon, *The Last 12 Verses of Mark*, Chapter VI, p. 73]

(3) Dean Burgon Quoted Two Other Scholars as to the Defects of the Vatican ("B") Manuscript. He wrote:

"They [the MISTAKES] **are chiefly OMISSIONS, OF ONE, TWO, OR THREE WORDS; but sometimes of HALF A VERSE, A WHOLE VERSE, or even several verses. . . . I hesitate not to assert that it would be EASIER to find a folio containing three or four such OMISSIONS than to light on one which should be WITHOUT ANY."** [p. 73]

"In the Gospels alone, Codex B LEAVES OUT WORDS OR WHOLE CLAUSES no less than 1,491 TIMES." [p. 73]

(4) Dean Burgon Was Also Disappointed in the Sinai ("Aleph") Manuscript. He wrote:

"And yet the Codex in question [that is, manuscript "Aleph" (Sinai)] **abounds with 'errors of the eye and pen, to an extent not unparalleled, but happily rather unusual in documents of first-rate importance.' . . . 'the state of the text** [that is, of "Aleph" (Sinai)], **as proceeding from the first scribe, may be**

regarded as VERY ROUGH.' . . Is, then, manuscript authority to be confounded with EDITORIAL CAPRICE--exercising itself upon the corrections of 'AT LEAST TEN DIFFERENT REVISERS,' who, from the 6th to 12th century have been endeavouring to lick into shape a text which its original author left 'VERY ROUGH'?" [Dean Burgon, *Last 12 Verses of Mark*, Chapter VI, pp. 75-76]

So we see "Aleph" is rough, and "B" is rough. Yes, both of them are rough!

(5) Herman Hoskier's Criticism of the Vatican ("B") Manuscript. Hoskier was a man who was in favor of Dean Burgon. He was a great scholar in the Anglican Church. He wrote:

"It is high time that the bubble of codex B should be pricked . . . I had thought that time would cure the extraordinary HORTIAN HERESY, . . . it seemed time to write a consecutive account of the CROOKED PATH pursued by the MS.B, which-- from ignorance I trow--most people STILL CONFUSE with PURITY and 'neutrality.' . . . I present therefore an indictment against the MS. B and against WESTCOTT AND HORT, subdivided into HUNDREDS OF SEPARATE COUNTS. . . . If I now throw some bombs into the inner citadel, it is because from that Keep there continues to issue a large amount of IGNORANT ITERATION of HORT'S CONCLUSIONS, without one particle of proof that his foundation theory is correct. . . . OVER 3,000 REAL DIFFERENCES between Aleph and B are recorded IN THE GOSPELS ALONE!"

That's Herman Hoskier with his comments on Westcott and Hort. I like to call them "Wayward" Westcott and "Heretic" Hort.) We have Hoskier's book-- *Codex "B" and its Allies.* It has over 900 pages and is in two volumes. It is a great scholarly work. It is hard to read but the evidence is all there. You can get a copy as **BFT #1643**, for a GIFT of **$46.00**.

e. The Blank Spaces in the Sinai ("Aleph") and Vatican ("B") Manuscripts.

(1) A Picture of the Sinai ("Aleph") Manuscript at Mark 16:9-20. The Sinai ("Aleph") manuscript is 13 and 1/8 inches by 13 inches in the original. In this manuscript, Mark 16 ends with verse 8, followed by a blank

space which would be sufficient for Mark 16:9-20.   Since the scribes never
began a new book on the same column as a previous book, they began the
Gospel of Luke on a new column.

(2) Dean Burgon's Explanation of the Blank Space in the Vatican ("B") Manuscript. Burgon uses the argument of silence when explaining the blank space to prove that Codex "B" (the Vatican manuscript) witnesses in favor of Mark 16:9-20. Here is Dean Burgon's explanation for the BLANK SPACE after Mark 16:8 and before Luke 1:1 in "B" (Vatican):

> "It is the only vacant column in the whole manuscript;--a blank space abundantly sufficient to contain the twelve verses which he nevertheless withheld. . . . The older MS. from which Codex B was copied must have infallibly contained the twelve verses in dispute. The copyist was instructed to leave them out,--and he obeyed; but he prudently left a BLANK SPACE *in memoriam rei.* NEVER WAS BLANK MORE INTELLIGIBLE! NEVER WAS SILENCE MORE ELOQUENT! By this simple expedient, strange to relate, the Vatican Codex is made to REFUTE ITSELF even while it seems to be bearing testimony against the concluding verses of S. Mark's Gospel, by withholding them. . . . The venerable Author of the original Codex from which Codex B was copied, is thereby brought to view. And thus, our supposed adversary (Codex B) proves our most useful ally: for it procures us the testimony of an hitherto unsuspected witness." (p. 87)

VI. The Evidence of the Greek Lectionaries Supporting the Genuineness of the Last Twelve Verses of Mark (Mark 16:9-20)

A. An Explanation of Lectionary Practice. Lectionaries were portions of the Greek New Testament that were read in the churches on certain days of the church year, such as on Easter or at the Christmas season.

Before each LECTION (or portion of Scripture to read from) it was customary to put the abbreviation of the word "archE" (beginning). At the end of the LECTION, they put the abbreviation of the word "to telos" (end). Since Mark 16:9-20 was one LECTION, and since Mark 16:2-8 was another LECTION, the LECTIONS were marked with some abbreviation of "to telos" after MARK 16:8. It is entirely possible that some scribe, not knowing this practice, thought "TO TELOS" meant the END of Mark, instead of the END of the LECTION (Mark 16:2-8) which was read on Easter day.

B. 100% of the Lectionaries Contain Mark 16:9-20. Dean Burgon shows that there is a UNITED TESTIMONY of ALL of the LECTIONARIES on record to the GENUINENESS of Mark 16:9-20. LECTIONARIES were portions of the Scripture used in the churches from the beginning of the Christian churches and even in the Jewish form of worship. He wrote:

> "ALL the Twelve Verses in dispute are found in EVERY KNOWN COPY OF THE VENERABLE LECTIONARY OF THE EAST. THOSE SAME TWELVE VERSES--NEITHER MORE NOR LESS--ARE OBSERVED TO CONSTITUTE one INTEGRAL LECTION. . . . [these 12 verses were] selected . . . from the whole body of Scripture for the special honour of being listened to once and again at EASTER time, as well as on ASCENSION DAY." [Dean Burgon, *The Last 12 Verses of Mark*, Chapter X, pp. 210-211]

Two days of the church year they read these verses. That's why 100% of the Lectionaries contain these verses. They were something the church read every single Easter and Ascension Day.

VII. Other Strong Evidences for the Genuineness of Mark 16:9-20

A. The Evidence of the Greek Manuscripts Showing the Genuineness of Mark 16:9-20. As mentioned before, here is the manuscript evidence.

Manuscript Evidence for Mark 16:9-20 SUMMARIZED (In Burgon's Day):

a. **AGAINST Mark 16:9-20:**
    (1) Codex "B" (Vatican) [p. 70]
    (2) Codex "Aleph" (Sinai) [p. 70]

b. **FOR Mark 16:9-20:**
    (1) 18 Uncials [p. 71]
    (2) c. 600 Cursive Copies [p. 71]
    (3) Every known Uncial or Cursive in existence! [p. 71]
    (4) Every known Lectionary of the East! [p. 210]

B. Ten Early Bible Versions that Support the Genuineness of Mark 16:9-20. Here is a list of ten early Bible versions supporting the last twelve verses of Mark. We are finally getting down to the documentation, and Burgon has it. He certainly does. These are early Bible versions. This evidence is found in *THE LAST 12 VERSES OF MARK* (pages 32-37) by Dean John William Burgon (**BFT #1139, 350 pages.**

	DATE	EARLY BIBLE VERSION
1.	100-199 A.D.	PESHITO SYRIAC
2.	100-199 A.B.	VETUS ITALA (OLD LATIN)
3.	200-299 A.D.	CURETONIAN SYRIAC
4.	200-299 A.D.	THEBAIC (SAHIDIC) EGYPTIAN
5.	300-399 A.D.	MEMPHITIC (COPTIC) EGYPTIAN
6.	350 A.D.	GOTHIC OF ULPHILAS
7.	382 A.D.	LATIN VULGATE
8.	400-499 A.D.	PHILOXENIAN SYRIAC
9.	300-699 A.D.(?)	ETHIOPIC
10.	500-599 A.D.(?)	GEORGIAN

All ten of these early versions contain Mark 16:9-20 without any doubt cast upon them at all. "B" and "Aleph" do not have Mark 16:9-20. Whom do you believe? Where did these early versions get these verses? Obviously from the original Gospel of Mark which contained them.

C. Nineteen Early Church Fathers Who Supported the Genuineness of Mark 16:9-20. These Church Fathers were leaders of the churches who wrote letters to their respective churches. In these letters, they would either quote various verses exactly, or make allusion to some Bible verse. This yields evidence as to what Greek text they held in their hands as they quoted from, or alluded to the New Testament. These men were from all different places in the Church world of their day. This evidence is found in *THE LAST 12 VERSES OF MARK* (pages 19-31) by Dean John William Burgon (**BFT #1139, 350 pages**). Where did these Church Fathers get these verses that they either quoted or alluded to? How could they manufacture them if they were not there in their copies of the Gospel of Mark? Remember now, it is not just the Church Fathers that vindicate Mark 16:9-20, but also every known lectionary. In addition, it is eighteen of the uncial manuscripts and in 600 of the cursive manuscripts. It is extremely strange that it is omitted from "B" and "Aleph"! Add ten early versions and now nineteen early Church Fathers, and the evidence is overwhelming!

	DATE	CHURCH FATHER	PLACE
1.	100	A.D. Papias (Mark 16:18)	
2.	151	A.D. Justin Martyr (Mark 16:20)	
3.	180	A.D. Irenaeus (Mark 16:19)	Lyons
4.	200	A.D. Hippolytus (Mark 16:17-18)	Portus (near Rome)
5.	256	A.D. Vincentius (Mark 16:17-18)	Africa
6.	250	A.D. Acta Pilati (Mark 16:15-18)	
7.	200's-300's	A.D. Apostolical Constitutions (Mark 16:16)	
8.	325	A.D. Eusebius (Mark 16:9-20)	
9.	325	A.D. Marinus (Mark 16:9-20)	
10.	337	A.D. Aphraates The Persian (Mark 16:9-20)	
11.	374-397	A.D. Ambrose (Mark 16:15-18, 20)	Milan
12.	400	A.D. Chrysostom (Mark 16:9, 19-20)	
13.	331-420	A.D. Jerome (Mark 16:9, 14)	
14.	395-430	A.D. Augustine (Mark 16:12, 15-16)	Hippo
15.	430	A.D. Nestorius (Mark 16:20	
16.	430	A.D. Cyril of Alexandria (Mark 16:20)	Egypt
17.	425	A.D. Victor of Antioch (Mark 16:9-20)	Syria
18.	500	A.D. Hesychius (Mark 16:19)	Jerusalem
19.	500'S	A.D. Synopsis Scripturae Sacrae (Mark 16:9-20)	

1. The Nineteen Early Church Fathers Vindicating Mark 16:9-20 Grouped by Dates. In the chart below, the 19 early Church Fathers are GROUPED BY DATES.

	19 EARLY CHURCH FATHERS GROUPED BY DATES		
	DATES	CENTURY	# of CHURCH FATHERS
1.	100-199 A.D.	(2nd CENTURY)	THREE
2.	200-299 A.D.	(3rd CENTURY)	FOUR
3.	300-399 A.D.	(4th CENTURY)	SIX
4.	400-499 A.D.	(5th CENTURY)	FOUR
5.	500-599 A.D.	(6th CENTURY)	TWO
	TOTALS:	5 CENTURIES	19 FATHERS

The information for the preceding chart was taken from *THE LAST 12 VERSES OF MARK* (pages 19-31) by Dean John William Burgon (**BFT #1139**, 350 pages).

2. The Nineteen Early Church Fathers Vindicating Mark 16:9-20 Grouped by Locations. The location of these nineteen early Church Fathers is important, too. The Westcott and Hort false theory teaches that there was collusion on the part of those who copied the manuscripts and that they all had duplicate copies of the Textus Receptus. But how could there be collusion when they were all working in such widely separated areas? Here are these same nineteen early Church Fathers bearing witness to Mark 16:9-20 grouped by their locations. It is found in *THE LAST 12 VERSES OF MARK* (pages 19-31) by Dean John William Burgon (**BFT #1139,** 350 pages).

---

19 EARLY CHURCH FATHERS
GROUPED BY 10 DIFFERENT LOCATIONS

	CITY	COUNTRY
1.	ANTIOCH	SYRIA
2.	CONSTANTINOPLE	ASIA MINOR
3.	HIERAPOLIS	ASIA MINOR (E. SYRIA)
4.	CAESAREA	JUDEA
5.	EDESSA	ASSYRIA
6.	CARTHAGE	N. AFRICA (BY ITALY)
7.	ALEXANDRIA	EGYPT
8.	HIPPO	AFRICA
9.	ROME	ITALY
10.	PORTUS	ITALY (BY ROME)

D. Seven Early Church Fathers Believed by Some to be Hostile to Mark 16:9-20, Shown to be Favorable Instead. [See *The Last Twelve Verses of Mark,* (pages 38-69)]

SEVEN ADDITIONAL FAVORABLE EARLY CHURCH FATHERS

1. GREGORY OF NYSA
2. EUSEBIUS
3. JEROME (331-420 A. D.)
4. SEVERUS OF ANTIOCH (6th Century)
5. HESYCHIUS OF JERUSALEM (6th Century)
6. VICTOR OF ANTIOCH (400-450 A. D.)
7. EUTHYMIUS ZIGABENUS (1116 A. D.)

Dean Burgon, with very incisive language and methods, takes up each of the above seven Church Fathers who are generally taken to be hostile critics so far as Mark 16:9-20 is concerned. Before he is finished, Burgon shows each of the seven to be favorable critics instead.

E. A Combined Table Showing Both the Ten Early Bible Versions and the Nineteen Early Church Fathers Supporting the Last Twelve Verses of Mark, Arranged by Dates.

<u>DATES</u>   <u>29 WITNESSES FOR MARK 16:9-20</u>

1. 2nd CENTURY   (1)   Papias (100 A. D.)
   (100-199 A.D.) (2)   Justin Martyr (151 A. D.)
                  (3)   Irenaeus (180 A. D.)
                  (4)   Peshito Syriac Version (100-199 A. D.)
                  (5)   Vetus Itala (Old Latin) Version (100-199 A. D.)

2. 3rd CENTURY   (6)   Hippolytus (200 A. D.)
   (200-299 A.D.) (7)   Vincentius (256 A. D.)
                  (8)   Acta Pilati (250 A. D.)
                  (9)   Curetonian Syriac Version (200-299 A. D.)
                  (10) Thebaic (Sahidic) Egyptian Version (200-299 A. D.)

3. 4th CENTURY   (11) Apostolical Constitutions (300-399 A. D.)
   (200's-300's) (12) Eusebius (325 A. D.)
                  (13) Marinus (325 A. D.)
                  (14) Aphraates The Persian (337 A. D.)
                  (15) Gothic of Ulphilas Version (350 A. D.)
                  (16) Ambrose (374-397 A. D.)
                  (17) Jerome (331-420 A. D.)
                  (18) Latin Vulgate Version (382 A. D.)
                  (19) Memphitic (Coptic) Egyptian Version (300-399 A. D.)
                  (20) Augustine (395-430 A. D.)

4. 5th CENTURY   (21) Chrysostom (400 A. D.)
   (400-499 A. D.) (22) Victor of Antioch (425 A. D.)
                  (23) Nestorius (430 A. D.)
                  (24) Cyril of Alexandria (430 A. D)
                  (25) Philoxenian Syriac (400-499 A. D.)

5. 6th CENTURY   (26) Hesychius (500 A. D.)
   (500-599 A. D.) (27) Synopsis Scripturae Sacrae (500's)
                  (28) Ethiopic Version (300-699 A. D. [?])
                  (29) Georgian Version (500-599 A. D. [?])

In the above chart, you can see the combined picture of the evidence for Mark 16:9-20 with the nineteen early Church Fathers and the ten early Bible versions grouped together by centuries. This was taken from *THE LAST 12 VERSES OF MARK* (pages 19-37) by Dean John William Burgon (**BFT #1139**, 350 pages)

VIII. The Internal Evidence or Style in Support of Mark 16:9-20

Here is Dean Burgon's handling of the internal evidence or style. Many would argue that Mark 16:9-20 could NOT possibly by written by Mark, because it lacks words he has used throughout his Gospel in other places. That's an argument from the internal evidence of the passage. The external evidence is strong in support of Mark 16:9-20! To answer this objection, Dean Burgon compared the vocabulary of Mark 16:9-20 with that of Mark 1:9-20. He examined closely the consecutive twelve verses in chapter one with those in chapter 16 to see if the vocabulary was similar.

What were Dean Burgon's conclusions on the INTERNAL EVIDENCE of the "style" of Mark 16:9-20 compared to Mark 1:9-20? He compared Mark 16:9-20 with Mark 1:9-20 and showed that the STYLE of the two twelve verse sections was that of the same author, that is, Mark. He concluded:

> **"I have shown that the supposed argument from 'STYLE,' (in itself a highly fallacious test,) DISAPPEARS under investigation. . . . it is rendered PROBABLE BY THE STYLE that the Author of the BEGINNING of this Gospel was also the Author of the end of it. . . . Instead of their being TWENTY-SEVEN SUSPICIOUS CIRCUMSTANCES in the PHRASEOLOGY of these Twelve Verses, it has been proved (pp. 170-3) that in twenty-seven particulars there emerge CORROBORATIVE CONSIDERATIONS. . . . A presumption of the highest order is created that these Verses must needs be the work of S. Mark."** [Dean Burgon, *Last 12 Verses of Mark*, Chapter IX, p. 190]

If the reader is interested in seeing just how Dean Burgon went about his defense and vindication of Mark 16:9-20 based on internal evidence, this may be found in Chapter IX of *THE LAST 12 VERSES OF MARK*.

IX. Dean Burgon's Conclusions in Vindication of Mark 16:9-20

Some of Dean Burgon's CONCLUSIONS on the LAST 12 VERSES OF MARK (Mark 16:9-20) are as follows:

- That Codex B and Codex Aleph must be henceforth allowed to be IN ONE MORE SERIOUS PARTICULARS UNTRUSTWORTHY AND ERRING WITNESSES. They have been convicted, in fact, of BEARING FALSE WITNESS in respect of S. Mark 16:9-20, where their evidence had been hitherto reckoned upon with the most undoubting confidence. . . .
- That, in all future critical editions of the New Testament, these 'Twelve Verses' will have to be restored to their rightful honours: never more appearing disfigured with brackets, encumbered with doubts, banished from their context, or molested with notes of suspicion. . . .
- Lastly, men must be no longer taught to look with distrust on this precious part of the Deposit; and encouraged to dispute the Divine sayings which it contains on the plea that PERHAPS they may not be Divine, after all; . . . NOT A PARTICLE OF DOUBT, that NOT AN ATOM OF SUSPICION, attaches to 'THE LAST TWELVE VERSES OF THE GOSPEL ACCORDING TO S. MARK.'" [Dean Burgon, *The Last 12 Verses of Mark*, Chapter XII, pp. 253-54]

There can be no doubt regarding the last twelve verses of Mark. Let me simply sum it up. We have a Bible that has the last twelve verses of Mark in it; and we have Dean Burgon, I think, showing his tremendous style and ability as he defends the Words of God. We have doctrines involved in this section, even though we have statements of Bible leaders to the effect that no doctrine is involved in any variant Greek text, or any variant version or translation. There are more than twenty-seven teachings contained in Mark 16:9-20. Is it not obvious who is right? Can you see the errors on the part of the Bible leaders who deny any doctrinal differences? These men either don't know the truth in the first place, of they are misrepresenting it. Perhaps they are simply repeating what has been told to them. There is serious trouble involved in either case.

Others have taken this up: not just the **New International Version** with its false notes on Mark 16:9-20; not just the **New American Standard Version**; not just the **New King James Version**, but almost ALL of the other modern versions have these same terrible doubts and notes. The Ryrie Study Bible also has doubted Mark 16:9-20. In Dallas Theological Seminary's Bible Commentary the doubts are very present. The Commentary suggests three or four different possibilities for the last twelve verses of Mark.

But Dean Burgon was a man who did his homework! I don't know of any more forceful writing on the last twelve verses of Mark. I think, as he pointed out, if "B" and "Aleph" are lying and false witnesses here in twelve large verses, against every other known uncial, every other known Gospel of Mark in existence, with all the Church Fathers who are involved and all the versions involved and all the lectionary evidence--every single one--100%, can they be depended upon in any of their statements? We do not believe they can!

And then, based also upon Herman Hoskier's exhaustive research comparing "B" (Vatican) with "Aleph" (Sinai), in the Gospels alone he found over 3,000 examples of where these two manuscripts contradiction each other. Yet the very basis and foundation of the new versions is "B"--the Vatican. And if "Aleph" disagrees with "B," then "B" finds some other manuscript to agree with it; and if it can't find any other manuscript to agree with it, "B" stands alone and is to be taken as truth. *"To 'B' or not to 'B,' that is the question."* The serious error of "B" (Vatican) and "Aleph" (Sinai) in Mark 16:9-20 shows how we must discard their validity throughout the entire Greek New Testament. The sooner every Bible believing Christian realizes this fact the better off we'll all be!

Though this short booklet has sought to sum up the major arguments of Dean John William Burgon in his tremendous book, *The Last Twelve Verses of Mark*, the reader is urged to get the entire volume and study it for himself. It is **BFT #1139** and is available from the Dean Burgon Society for a GIFT of **$15.00**.

When the Words of Inspiration Are Imperilled
(By Dean Burgon)

"If, therefore, any do complain that I have sometimes hit my opponents rather hard, I take leave to point out that 'to every thing there is a season, and a time to every purpose under the sun': 'a time to embrace, and a time to be far from embracing': a time for speaking smoothly, and a time for speaking sharply. And that when the words of Inspiration are seriously imperilled, as now they are, it is scarcely possible for one who is determined effectually to preserve the Deposit in its integrity, to hit either too straight or too hard." (*The Revision Revised*, by Dean John William Burgon, pp. vii-viii).

SEND GIFT SUBSCRIPTIONS!
All gifts to Dean Burgon Society are tax deductible!

THE DEAN BURGON SOCIETY
Box 354, Collingswood, New Jersey 08108, U.S.A. • Phone (609) 854-4452

MEMBERSHIP FORM

I have a copy of the **"Articles of Faith, Operation, and Organization"** of **The Dean Burgon Society, Incorporated.** After reading these **"Articles,"** I wish to state, by my signature below, that I believe in and accept such **"Articles."** I understand that my "Membership" is for one year and that I must renew my "Membership" at that time in order to remain a "Member" in good standing of the Society.

( ) I wish to become a member of **The Dean Burgon Society** for the first time.

( ) I wish to **renew** my membership subscription which has expired as of: _____

SIGNED _____

DATE _____

I enclose   **Attention: The Dean Burgon Society**
           Box 354, Collingswood, New Jersey 08108

*Membership Donation ($7.00/year) $ _____
*Life Membership Donation ($50.00) $ _____
*Additional Donation to the Society $ _____
           TOTAL $ _____

Please PRINT in CAPITAL LETTERS your name and address below:

NAME _____

ADDRESS _____

CITY _____ STATE _____ ZIP _____

Although I am not a member of **The Dean Burgon Society,** I do wish to subscribe to the **newsletter** by making a gift of $3.50 to the Society.

NAME _____

ADDRESS _____

CITY _____ STATE _____ ZIP _____

*I understand that, included in my first **$3.50 gift** accompanying any donatioin or order — regardless of the amount of the order or donation — is my year's subscription to **The Dean Burgon Society NEWSLETTER.**

Canada and All Foreign Subscriptions $7.00 Yearly

Order Blank

Name:_____

Address:_____

City & State:_____Zip:_____

[ ] Enclosed is $_____. Send _____copy(ies) of *The Last Twelve Verses of Mark* (c. 400 pages) each for a GIFT of **$15.00 + $3.00** for postage & handling.

[ ] Send the **"DBS Articles of Faith & Organization"** (N.C.)

[ ] Send **Brochure #1: "900 Titles Defending KJB/TR"** (N.C.)

[ ] Send information on **DBS pamphlets** on KJB & T.R. (N.C.)

[ ] Send *The Revision Revised* by Dean Burgon (**$25 + $3**)

[ ] Send *The Traditional Text* by Dean Burgon (**$15 + $3**)

[ ] Send *The Causes of Corruption* by Dean Burgon (**$14 + $3**)

[ ] Send *Inspiration and Interpretation* by Dean Burgon (**$25 + $3**)

[ ] Send *Defending the King James Bible* by Dr. Waite (**$12 + $3**)

[ ] Send *Guide to Textual Criticism* by Edward Miller·(**$7 + $3**)

The
Dean Burgon
Society
In Defense of Traditional Bible Texts
Box 354
Collingswood, New Jersey 08108, U.S.A.

The
Last Twelve Verses
of Mark

**Vindicated Against Recent
Critical Objectors & Established**

*The Fatal Blow to Manuscripts
"B" and "Aleph"*

by

Dean John William Burgon